Clinical Updates for Family Therapists:

Research and Treatment Approaches for Issues Affecting Today's Families

Volume 4

AA
MFT

Published by the
American Association for Marriage and Family Therapy
Alexandria, VA

The American Association for Marriage and Family Therapy promotes and advances the common professional interests of marriage and family therapists.

This book is published by:

The American Association for Marriage and Family Therapy
112 South Alfred Street
Alexandria, VA 22314
703-838-9808
www.aamft.org

ISBN 978-1-931846-13-4

PREFACE

The *Clinical Updates* articles were launched in 1999 and published every two months thereafter in the AAMFT's *Family Therapy Magazine*. Numerous requests for copies of the *Clinical Updates* led to the publication of the *Clinical Updates for Family Therapists* book series, the fourth and final edition of which you hold in your hand. This volume contains those articles published in 2008, 2009, and 2010. The *Clinical Updates* articles, as such, were retired at the beginning of 2011.

Each *Clinical Update* is written by an author with expertise in the topic area and includes an overview of the current research, terminology, treatment approaches and additional resources for the issues being addressed. Each author reviewed their chapter prior to this publication, to ensure that the information was current at the time of publication.

We are grateful to the authors who so generously shared their time and expertise through these articles. You will notice that this particular volume emphasizes medical issues. Special appreciation goes to the faculty and students at East Carolina University's medical family therapy doctoral program who wrote or coordinated many of these articles.

Kimberlee Bryce, the managing editor of the AAMFT *Family Therapy Magazine*, also deserves recognition for years of identifying authors, gently enforcing deadlines, editing each article, and managing the production of this fourth volume.

Our hope is that these volumes, singly and collectively, will offer a ready reference to family therapy clinicians. (Topics addressed in the first three volumes are listed in the back of this book.) While not exhaustive, these volumes will help you expand your knowledge and begin to develop your own expertise in numerous issues that impact your clients.

Karen Gautney, MS
Deputy Executive Director
American Association for Marriage and Family Therapy

TABLE OF CONTENTS

MEDICAL TOPICS

OTHER TOPICS

Adult Cancer

Patrick Meadors, PhD

Originally Published as Clinical Update in Family Therapy Magazine
January-February 2009

PREVALENCE AND SURVIVORSHIP

There are currently over 10.5 million people in the United States with a history of cancer and another 1.4 million new cases expected by the end of 2008 (excluding in-situ, basal cell, and squamous cell skin cancers) (Ries et al., 2007). Nearly 41 percent of Americans can expect to be diagnosed with cancer at some point in their lifetime (Ries et al.). Furthermore, cancer is responsible for one in four deaths in the U.S., with close to 1,500 cancer related deaths happening daily and almost 600,000 annually (American Cancer Society [ACS], 2008). Despite a steady increase in the five-year survival rate from 50 to 66 percent (between 1975-2003), cancer is still the second leading cause of death in the U.S. behind heart disease (ACS).

As the survival rate for those diagnosed with cancer has increased, so has attention to improving the quality of life and the notion of survivorship. Once someone is diagnosed with cancer, they are considered to be a cancer survivor for their lifetime (National Cancer Institute, 2008). While much of the attention in the field of oncology has pertained to how long someone lives, increased attention has been given to the quality of life during these extended time frames (Jacobson & Jim, 2008). With more than 60 percent of individuals surviving five years after diagnosis, it is imperative that mental health clinicians focus on improving the quality of life and helping individuals, couples, and families adjust to cancer's prolonged effects.

It is troublesome that despite the advancements in the treatment of the biomedical needs for cancer, the psychosocial needs have been grossly overlooked in oncology practices with no major advancements in this part of their treatment (Adler & Page, 2008). In fact, cancer survivors and families have stated that medical cancer care providers did not address their psychosocial concerns and failed to assess for depression or other stress related reactions. Those diagnosed with cancer face the risk for significant physical impairment, disability, and numerous psychological and social issues that can develop from cancer and its treatment (Adler & Page). To assist our clients and complement the work of medical providers, mental health professionals should familiarize themselves with the specific types of cancers impacting their client population, treatment methods, and side effects of each. Although some cancers are aggressive and the treatments for them are equally so, mental health providers may find themselves working with families from only a few weeks to a prolonged period of time. This may present a challenge to mental health providers as to how to structure therapeutic sessions due to erratic time frames and the debilitating/grueling nature of treatment.

Many individuals diagnosed with cancer technically meet the criteria for a chronic disease. Chronic diseases may be "permanent, leave residual disability, caused by nonreversible pathological alteration, require special training of the patient for rehabilitation, or require a long period of supervision, observation, or care" (Timmreck, 1987, p. 100). Due to the chronic nature of some types of cancer, a focal point for many clinicians, then, is to provide the guidance needed for the individual, couple, and family to successfully adjust to the illness. Rolland (1994) suggested that many enter the world of illness and disability without a biopsychosocial map to assist and assure them that they are adjusting to the illness normally.

BIOMEDICAL ISSUES

Staging. Cancer diagnoses are accompanied with staging that describes the extent/severity of the disease at time of diagnosis. The staging process is essential in determining the appropriate course of treatment and is significantly tied to prognostic assessments (ACS, 2008). Mental health professionals will find this important to understand, as it may guide their work with individuals, couples, and families who are facing a certain stage of the disease. Depending on the type of cancer, the stage of cancer is determined by a combination of tests (i.e., physical exam, imaging studies, laboratory tests, pathology reports, and surgical reports) to evaluate the extent of the disease. The most relevant staging criteria for mental health clinicians are presented in Table 1.

Treatment. Once mental health providers become aware of the diagnostic stage of cancer for their client, they should familiarize themselves with the main treatments for cancer and their biomedically toxic and psychosocially altering side effects from each treatment. Most patients will be treated with radiation therapy, chemotherapy, and/or surgery.

Radiation therapy consists of multiple methods of delivering high doses of radiation to a defined area, with capability of targeting very minute tumors. The high doses of radiation alter the cell DNA, or molecules of the cell, so that it controls which cells can divide (ACS, 2008). Unfortunately, some normal tissue is also altered, thus technology has improved that drastically spares normal tissues while applying the high doses directly to the tumor. External beam radiation has improved as a treatment option since the inclusion of enhanced imaging and targeting technology whereby an external beam of radiation is

TABLE 1: STAGING CRITERIA FOR CANCER[1, 2]

Numerical Staging	1. Stage 0 – carcinoma in situ – only present in tissue where it originated
	2. Stage I, Stage II, Stage III – higher number stage represents a larger tumor size, higher instance of metastasis, invasion of organs, etc.
	3. Stage IV – Cancer has spread extensively to other organs.
Summary Staging	1. In Situ – cancer only present in tissue where it began
	2. Localized – limited to the organ in which it started with no evidence of spread
	3. Regional – Spread from the original (primary) tissue to surrounding lymph nodes, organs or tissues
	4. Distant – Spread from original tissue to distant organs or lymph nodes

[1] It should be noted that the presented staging criteria has been simplified and the staging process varies based on the type of cancer.

[2] While the TNM staging may be helpful for oncologists, these staging descriptions are most commonly spoken about by patients in treatment and their family members

precisely aimed at the cancerous locations. **Chemotherapy** is used to control the systemic spread of the disease by introducing toxic chemicals into the patient's body. The problem with this treatment is that many patients describe it as being worse than the cancer itself, with side effects that are excruciating. New clinical trials are consistently unveiling new effective chemotherapy regimens, methods of delivery and improved combinations of existing drugs to better eliminate the cancer cells. **Surgical procedures** are becoming less invasive, while saving more normal tissue when removing the cancerous tumors.

Surgical treatments can be prophylactic (preventative), diagnostic, staging, curative, debulking (removing some of tumor), palliative, reconstructive or supportive (placing a port for chemo). While an exhaustive review of the newest technology and treatments may not be most prudent, a general understanding of the most common types of cancer and related treatments is needed. For more information about the different treatment options, please see the ACS Web site, www.cancer.org, for the latest techniques and in depth descriptions of the different treatment options.

COMMON TYPES OF CANCER AND DEMOGRAPHIC CORRELATES

Breast Cancer. Without accounting for skin cancer, breast cancer is the second leading cancer related death in adult women behind lung cancer (ACS, 2008). Early detection, improved awareness, and enhanced treatments have increased survival rates while decreasing the number of associated deaths. The earliest of breast cancers are usually detected by a mammogram or Magnetic

Resonance Imaging (MRI) (typically for those women who are either younger or have a lifetime susceptibility to breast cancer). The larger tumors are usually palpable, painless nodules. Genetic testing is available for those individuals who may have a strong family history of breast cancer and/or have a history of ovarian cancer. However, those individuals who carry the mutated BRCA1 and BRCA2 genes makeup less than 1 percent of the population (and account for 10% of breast cancer cases), so extensive genetic testing is not recommended for everyone and those interested should first consult a genetic counselor. This may prove to be difficult, as there may be few genetic counselors in a particular region, thus consultation with an oncologist may be the most prudent. While genetics is considered a significant risk factor for breast cancer, the strongest risk factor is aging (ACS).

Multiple treatment methods accompany a diagnosis of breast cancer, depending on the location, size, and type of breast cancer. The most common treatment methods are one or more of the following: lumpectomy, mastectomy, radiation therapy, chemotherapy, hormone therapy, or targeted biological therapy (ACS, 2008). Many of the treatment decisions must take into account patient preferences and joint decisions with partners and family members, as some of the treatment options entail significant disfigurement and reconstruction. Regardless of the treatment option chosen (mastectomy or lumpectomy with subsequent radiation therapy), survival rates for those women with localized disease (e.g., in situ) are nearly identical. However, African American women have a lower five-year survival rate than white women and also have a higher mortality rate from breast cancer than white women. While research on the disparities is ongoing, preliminary results point toward difference in screening practices, stage at diagnosis, and biology of the disease (ACS). The five-year survival rate for localized breast cancer is close to 98%, while the five-year survival rate for those individuals with regional metastasis is close to 84%. If distant metastasis (cancer has spread to distant organs or tissues from the primary tumor) is present from breast cancer, the survival rate goes down to 27 percent (ACS, 2008).

Prostate Cancer. Prostate cancer is the most frequently diagnosed cancer in adult men with close to 187,000 cases expected to be diagnosed in 2008 (ACS, 2008). While it is not readily known, the incidence of prostate cancer is twice as high in African American men as in white men. In addition, while the death rates related to prostate cancer have been steadily decreasing, it is still the second leading cancer related death among men behind lung cancer.

Prostate cancer is typically detected following a prostate-specific antigen (PSA) blood test and/or a digital rectal exam in which the prostate is palpated for any notable abnormalities (ACS, 2008). It is recommended that men have their PSA levels checked annually if they are over the age of 50 or over the age of 45 if a family history of prostate cancer is present. Most prostate cancers are diagnosed in men over 65 and the only significant established risk factors are age, ethnicity, and family history. Treatment for prostate cancer varies based on stage of cancer, age, and other medical concerns. The most common methods to treat early stage prostate cancer would be a prostatectomy, external beam radiation (Intensity-Modulated Radiation Therapy [IMRT] and Image-Guided Radiotherapy [IGRT]), and radioactive seed implants. Hormonal therapy can also be used in conjunction with radiation or chemotherapy, or as a primary treatment option. Hormonal treatment, radiation, and/or chemotherapy are commonly used to treat advanced prostate cancer. However, more than 90 percent of prostate cancers are detected when it is localized and has not metastasized. The five-year survival rate is close to 100 percent for those with early stage prostate cancer; yet there is usually significant impairment to sexual functioning (ED prevalence is 75 to 85 percent following prostatectomy with slightly lower percentages with external radiation) and many who have surgery become incontinent (Schover, 2009). See sidebar for additional information regarding sexual dysfunction as a result of cancer.

BIOPSYCHOSOCIAL-SPIRITUAL PERSPECTIVE

While it is evident that the diagnosis of cancer involves a host of complex biomedical issues, collaboration between the medical and mental health systems is essential in providing high quality biopsychosocial-spiritual care and effective assessment of the patient and family's needs. Replete in the literature are articles about how cancer is primarily treated organically, despite rich evidence that it is a biopsychosocial-spiritual (BPS-S) disease (e.g., loss of savings, changing caregiver roles, fears associated with the illness).

The need to integrate the biopsychosocial (BPS) perspective in medicine was established over three decades ago (Engel, 1977); with the spiritual component only recently deemed a significant element to the BPS assessment and understanding of the utilization of medical treatment options (Wright, Watson & Bell, 1996). Considering that the three biggest barriers to receiving high quality treatment for cancer are inadequate healthcare coverage, inability to pay treatment related expenses, and transportation, none of which are biomedical (Association of Oncology Social Work [AOSW], 2006), it is evident that biomedical problems are not devoid of psychosocial or spiritual issues, and at times, vice versa (McDaniel, Hepworth, & Doherty, 1992).

To develop a BPS-S treatment plan, the mental health clinician should obtain a signed release to talk to the other providers involved, to be biopsychosocial-spiritually sensitive in the patient's cultural and care milieu. The goal is to assess the psychosocial concerns and to develop a treatment plan that is collaborative, non-competing, and without duplicating services or history taking. Although mental health clinicians do not diagnose cancer, we often become part of the treatment team at some point during the diagnosis, treatment, or recovery process. Many biomedical factors (level of disability, severity, and potential chronic nature of the illness) may substantially enhance the risk for numerous mental health concerns, which further emphasizes the need to assess the whole patient (Adler & Page, 2008). A list of the more common collaborative partners who could participate in a patient's cancer care is included in Table 2. Our role as mental health providers is to identify appropriate psychosocial reactions to a cancer diagnosis and to assist the patient and their families as they maneuver through one of the most challenging times of their lives. Psychosocial care that focuses on improving family dynamics and reducing emotional distress is at the forefront of improving the quality of life for many cancer survivors (Jacobson & Jim, 2008). For mental health clinicians who are interested in a structured interview process to gain a more complete history of the illness, Hodgson, Lamson, and Reese (2007) developed the BPS-S interview method that could easily be adapted to work with clients who have cancer.

PSYCHOSOCIAL ISSUES

Depression and Anxiety. Depressive and anxiety disorders are commonly diagnosed among cancer patients and represent the two most researched mood disorders in cancer patients (Bruce, 2006; Carlsen, Jensen, Jacobsen, Krasnik, & Johansen, 2005). While the depression (25 percent) and anxiety rates (30 percent) have been found to fluctuate depending on the stage and type of cancer (1-50 percent), the rates of depression, anxiety and distress for cancer survivors are similar to the general population (Alfano & Rowland, 2009; Massie, 2004; McDaniel, Musselman, Porter, Reed, & Nemeroff, 1995). Multiple methods exist to assess for depression and anxiety in cancer patients, however a multisymptom approach is most commonly used (Jacobson & Jim, 2008). The strength of this approach centers on being able to reliably detect changes in mood and/or anxiety over time; however, when working specifically with cancer patients, many symptoms of depression and anxiety could be confounded by treatment side effects or physical changes (loss of appetite, fatigue, etc.). The 14-item Hospital Anxiety and Depression Scale (HADS; Zigmund & Snaith, 1983) is effective in diagnosing major depressive disorder (MDD), and mood disturbances in cancer patients; however, the authors also recommended that a subsequent clinical interview be conducted to confirm the diagnosis (Walker et al., 2007). The Functional Assessment of Cancer Therapy-General (FACT-G; Jang, Ackler, Braitman, & Tester, 2007) also has a strong predictive factor in diagnosing those with MDD. However, diagnostic categories and assessments do not do justice to the myriad of psychosocial strengths and difficulties that cancer patients and their family members may reveal.

RELATIONAL ISSUES

The systemic implications of cancer on the family should not be overlooked, and is at times a vital focus of the patient's assessment and psychosocial treatment. In many instances, family members are expected to assist the patient in achieving treatment goals as well as managing side effects. To properly fulfill this role, family members have to make significant changes to their social and occupational roles (e.g., working different hours, changing jobs, more household responsibility), in addition to altering established communication patterns. In fact, Rolland (1994) stated that chronic illness, along

---

TABLE 2: POTENTIAL COLLABORATORS IN TREATMENT OF WHOLE PATIENT

1. **Medical Oncologist*** – responsible for the management of chemotherapy
2. **Radiation Oncologist*** – responsible for the management of radiation therapy
3. **Radiologist*** – responsible for the radiology report and diagnostics
4. **Pathologist*** – analyzes tissue samples and determines type of cancer cell
5. **Medical Family Therapist** – collaborative partner in the biopsychosocial-spiritual and systemic understanding of illness and the impact on the family
6. **Dietitian** – monitors nutritional health patients during treatment of cancer
7. **Social Worker** – coordination of services for cancer patients, patient assistance programs, insurance concerns, etc.
8. **Genetic Counselor** – responsible for screening the individual for genetic links to certain types of cancer.
9. **Child Life Specialist** – works with a child(ren) who have a parent diagnosed with cancer; appreciates the developmental stage of the child(ren) and combines it with the best method for delivering information about the disease; conducts ongoing assessment of the child(ren)'s coping mechanisms and their role in the family
10. **Psychiatrist** – provides psychopharmacological and diagnostic expertise related to the treatment of mental illnesses
11. **Chaplain** – provides spiritual support for patient and family
12. **Primary Care Physician** – may have most extensive history of patient, and be in charge of follow-up care once treatment is finished
13. **Hospice Care** – terminal patients are referred to hospice care to help coordinate end of life concerns.

* If provider is unavailable, it may be more helpful to collaborate with the nurse or physician assistant affiliated with each respective profession.

---

with threatened loss of life, can be one of the biggest challenges to a couple and family's communication patterns. Couples reported that ineffective communication is one of their biggest concerns and couples dealing with breast cancer have shown patterns of disengagement (withdrawing or avoidance strategies) when discuss difficult aspects of the treatment and recovery process (Hodgson, Shields, & Rousseau, 2003; Neuling & Winefield, 1988). Systemic assessment could reveal that the communication difficulties stem from a family's unsupportive behaviors, strained responses, or protective mechanisms (Helgeson & Cohen, 1996).

A cancer diagnosis is filled with uncertainties (treatments, progression, recurrence, prognosis) that are accompanied by a myriad of emotional reactions as the family desperately tries to maintain hope, prepare for loss, and

---

cope with the varying degrees of illness (Rolland, 1994). Interestingly, many spouses and family members will exhibit more emotional distress than the actual patient, which may be indicative of feelings of helplessness and loss of control. Some of the emotional distress can be attributed to anticipatory loss and can be exacerbated by the fluctuations of a chronic/relapsing illness such as cancer (Rolland). The anticipation of losing someone from cancer, in conjunction with the ebbs and flows of the disease progression, can be as debilitating as the illness itself. A client and his or her family may exhibit symptoms of denial, overprotection, disappointment, guilt, sadness, exhaustion; all of which are characteristics of anticipatory loss. While this emotional despair may be most prominent, the family members may fluctuate between despair and moments of hope and positivity (Rolland). Even years following a diagnosis, the impact of cancer on the family should be at the forefront of a clinician's psychosocial assessment and treatment. As a clinician, familiarity with this type of disease and biomedical treatment could prove essential in helping the couple overcome interpersonal and relational distress.

PSYCHOSOCIAL TREATMENT OPTIONS

The psychosocial treatment process for clients who have cancer should be predicated on the biomedical characteristics of the type of cancer, staging, and subsequent treatment options. For instance, a mental health clinician would undoubtedly approach someone who had localized, stage 1 breast cancer very differently than they would a client who had a large glioblastoma (aggressive brain cancer). Localized breast cancer is highly curable, and while it may involve temporary disruption and distress within the family, it can result in minimal long-term impact. Glioblastomas are highly aggressive and only one in 20 people will survive past three years and many exhibit substantial impairment and disability (emotional changes, difficulty walking, memory difficulties) depending on where the brain tumor is located (Krex et al., 2007). Treatment for these types of cancers is often palliative or designed to improve quality of life.

In an effort to assist the clinician in identifying psychosocial implications of each illness, Rolland (1994) developed the "psychosocial typology of illness," which is especially useful for clinicians as they examine and help each family overcome the effects of cancer (or any illness). Five distinct illness characteristics (onset, course, outcome, incapacitation, and degrees of uncertainty) are identified as having significant impact on the psychosocial dynamics of a family. Consideration of these five characteristics provides the clinician with a typology that can identify individual and family dynamics (i.e., financial concerns, end-of-life concerns, level of disability, etc.) that could be a focal point for treatment.

Individually-Based Treatment. Even though cancer is inherently an organic disease which is best viewed through a BPS-S lens, treatment of a patient's intra and interpersonal needs is essential. Depression and anxiety are commonly treated organically with pharmaceuticals such as antidepressants (Lexapro,

Prozac, Paxil, etc.) and benzodiazepines (Xanax, Lorazepam, etc.). However, researchers have shown that cognitive behavioral therapy (CBT) is also effective in the reduction of depression symptoms in cancer patients, especially on the short term (Kuijer, Buunk, Jong, Ybema, & Sanderman, 2004). CBT prevents and relieves depressive symptoms and anxiety in those patients with metastatic disease and those undergoing surgery (Edelman, Lemon, Bell, & Kidman, 1999; Moynihan, Bliss, Davidson, Burchell, & Horwich, 1998) by restructuring cognitions, easing fears of recurrence, and controlling behaviors that can be destructive. Regardless of the type of cancer, ambiguity of cancer and fear of recurrence seem to be prominent in many patients. While systemic therapy can be helpful, CBT has been found to be most effective in helping patients overcome these debilitating fears and thoughts. Furthermore, there are multiple interpersonal factors that have been found to be predictive of poor adjustment to cancer, such as patients who exhibited regrets in life, marital problems, pessimism, poor self esteem and perceived lack of social support (Weisman & Worden, 1976). Thus, enhancing the individual's social supports (e.g., Internet support groups, support groups, supportive dyads) are also effective in reducing symptoms of depression and anxiety (Winzelberg et al., 2003).

Familial-Based Treatment. The difficulty for many families who are faced with the task of overcoming cancer is maintaining effective communication and enhancing problem solving skills in the face of the diagnostic crisis. Psychoeducation at the beginning of treatment can provide essential information to the patient and family and help them overcome many of the rational and irrational fears regarding the treatment process (McQuellon et al., 1998). Furthermore, psychotherapy at the time of diagnosis seems to promote more active decision making for the individual and the family which can ultimately lead to timely decisions on treatment (Davidson, Goldenberg, Gleave, & Degner, 2003). Effective decision making can increase feelings of mastery, reduce distress in the patient and family, and potentially improve treatment outcome. Furthermore, it should not be assumed that couples and families discuss their worries and fears about cancer with each other (or a healthcare professional) (Bischoff, 2005). Thus, clinicians should be astute at encouraging these discussions. Otherwise, these disengaging patterns of communication, such as avoidance or withdrawing, can impede effective problem solving during a time of crisis. Hodgson et al. (2003) recommended helping couples discuss painful topics that may be difficult to discuss on their own, such as fear of recurrence, threatened loss, intimacy, and relationship satisfaction.

One of the most distressing aspects of cancer is the perceived loss of control in their lives for every member of the family including the patient. The family is flooded with uncertainties about treatment, prognosis, new medical technologies, new medical personnel, and many changing roles within the family. Many patients will attempt to take on the illness as "my" illness and fail to include the rest of the family. Rolland (1994) suggested that this places the illness within the individual and creates an unbalanced skew in the family that can result in changes in intimacy, exercise of power, and unbalanced decision making. A clinician has to be wary of this caregiver-patient role replacing the existing spousal role or familial role. In addition, there is increased potential for an influx of negative communication about the illness replacing other more positive interactions. Uniting the family against the illness, balancing new roles with existing ones, and creating balance through positive familial communications are essential tasks for the clinician. A unified, balanced couple or family front can create a supportive environment that does not single out the individual cancer patient. This balancing can be a crucial component for effective management of the psychosocial effects. The individual and family must reach a new definition of mastery and control in their lives with the cancer included (Rolland). Mental health clinicians can help the family overcome their feelings of helplessness and focus their energies on redefining the illness as "our" illness and identify parts of their situation that are controllable.

Facing a potential loss of a spouse or family member from cancer is a devastating realization and can have systemic effects throughout the family. Many patients and family members are faced with the notion of their own mortality for the first time. Undoubtedly, this realization creates a loss experience of the "life that used to be." These grief reactions can shock the fabric of a family and challenge the most secure of attachments. Emotionally focused therapy (Johnson & Greenberg, 1985) is an example of a systemic approach that can enhance the feelings of connectedness between the cancer patient and a partner through open communication and empathic responses (Kowal, Johnson, & Lee, 2003). Researchers suggested that the couple's attachment styles may be interrelated to the ability to cope effectively with cancer (Shields, Travis, & Rousseau, 2000). Secure attachment styles that are prevalent prior to a cancer diagnosis can be predicative of a better adjustment process to cancer.

While a number of overarching issues and treatment suggestions are mentioned, it is equally important to appreciate the uniqueness of each client and family. Each family has their own culture, communication pattern, attachment process and may handle the diagnosis and treatment of cancer differently. Thus, significant importance is placed on understanding the family system and dynamics that were present prior to the illness. Regardless of the practice domain, mental health clinicians working with cancer patients and/or their families should also incorporate the client's health concerns into their own therapeutic process, collaborate with medical professionals, and remain cognizant of the impact of health concerns on the family system. Cancer is an illness that affects the whole family, thus it is equally important to supplement some of the individually focused treatment strategies and incorporate a relational, systemic dynamic.

WORKING WITH CANCER AND SEXUAL DYSFUNCTION

Sexual dysfunctions can result from numerous organic, psychological, and relational origins. The physiological changes (e.g., hormonal, vascular) are typically more prominent in presentation, however often require a biopsychosocial treatment perspective. Many of the physiological changes are accompanied with psychological latent effects (e.g., negative body image, relational distress, stigmatization) that may go unnoticed or addressed because they are never disclosed to a healthcare professional (Schover, 2009). These psychological effects could be responsible for the different adjustment patterns that couples exhibit in maintaining their sexual functioning despite physical impairment.

Individuals with cancer often report similar types of sexual dysfunction. Most men will experience a loss of desire or have difficulty becoming aroused (Schover, 2009). Erectile dysfunction (ED) is the most common complaint for men. Organically speaking, radiation therapy to the pelvic region is often responsible for significant scarring of the reproductive tissues. Thus, men will often have difficulty maintaining an erection due to vascular difficulties, or the destruction of the nerves controlling the erection of the penis. Surgery and hormonal treatments do not seem to reduce these side effects. Close to 85% of men who had a radical prostatectomy experience long term ED (Walsh, Marschke, Ricker, & Burnett, 2000). Blood is often present in the ejaculate as the prostate continues to heal following treatment, which can create psychological barriers about performance or negative sexual attitude. In addition, hormonal treatment often causes men to lose all desire and feelings of arousal (Schover et al. 2002).

Women who have endured pelvic radiation or removal of the reproductive organs through prophylactic or curative surgery will often lose elasticity and lubrication essential for sexual intercourse (Schover, 2009). Following chemotherapy or pelvic irradiation, reports of vaginal tightness, dryness, and pain during intercourse, may mimic the symptoms many post-menopausal women experience (Robson et al., 2003). Many women who go through chemotherapy for breast cancer or ovarian cancer will experience a reduction in their estrogen production that can force younger women into menopause at a much younger age (Ganz et al., 2002). The post-menopausal symptoms can often result in painful sex, difficulty having an orgasm, significant weight gain and lead many women to avoid sex with their partner. Some researchers have found that loss of desire could be a result of anticipatory pain during sex that causes them to not initiate sexual intercourse (Schover).

Despite the dearth of research on the topic of sexual dysfunctions, very little empirically supported treatment options have been developed that could easily be implemented in oncology clinics (Schover, 2009). Collaboratively with participating healthcare professionals, mental health providers should assess the couple and develop the appropriate joint treatment method that includes many of the traditional sex therapy techniques (i.e., sensate focus, cognitive behavioral therapy, and communication training/marital therapy) and the physiological treatments (i.e., pharmaceutical, vacuum and ring, injections, lubrications, dilators). It may be especially important to focus on the sexual dysfunction as a couple concern and not focus solely on the cancer survivor. In order for the treatment of the sexual dysfunction to be successful, it must encompass the biopsychosocial-spiritual implication of the dysfunction and avoid focusing solely on the organic or psychological origins of the dysfunction.

TERMINOLOGY

Basal Cell – most common form of skin cancer

Biopsy – removal of tissue for examination under a microscope

BRCA I and II – human gene associated with increased risk in breast cancer; responsible for tumor suppression and regulates divisions of cells

Chemotherapy – use of chemicals to control cancer growth systemically throughout the body

Computed Tomography (CT) – medical imaging using tomography; creates 3-D image of what is inside the body

Erectile Dysfunction (ED) – inability for a man to maintain a firm erection long enough to have intercourse

Hormone Therapy – manipulation of the endocrine system through the administration of hormones to suppress the production or activity of other hormones; effective with hormone responsive tissues like the prostate and breast

In-Situ – absence of invasion of cancer cells into surrounding tissues

Imaging Studies – produce pictures of inside the body (i.e., CT, PET, MRI). Important in determining location, size, and metastasis of cancer

Image Guided Radiation Therapy (IGRT) – use of 3D or 2D imaging during the course of radiation therapy to improve accuracy

Intensity Modulated Radiation Therapy (IMRT) –creates the ability to focus intensity of radiation on the bulk of the disease while sparing normal tissues

Lumpectomy – a surgical procedure to remove a lump from a man or woman's breast; viable means for saving the rest of the breast

Mastectomy – a surgical procedure to remove the breast either partially or fully

Metastasis – spread of a malignant disease to other parts of the body

Magnetic Resonance Imaging (MRI) – a test that uses radio waves and powerful magnets to produce images of tissues in the body; capable of showing the difference between normal and diseased tissue

Pathology Report – can provide information about type of tumor cells, extent of invasion into organs, and grade of cancer cells (how closely the cancer cells resemble normal cells)

Position Emission Tomography (PET) – a procedure where radioactive glucose is administered intravenously and imaging notes "hot spots" where the glucose is being used by the body; since cancer cells use more glucose than normal cells the imaging can identify clusters of cancer cells

Prostate Specific Antigen (PSA) – protein produced by cells of the prostate; usually elevated when cancer is present

Radiation Therapy – medical use of radiation for controlling cancer cells; multiple angles used to prevent problems in normal surrounding tissue; usually treats specific regions

Sensate Focus – Highly structured touching activities that are designed to help individuals overcome performance anxiety and increase comfort with physical intimacy; sexual intercourse is discouraged while full attention is given to engaging one's senses

Squamous cell skin cancer – a faster growing form of skin cancer with more risk for metastasis

ABOUT THE AUTHOR

Patrick Meadors, PhD, LMFT is a licensed MFT, AAMFT Clinical Member, and CFHA Professional Member. He is currently a practicing medical family therapist at Robert Boissoneault Oncology Institute in Ocala, FL. This radiation oncology practice has five offices in Central Florida. He was in the first graduating class from the nation's first Medical Family Therapy doctoral program at East Carolina University.

RESOURCES FOR PRACTITIONERS

ONLINE

National Cancer Institute
www.cancer.gov
Offers up-to-date information regarding cancer and the prevention, early detection, treatment, survivorship of cancer.

American Cancer Society
www.cancer.org
Information about cancer, treatment, support groups and psychosocial services available to patients.

Cancer Care
www.cancercare.org
Provides information on cancer, treatments, support group, counseling, and financial assistance options.

Needy Meds
www.needymeds.com
Multiple programs that help with cost of medicine and other healthcare expenses.

BOOKS

Adler, N. & Page, A. (Eds.) (2008). *Cancer care for the whole patient: Meeting psychosocial health needs.* Washington: Institute of Medicine of the National Academies.
This text outlines a standard of care for psychosocial services provided to patients with cancer. There is a focus on the improvement of the quality of care for patients with chronic illnesses and discussion about models of implementation.

Miller, S., Bowen, D., Croyle, R., Rowland, J. (Eds.) (2009). *Cancer control and behavioral science: A resource for researchers, practitioners, and policy makers.* Washington: American Psychological Association.
This text provides research based behavioral approaches to the treatment of psychosocial issues in cancer patients. While empirically supported models are discussed, this text is particularly useful to researchers interested in the effectiveness of psychosocial interventions.

REFERENCES

Adler, N., & Page, A. (Eds.) (2008). *Cancer care for the whole patient: Meeting psychosocial health needs.* Washington, DC: Institute of Medicine of the National Academies.

Alfano, C., & Rowland, J. (2009). The experience of survival for patients: Psychosocial adjustment. In S. Miller, D. Bowen, R. Croyle, & J. Rowland (Eds.), *Cancer control and behavioral science: A resource for researchers, practitioners, and policy makers.* (pp.413-430). Washington, DC: American Psychological Association.

American Cancer Society (2008). *Cancer facts and figures: 2008,* Atlanta: American Cancer Society. Retrieved November 10, 2008, from http://www.cancer.org/downloads/STT/2008CAFFfinalsecured.pdf.

Association of Oncology Social Work. (2006). Member survey report. *The Association of Oncology Social Work.* Retrieved November 3, 2008, from http://www.aosw.org/docs/Member Survey.pdf.

Bischoff, R. (2005). Cancer and the couple relationship: The implications of recent findings for couple therapy. *Journal of Couple and Relationship Therapy, 4,* 93-99.

Bruce, M. (2006). A systematic and conceptual review of posttraumatic stress in childhood cancer survivors and their parents. *Clinical Psychology Review, 26,* 233-256.

Carlsen, K., Jensen, A., Jacobsen, E., Krasnik, M., & Johansen, C. (2005). Psychosocial aspects of lung cancer. *Lung Cancer, 47,* 293-300.

Davidson, B., Goldenberg, S., Gleave, M., & Degner, L. (2003). Provision of individualized information to men and their partners to facilitate treatment decision making in prostate cancer. *Oncology Nursing Foundation, 30,* 107-114.

Edelman, S., Lemon, J., Bell, D., Kidman, A. (1999). Effects of group CBT on the survival time of patients with metastatic breast cancer. *Psycho-Oncology, 8,* 474-481.

Engel, G. (1977). The need for a new medical model. *Science, 196,* 129-136.

Ganz, P., Greendale, G., Petersen, L., Zibecchi, L., Kahn, B., & Belin, T. (2002). Quality of life in long-term, disease-free survivors of breast cancer: A follow-up study. *Journal of the National Cancer Institute, 94,* 39-49.

Helgeson, V., & Cohen, S. (1996). Social support and adjustment to cancer: Reconciling descriptive, correlational, and intervention research. *Health Psychology, 15,* 135-148.

Hodgson, J., Shields, C., & Rousseau, S. (2003). Disengaging communication in later-life couples coping with breast cancer. *Families, Systems, & Health, 21,* 145-163.

Hodgson, J., Lamson, A., & Reese, L. (2007). The biopsychosocial-spiritual interview method.

In D. Linville, & K. Hertlein (Eds.), *The therapist's notebook for family health care* (pp. 3-12). New York: Haworth Press.

Jacobsen, P., & Jim, H. (2008). Psychosocial interventions for anxiety and depression in adult cancer patients: Achievements and challenges. *A Cancer Journal for Clinicians, 58,* 214-230.

Jang, S., Ackler, J., Braitman, L., & Tester, W. (2007). The value of FACT-G in screening cancer patients for depression. *Journal of Clinical Oncology, 25,* 19557.

Johnson, S., & Greenberg, L. (1985). The differential effects of experiential and problem
solving interventions in resolving marital conflict. *Journal of Consulting and Clinical-Psychology, 53*, 175-183.

Kowal, J., Johnson, S., & Lee, A. (2003). Chronic illness in couples: A case for emotionally focused therapy. *Journal of Marital and Family Therapy, 29*, 299-310.

Krex, D., Klink, B, Hartmann, C., et al. (2007). Long-term survival with glioblastoma multiforme. *Brain, 130*, 2596-2606.

Kuijer, R., Buunk, B., Jong, M., Ybema, J., Sanderman, R. (2004). Effects of a brief intervention program for patients with cancer and their partners on feelings of inequity, relationship quality, and psychological distress. *Psycho-Oncology, 13*, 321-334.

Massie, M. (2004). Pervalence of depression in patients with cancer. *Journal of the National Cancer Institute Monographs, 32*, 57-71.

McDaniel, S., Doherty, W., & Hepworth, J. (1992). *Medical family therapy: A biopsychosocial approach to families with health problems.* New York: Basic Books.

McDaniel, J., Musselman, D., Porter, M., Reed, D., & Nemeroff, C. (1995). Depression in patients with cancer. *Archives of General Psychiatry, 52*, 89-99.

McQuellon, R., Wells, M., Hoffman, S., Craven, B., Russell, G., Cruz, J., et al. (1998). Reducing distress in cancer patients with an orientation program. *Psycho-Oncology, 7*, 207-217.

Moynihan, C., Bliss, J., Davidson, J., Burchell, L., & Horwich, A. (1998). Evaluation of adjuvant psychological therapy in patients with testicular cancer: Randomised controlled trial. *British Medical Journal, 316*, 429-435.

National Cancer Institute (2008). Facing forward: Life after cancer treatment. Retrieved November 10, 2008, from http://www.cancer.gov/cancertopics/life-after-treatment.

Neuling, S., & Winefield, H. (1988). Social support and recovery after surgery for breast cancer:
Frequency and correlates of supportive behaviors by family, friends, and surgeon. *Social Science and Medicine, 27*, 385-392.

Reis, L., Melbert, D., Krapcho, M., Mariotto, A., Miller, B., Feuer, E., et al. (Eds.) (2007). *SEER cancer statistics review, 1975-2004 National Cancer Institute.* Retrieved October 27, 2008, from https://seer.cancer.gov/csr/1975_2004.

Robson, M., Hensley, M., Barakat, R., Brown, C., Chi, D., Poyner, E., & Offit, K. (2003). Quality of life in women at risk for ovarian cancer who have undergone risk-reducing oophorectomy. *Gynecologic Oncology, 89*, 281-287.

Rolland, J. (1994). *Families, illness, and disability.* New York: Basic Books.

Shields, C., Travis, L., & Rousseau, S. (2000). Marital attachment and adjustment in older couples coping with cancer. *Aging and Mental Health, 4*, 223-233.

Schover, L. (2009). Reduction of psychosexual dysfunction in cancer patients. In S. Miller, D.
Bowen, R. Croyle, & J. Rowland (Eds.), *Cancer control and behavioral science: A resource for researchers, practitioners, and policymakers.* (pp. 379-389). Washington, DC: American Psychological Association.

Schover, L., Fouladi, R., Warneke, C., Neese, L., Klein, E., Zippe, C., & Kupelian, P. (2002).
Defining sexual outcomes after treatment for localized prostate cancer. *Cancer, 95*, 1773-1778.

Timmereck, T. (1987). *Dictionary of health services management* (2nd ed). Owings

Mills, MD: National Health Publishing.

Walker, J., Postma, K., McHugh, G., Rush, R., Coyle, B., Strong, V., & Sharpe, M. (2007). Performance of the hospital anxiety and depression scale as a screening tool for major depressive disorder in cancer patients. *Journal of Psychosomatic Research, 63*, 83-91.

Walsh, P., Marschke, P., Ricker, D., & Burnett, A. (2000). Patient-reported urinary continence and sexual function after anatomic radical prostatectomy. *Urology, 55*, 58-61.

Weisman, A., & Worden, J. (1976). The existential plight in cancer: Significance of the first 100 days. *International Journal of Psychiatry in Medicine, 7*, 1-15.

Winzelberg, A., Classen, C., Alpers, G., Roberts, H., Koopman, C., Adams, R., et al. (2003). Evaluation of an internet support group for women with primary breast cancer. *Cancer, 97*, 1164-1173.

Wright, L., Watson, W., & Bell, J. (1996). *Beliefs: The heart of healing in families and illness.* New York: Basic Books.

Zigmund, A, & Snaith, R. (1983). The hospital anxiety and depression scale. *Acta Psychiatrica Scandinavica, 67*, 361-370.

Autoimmune Diseases in Women

Mark B. White, PhD & Carmel Parker White, PhD

*Originally published as Clinical Update in Family Therapy Magazine
September-October 2009*

WOMEN AND AUTOIMMUNITY

As you review the intake for your 2pm appointment, you see that the client is a 38-year-old woman reporting fatigue, aches and pains, difficulty concentrating, and depressed mood. She could be experiencing major depressive disorder. However, she could also have an autoimmune disease, like multiple sclerosis (MS) or systemic lupus erythematosus (SLE).

The autoimmune diseases are a heterogeneous collection of disorders that share one key feature—the immune system malfunctions and turns on the patient's body, resulting in tissue and organ damage. For example, in MS the immune system attacks myelin, the protective coating of the nerve cells in the brain and spinal cord, resulting in sclerosis or scarring. There are many autoimmune diseases—estimates range from 70 (Whitacre, 2001) to over 100 (American Autoimmune Related Disease Association [AARDA], 2009). They are the third most prevalent category of disease in the United States, after cancer and heart disease (Fairweather & Rose, 2004). Somewhere between three to eight percent of the U.S. populace are estimated to have an autoimmune disease (Cooper & Stroehla, 2003).

In the past, the autoimmune disorders were considered individually, resulting in fragmented attention and research activity (Whitacre, 2001). However, in recent years there has been a push to group and study them as a family of diseases, like cancers (AARDA, 2004-2009; Whitacre, 2001). While there appears to be a genetic predisposition associated with virtually all of the autoimmune diseases, environmental (e.g., infections, viruses, medications, chemical exposure) and chance factors are important as well, since the genetic contribution is usually relatively minor (Davidson & Diamond, 2006; Rose & Mackay, 2006).

A perplexing aspect of the autoimmune diseases is that almost all are more common in females. Approximately two-thirds to three-fourths of patients with an autoimmune disease are female (Cooper & Stroehla, 2003; Fairweather & Rose, 2004). In fact, autoimmune diseases are "among the leading causes of death among young and middle-aged women in the United States" (Cooper & Stroehla, 2003, p. 119).

The reasons for the sex differences are only partially understood. One complicating factor is that the degree of sex-discordance varies. Sjögren's Syndrome and SLE are the most sex-discordant, with sex ratios of 9:1 (females:males) (Manoussakis & Moutsopoulos, 2006; Petri, 2006), while Type 1 diabetes may be slightly more prevalent in males (Whitacre, 2001). Thus, sex-linked factors vary across the different diseases. However, there is some evidence that sex differences in the basic immune response exist (Whitacre, 2001). Researchers have noted that in response to an antigen, immune system activation appears to be more pronounced in women than in men (Fairweather & Rose, 2004; Whitacre, 2001). Attention has also been paid to the sex hormones (estrogen, testosterone, and progesterone). Fluctuating levels of sex hormones have been associated with differential disease patterns. For example, during the third trimester of pregnancy, the levels of estrogen and progesterone increase. Pregnant women with MS or rheumatoid arthritis (RA) typically experience decreased symptoms over the course of the pregnancy, particularly during the third trimester. In contrast, the symptoms of women with SLE stay the same or worsen during pregnancy. Certain immune system responses appear to be favored or minimized in the face of increased or decreased levels of sex hormones (Whitacre, 2001). It has also been found that sex hormones can communicate directly with immune cells themselves. Furthermore, genetic factors may make some individuals more susceptible to certain autoimmune diseases, as well as impact the expression of sex hormones and the immune response (Whitacre, 2001).

In following sections we focus on three autoimmune disorders, MS, RA, and SLE, in order to provide more specific illustrations of the issues facing women with these diseases and their families.

DIAGNOSIS AND ASSESSMENT

Medical family therapists and family therapists who are informed about the challenges associated with living with a chronic illness can be a resource to patients and their families at any stage of the process of seeking, receiving, and living with the diagnosis of an autoimmune disease. Women who are symptomatic have often seen several physicians and may even have been referred to a mental health provider for a mood, anxiety, or somatization disorder before obtaining a definitive diagnosis. While the diagnosis of an autoimmune disorder can be traumatic, it can also bring relief—"there is a name for what I am going through and I'm not crazy." A brief discussion of each disease and the respective diagnostic process follows.

MS. Multiple sclerosis, a disease that appears to be a mixture of both an autoimmune disorder and a degenerative neurological disease, is the "most common chronic disabling disease of the central nervous system in young adults" (Confavreux, Vukusic, Moreau, & Adeleine, 2000, p. 1430). Autoimmune activity within the person attacks the myelin of nerve cells in the central nervous system (brain, spinal cord, and optic nerves). The resulting impairment ranges from mild to severe. The disease is more common among women, has both progressive and relapsing forms, and is generally diagnosed between the ages of 20 and 50. The National Multiple Sclerosis Society (NMSS) (2008) estimates that approximately 400,000 individuals in the U.S. have MS. Symptoms of MS can include extreme fatigue, pain, depression and anxiety, sensory symptoms (burning, tingling, numbness, and itching), cognition (short-term memory, problems with organization) vision (blurred, double vision), speech (slurred, fluency), bladder (overactive, infections), bowel, mobility (paralysis), spasticity, weakness, balance and dizziness, and tremor (Kalb, 2000; Schapiro, 2007).

Over the years neurologists have developed various diagnostic criteria to organize the clinical data into a coherent diagnosis; the revised McDonald Diagnostic Criteria for MS is the latest iteration (Polman et al., 2005). In essence, these criteria rely on various combinations of clinical evidence, including one or more MS attacks, magnetic resonance imaging (MRI) evidence of lesions (damage to the myelin as a result of autoimmune activity), and/or evidence of immunoglobulins or specific proteins in the patient's cerebral spinal fluid that suggest autoimmune attacks on the nerve cells. Depending upon the symptom profile, there can be a significant diagnostic lag or time period between the emergence of initial symptoms and the receipt of a definitive diagnosis. In our reviews of the literature, we found reported lags ranging from 6 months to 46 years, although the typical lag was between 4 to 5 years (White, White, & Fox, in press). However, routine use of MRIs in diagnosing MS has likely reduced the duration of the diagnostic lag.

Perhaps the most useful way to classify the clinical course of MS is to distinguish between the relapsing and progressive subtypes. At the time of initial diagnosis, approximately 85% of persons with MS have a relapsing form of the illness and 15 percent have a progressive form (McDonnell, 2007). The former involves attacks or exacerbations followed by remission or periods of return to baseline functioning; the latter involves a worsening of symptoms, whether or not there are periods of discrete attacks or exacerbations. Over time, especially if not treated, many of those initially diagnosed with a relapsing form of the illness end up with a progressive form (secondary progressive).

RA. In RA, the immune system attacks the synovium or lining of the joints. The resulting inflammation, *synovitis*, brings joint pain and stiffness, and eventual cartilage breakdown and erosion of nearby bones, especially if treatment is not initiated. If the disease progression is not halted, the continuing inflammatory process can affect other organ systems, including the heart and lungs. RA is more common in women and is usually diagnosed between the ages of 30 and 50. The Arthritis Foundation (AF) estimates that about 1.3 million Americans have RA (2008). Although symptoms of RA may vary across persons with the illness, RA is considered a singular disease rather than one with distinct subtypes like MS or lupus. Although the course of RA varies from mild to severe, it often follows a progressive course, with patients experiencing periods of relapse, referred to as flares, followed by a return to some degree of improved functioning; in this sense for many women it can be considered a progressive, relapsing disease.

Patients are typically diagnosed by a rheumatologist. The present diagnostic criteria require that patients meet at least four of seven criteria. The criteria include morning stiffness, arthritis in three or more joint areas, arthritis in hand joints, symmetric arthritis (in both sides of the body), rheumatoid nodules, serum rheumatoid factor, and visible changes in x-rays of affected areas (Arnett et al., 1988). RA can also have a diagnostic lag as initial symptoms can mimic other diseases and patients may not initially seek care from a rheumatologists, although the lag times in the literature tend to be shorter than for MS (e.g., from a few weeks to more than six months once a person realizes the necessity for a rheumatology consult; Kim & Weisman, 2000; a median lag of 17 months in another study, Hernández-García et al., 2000).

Lupus. There are four lupus subtypes (Wallace, 2005). The most common and serious type, SLE (approximately 70 percent of lupus patients), involves autoimmune attacks on a wide range of cells and tissues within the body, including the skin, joints, blood, kidneys, heart, lungs, and nervous system. Antibodies created by the immune system attack and inflame the body's own tissues, resulting in pain, swelling, rashes, anemia, and ulceration. SLE is much more common in women, and is more likely to be diagnosed in women of color. Most individuals are diagnosed between the ages of 15 and 45. The other subtypes are (a) Discoid lupus erythematosus (about 10 percent of cases—the skin is the only organ affected); (b) Drug-induced lupus erythematosus (another 10 percent of cases—begins as a result of the use of a few specific prescription drugs; typically remits once the drugs have been discontinued); and (c) Crossover or overlap syndrome or Mixed connective tissue disease (approximately 5 to 10 percent of cases; these persons also meet criteria for another lupus-like autoimmune disorder, such as RA or scleroderma; a disease involving tight skin and arthritis) (Wallace, 2005). The Lupus Foundation of America (LFA) estimates that approximately 1.5 million Americans have some form of lupus (2008).

The diagnostic criteria for SLE involve 11 criteria (Wallace, 2005). These 11 consist of 3 skin criteria (e.g., butterfly rash over the cheeks and nose, sun sensitivity); 4 systemic criteria (e.g., arthritis, kidney disorder); and 3 laboratory criteria (e.g., blood abnormalities, a positive antinuclear antibody blood test). Patients are diagnosed with SLE if 4 of the 11 criteria are present (2005). The diagnostic lag for lupus is estimated between two to three years, but can be longer for patients who are first diagnosed after the age of 60 (2005). About half of patients in one survey had symptoms for more than five years before being diagnosed (Baron-Faust & Buyon, 2003). There is a wide range of severity over the course of SLE with most cases resulting in mild to moderate symptoms, although for a minority the disease is fatal as a result of damage to the heart, lungs, and/or kidneys.

Clinical Issues. There are a wide range of relevant clinical issues that may arise when working with women with MS, RA, or SLE in individual, couple, or family therapy. At a minimum, we encourage family therapists to evaluate (a) how the client is coping with and making sense of having the illness; (b) the relational impact of the illness; and (c) any comorbid symptoms of a mental disorder.

To gain greater insight into how these women are coping with their illness, therapists might administer a measure like the Illness Cognition Questionnaire (Evers et al., 2001), a brief measure of how individuals view their illness and assesses the degree to which individuals have accepted their illness, feel helpless in dealing with it, and have identified any benefits to having the illness. Illness-specific coping measures might also be used (cf., MS, Pakenham, 2001; RA, van Lankveld, van't Pad Bosch, van De Putte, Näring, & van der Staaks, 1994; SLE, Büchi et al., 2000). In our research with persons with MS, higher illness related personal meaning with higher quality of life (Russell, White, & White, 2006), suggesting that this may be an important area of intervention for therapists.

Because MS, RA, and SLE have the potential to dramatically alter the daily life and interactions of women and their families, therapists should seek to assess the relational impact of the disease. One resource is Rolland's Family Systems-Illness Model (Rolland, 1994), which provides therapists with a valuable template for helping ill individuals and their families view and manage illness systemically. One facet of this exploration could be the degree of caregiver burden. For many families of a woman with MS, RA, or SLE, the impact of the illness on family roles and relationships is relatively minor; however, for others, issues of caregiver burden are significant. Accordingly, the same measures discussed for assessing symptoms of depression and anxiety could be administered to caregivers. In addition, numerous measures of positive and negative aspects of caregiving are available (cf. Buhse, 2002; Family Caregiver Alliance, 2002; Jacobi, 2003), such as the Coping with MS Caregiving Inventory (Pakenham, 2002), which includes five subscales: avoidance, criticism and coercion, positive reframing, supportive engagement, and practical assistance.

Figure 1 provides the lifetime prevalence of either anxiety or mood disorders obtained in various samples of persons with MS, RA, and SLE. Given that a significant proportion of individuals with these illnesses may also develop a mood or anxiety disorder, routine use of screening measures for anxiety and mood symptoms should be standard practice (e.g., PHQ-9 [Kroenke & Spitzer, 2002] or Zung's Self-Rating Anxiety Scales (SAS) [Zung, 1971]). It is vital that therapists be prepared to help these clients find a way to identify and manage their mood and anxiety symptoms. The challenge in doing so is that anxiety and depression can be (a) a physical consequence of the autoimmune disease; (b) a side effect of the treatments for the illness (e.g., the interferons or corticosteroids); and/or (c) a result of the burden of living with a chronic illness. While it may not be possible or necessary to ascertain the specific cause of the mental health symptoms, patients and their families should benefit from reaching a shared agreement about how to view and

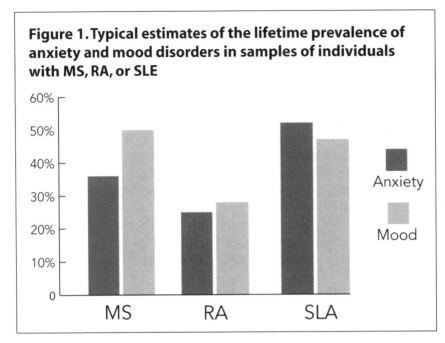

Figure 1. Typical estimates of the lifetime prevalence of anxiety and mood disorders in samples of individuals with MS, RA, or SLE

manage these symptoms.

Because the prognosis, course, and treatment options for these three autoimmune diseases and their subtypes can be different, it is important that therapists should be familiar with the unique aspects of these illnesses, including the various subtypes. For example, the coping skills required of patients and families are different for a woman with a relapsing illness like relapsing-remitting MS, versus one with a progressive illness like RA or SLE. The former must adjust to normal functioning being disrupted by attacks that are unpredictable and can come on suddenly. During the attack, the patient and her family will not know how long the attack will last and if she will return to her former level of functioning. In contrast, the certainty that comes with a progressive form of an illness brings its own challenges. The patient and her family know she is only going to get worse, which can be a painful and difficult adjustment. Further, at present there are few real treatment options for the progressive forms of MS, which can be disheartening to individuals and families.

Collaboration. Family therapists can also play an important role in assisting individuals and families who are navigating the healthcare system, including helping individuals and families communicate with healthcare providers to ensure their questions about the illness and medical treatment are answered and that their emotional needs are being met in interactions with healthcare providers (White, White & Russell, 2007).

TREATMENT OPTIONS AND BIOMEDICAL ISSUES

At present, a cure does not exist for MS, RA, or SLE. Accordingly, the goal of treatment is to manage symptoms and slow the progression of the illness. While there are some commonalities across treatments for MS, RA, and SLE (e.g., the use of pain medications and corticosteroids; Baron-Faust & Buyon, 2003), each illness is typically treated by different medical specialists (neurologists for MS and rheumatologists for RA and SLE). Patients and their families often need to coordinate their medical treatments between these specialists and their primary care physician, and as noted previously, can be supported by family therapists in doing so. Individuals who experience symptoms that impede or interfere with bodily movements also may need to be treated by occupational, physical, speech, and/or vestibular rehabilitation therapists (Cabrera-Gómez, 2007).

A healthy lifestyle, including adequate nutrition, rest and relaxation, and appropriate exercise are essential for individuals living with these chronic illnesses (Saydah & Eberhardt, 2002; Shapiro et al., 1996; Stuifbergen & Roberts, 1997). An exercise regimen can be adapted to an individual's specific needs and has been associated with reduced fatigue and improved mood (Krupp, 2004; Mostert & Kesselring, 2002). For example, some evidence exists that forms of low impact exercise like yoga or t'ai chi may be beneficial to individuals with MS, RA, and SLE (e.g., Oken et al., 2004; Taibi & Bourguignon, 2003; Wallace, 2006). Diets rich in Omega-3 fatty acids, commonly found in fish oil, have been beneficial for persons with SLE, MS, and RA (Bates, 1990; Geusens, Wouters, Nijs, Yebin, & Dequeker, 1994; Simopoulos, 2002; Wallace, 2005). Mediation and mindfulness assist those with chronic illnesses to experience feelings of well-being (Bonadonna, 2003; Reibel, Greeson, Brainard, & Rosenzweig, 2001; Wallace, 2005) and those with chronic illnesses can carefully attend to their bodies' signals in order to maximize their feelings of well-being (e.g., what types of stress negatively impact them, foods that influence their energy, what medical symptoms need medical attention) (Register, 1987). Individuals with autoimmune disease are also usually encouraged to avoid exposure to others with infections or viruses, such as the flu, and remain current on their immunizations.

The role of stress in autoimmune illnesses is still being debated. Some researchers have found that stress plays a role in causing an exacerbation of symptoms, while other researchers have not (Kozora, Ellison, Waxmonsky, Wamboldt, & Patterson, 2005; Schwartz et al., 1999). Accordingly, it cannot hurt and may be beneficial for individuals and families to minimize stress and maximize feelings of well-being. The ideal therapist for individuals and families living with chronic illness is one who is familiar with the unique challenges of living with chronic illness, especially the patient's specific illness. In some instances, the National Multiple Sclerosis Society, the Arthritis Foundation, or the Lupus Foundation can provide names and contact information of local therapists. Individuals could ask questions of the therapist to ascertain their familiarity with chronic illness issues. Helpful questions include, "Have you ever treated a woman living with SLE and her family?" "How familiar are you with the symptoms of MS and their impact on an individual and her family?" or "Are you familiar with the challenges of living with a chronic illness, especially a chronic illness with invisible symptoms (see sidebar)?"

Individuals with MS, RA, and SLE can experience fatigue, which may be one of their most severe and debilitating symptoms (Baker & Pope, 2009; Johnson, 2008; Patrick, Christodoulou, & Krupp, 2009; Repping-Wuts, van Riel, & van Achterberg, 2008; Yount et al., 2007). This fatigue is categori-

INVISIBLE SYMPTOMS

Illness does not occur in a vacuum—there are social considerations associated with illness. Over 50 years ago, Talcott Parsons (1951) asserted that being sick is not just a condition, it is a social role that comes with a set of behavioral expectations. Sick people are to act like they are ill. Accordingly, there are advantages to having visible symptoms. If one is visibly ill—in a wheelchair, bandaged, breathing supplemental oxygen— then individuals are validated in the sick role. However, there are also disadvantages to being in the sick role. Sick persons may experience stigma or differential treatment. For example, when encountering individuals in a wheelchair, strangers may speak to the companion of the person rather than to the person in the chair, or raise their voice and speak louder or in an exaggerated manner.

Many of the symptoms experienced by women with autoimmune diseases are not readily visible or apparent to others. Common invisible symptoms for these illnesses include:

MS	RA	SLE
cognitive difficulties	joint pain	fatigue
fatigue	pleurisy	anemia
depression	fatigue	memory and concentration problems
numbness and tingling	feelings of malaise	arthritis
bowel and bladder dysfunction	anemia	elevated blood pressure
	dry eyes	sensitivity to the sun

Women who experience a host of invisible symptoms may escape the stigma associated with the sick role, but at the same time may not receive the validation that comes with it. Accordingly, people may not perceive or believe that the person is ill ("But you look so good") or may be critical (e.g., a woman with MS who has some trouble walking may be thought to be intoxicated; a person with movement issues that come and go may be criticized for parking in a handicapped spot).

Family therapists can help women with an autoimmune illness initiate conversations with the significant people in their lives about their illness and its impact. In particular, therapists can help these women explore ways to validate their experience of being ill, and at the same time resist being marginalized or stigmatized. Participating in support groups with other individuals who have the same illness can be one way to accomplish this. Therapists who have developed a specialty working with a specific illness might facilitate such groups, or can encourage their patients to contact their local chapters of the NMSS, AF, or LFA. Each provides referral information on available support groups and other local resources available.

cally different than what healthy individuals experience and can be extremely distressing to the individual. Fatigue can impact an individual's ability to perform in her roles as a family member, worker, and friend. Given the central role that most women play in families, it is important for family therapists to ascertain if women are able to perform their roles and if they are unable to do so, what types of social support they have access to (White, White, & Martin, in press). Further, the invisibility (see sidebar) of fatigue necessitates that individuals learn how to communicate with others about their fatigue and how it is impacting them (White, White, & Russell, 2008). While there are some pharmacological treatments for fatigue, fatigue is typically dealt with by appropriate exercise, staying cool, appropriate nutrition, and energy conservation strategies through modifications to the patient's schedule, environment, and social interactions (Krupp, 2004; White et al., in press).

Because many of the disease symptoms or side effects of medication may interfere with body image (e.g., weight gain, disfigured joints, skin rashes) or ability to perform important roles (e.g., parent, partner), family therapists need to be aware of and address the implications of identities being changed by illness or the treatment of illness. Furthermore, there can be numerous issues for women with MS, RA, or SLE who are trying to become pregnant, who are pregnant or are breastfeeding that are beyond the scope of this article, including the need to work closely with their healthcare provider to ensure the medications are safe. In the next section, we will briefly review the approaches to treating MS, RA, and SLE.

While the discussion that follows focuses more on biomedical treatments in order to inform family therapists about standard treatment for these illnesses, we also want to stress that data exist that talk therapy, often including elements of psychoeducation or cognitive-behavioral therapy, has a role in helping individuals with MS (Thomas, Thomas, Hillier, Galvin & Baker, 2006), RA (Astin, Beckner, Soeken, Hochberg, & Berman, 2002) and SLE (e.g., Karlson et al., 2004) cope with their illnesses. Behavioral interventions that have empirical support include cognitive-behavioral interventions focusing on managing the illness, psychoeducation about the disease and its psychosocial impact, a focus on enhancing patient self-efficacy, an emphasis on health promotion, mindfulness components (e.g.,. progressive relaxation, meditation), and stress management (e.g., Karlson et al., 2004; Kraaimaat, Brons, Geenen, Bijlsma, 1995; Stuifbergen, Becker, Blozis, Timmerman, Kullbert, 2003).

Some literature on the relational issues and/or treatments for these diseases is available. For example, a study of individuals with an episodic neurological interview (epilepsy or MS) and a family member identified the issues facing them, which can guide the domains addressed in family interventions (i.e., relationship issues with family members and significant others; intrapersonal issues; psychosocial, vocational, and educational issues; issues of disability, symptoms and medical concerns; Long, Glueckauf, & Rasmussen, 1998). A psychoeducational group for couples living with MS is available (Rolland, McPheters, & Carbonell, 2008). Clinical outcome studies have utilized a treatment condition that provided psychoeducation about the disease, and skill training for the patient and a family member related to issues like pain management, coping, and treatment compliance (RA patients and a family member, Radojevic, Nicassio, & Weisman, 1992) or self-efficacy, communicating about the disease, social support and problem solving (SLE patients and a family member, Karlson et al., 2004). Hopefully the future will bring randomized clinical trials of true family therapy treatments for these illnesses.

There are two main categories of pharmaceutical treatments for autoimmune illnesses that will be described in the next section—medications to (a) manage the symptoms caused by the illness; and (b) slow the progression of the disease (Baron-Faust & Buyon, 2003; Holland, Murray, & Reingold, 2002; Oger, 2007; Schapiro, 2007). It should be noted that the side effects of some of the pharmacological treatments listed below can be serious and extensive and can greatly impact the quality of life for patients and their families. Family therapists should work with patients and their physicians in dealing with the side effects. If the medication is designed to treat a symptom but the side effects of the symptom are more difficult to live with, patients may decide to discontinue the medication. However, for medications designed to slow the progression of the disease, patients and their families need to clearly understand that while the side effects may be difficult to live with, there is a definite benefit to the medication in the long-term, even if the progression of the disease may be unobservable to the patient.

MULTIPLE SCLEROSIS

Symptom Management. Individuals with MS can have vastly different symptoms, and even within the same person can be variable over time. Therefore, treatments can widely vary from individual to individual and over time. Given the wide array of possible symptoms and treatments, individual treatments for each of the symptoms will not be discussed here. However, Holland et al. (2002) and Schapiro (2007) offer detailed discussions of symptoms and possible treatments. At the same time, we should point out that when an individual with MS experiences new symptoms or an increase in existing symptoms, frequently corticosteroids like prednisone are prescribed to reduce inflammation with the hope that the new symptom will disappear or symptoms will return to previous levels.

Slowing the Progression of the Disease. Several treatments are now available to slow the progression of the disease. They are referred to as disease modifying agents (DMAs). Immunomodulators designed to "turn down" the overreaction of the immune system include interferons (Avonex®, Betaseron®, or Rebif®), monoclonal antibodies (Tysabri®), glatiramer acetate (Copaxone®), and mitoxantrone (Novantrone®) (Holland et al., 2002; Oger, 2007). One caveat about DMAs, however, is that they are primarily designed for individuals with relapsing-remitting MS. Some of the mentioned treatments can be used by those with secondary progressive MS (a form of MS that began as relapsing-remitting but changed to gradual decline without periods of remission), usually mitoxantrone, but unfortunately there are currently no specific

TERMINOLOGY

Antibody: A specialized protein created by the immune system in response to an antigen. Also known as immunoglobulins, antibodies bind to the invading substance in order to destroy it or make it easier to destroy.

Antigen: Any substance that triggers the immune system to produce an antibody to fight the perceived threat.

Autoimmunity: The condition in which the immune system is activated by one's own tissue and creates antibodies that attack one's own organs and tissues.

Autoimmune diseases: A diverse group of illnesses that share one feature—the immune system mistakenly identifies some component of the individual's own body as an antigen and manufactures antibodies and mounts an attack on the substance, such as the synovium in RA or a wide range of body cells or parts of cells in SLE.

Magnetic Resonance Imaging (MRI): A diagnostic scanning procedure that uses a magnetic field and radio waves, instead of X-rays, to create pictures of human tissue based on a computerized composite of multiple "slices" of the body.

Medical family therapy: A subspeciality within family therapy that focuses on the intersection between families and illness, health, loss, or trauma. Medical family therapists operate from a biopsychosocial-spiritual framework in their work with individuals, couples, families, and larger systems coping with acute and chronic challenges associated with health. They are commonly employed as academicians, researchers, policy makers, administrators and/or clinicians. Regardless of the work context, medical family therapists are innovators in integrated care and are trained to collaborate with a variety of medical providers, researchers, and educators.

Sjögren's Syndrome: An autoimmune disease that can be a primary disorder or a secondary complication of other autoimmune disease like SLE and RA. As a result of autoimmune activity, cells that provide moisture for the body are attacked (including the tear and saliva glands), resulting in dry eyes and mouth and damage to other organ systems. The disease is nearly always diagnosed in women, usually after age 50.

Synovitis: Inflammation of the synovium.

Synovium: The fluid-filled membrane in the space between joints that acts to cushion and lubricate the joints.

MS & Anxiety. Source: Korostil & Feinstein (2007). Lifetime prevalence of an anxiety disorder based on a structured clinical interview from a clinical sample of patients at an MS clinic in Toronto (n=140).

MS & Mood. Source: Minden & Schiffer (1990). Estimates of the lifetime prevalence of depression in individuals with MS based on a review of the literature.

RA & Anxiety. Source: Arnold et al. (2006). Lifetime prevalence of any anxiety disorder based on a structured clinical interview from a clinical sample of patients at a rheumatology clinic in Cincinnati, OH (n=40).

RA & Mood. Source: Fifield, Tennen, Reisinne, & McQuillan. (1998). Lifetime prevalence of a mood disorder based on CES-D scores from a cohort study of individuals with RA from a national RA panel (n=203).

SLE & Anxiety. Source: Nery et al. (2008). Lifetime prevalence of an anxiety disorder based on a structured clinical interview from a clinical sample of female patients at a lupus clinic in San Paolo, Brazil (n=71).

SLE & Mood. Bachen, Chesney, & Criswell. (2009). Lifetime prevalence of major depressive disorder based on a diagnostic interview in a sample of women with SLE enrolled in a lupus genetics project (n=301).

DMAs designed to slow the progression of primary progressive MS (a form of MS involving gradual worsening without periods of remission).

RHEUMATOID ARTHRITIS

Symptom Management. Typical symptoms of RA include morning stiffness and soreness and sore and aching joints. Although any joint in the body can be a target, the hands and feet are usually the first areas affected (Baron-Faust & Buyon, 2003). The associated inflammation is also linked to body aches, low-grade fever, and malaise (Baron-Faust & Buyon). Over half of persons with RA will also develop pleurisy or swelling of the lining of the chest and lungs—some also develop pericarditis or swelling of the sac around the heart (Baron-Faust & Buyon). Nearly 30 percent of individuals with RA may develop firm raised lumps—rheumatoid nodules—most commonly in places like the elbows and finger joints, but in other body systems as well (Kent & Matteson, 2004). Over time, erosion and bone loss also occurs.

The primary components of symptom-focused RA treatment are pain control and reducing inflammation. Women with RA may be prescribed a range of medications including aspirin, nonsteroidal anti-inflammatory drugs (NSAIDs) (e.g., ibuprofen, Motrin®), naproxen sodium (Alleve®) or nabumetone (Relafen®), or newer NSAIDs, known as COX-2 inhibitors, like celecoxib (Celebrex®) or rofecoxib (Vioxx®) (Baron-Faust & Buyon). As was noted, corticosteroids are also used on an intermittent basis to reduce inflammation and pain.

Slowing the Progression of the Disease. A central aspect of treating RA involves the use of disease-modifying antirheumatic drugs (DMARDs). These drugs may alter the course of RA by targeting specific immune cells that cause the damage, thus slowing the rate of further injury to the joints, bones, and cartilage. Although there are several, the most commonly used DMARD is methotrexate (Rheumatrx®, Trexall®) (Baron-Faust & Buyon, 2003). Methotrexate is typically viewed as a first line treatment, often in combination with the medications classified as biological agents, like infliximab (Remicade®) or entanercept (Embrel®) (Baron-Faust & Buyon; Lee & Weinblatt, 2004). Antimalarial drugs like hydroxychloroquine (Plaquenil®) are also utilized for their ability to suppress inflammation, often in combination with methotrexate (Baron-Faust & Buyon). Surgical treatments for RA include joint replacement and tendon reconstruction (Baron-Faust & Buyon). It should be noted that the standard of care in RA is quite complex and depends on a host of factors including prognosis, disease activity, and pattern of response to other drugs (Saag et al., 2008).

SYSTEMIC LUPUS ERYTHEMATOSUS

Symptom Management. Because the autoimmune activity in SLE can target a host of different cells within the body, the range of symptoms is extensive. They include joint pain, fevers, skin rashes, sensitivity to the sun, fatigue, anemia, arthritis, hair loss, kidney problems, pleurisy, pericarditis, oral or nasal ulcers, and seizures or psychosis (Baron-Faust & Buyon, 2003). There can be considerable overlap between the treatments for RA and SLE. The same pain medications listed for RA (NSAIDS and COX-2 inhibitors) are also used for patients with SLE. Other treatments are also utilized as necessary to target the specific organ systems impacted by SLE activity (e.g., dialysis for kidney problems, lasers for removing skin lesions) (Wallace, 2005). Part of managing SLE involves controlling environmental factors. For example, patients with SLE should limit their exposure to the sun and ultraviolet light, but with appropriate use of sunscreen, hats, appropriate clothing, sunglasses, and tinted windows, need not become phobic about exposure to the sun or UV rays (2005).

Slowing the Progression of the Disease. Rheumatologists utilize several classes of drugs to slow the progression of SLE. The DMARDs noted for RA are also used for patients with SLE, including antimalarial drugs like hydroxychloroquine. A wide range of corticosteroids are also employed in treating various aspects of SLE. They have a more central role in treating SLE than in MS or RA, because they can be very effective in slowing disease activity associated with major organs like the heart, kidneys, lungs, liver, or blood (Wallace, 2005). Corticosteroids are also used to manage SLE exacerbations or flares. Many individuals with SLE are on low doses of corticosteroids for extended periods of time. Wallace discussed the negative consequences that are often associated with long-term use of these medications and the trade-offs that patients must make (e.g., agitation, insomnia, aggression, thinning skin and hair, impaired wound healing, glucose intolerance, fat redistribution, water retention, osteoporosis).

A wide range of other medications are sometimes used in treating SLE (cf. Wallace, 2005), including immunosuppressive drugs, which typically are a form of chemotherapy (e.g., cyclophosphamide, Cytoxan®; cyclosporine A, Neoral®; tacrolimus, Prograf®). These drugs are considered cytotoxic (cell killing), in that they reduce the number of immune cells (Baron-Faust & Buyon, 2003). These medications are typically used when the SLE is threatening key organs and corticosteroids alone cannot treat the problems (2005).

ABOUT THE AUTHORS

Mark B. White, PhD, an AAMFT Clinical Member and Approved Supervisor, is an associate professor of medical family therapy and marriage and family therapy in the Department of Child Development and Family Relations at East Carolina University. His research interests focus on couples and chronic illness, and family therapy process and outcome.

Carmel Parker White, PhD, is an assistant professor in the Department of Child Development and Family Relations at East Carolina University. Her research interests focus on families and chronic illness, specifically considering the role fatigue, pain, and depression play in family interaction.

RESOURCES FOR PRACTITIONERS

American Autoimmune Related Diseases Association
www.aarda.org
National nonprofit health agency dedicated to bringing a national focus to the autoimmune diseases. Web site includes a wide range of resources for patients with an autoimmune disease and healthcare professionals.

Arthritis Foundation
www.arthritis.org
National organization supporting research, advocacy, information and services for persons with osteoarthritis, RA, and juvenile arthritis, their family members, and healthcare professionals.

Baron-Faust, R., & Buyon, J. P. (2003). *The autoimmune connection: Essential information for women on diagnosis, treatment, and getting on with your life.* Comprehensive and practical overview of the diagnostic process, treatment options, and management of several autoimmune diseases. Written by a medical journalist who was diagnosed with hyperthyroidism in 1971 and a physician specializing in treating SLE and other rheumatic illnesses.

Lupus Foundation of America
www.lupus.org
National organization supporting research, advocacy, information and services for persons with lupus, their family members, and healthcare professionals.

National Multiple Sclerosis Society
www.nmss.org
National organization supporting research, advocacy, information and services for persons with MS, their family members, and healthcare professionals.

Wallace, D. L. (2005). *The lupus book: A guide for patients and their families* (3rd ed.). New York: Oxford University Press. Comprehensive overview of the immune system, the signs and symptoms of lupus, and its treatment and management by a board certified rheumatologist.

REFERENCES

American Autoimmune Related Diseases Association. (2004-2009). Autoimmune disease in women. Retrieved June 29, 2009, from http://www.aarda.org/research_display.php?ID=47.

American Autoimmune Related Diseases Association. (2009). List of autoimmune diseases. Retrieved June 29, 2009, from http://www.aarda.org/research_display.php?ID=47.

Arnett, F. C., Edworthy, S. M., Bloch, D. A., McShane, D. J., Fries, J. F., Cooper, N. S., et al. (1988). The American Rheumatism Association 1987 Revised Criteria for the classification of rheumatoid arthritis. *Arthritis & Rheumatism, 31,* 315-

324.

Arnold, L. M., Hudson, J. I., Keck, P. E., Jr., Auchenbach, M. B., Javaras, K. N., & Hess, E. V. (2006). Comorbidity of fibromyalgia and psychiatric disorders. *Journal of Clinical Psychiatry, 67,* 1219-1225.

Arthritis Foundation. (2008). Rheumatoid arthritis: What is it? Retrieved July 20, 2009, from http://www.arthritis.org/disease-center.php?disease_id=31.

Astin, J. A., Beckner, W., Soeken, K., Hochberg, M. C., & Berman, B. (2002). Psychological interventions for rheumatoid arthritis: A meta-analysis of randomized controlled trials. *Arthritis & Rheumatism, 47,* 291-302.

Bachen, E. A., Chesney, M. A., & Criswell, L. A. (2009). Prevalence of mood and anxiety disorders in women with systemic lupus erythematosus. *Arthritis & Rheumatism, 61,* 822-829.

Baker, K., & Pope, J. (2009). Employment and work disability in systemic lupus erythematosus: A systemic review. *Rheumatology,* 48, 281-284.

Baron-Faust, R., & Buyon, J. P. (2003). *The autoimmune connection: Essential information for women on diagnosis, treatment, and getting on with your life.* New York: McGraw-Hill.

Bates, D. (1990). Dietary lipids and multiple sclerosis. *Upsala Journal of Medical Sciences Supplement, 48,* 173-187.

Bonadonna, R. (2003). Meditation's impact on chronic illness. *Holistic Nursing Practice, 17,* 309-319.

Büchi, S., Villiger, P., Kauer, Y., Klaghofer, R., Sensky, T., & Stoll, T. (2000). PRISM (Pictorial Representation of Illness and Self Measure)—A novel visual method to assess the global burden of illness in patients with systemic lupus erythematosus. *Lupus, 9,* 368-373.

Buhse, M. (2008). Assessment of caregiver burden in families of persons with multiple sclerosis. *Journal of Neuroscience Nursing, 40,* 25-31.

Cabera-Gómez, J. A. (2007). Rehabilitation in multiple sclerosis. In T. L. Munstat (Series Ed.) & J. Oger & A. Al-Araji (Co-Chairs), *Multiple sclerosis for the practicing neurologist,* World Federation of Neurology Seminars in Clinical Neurology (Vol. 5, pp. 75-83). New York: Demos.

Carson, M. J., Anglen, C. S., & Ploix, C. (2005). In A. Minagar & J. S. Alexander (Eds.), *Inflammatory disorders of the nervous system: Pathogenesis, immunology, and clinical management* (pp. 17- 40). Totowa, NJ: Humana Press.

Confavreux, C., Vukusic, S., Moreau, T., & Adeleine, P. (2000). Relapses and progression of disability in multiple sclerosis. *New England Journal of Medicine, 343,* 1430-1438.

Cooper, G. S., & Stroehla, B. C. (2003). The epidemiology of autoimmune diseases. *Autoimmunity Reviews, 2,* 119-125.

Davidson, A., & Diamond, B. (2006). General features of autoimmune disease. In N. R. Rose & I. R. Mackay (Eds.), *The autoimmune diseases* (4th ed., pp. 25-36). San Diego, CA: Elsevier Academic Press.

Evers, A. W. M., Kraaimaat, F. W., van Lankveld, W., Jongen, P. J. H., Jacobs, J. W. G., & Bijlsma, J. W. J. (2001). Beyond unfavorable thinking: The Illness Cognition Questionnaire for chronic diseases. *Journal of Consulting and Clinical Psychology, 69,* 1026–1036.

Fairweather, D., & Rose, N. R. (2004). Women and autoimmune disease. *Emerging Infectious Diseases, 10*(11), 2005-2011.

Family Caregiver Alliance. (2002). *Selected caregiver assessment measures: A resource inventory for practitioners.* San Francisco, CA: Author.

Fifield, J., Tennen, H., Reisine, S., & McQuillan, J. (1998). Depression and the long-term risk of pain, fatigue, and disability in patients with rheumatoid arthritis. *Arthritis & Rheumatism, 41,* 1851-1857.

Geusens, P., Wouters, C., Nijs, J., Yebin, J., Dequeker, J. (1994). Long-term effect of Omega-3 fatty acid supplementation in active rheumatoid arthritis: A 12-month, double-blind, controlled study. Arthritis and Rheumatism, *37,* 824-839.

Hernández-García, C., Vargas, E., Abásolo, L., Lajas, C., Bellajdell, B., Morado, I. C., et al. (2000). Lag time between onset of symptoms and access to rheumatology care and DMARD therapy in a cohort of patients with rheumatoid arthritis. *Journal of Rheumatology, 27,* 2323-2328.

Holland, N. J., Murray, T. J., & Reingold, S. C. (2002). *Multiple sclerosis: A guide for the newly diagnosed* (2nd ed.). New York: Demos.

Jacobi, C. E., van den Berg, B., Boshuizen, H. C., Rupp, I., Dinant, H. J., van den Bos, G. A. (2003). Dimension-specific burden of caregiving among partners of rheumatoid arthritis patients. *Rheumatology (Oxford), 42,* 1226-1233.

Johnson, S. L. (2008). The concept of fatigue in multiple sclerosis. *Journal of Neuroscience Nursing, 40,* 72-77.

Kalb, R. C. (2000). *Multiple sclerosis: The questions you have, the answers you need.* New York: Demos Medical Publishing.

Karlson, E. W., Liang, M. H., Eaton, H., Huang, J., Fitzgerald, L., Rogers, M. P., & Daltroy, L. H. (2004). A randomized clinical trial of a psychoeducational intervention to improve outcomes in systemic lupus erythematosus. *Arthritis & Rheumatism, 50,* 1832-1841.

Kim, J. M., & Weisman, M. H. (2000). When does rheumatoid arthritis begin and why do we need to know? *Arthritis & Rheumatism, 43,* 473-484.

Korostil, M., & Feinstein, A. (2007). Anxiety disorders and their clinical correlates in multiple sclerosis patients. *Multiple Sclerosis, 13,* 67-72.

Kozora, E., Ellison, M. C., Waxmonsky, J. A., Wamboldt, F. S., & Patterson, T L. (2005). Major life stress, coping styles, and social support in relation to psychological distress in patients with systemic lupus erythematosus. *Lupus, 14,* 363-372.

Kroenke, K., & Spitzer, R. L. (2002). The PHQ-9: A new depression diagnostic and severity measure. *Psychiatric Annals, 32*(9), 1-7.

Kraaimaat, F. W., Brons, M. R., Geenen, R., Bijlsma, J. W. J. (1995). The effect of cognitive behavior therapy in patients with rheumatoid arthritis. *Behaviour Research and Therapy 33,* 487–95.

Krupp, L. B. (2004). *Fatigue in multiple sclerosis: A guide to diagnosis and management.* New York: Demos.

Lee, D. M., & Weinblatt, M. E. (2004). Methotrexate and Azathioprine. In E. W. St. Clair, D. S. Pisetsky, & B. F. Haynes (Eds.), *Rheumatoid Arthritis.* (pp. 303-314). Philadelphia, PA: Lippincott Williams & Wilkins.

Long, M. P., Glueckauf, R. L., & Rasmussen, J. L. (1998). Developing family counseling interventions for adults with episodic neurological disabilities: Presenting problems, persons involved, and problem severity. *Rehabilitation Psychology, 43,* 101-117.

Lupus Foundation of America (2008). *What is lupus?* Retrieved July 20, 2009, from http://www.lupus.org/webmodules/webarticlesnet/templates/new_learnunderstanding.aspx?articleid=2232&zoneid=523.

Manoussakis, M. N., & Moutsopoulos, H. M. (2006). Sjögren syndrome. In N. R.

Rose & I. R. Mackay (Eds.), *The autoimmune diseases* (4th ed., pp. 401-416). San Diego, CA: Elsevier Academic Press.

McDonnell, G. V. (2007). Clinical features of multiple sclerosis. In T. L. Munstat (Series Ed.) & J. Oger & A. Al-Araji (Co-Chairs), *Multiple sclerosis for the practicing neurologist*, World Federation of Neurology Seminars in Clinical Neurology (Vol. 5, pp. 7-18). New York: Demos.

Minden, S. L., & Schiffer, R. B. (1990). Affective disorders in multiple sclerosis: Review and recommendations for clinical research. *Archives of Neurology, 47,* 98-104.

Mostert, S., & Kesselring, J. (2002). Effects of a short-term exercise training program on aerobic fitness, fatigue, health perception and activity level of subjects with multiple sclerosis. *Multiple Sclerosis, 8,* 161-168.

National Multiple Sclerosis Society. (2008). *Just the facts, 2007-2008: General information.* New York: Author.

Nery, F. G., Borba, E. F., Viana, V. S. T., Hatch, J. P., Soares, J. C., Bonfá, E., & Neto, F. L. (2008). Prevalence of depressive and anxiety disorders in systemic lupus erythematosus and their association with anti-ribosomal P antibodies. *Progress in Neuro-Psychopharmacology & Biological Psychiatry, 32,* 695-700.

Oger, J. (2007). Immunotherapy of multiple sclerosis: Theoretical basis and practical approach. In T. L. Munstat (Series Ed.) & J. Oger & A. Al-Araji (Co-Chairs), *Multiple sclerosis for the practicing neurologist*, World Federation of Neurology Seminars in Clinical Neurology (Vol. 5, pp. 65-74). New York: Demos.

Oken, B. S., Kishiyama, S., Zajdel, D., Bourdette, D., Carlsen, J., Hass, M. et al. (2004). Randomized controlled trial of yoga and exercise in multiple sclerosis. *Neurology, 62,* 2058-2064.

Olek, M. J. (2005). Differential diagnosis, clinical features, and prognosis of multiple sclerosis. In M. J. Olek (Ed.), *Multiple sclerosis: Etiology, diagnosis, and new treatment strategies* (pp. 15-53). Totowa, NJ: Humana Press.

Pakenham, K. K. (2001). Coping with multiple sclerosis: Development of a measure. *Psychology, Health & Medicine, 6,* 411-428.

Patrick, E., Christodoulou, C., Krupp, L., & on behalf of the New York State MS Consortium. (2009). Longitudinal correlates of fatigue in multiple sclerosis. *Multiple Sclerosis, 15,* 258-261.

Petri, M. (2006). Systemic lupus erythematosus and related diseases: Clinical features. In N. R. Rose & I. R. Mackay (Eds.), *The autoimmune diseases* (4th ed., pp. 351-356). San Diego, CA: Elsevier Academic Press.

Polman, C. H., Reingold, S. C., Edan, G., Filippi, M., Hartung, H-P, Kappos, L., et al. (2005). Diagnostic criteria for multiple sclerosis: 2005 revisions to the "McDonald Criteria." *Annals of Neurology, 58,* 840-846.

Register, C. (1987). *The chronic illness experience: Embracing the imperfect life.* Center City, MN: Hazelden.

Reibel, D. K., Greeson, J. M., Brainard, G. C., & Rosenzweig, S. (2001). Mindfulness-based stress reduction and health-related quality of life in a heterogeneous patient population. *General Hospital Psychiatry, 23,* 183-192.

Repping-Wuts, H., Fransen, J., van Achterberg, T., Bleijenberg, G., & van Riel, P. (2007). Persistent severe fatigue in patients with rheumatoid arthritis. *Journal of Clinical Nursing, 16,* 377-83.

Rolland, J. S. (1994). *Families, illness, and disability: An integrative treatment model.* New York: Basic Books.

Rolland, J. S., McPheters, J. K., & Carbonell, E. (2008, November). *Resilient partners: A collaborative project with the MS Society.* Presentation at the annual conference of the Collaborative Family Healthcare Association, Denver, CO.

Rose, N. R., & Mackay, I. R. (2006). Prospectus: The road to autoimmune disease. In N. R. Rose & I. R. Mackay (Eds.), *The autoimmune diseases* (4th ed., pp. xix-xxv). San Diego, CA: Elsevier Academic Press.

Russell, C. S., White, M. B., & White, C. P. (2006). Why me? Why now? Why multiple sclerosis? Meaning making and perceived quality of life in a midwestern sample of patients with multiple sclerosis. *Families, Systems, & Health, 24,* 65-81.

Saag, K. G., Teng, G. G., Patkar, N. M., Anuntiyo, J., Finney, C., Curtis, J. R., et al. (2008). American College of Rheumatology 2008 recommendations for the use of nonbiologic and biologic disease-modifying antirheumatic drugs in rheumatoid arthritis. *Arthritis & Rheumatism, 59,* 762-784.

Saydah, S. H., & Eberhardt, M. S., (2006). Use of complementary and alternative medicine among adults with chronic diseases: United States 2002. *The Journal of Alternative and Complementary Medicine, 12,* 805-812.

Schapiro, R. T. (2007). Symptomatic management of multiple sclerosis. In T. L. Munstat (Series Ed.) & J. Oger & A. Al-Araji (Co-Chairs), *Multiple sclerosis for the practicing neurologist,* World Federation of Neurology Seminars in Clinical Neurology (Vol. 5, pp. 51-57). New York: Demos.

Shapiro, J. A., Koepsell, T. D., Voigt, L. F., Dugowson, C. E., Kestin, M., & Nelson, J. L. (1996). Diet and rheumatoid arthritis in women: A possible protective effect of fish consumption. *Epidemiology, 7,* 256-263.

Simopoulos, A. P. (2002). Omega-3 fatty acids in inflammation and autoimmune diseases. *Journal of the American College of Nutrition, 21,* 495-505.

Singhal, B. S. (2007). Corticosteroids in the treatment of multiple sclerosis. In T. L. Munstat (Series Ed.) & J. Oger & A. Al-Araji (Co-Chairs), *Multiple sclerosis for the practicing neurologist,* World Federation of Neurology Seminars in Clinical Neurology (Vol. 5, pp. 59-64). New York: Demos.

Schapiro, R. T. (2007). Symptomatic management of multiple sclerosis. In T. L. Munstat (Series Ed.) & J. Oger & A. Al-Araji (Co-Chairs), *Multiple sclerosis for the practicing neurologist,* World Federation of Neurology Seminars in Clinical Neurology (Vol. 5, pp. 51-57). New York: Demos.

Schwartz, C. E., Foley, F. W., Rao, S. M., Bernardin, L. J., Lee, H., & Genderson, M. W. (1999). Stress and course of disease in multiple sclerosis. *Behavioral Medicine, 25,* 110-116.

Stuifbergen, A. K., & Roberts, G. J. (1997). Health promotion practices of women with multiple sclerosis, *Archives of Physical Medicine and Rehabilitation, 78,* S3-S9.

Stuifbergen, A. K., Becker, H., Blozis, S., Timmerman, G., & Kullbert, V. (2003). A randomized clinical trial of a wellness intervention for women with multiple sclerosis.

Taibi, D. M., & Bourguignon, C. (2003). The role of complementary and alternative therapies in managing rheumatoid arthritis. *Family & Community Health, 26,* 41-52.

Thomas, P. W., Thomas, S., Hillier, C., Galvin, K., & Baker, R. (2006). Psychological intervention for multiple sclerosis. *Cochrane Database of Systematic Reviews,* Issue 1. Art. No.: CD004431. DOI: 10.1002/14651858.CD00431.pub2.

van Lankveld, W., van't pad Bosch, P., van De Putte, L., Näring, G., & van der

Staaks, C. (1994). Disease-specific stressors in rheumatoid arthritis: Coping and well-being. *British Journal of Rheumatology, 33,* 1067-1073.

Wallace, D. J. (2005). *The lupus book: A guide for patients and their families* (3rd ed.). New York: Oxford University Press.

Wallace, D. J. (2006). What's new in the management of lupus since 2000? *Journal of Clinical Rheumatology, 12,* 307-313.

Whitacre, C. C. (2001). Sex differences in autoimmune disease. *Nature Immunology, 2,* 777-780.

White, C. P., White, M. B., & Martin, J. K. (in press). The aftermath of the diagnostic lag: Working with women recently diagnosed with multiple sclerosis. In *Women and multiple sclerosis: Symptoms, diagnosis, and quality of life.* New York: Nova Science.

White, C. P., White, M. B., & Martin, J. K. (in press). Relational coping strategies used by mothers with multiple sclerosis to cope with fatigue. In *Women and multiple sclerosis: Symptoms, diagnosis, and quality of life.* New York: Nova Science.

White, C. P., White, M. B., & Russell, C. S. (2008). Invisible and visible symptoms of multiple sclerosis: Which are more predictive of health distress? *Journal of Neuroscience Nursing, 40,* 85-95, 102.

White, C. P., White, M. B., & Russell, C. S. (2007). Multiple sclerosis patients talking with healthcare providers about emotions. *Journal of Neuroscience Nursing, 39,* 89-101.

Yount, S., Sorensen, M. V., Cella, D., Senqupta, N., Grober, J., & Chartash, E. K. (2007). Adalimumab plus methotrexate or standard therapy is more effective than methotrexate or standard therapies alone in the treatment of fatigue in patients with active, inadequately treated rheumatoid arthritis. *Clinical and Experimental Rheumatology, 25,* 838-846.

Zung, W. W. K. (1971). A rating instrument for anxiety disorders. *Psychosomatics, 12,* 371-379.

Bariatric Surgery

Maria J. Frisch, MS, Carol Signore, MAT & Ellen S. Rome, MD

*Originally published as Clinical Update in Family Therapy Magazine
January-February 2011*

O besity is a major health problem. During the past 25 years, rates of adult obesity have doubled and rates of childhood obesity have nearly tripled; that rate is as high as one in three for 8 to 19 year olds in many states (Ogden, Carroll, McDowell, & Flegal, 2007; Ogden, Carroll, Curtin, Lamb, & Flegal, 2010; Skelton, Cook, Auinger, Klein, & Barlow, 2009). Approximately 34 percent of US adults and on average 18 percent of US adolescents are currently obese (a BMI of 30 or greater for adults and a BMI at or above the 95th percentile for children of the same age and sex) (Flegal, Carroll, Ogden, & Curtin, 2010; Ogden et al., 2010). Around 75 percent among this group will suffer from one or more obesity-related medical comorbidities (Must et al., 1999).

Bariatric surgery has emerged as a viable option (and often a medical necessity) for obese individuals suffering from related medical complications, who have not responded to non-surgical interventions (Allen, Lawson, Garcia, & Inge, 2005; Nguyen et al., 2005; Santry et al., 2007; Steinbrook, 2004; T. A. Wadden & Phelan, 2002). For many, bariatric surgical procedures provide greater and more durable weight reduction than both behavioral and pharmacological interventions alone **(Santry et al., 2007).**

Marriage and family therapists can use their training and expertise with couples and families to help bariatric surgery patients navigate challenges before and after surgery. In addition to the physical and behavioral alterations that follow weight loss surgery, personal relationships and family loyalties may undergo significant changes as a result of dramatic weight loss. (Mamplekou, 2005; van Hout 2005; Green et al., 2004; Hafner, 1991; Rand et al., 1982)

DEFINITION

Bariatric surgery involves a combination of techniques that cause gastric restriction, malabsorption and/or changes in neural and endocrine hormones.

The procedures are typically performed laparoscopically, through a small incision in the abdomen.

Adjustable Gastric Banding. Gastric restriction is accomplished by placement of a belt-like band (such as Lap Band or Realize Band) around the stomach. Once tightened, it constricts the stomach into an hourglass shape, leaving a very small pouch that receives food via the esophagus. The band functionally slows movements down through the stomach, causing one to feel full for a longer period of time, following consumption of smaller than usual meals. The overall effect of this is calorie reduction.

Roux-en-Y. This technique combines the process of gastric restriction along with malabsorption. First, the stomach size is drastically reduced (usually with staples or a band), allowing for less intake of calories. Second, the first part of the small intestine (duodenum), where substantial calories are absorbed, is surgically bypassed. Ingested nutrients thus mix directly in the lower intestine, causing reduced absorption. This method advantageously allows one to consume more calories than with gastric restriction alone, while still maintaining weight reduction over time. However, there are also disadvantages to this method. Mainly, the pyloric valve is bypassed during banding. This sometimes leads to dumping syndrome, whereby undigested stomach contents are rapidly dumped into the small intestine causing nausea, bloating or abdominal cramping.

Bilopancreatic Diversion with a Duodenal Switch. This method also works by combining gastric restriction and malabsorption. First, a large portion of the stomach is removed, creating a "gastric sleeve." This decreases the amount of food one is able to consume in a single sitting. Next, a significant amount of the smaller intestine is removed (via rearrangement) in order to impair food absorption. But unlike Roux-en-Y, a portion of the duodenum is preserved. This allows for greater absorption of vitamins and nutrients. As a result of the small intestine rearrangement, bile and pancreatic juices are separated from food during a portion of digestion, directly impairing fat absorption. This complex procedure tends to be higher risk than the others mentioned.

Some morbidly obese individuals who weigh too much to qualify for the full procedure may undergo only the first part. This procedure is known as vertical sleeve gastrectomy. Some patients may lose significant amounts of weight through this procedure alone. It is thought that removal of much of the stomach may reduce a hormone called grehlin, which leads to reduced feelings of hunger. Reduction of grehlin levels is not seen in gastric banding, where the cells secreting grehlin are not disturbed.

Gastric Pacing. Gastric pacing is a form of electrical stimulation that involves placing a gastric pacemaker on the stomach, near the vagus nerve. The stimulations likely mimic the actions of extragastric neurohormones like CCK, giving a sensation that one is full. However, proposed mechanisms of action are still under investigation. This procedure is currently in clinical trials (Hasler, 2009; Sanmiguel et al., 2009; Shikora et al., 2009).

EFFICACY

Dallal and colleagues used mixed-effects linear modeling to calculate patient weight loss in multiple clinical settings (Dallal, Quebbemann, Hunt, et al., 2009). Average percentage of weight loss following bariatric surgery was 71 percent, 79 percent, and 76 percent at one, two, and three years post-surgery, respectively. Previous studies have reported results up to 20 percent lower (Cunneen, 2008; Garb, Welch, Zagarins, Kuhn, & Romanelli, 2009), however their methods of statistical analysis (uncontrolled t-tests) may have been less ideal (Singer & Willett, 2003).

Improvements are seen in several areas of medical and psychological comorbidity. Diabetes is completely resolved in 64-100 percent of patients, hyperlipidemia improved in 60-100 percent, hypertension resolved in 60-88 percent, and obstructive sleep apnea resolved in 85 percent (Buchwald & Consensus Conference Panel, 2005; Kushner & Noble, 2006; Pories et al., 1995). Significant improvements are also seen in quality of life and mental health (de Zwaan et al., 2002; Larsen et al., 2003; Mamplekou, Komesidou, Bissias, Papakonstantinou, & Melissas, 2005; Vage, Solhaug, Viste, Bergsholm, & Wahl, 2003). Risk of suicide, binge eating, and issues related to past abuse have been shown to persist after surgery (Clark et al., 2007; Pekkarinen, 1994; Sarwer, 2008a; Sarwer, 2008b). Thus, post-surgical psychological follow-up should include ongoing assessment of these areas. Longitudinal follow up is ideal, as problems may not resurface during the first few months of weight loss. Weight loss often slows following the first year of surgery. During this period of transition, old coping strategies may resurface or new stressors may occur. The shift in body image that comes with precipitous weight loss may also alter relationships, with literature documenting post-operative marital stress (Hafner, 1991; Rand et al., 1992). The need for plastic surgery for excess skin folds can also cause stresses on body image, both pre- and post-surgery, requiring psychological follow up and support to adjust to a changing figure.

MORTALITY

A recent prospective longitudinal study sponsored by the National Institutes of Health (NIH) and published in the New England Journal of Medicine (Longitudinal Assessment of Bariatric Surgery (LABS) Consortium, 2009) likened the risks of bariatric surgery to that of gallbladder or hip replacement surgery. From 2005-2007, a total of 4,776 first-time bariatric surgery patients from 10 US clinical sites were followed for 30 days post-surgery. The 30-day mortality rate among patients who underwent a Roux-en-Y gastric bypass or laparoscopic adjustable gastric banding was 0.3 percent, with 4.3 percent of patients reporting at least one major adverse event. These mortality rates are lower than the long-term risk of dying from heart disease or diabetes.

Another large study (Adams et al., 2007) looked at mortality by comparing a large sample size of people who had undergone bariatric surgery (9,949) with obese individuals who had not undergone surgery (9,628). The one-year mortality rate among patients who had undergone bariatric surgery was 0.53 percent, which was the same as the control group (0.53 percent). By 7 years post-surgery, likelihood of mortality decreased by 40 percent as compared to the control. Those who had undergone bariatric surgery were also 92 percent, 60 percent, and 52 percent less likely to die from diabetes, cancer, and coronary artery disease, respectively.

PATIENT SELECTION

Patient selection is often based on standards published by the National Institutes of Health (NIH, 1992) Candidates typically have a body mass index (BMI) of 35 or more, along with one or more severe comorbidities that are expected to have a meaningful clinical improvement with weight reduction (for example, diabetes, hypertension, obstructive sleep apnea, etc.). It is recommended that patients show evidence of completion of a structured weight management program that covered diet, physical activity, and psychological and drug interventions, but did not result in significant and sustained improvement in weight-related comorbidities. Patients should be well informed of risks and complications, motivated to make lifestyle and eating habit changes, and able to participate in long-term follow-up (Association of periOperative Registered Nurses, 2004; Greenberg, Sogg, & M. Perna, 2009; Pull, 2010).

Morbid obesity is associated with somatic and psychiatric comorbidity, including depression, anxiety, eating disorders, abnormal personality traits and personality disorders (Pull, 2010). However, personality traits and history of psychological or psychiatric treatment do not predict long-term post-surgery weight loss (Herpertz, Kielmann, Wolf, Hebebrand, & Senf, 2004). As such, psychiatric comorbidity is not necessarily a contraindication for surgery. In fact, bariatric surgery often improves mental health and overall quality of life (e.g. somatization, depression, anxiety, interpersonal sensitivity, social functioning, etc.) (de Zwaan et al., 2002; Larsen et al., 2003; Mamplekou et al., 2005). Improvements, particularly in the areas of depression and anxiety, have been reported up to 25 years post-surgery (Vage et al., 2003).

EXPERT RECOMMENDATIONS FOR HEALTHCARE PROVIDERS

The 1991 NIH Consensus Statement on "Gastrointestinal Surgery for Severe Obesity," which has since been updated (Buchwald et al., 2004), was a watershed document in promoting bariatric surgery as a legitimate intervention. This publication was followed by increased utilization of bariatric surgery in both the United States and Canada (Davis, Slish, Chao, & Cabana, 2006). Other countries have followed with similar guidelines. (CMAJ, 2007; NHS, 2007; SIGN, 2010). Many professional journals have also published

TABLE 1. GUIDELINES FOR ADOLESCENTS (12-18 YRS) WITH A BMI OF ≥ 40

	On maximum medical therapy	NOT on maximum medical therapy
Diabetes - severity defined by Hgb A1c levels		
Severe	✔	✔
Moderate	✔	
Mild		
Hypertension – normal defined as ≤ 140/ ≤ 90 ≥ 140 SBP and/or ≥ 90 DBP	✔	
Dyslipidemia - excess lipids in blood or excess cholesterol levels	✔	✔
Chronic joint pain that severely affects work and leisure	✔	✔

	Regardless of therapy
Prediabetes (fasting blood glucose of 101-125 mg/dl)	✔
Sleep Apnea – as confirmed by a sleep study test	
Severe	✔
Moderate	✔
Mild	✔
Venous stasis disease	✔
Impaired quality of life - as measured by a formal and previously validated quality of life (QOL) questionnaire.	✔
Reflux esophagus – any symptoms 2 + of any of the above comorbidities	✔
No comorbidities	

✔ = surgery recommended

bariatric surgery guidelines targeted at specific needs within the health professions.

Revisions to the 1991 NIH Patient Selection Criteria. The NIH-supported patient selection criteria for bariatric surgery include BMI, medical comorbidities, and history of weight loss attempts. However, recent trends, such as positive outcomes in adolescents who have undergone surgery, support incorporation of additional factors, such as age and severity of medical comorbidities. Yermilov and colleagues (2009) recently published revised selection criteria that addressed the wider spectrum of patients currently presenting for bariatric surgery, whereby the benefits of bariatric surgery outweigh the risks. In particular, they provide detailed guidelines for adults and adolescents presenting with a BMI between 35 and 39. For adults with a BMI as low as

34 through 39, most medical comorbidities (along with a history of failed weight loss attempts) were grounds for surgical intervention. For those with no medical comorbidities, it was unclear if the benefits outweighed the risks. In general, surgical intervention was not recommended for adults with a BMI of less than 34. The guidelines for adolescents were more dependent on severity of specific comorbidities and are summarized in the table below for those with a BMI of 40 or greater. For adolescents with a BMI between 35 and 39, only the following are appropriate candidates: those with moderate to severe diabetes (despite maximal medical therapy), severe hypertension (despite maximal medical therapy), moderate to severe sleep apnea, or two or more medical comorbidities from Table 1. Surgery is generally not recommended for adolescents who have a BMI of less than 34.

Pre- and Post-operative Assessment. The purpose of assessment is to identify psychological risk factors that may compromise treatment outcomes. Most recently, these authors were involved in publication of recommendations for professionals working within the field of eating disorders (McAlpine, Frisch, Rome, et al., 2010). This document outlined pre- and post-operative assessment guidelines for healthcare providers. In summary:

1. Preoperative evaluation followed by postoperative, longitudinal follow-up by a multidisciplinary team specializing in surgery, medicine, psychiatry/psychology, exercise science, and nutrition. Follow-up should be monthly for the first six months, then bimonthly for the rest of the first year post surgery.
2. Each preoperative patient should have full understanding of postoperative dietary requirements, necessary postsurgical support, and the importance of stress management strategies.
3. Candidates with disordered eating should receive preoperative dietary, psychological, and psychiatric care so that they can successfully adapt to the required changes.
4. All patients should be screened for the presence of severe psychiatric comorbidities and receive clearance by a licensed mental health professional. An extended (e.g., 12-month) period of recovery from an eating disorder, substance abuse, manic episode, psychosis, psychiatric hospitalization, suicide attempt, and resolution of trauma survivorship issues before having bariatric surgery is recommended.
5. Preoperative and postoperative counseling and education are suggested for all candidates for assistance with lifestyle change, and additional individualized treatment should be provided to those with an Axis I or II psychiatric disorder

Assessment Instruments. Utilization of well-validated assessment instruments used in both research and clinical practice is important for purposes of standardization and optimal outcome measurements. Several instruments are suggested in Table 2. All instruments may be administered by a clinician or trained professional.

Child-focused Recommendations. Morbidly obese children and adolescents demonstrate sustained and clinically significant weight loss following bariatric

TABLE 2. PSYCHOLOGICAL ASSESSMENT INSTRUMENTS

Instrument	Admin. time	Major areas of assessment
Adult Psychopathology		
Structured Clinical Interview for DSM-IV Axis I Disorders (SCID-I) (M. B. First, Spitzer, Gibbon, & Williams, 1996) and the Structured Clinical Interview for DSM-IV Axis II Personality Disorder Diagnoses (SCID-II) (M. B. First, Gibbon M., Spitzer, Williams, & Benjamin, 1997).	1.5 – 3 hr. clinical interview	DSM-IV axis I and II diagnoses.
Minnesota Multiphasic Personality Inventory-2 (MMPI-2)	1 – 1.5 hr. written	Social and personal maladjustment
Pre-Surgical Readiness		
PsyBari (Mahony, 2010)	30 min. written	Psychological readiness for surgery: response bias, high risk factors, diet risk factors, emotional eating risk factors, weight related depression, weight related anxiety, anger index, weight-related impairment, medical health index, psychosocial supports, coping skills, and post-surgical expectations.
The Boston Interview for Bariatric Surgery (Sogg & Mori, 2004; Sogg & Mori, 2008)	1 – 1.5 hr. clinical interview	Psychological suitability for bariatric surgery: weight, diet, and nutrition history; eating pathology; medical history; understanding of surgical procedures, risks, and the post-surgical regimen; motivation and outcome ·expectations; relationships and support system; and psychiatric functioning.
Weight- and Eating-Related		
Weight and Lifestyle Inventory (WALI)(T. A. Wadden & Foster, 2006)	1 – 1.5 hr. written	Weight history, past weight loss attempts, weight loss goals, historical eating habits and associated patterns of behavior, physical activity, self-perceptions, psychological/emotional status and medical history.
Eating Disorders Examinations (EDE) (Cooper & Fairburn, 1987)	0.5 – 2 hr. clinical interview	Eating disorder related psychopathologies in the areas of restraint, eating concern, weight concern, and shape concern.
The Binge Eating Scale (BES) (Gormally, Black, Daston, & Rardin, 1982)	5 - 10 min. written	Severity of binge eating
Surgical Outcomes		
Bariatric Analysis and Reporting Outcome System (BAROS) (Oria & Moorehead, 2009).	5-10 min. written	Postoperative outcomes in obese patients: weight loss, changes in co-morbidities, and quality of life
Moorehead-Ardelt Quality of Life Questionnaire II (Moorehead, Ardelt-Gattinger, Lechner, & Oria, 2003). Incorporated into the BAROS, but may be given alone for pre- to post-surgery comparisons.	1 min. written	Postoperative outcomes of self-perceived quality of life (QoL) in obese patients: self-esteem, physical well-being, social relationships, work, and sexuality

surgery. However, some may face post-operative complications (Pratt et al., 2009). Thus, surgery is not generally recommended unless there is a clear and favorable risk to benefit profile (Caniano, 2009). The RAND/UCLA modified Delphi method is an objective and effective tool that may be used to weigh benefits vs. harm within a pediatric population (www.Rand.org).

While there have been reports of successful outcomes in children as young as six (Dan, Harnanan, Seetahal, Naraynsingh, & Teelucksingh, 2010), most surgeons reserve bariatric surgery for post-pubertal adolescents with morbid obesity and severe weight-related comorbidities (Logue et al., 2010). As an initial screening tool, the 1991 NIH consensus criteria and the 2009 comorbidity profile (outlined by Yermilov and colleagues) provide excellent resources (Nadler, Brotman, Miyoshi, Fryer, & Weitzman, 2009; Yermilov, McGory, Shekelle, Ko, & Maggard, 2009).

Recent studies report positive outcomes comparable to that seen in adults (Sjostrom, Lissner, Wedel, & Sjostrom, 1999): significant weight reduction up to six years post surgery; correction of obesity-related comorbidities; improvements in self-image, socialization and overall functioning, and an elevated quality of life (Barnett et al., 2005; Fielding & Duncombe, 2005; Papadia, Adami, Marinari, Camerini, & Scopinaro, 2007; Strauss, Bradley, & Brolin, 2001; Sugerman et al., 2003)

In lieu of these positive outcomes, those working with pediatric/adolescent populations must also consider ethical considerations present within this unique population. First, pediatric and adolescent populations are in the process of physiological and psychological maturation. The direct impact of restrictive and/or malabsorptive surgical procedures on this development is unclear. As a result, it is difficult to pinpoint an ideal age or stage for surgery.

Second, both parent and child are required to consent to the surgery. Assent procedures are adapted to a child's developmental level. However, a desire to have a surgical procedure, along with an ability to understand and approve of the procedure, does not infer physiological or psychological readiness. There are significant differences between the adolescent and the adult brain that yield implications for compromised decisional capacity (Partidge, 2010). Adolescents often have a limited ability to adequately assess risk (Bessant, 2008). This phenomenon is likely associated with the delayed maturation of the frontal lobes (Geidd, Blumenthal, & Jeffries, 1999). Full maturation of this area (in late adolescence to early adulthood) is required for fully developed executive functioning, decision-making capacity, and appreciation of long-term consequences associated with a decision. Children and adolescents may face a disadvantage in their assent for the procedure because their physiological development does not afford them with the same, well developed decision-making capacity found in an adult patient. It is important that parents understand this aspect of their child's consent.

Family-focused Recommendations. The expertise of marriage and family therapists makes them ideally suited for working with bariatric surgery patients. The families and partners of weight loss surgery patients are integrally involved in, and heavily impacted by, the behavior changes required in order for bariatric surgery to succeed. Food shopping, mealtime and even relaxing in front of the family TV can be charged with emotion and difficulty following surgery. Formerly comfortable familial patterns must shift to accommodate healthier habits. Change is often difficult, for everyone.

Family loyalties, friendships, and marital bonds are tested and sometimes traumatized in the first 6-8 months after surgery. Patients report strong interpersonal experiences of anger, embarrassment, and euphoria. An innocent observation from a spouse, friend or co-worker may be experienced as intrusive. A well-meant compliment at home or at work may cause confusion, discomfort and anger for patients. Research has labeled "oversensitivity in personal relationships" as a common source of post-op anxiety (Mamplekou, 2005).

Divorce rates appear to climb among couples with a bariatric surgery partner, especially in the first year after surgery (Rand et al., 1982). Hafner (1991) described altered partner perceptions following bariatric surgery. Patients saw their partners as less interesting and less social than they remember. Another study noted that partners and friends of bariatric patients sometimes felt abandoned or threatened by their new, thinner friend or partner.

Drastic physical transformations often lead to changes in self- and society perceptions. This may stress the patient's family and friends, forcing relationships to evolve. Also threatening to partnerships are the new and intense relationships patients often form with others who have had surgery. These relationships hold great importance for patients in the early months after surgery, but recede naturally as patients learn to navigate their own recoveries and their own conflicting feelings about self and others.

Marriages that fail following one partner's surgery are typically unions that were problematic beforehand. For example, some patients experience physical or emotional abuse in their relationship as a result of their morbid obesity. Strong, healthy relationships are more likely to survive the experience (van Hout 2005; Green et al 2004).

Near the end of the first post-operative year, some patients may display an intense and uncharacteristic self-assertiveness. They may explode with strident needs and opinions after years of accommodating and caretaking others. Friends, families and even patients are shocked at these strange changes in personality and in behavior. Individual or family counseling may be needed to help patients separate their true feelings from those that represent a normal reaction to years of personal invisibility.

There is growing anecdotal evidence that bariatric surgery patients are at risk for symptom substitution (Ertelt, Mitchell, & Lancaster, 2008). They may need guidance and individual support to develop new healthy behaviors and activities to replace the core role food has previously played in their lives. Couples and family therapy is recommended. Intervention and guidance for weight loss surgery patients and their families or partners is particularly important if eating was formerly experienced as an addiction or was used compulsively to organize and/or manage mood states.

CONCLUSION

Marriage and family therapists are ideally suited for providing effective after care to bariatric surgery patients and their families. Long-term success may be dramatically improved by coaching and individual care from pre-surgical evaluation through the first two to three years post-operation. We strongly encourage marriage and family therapists to pursue the additional education they may need to become familiar with the postoperative stages of change for bariatric surgery patients and the psychological issues facing this unique population. The American Society for Metabolic and Bariatric Surgery (www. asmbs.org) offers continuing education for mental health professionals.

ABOUT THE AUTHORS

Maria J. Frisch, MS, holds her graduate degree in health services research and policy from the University of Minnesota. She completed post-graduate research fellowships in the area of eating disorders at both Harvard University and Mayo Clinic. She is currently a second-year medical student at St. George's University.

Carol Signore, MAT, is a licensed Pennsylvania marriage and family therapist and a Clinical Member of the AAMFT. She is also a Fellow of the Academy for Eating Disorders and a member of the International Coaching Federation and the Tucson Professional Coaches Alliance. In 2002, Signore founded the nationally recognized bariatric surgery aftercare program, My Self Design, which provides individual assistance to weight loss surgery patients and certification training in bariatric surgery aftercare to qualified professionals.

Ellen S. Rome, MD, MPH, currently serves as the head of Adolescent Medicine at the Cleveland Clinic. She is a board certified pediatrician and an expert in the field of eating disorders and obesity. Rome holds an undergraduate degree in psychology from Yale, a medical degree from Case Western Reserve's School of Medicine, and a master's degree in Public Health from Harvard University. She also serves as an associate professor of pediatrics at the Cleveland Clinic Lerner College of Medicine at Case and runs the Cleveland Clinic's Pediatric Obesity Initiative, working to decrease childhood obesity through healthier exercise and eating habits.

REFERENCES

Adams, T. D., Gress, R. E., Smith, S. C., Halverson, R. C., Simper, S. C., Rosamond, W. D., et al. (2007). Long-term mortality after gastric bypass surgery. *The New England Journal of Medicine, 357*(8), 753-761.

Allen, S. R., Lawson, L., Garcia, V., & Inge, T. H. (2005). Attitudes of bariatric surgeons concerning adolescent bariatric surgery (ABS). *Obesity Surgery, 15*(8), 1192-1195.

ASMBS significant study on the safety of bariatric surgery. Retrieved July 8, 2010, from http://www.asmbs.org/Newsite07/resources/asmbs_news_study.html.

Association of periOperative Registered Nurses. (2004). AORN bariatric surgery guideline. *AORN Journal, 79*(5), 1026-40, 1043-4, 1047-52.

Barnett, S. J., Stanley, C., Hanlon, M., Acton, R., Saltzman, D. A., Ikramuddin, S., et al. (2005). Long-term follow-up and the role of surgery in adolescents with morbid obesity. *Surgery for Obesity and Related Diseases: Official Journal of the American Society for Bariatric Surgery, 1*(4), 394-398.

Bessant J. (2008). Hard wired for risk: Neurological science, 'the adolescent brain' and developmental theory. *Journal of Youth Studies:347, 11-60.*

Bocheri, L.E., Meana, M., & Fisher, B.L. (2002). *Perceived Psychosocial Outcomes of Gatric Bypass Surgery: A Qualitative Study, 12*(6), 781-788.

Buchwald, H., Avidor, Y., Braunwald, E., Jensen, M. D., Pories, W., Fahrbach, K., et al. (2004). Bariatric surgery: A systematic review and meta-analysis. *JAMA: The Journal of the American Medical Association, 292*(14), 1724-1737.

Buchwald, H., & Consensus Conference Panel. (2005). Bariatric surgery for morbid obesity: Health implications for patients, health professionals, and third-party payers. *Journal of the American College of Surgeons, 200*(4), 593-604.

Caniano, D. A. (2009). Ethical issues in pediatric bariatric surgery. *Seminars in Pediatric Surgery, 18*(3), 186-192.

Clark, M. M., Hanna, B. K., Mai, J. L., Graszer, K. M., Krochta, J. G., McAlpine, D. E., et al. (2007). Sexual abuse survivors and psychiatric hospitalization after bariatric surgery. *Obesity Surgery, 17*(4), 465-469.

Cooper, Z., & Fairburn, C. (1987). The eating disorder examination: A semi-structured interview for the assessment of the specific psychopathology of eating disorders. *International Journal of Eating Disorders, 6,* 1.

Cunneen, S. A. (2008). Review of meta-analytic comparisons of bariatric surgery with a focus on laparoscopic adjustable gastric banding. *Surgery for Obesity and Related Diseases: Official Journal of the American Society for Bariatric Surgery, 4*(3 Suppl), S47-55.

Dallal, R. M., Quebbemann, B. B., Hunt, L. H., & Braitman, L. E. (2009). Analysis of weight loss after bariatric surgery using mixed-effects linear modeling. *Obesity Surgery, 19*(6), 732-737.

Dan, D., Harnanan, D., Seetahal, S., Naraynsingh, V., & Teelucksingh, S. (2010). Bariatric surgery in the management of childhood obesity: Should there be an age limit? *Obesity Surgery, 20*(1), 114-117.

Davis, M. M., Slish, K., Chao, C., & Cabana, M. D. (2006). National trends in bariatric surgery, 1996-2002. *Archives of Surgery, 141*(1), 71-74.

de Zwaan, M., Lancaster, K. L., Mitchell, J. E., Howell, L. M., Monson, N., Roerig, J. L., et al. (2002). Health-related quality of life in morbidly obese patients: Effect of gastric bypass surgery. *Obesity Surgery: The Official Journal of the American Society for Bariatric Surgery and of the Obesity Surgery Society of Australia and New Zealand, 12*(6), 773-780.

Ertelt, T.W., Mitchell J.E., Lancaster, K., et al., (2008). Alcohol abuse and dependence before and after bariatric surgery: a review of the literature and report of a new data set. *JM Surg Obes Relat Dis.* 4(5):647-50.

Fielding, G. A., & Duncombe, J. E. (2005). Laparoscopic adjustable gastric banding in severely obese adolescents. *Surgery for Obesity and Related Diseases: Official Journal of the American Society for Bariatric Surgery, 1*(4), 399-405; discussion 405-7.

First, M. B., Gibbon M., Spitzer, R. L., Williams, J. B. W., & Benjamin, L. S.

(1997). *Structured clinical interview for DSM-IV axis II personality disorders, (SCID-II)*. Washington, D.C.: American Psychiatric Press, Inc.

First, M. B., Spitzer, R. L., Gibbon, M., & Williams, J. B. W. (1996). *Structured clinical interview for DSM-IV axis I disorders, clinician version (SCID-CV)*. Washington, D.C.: American Psychiatric Press, Inc.

Flegal, K. M., Carroll, M. D., Ogden, C. L., & Curtin, L. R. (2010). Prevalence and trends in obesity among US adults, 1999-2008. *JAMA: The Journal of the American Medical Association, 303*(3), 235-241.

Garb, J., Welch, G., Zagarins, S., Kuhn, J., & Romanelli, J. (2009). Bariatric surgery for the treatment of morbid obesity: A meta-analysis of weight loss outcomes for laparoscopic adjustable gastric banding and laparoscopic gastric bypass. *Obesity Surgery, 19*(10), 1447-1455.

Gastrointestinal surgery for severe obesity: National institutes of health consensus development conference statement.(1992). *The American Journal of Clinical Nutrition, 55*(2 Suppl), 615S-619S.

Giedd J.N., Blumenthal J., Jeffries N.*(1999)* Brain development during childhood and adolescence: A longitudinal MRI study. *Nature Neuroscience, 2:861-3.*

Gormally, J., Black, S., Daston, S., & Rardin, D. (1982). The assessment of binge eating severity among obese persons. *Addictive Behaviors, 7*(1), 47-55.

Green, A.E.C., Dymek-Valentine, M., Pytluk, S. et al. (2004). Psychosocial Outcome of Gastric Bypass Surgery for Patients with and without Binge Eating. *Obesity Surgery, 14*(7), 975-985.

Greenberg, I., Sogg, S., & M Perna, F. (2009). Behavioral and psychological care in weight loss surgery: Best practice update. *Obesity (Silver Spring, Md.), 17*(5), 880-884.

Hafner, R.J. (1991). Effects on the marital system of weight loss after gastric restriction. *Psychotherapy Psychosomatics, 56*, 162-166.

Hasler, W. L. (2009). Methods of gastric electrical stimulation and pacing: A review of their benefits and mechanisms of action in gastroparesis and obesity. *Neurogastroenterology and Motility: The Official Journal of the European Gastrointestinal Motility Society, 21*(3), 229-243.

Hassink, S.G. (2007). *Pediatric obesity: prevention, intervention, and treatment strategies for primary care, strategies for primary care*. Elk Grove, IL: American Academy of Pediatrics.

Herpertz, S., Kielmann, R., Wolf, A. M., Hebebrand, J., & Senf, W. (2004). Do psychosocial variables predict weight loss or mental health after obesity surgery? A systematic review. *Obesity Research, 12*(10), 1554-1569.

Herpertz, S., Kielmann, R., Wolf, A.M., Langkafel, M., Senf, W., Hebebrand, J. (2003). Does obesity surgery improve psychosocial functioning? A systematic review. *International Journal of Obesity. 27*, 1300-1314

Kushner, R. F., & Noble, C. A. (2006). Long-term outcome of bariatric surgery: An interim analysis. *Mayo Clinic Proceedings. Mayo Clinic, 81*(10 Suppl), S46-51.

Larsen, J. K., Geenen, R., van Ramshorst, B., Brand, N., de Wit, P., Stroebe, W., et al. (2003). Psychosocial functioning before and after laparoscopic adjustable gastric banding: A cross-sectional study. *Obesity Surgery: The Official Journal of the American Society for Bariatric Surgery and of the Obesity Surgery Society of Australia and New Zealand, 13*(4), 629-636.

Lau, D. C.W., Douketis, J.D., Morrison, K.M., Hramiak, I.M., Sharma, A.M., Ur, Ehud, for members of the Obesity Canada Clinical Practice Guidelines Expert Panel. (2007). 2006 Canadian clinical practice guidelines on the management and prevention of obesity in adults and children [summary]. *Canadian Med Assoc J*, 176: S1-13

Logue, J., Thompson, L., Romanes, F., Wilson, D. C., Thompson, J., Sattar, N., et al. (2010). Management of obesity: Summary of SIGN guideline. *BMJ (Clinical Research Ed.), 340,* c154.

Longitudinal Assessment of Bariatric Surgery (LABS) Consortium, Flum, D. R., Belle, S. H., King, W. C., Wahed, A. S., Berk, P., et al. (2009). Perioperative safety in the longitudinal assessment of bariatric surgery. *The New England Journal of Medicine, 361*(5), 445-454.

Mahony, D. (2010). Psychological assessments of bariatric surgery patients. development, reliability, and exploratory factor analysis of the PsyBari. *Obesity Surgery,*

Mamplekou, E., Komesidou, V., Bissias, C., Papakonstantinou, A., & Melissas, J. (2005). Psychological condition and quality of life in patients with morbid obesity before and after surgical weight loss. *Obesity Surgery: The Official Journal of the American Society for Bariatric Surgery and of the Obesity Surgery Society of Australia and New Zealand, 15*(8), 1177-1184.

McAlpine, D.E., Frisch, M.J., Rome, E.S. Clark, M.M., Signore, C., Lindroos, A.K., Allison, K.C. (2010). Bariatric surgery: a primer for eating disorder professionals. *Eur Eat Disord Rev, 18*(4), 304-317

Moorehead, M. K., Ardelt-Gattinger, E., Lechner, H., & Oria, H. E. (2003). The validation of the moorehead-ardelt quality of life questionnaire II. *Obesity Surgery, 13*(5), 684-692.

mr1269.ch1.pdf (application/pdf object) Retrieved July 2, 2010, from http://www.rand.org/pubs/monograph_reports/MR1269/mr1269.ch1.pdf.

Must, A., Spadano, J., Coakley, E. H., Field, A. E., Colditz, G., & Dietz, W. H. (1999). The disease burden associated with overweight and obesity. *JAMA: The Journal of the American Medical Association, 282*(16), 1523-1529.

Nadler, E. P., Brotman, L. M., Miyoshi, T., Fryer, G. E.,Jr, & Weitzman, M. (2009). Morbidity in obese adolescents who meet the adult national institutes of health criteria for bariatric surgery. *Journal of Pediatric Surgery, 44*(10), 1869-1876.

National Institute for Health and Clinical Excellence: Bariatric surgery for the treatment of people with severe obesity. (2007) London: National Institute for Health and Clinical Excellence.: NHS guidelines.

Nguyen, N. T., Morton, J. M., Wolfe, B. M., Schirmer, B., Ali, M., & Traverso, L. W. (2005). The SAGES bariatric surgery outcome initiative. *Surgical Endoscopy, 19*(11), 1429-1438.

Ogden, C. L., Carroll, M. D., Curtin, L. R., Lamb, M. M., & Flegal, K. M. (2010). Prevalence of high body mass index in US children and adolescents, 2007-2008. *JAMA: The Journal of the American Medical Association, 303*(3), 242-249.

Ogden, C. L., Carroll, M. D., McDowell, M. A., & Flegal, K. M. (2007). Obesity among adults in the united states--no statistically significant chance since 2003-2004. *NCHS Data Brief, (1)*(1), 1-8.

Oria, H. E., & Moorehead, M. K. (2009). Updated bariatric analysis and reporting outcome system (BAROS). Surgery for Obesity and Related Diseases: Official *Journal of the American Society for Bariatric Surgery, 5*(1), 60-66.

Papadia, F. S., Adami, G. F., Marinari, G. M., Camerini, G., & Scopinaro, N. (2007). *Bariatric surgery in adolescents: A long-term follow-up study. Surgery for Obesity and Related Diseases: Official Journal of the American Society for Bariatric Surgery, 3*(4), 465-468.

Partridge, B.C. (2010). Adolescent Psychological Development, Parenting Styles, and Pediatric Decision Making. *J Med Philos* [Epub ahead of print].

Perioperative Safety in the Longitudinal Assessment of Bariatric Surgery by the Longitudinal Assessment of Bariatric Surgery (LABS) Consortium. (2009) *N Engl J Med*, 361:445-54.

Pekkarinen. (1994). Long-term results of gastroplasty for morbid obesity: binge-eating as a predictor of poor outcome. *Obesity Surgery, 4,* 248-255.

Pories, W. J., Swanson, M. S., MacDonald, K. G., Long, S. B., Morris, P. G., Brown, B. M., et al. (1995). Who would have thought it? an operation proves to be the most effective therapy for adult-onset diabetes mellitus. *Annals of Surgery, 222*(3), 339-50; discussion 350-2.

Pratt, J. S., Lenders, C. M., Dionne, E. A., Hoppin, A. G., Hsu, G. L., Inge, T. H., et al. (2009). Best practice updates for pediatric/adolescent weight loss surgery. *Obesity (Silver Spring, Md.), 17*(5), 901-910.

Pull, C. B. (2010). Current psychological assessment practices in obesity surgery programs: What to assess and why. *Current Opinion in Psychiatry, 23*(1), 30-36.

Rand, C.S., Kuldau, J.M., Robbins, L. (1982). Surgery for obesity and marriage quality. *JAMA. 247,* 1419-1422.

Sanmiguel, C. P., Conklin, J. L., Cunneen, S. A., Barnett, P., Phillips, E. H., Kipnes, M., et al. (2009). Gastric electrical stimulation with the TANTALUS system in obese type 2 diabetes patients: Effect on weight and glycemic control. *Journal of Diabetes Science and Technology, 3*(4), 964-970.

Santry, H. P., Lauderdale, D. S., Cagney, K. A., Rathouz, P. J., Alverdy, J. C., & Chin, M. H. (2007). Predictors of patient selection in bariatric surgery. *Annals of Surgery, 245*(1), 59-67.

Sarwer. (2008a). Preoperative eating behavior, postoperative dietary adherence, and weight loss after gastric bypass surgery. *Surgery for Obesity and Related Diseases, 4,* 640-646.

Sarwer. (2008b). Psychological issues following bariatric surgery. *Primary Psychiatry, 15,* 50-55.

Scottish intercollegiate guidelines network (SIGN) Retrieved July 2, 2011, from http://www.sign.ac.uk/.

Shikora, S. A., Bergenstal, R., Bessler, M., Brody, F., Foster, G., Frank, A., et al. (2009). Implantable gastric stimulation for the treatment of clinically severe obesity: Results of the SHAPE trial. Surgery for Obesity and Related Diseases: *Official Journal of the American Society for Bariatric Surgery, 5*(1), 31-37.

Singer, J. D., & Willett, J. B. (2003). *Applied longitudinal data analysis: Modeling change and event occurrence.* New York: Oxford University Press.

Sjostrom, C. D., Lissner, L., Wedel, H., & Sjostrom, L. (1999). Reduction in incidence of diabetes, hypertension and lipid disturbances after intentional weight loss induced by bariatric surgery: The SOS intervention study. *Obesity Research, 7*(5), 477-484.

Skelton, J. A., Cook, S. R., Auinger, P., Klein, J. D., & Barlow, S. E. (2009). Prevalence and trends of severe obesity among US children and adolescents. *Academic Pediatrics, 9*(5), 322-329.

Sogg, S., & Mori, D. L. (2004). The boston interview for gastric bypass: Determining the psychological suitability of surgical candidates. *Obesity Surgery, 14*(3), 370-380.

Sogg, S., & Mori, D. L. (2008). Revising the boston interview: Incorporating new knowledge and experience. *Surgery for Obesity and Related Diseases: Official Journal of the American Society for Bariatric Surgery, 4*(3), 455-463.

Steinbrook, R. (2004). Surgery for severe obesity. *The New England Journal of Medicine, 350*(11), 1075-1079.

Strauss, R. S., Bradley, L. J., & Brolin, R. E. (2001). Gastric bypass surgery in adolescents with morbid obesity. *The Journal of Pediatrics, 138*(4), 499-504.

Sugerman, H. J., Sugerman, E. L., DeMaria, E. J., Kellum, J. M., Kennedy, C., Mowery, Y., et al. (2003). *Bariatric surgery for severely obese adolescents. Journal of Gastrointestinal Surgery: Official Journal of the Society for Surgery of the Alimentary Tract, 7*(1), 102-7; discussion 107-8.

Vage, V., Solhaug, J. H., Viste, A., Bergsholm, P., & Wahl, A. K. (2003). Anxiety, depression and health-related quality of life after jejunoileal bypass: A 25-year follow-up study of 20 female patients. *Obesity Surgery: The Official Journal of the American Society for Bariatric Surgery and of the Obesity Surgery Society of Australia and New Zealand, 13*(5), 706-713.

Van Hout. (2005). Psychosocial effects of bariatric surgery. *Acta Chir Belg, 105*, 40-43

Wadden, T. A., & Phelan, S. (2002). Behavioral assessment of the obese patient. In T. A. Wadden, & S. Phelan (Eds.), *Handbook of obesity treatment* (pp. 186). New York: Guilford Press.

Wadden, T. A., & Foster, G. D. (2006). Weight and lifestyle inventory (WALI). *Surgery for Obesity and Related Diseases: Official Journal of the American Society for Bariatric Surgery, 2*(2), 180-199.

Yermilov, I., McGory, M. L., Shekelle, P. W., Ko, C. Y., & Maggard, M. A. (2009). Appropriateness criteria for bariatric surgery: Beyond the NIH guidelines. *Obesity (Silver Spring, Md.), 17*(8), 1521-1527.

Childhood Obesity: The Epidemic of Today's Youth

Keeley Pratt, PhD & Angela Lamson, PhD

Originally published as Clinical Update in Family Therapy Magazine
July-August 2009 • Revised by author June 2011

PREVALENCE

Obesity has been identified by researchers as an established pediatric condition for over 50 years (Gordon & Hill, 1957). Of late, however, childhood obesity is considered a nationwide epidemic that impacts children regardless of sex, age, race, and ethnic group (Federal Interagency Forum on Child and Family Statistics [FIFCFS], 2007; Hedley et al., 2004; Institute of Medicine, 2005). According to the 2007-2008 National Health and Nutrition Examination Survey (NHANES), 31.7 percent of youth aged 2-19 were at or above the 85th percent percentile for BMI and age (i.e., overweight, obese, or severely obese); which has led policy makers to rank childhood obesity as a critical public health threat (Ogden et al., 2010).

DEFINITIONS OF OVERWEIGHT & OBESITY

In order to comprehend the prevalence of obesity, it is important to know how obesity is defined in child populations. According to 2007 recommendations (see Expert Recommendations for Healthcare Providers), weight is categorized by age and gender-specific Body Mass Index (BMI). There are four weight categories for children: underweight (< 5th percentile), healthy weight (5th - <85th percentile), overweight (85th - <95th percentile) and obese (≥ 95th percentile).

CONTEXTUAL VARIABLES

The significant and rapid increase in the number of children who are overweight or obese has left researchers scrambling to understand the healthcare determinants for over 13 million children and families impacted by this condition. Researchers have found that 80 percent of children who were overweight or obese from 10-15 years old remained obese when they were 25 years old (Whitaker, Wright, Pepe, Siedel, & Dietz, 1997). A variety of factors likely explain this continuity, but researchers have found some contextual variables that tend to be correlated with higher rates of obesity including ethnicity, socioeconomic status (SES), and parental constellation (Golan, Fainaru, & Weizman, 1998; Institute of Medicine, 2005; U.S. Department of Health and Human Services [DHHS], Health Resources and Services Administration [HRSA], Maternal and Child Health Bureau [MCHB], 2005).

Ethnicity. Nationally, obesity in children was most prevalent in middle and high school-aged children and those from ethnic minority populations (Hedley et al., 2004; Ogden, Carroll, & Flegal, 2002, 2008). According to National Health and Nutrition Examination Survey (NHANES) data, non-Hispanic Black children had the highest rate of obesity (22.9 percent), with Mexican American and non-Hispanic White children having lower prevalence, at 21.1 percent and 16 percent, respectively (Hedley et al., 2004; Ogden, Carroll, & Flegal, 2002, 2008; Freedman, Dhan, Serdula, Ogden, & Dietz, 2006; DHHS, HRSA, MCHB, 2005). Asian children appeared to have an obesity prevalence similar to that of White children (Freedman et al., 2008). Specifically, child populations that had the highest prevalence of obesity included adolescent Mexican American boys and non-Hispanic Black girls (Hedley et al., 2004; Ogden, Carroll, & Flegal, 2008; Ogden, Flegal, Carroll, & Johnson, 2002; IOM, 2005; Center for Disease Control and Prevention, 2007). These differences may be due to multiple complex variables interacting with ethnicity, sex, and SES.

Socioeconomic Status. Assessment of SES is often confounded by related demograpnic variables such as family income, caregiver education, and residential proximity. All of these variables appear to be associated with the prevalence of childhood obesity. For instance, family income has been shown to have an inverse relationship with childhood obesity; as income increased, the prevalence of overweight in children decreased (DHHS, HRSA, MCHB, 2005). Additionally, those children residing in southern regions of the U.S. had an increased prevalence of obesity (IOM, 2005). SES, income, residential location, and caregiver education level are all fundamental components to understanding childhood obesity; however, family factors must also be considered.

Parental Constellation. In the National Survey of Children's Health (2003-2004), parental/family structure (e.g., single parent or children from blended families) were found to be factors that influenced overweight in childhood. For example, children who dwelt in two-parent (biological or adoptive) households were least likely to be overweight as compared with children who lived with a step parent; children who lived with single mothers had the greatest prevalence of overweight (DHHS, HRSA, MCHB, 2005). While some have speculated that family/parental structures (e.g., single or two-parent families) have implications into childhood overweight patterns, others suggested that parental behaviors (e.g., physical activity and food choices) have significant correlates with children's health (DHHS, HRSA, MCHB, 2005).

BIOPSYCHOSOCIAL APPROACH

George Engel introduced the biopsychosocial (BPS) approach in 1977 to explore and explain health as an interplay of biological, psychological, and social systems. Engel's approach allowed researchers and clinicians to better understand a condition such as obesity from a comprehensive BPS perspective, whereby a diagnosis that began at the cellular level was influential up to the societal or cultural levels. A formal assessment of quality of life is one method to comprehensively assess how weight may impact a child from a BPS perspective. Numerous clinicians have utilized quality of life (QOL) inventories in assessing children who are struggling with a medical diagnosis, particularly the PedsQL4.0TM (Chan, Mangione-Smith, Burwinkle, Rosen, & Varni, 2005; Varni, 1999, 2001, 2002, 2003.) The PedsQL inventory is used to assess physical, emotional, social, and school functioning, thus providing both physical and psychosocial assessment in one tool. The domains measured by the PedsQL inventory appeared to be comparable to the systems described in Engel's BPS model: the biological system links to the physical domain, the psychological system links to the emotional domain, and the social system links to the social and school domains.

The relationship between weight and QOL in children has been researched previously with inconsistent findings. Researchers have documented the relationship between overweight and decreased quality of life in children and adolescents (Ravens-Sieberer, Redegeld, & Bullinger, 2001; Schwimmer, Burwinkle, & Varni, 2003; Swallen, Reither, Haas, & Meier, 2005). For example, Schwimmer et al. (2003) found that obese children were 5.5 times more likely than healthy children to have impaired QOL, making QOL for an obese child similar to that of a child diagnosed with cancer (Schwimmer et al., 2003). Quality of life appeared to be inversely related to weight. As a child's weight increased, her quality of life decreased, so the most overweight children had the most significantly impaired QOL (Williams, Wake, Hesketh, Maher, & Waters, 2005; Zeller, Roehrig, Modi, Daniels, & Inge, 2006). However, other researchers have found no significant association between weight and QOL (Janicke, 2007). The apparent inconsistent QOL findings have prompted researchers to include additional psychological assessments (e.g., the PHQ-9) to enhance the exploration of the relationship between systems (biological, psychological, and social) and QOL.

Biological. The medical literature has documented several biological comorbidities of childhood obesity including type-2 diabetes, heart disease, high cholesterol, hypertension, early puberty, enuresis, polycystic ovarian syndrome, and trouble sleeping/sleep apnea (see Table 4 for more medical comorbidities) (Dietz, 1998; IOM, 2005; Kiess et al., 200; DHHS, HRSA, MCHB, 2005). These additional medical conditions can add complexity for overweight children who are expected to meet with multiple providers and thus follow multiple treatment plans specific to each individual comorbidity. These weight-related biological comorbidies are further influenced by contextual variables such as sex and race.

Sex and race have played a significant role in quality of life for overweight and obese adolescents (Ogden et al., 2002). Specifically, in regard to sex differences and QOL, boys reported higher physical functioning (Janicke, 2007); while girls reported lower social functioning (Zeller et al., 2006). Furthermore, race was found to be an indicator of low QOL scores with African American obese girls. Overall, across all races surveyed, impairments in physical functioning were more frequently reported than those of emotional, social, or school functioning (Pinhas-Hamiel et al., 2006; Swallen et al., 2005). However, impaired physical functioning may relate to impaired functioning in other psychological or social areas over time.

Psychological. Treatment seeking children who are overweight reported more depressive symptoms when compared with their normal weight and non treatment seeking peers (Britz, Seigfried, Ziegler, et al, 2000). In a sample of 166 overweight youth, Zeller and colleagues (2006) found children with increased depressive symptoms had lower reported QOL. Epstein, Valoski, Wing, and McCurley (1994) completed a 10-year follow-up study of family-centered treatment for childhood obesity and found the most prevalent psychiatric problem to be depression. Depressive symptoms in overweight and obese children have been significantly related to child-reported QOL (Janicke, 2007). In a sample of obese children entering treatment, it was found that 29 percent met or exceeded clinical levels for psychosocial problems on the Child Behavior Checklist, specifically with regard to anxiety and depression (Achenbach, 1991). In another sample of obese adolescents presenting for bariatric surgery, 30 percent met criteria for clinically significant depressive symptoms (Zeller et al., 2006). Obese or overweight adolescents who did not live in two-parent homes were more likely to be depressed, have low self-esteem, and have poorer school functioning (Swallen et al., 2005).

Given the finding that children who are obese had increased psychological problems that may persist into adulthood as compared to children who are not obese, researchers have attempted to explore and examine the psychological complications (Epstein, Paluch, Gordy, Saelens, & Ernst, 2000). Psychological impairments included poor self-esteem, low self-worth, depression (IOM, 2005; Speiser et al., 2005), loneliness, poor self image, suicide, drug and alcohol addiction, bulimia, binge eating, and smoking (Hoot & Lynn-Garbe, 2005; Kiess et al., 2001; DHHS, HRSA, MCHB, 2005). Due to the lack of longitudinal data, it was unclear whether specific psychological issues (e.g., depression, anxiety) persisted from youth to adulthood or disproportionately affected specific sex and/or ethnic populations. Psychological issues associated with being at an increased weight may have social consequences as well (e.g., social isolation associated with depressive feelings from being teased or bullied).

Social. According to Edmunds, Waters, and Elliott (2001) the social implications for children who are overweight were evident in children as early as six years of age, when children begin to understand societal messages that being overweight is not desirable. Not surprisingly, children who are overweight were more likely to be at risk for peer victimization such as teasing (Griffiths,

Wolke, Page, Horwood, & Team, 2006; Janssen, Craig, Boyce, & Pickett, 2004; Latner, & Stunkard, 2003). Additional social issues for children who are obese included problems associated with school (e.g., performance or poor school attendance), relational issues (e.g., child and parent or peer group conflict), social isolation, promiscuity, and bullying (Janssen et al., 2004). Peer perceptions of children who are obese included characteristics such as selfishness, poor academic success, and lower intelligence (Epstein, Roemmich, & Raynor, 2001). Evidence of such peer perceptions merits exploration into BPS comorbidities that may be impacting the health of children and their relationships with others.

The social contexts on the PedsQL encompassed overweight children's functioning in relationships with their friends, families, and peers at school. In addition, the social area included bullying, teasing, social isolation, etc. Socially, QOL assessments have identified child and caregiver risks and discrepancies among interpretations. For example, a large disagreement among a child's perceived QOL and the caregiver's perception of their child's QOL can merit further exploration. Income has been associated with higher parent-reported QOL physical functioning (Janicke, 2007) and discrepancies among child and caregiver perceptions of the child's QOL. There is not sufficient evidence about communication between caregivers and their children about weight and weight-related psychosocial impairments. Pratt and colleagues (2011a, 2011b) have looked at child and caregiver QOL congruence in a sample of treatment seeking overweight youth and caregivers. They have identified that there are several contextual differences in child and caregiver QOL agreement based on child age, race, gender, and reported depressive symptoms of the child and caregiver. Therefore, discrepancies in child and caregiver perceptions of QOL scores could be classified as a social concern, due to the potential for miscommunication surrounding weight-related issues.

DIAGNOSIS

When diagnosing obesity in children, the following protocol is recommended by the Expert Recommendations (see Expert Recommendations for Healthcare Providers): a medical provider will typically begin with a physical examination that includes finding the child's Body Mass Index (BMI), which is based on the child's height, weight, and sex (see Table 2), then the child's BMI value is plotted on age and sex adjusted growth charts. Finally, the appropriate BMI category is determined (See Table 2 for classification of underweight, healthy weight, overweight, or obese).

Adolescents who are obese may inquire about surgical means to control their obesity. Weight-related surgeries such as the Roux-en-Y gastric **bypass (Sugerman et. al, 2003) and** adjustable gastric **band**ing (AGB) (Dolan, Creighton, Hopkins, & Fielding, 2003) have been effective in treating severe obesity in adolescence. However, a number of biopsychosocial assessments must be conducted for adolescents to be considered an appropriate candidate for the procedure. These assessments include: adolescent growth and development principles (e.g., charting growth for physical development), decision capacity (of the adolescent), potential barriers to adopting a healthy lifestyle, prior attempts at weight loss via a plan or program (for more than six months), severe obesity (BMI greater than 40), generally have reached puberty and skeletal maturity, and multiple obesity related comorbidities that could be reduced through surgery (Inge et al., 2004). Additionally, surgery candidates should have a family-based assessment, meaning the child and caregiver (typically the parent) are interviewed about: the family dynamics (i.e., sources of support and conflicting relationships), including family strengths and challenges, the candidate's coping skills, and any additional psychosocial comorbidities (e.g., depression) (Inge et al., 2004).

EXPERT RECOMMENDATIONS FOR HEALTHCARE PROVIDERS

The American Medical Association (AMA), Health Resources and Services Administration (HRSA), and Centers for Disease Control and Prevention (CDC) brought together an expert committee including representatives from the areas of medicine, mental health, and epidemiology to develop recommendations for the care of overweight and obese children (Barlow, 2007). The report, entitled *Expert Committee Recommendations Regarding the Prevention, Assessment, and Treatment of Child and Adolescent Overweight and Obesity* (2007), summarized current accepted practices for pediatric obesity prevention, assessment, intervention, and treatment. A concurrent publication by the National Initiative for Children's Healthcare Quality (NICHQ), entitled *An Implementation Guide from the Childhood Obesity Action Network*, offered a combination of important aspects of the expert recommendations with real-world practice tools identified by NICHQ from primary care groups who developed obesity care strategies (NICHQ, 2007). Thus, the implementation guide offered practical application of the expert recommendations. The expert committee recommendations described four stages of childhood obesity treatment: 1) prevention plus; 2) structured weight management; 3) comprehensive, multidisciplinary intervention; and 4) tertiary care intervention (Barlow, 2007). The recommendations below describe the management of pediatric obesity from preventive care to surgical options. Additionally, there is a case example provided based on a level-three intervention done in a pediatric obesity specialty clinic.

Prevention Plus. A stage one visit most commonly takes place at a child's primary care office during a yearly well care visit. At a stage one well care visit, the following should be conducted by the healthcare provider: plot a body mass index (BMI), identify a weight category (see Table 2), measure blood pressure, take a family focused medical history, take a focused review of systems, perform a thorough medical physical examination, order appropriate laboratory tests, and give consistent evidence-based messages for physical activity and nutrition. In addition, healthcare providers should assess beyond dietary and physical activity behaviors by looking at the child's attitude, including self-perceptions or concerns about weight, readiness to change, successes, barriers, and challenges (Barlow, 2007; NICHQ, 2007; Spear et al., 2007). Finally, it is recommended that the physician follow certain communication strategies (e.g., empathize, elicit, and provide) to improve the effectiveness of counseling.

In a prevention plus encounter, which could take place in a variety of settings including private practice offices, agencies, or healthcare settings, a family therapist's initial interaction should include joining and exploration of family dynamics for potential strengths and challenges in the adaptation of a healthy lifestyle. In this stage, family therapists should maximize collaboration through facilitating patient and provider communication about health-related concerns of the child and family.

Structured Weight Management. Stage two visits take place at a primary care office with the added support of a healthcare provider who has specific training in weight management. Visits provide an increase in structure and support, specifically toward setting physical activity and nutritional goals and creating rewards. Stage two visits ideally occur on a monthly basis either with the child seen individually or as part of a group visit.

In a stage two visit, a family therapist may be on staff at a healthcare setting or collaborating with healthcare providers about a child they are seeing for therapy services at a different location. In addition to joining and exploration of family dynamics (as in a prevention encounter), a family therapist should assess for readiness to change (see Table 1) for the child and the caregivers in a structured weight management encounter. Assessing for readiness to change allows all healthcare providers to understand the family's motivation for lifestyle changes (e.g., nutrition and physical activity). A family therapist is

TABLE 1: Classification of Readiness to Change Nutrition and Physical Activity Behaviors

Stage	Description
Precontemplation	Child or family is not yet considering changing a lifestyle behavior
Contemplation	Child or family is evaluating reasons for and against change
Preparation	Child or family is planning to change
Action	Child or family has carried out a change for less than six months
Maintenance	Child or family has maintained a change for at least six moths

(Krebs, Himes, Jacobson, Nicklas, Guilday, Styne, 2007)

TABLE 2: The weight status category for the calculated BMI-for-age-percentile based on the Expert Committee recommendations.

Weight Status Category	Percentile Range
Underweight	Less than the 5th percentile
Healthy Weight	5th percentile to less than the 85th percentile
Overweight	85th to less than the 95th percentile
Obese	Equal to or greater than the 95th percentile

(CDC, 2009)

TABLE 3. BMI Chart at the 99th percentile		
	Boys	Girls
Age	BMI	BMI
5	20.1	21.5
6	21.6	23.0
7	23.6	24.6
8	25.6	26.4
9	27.6	28.2
10	29.3	29.9
11	30.7	31.5
12	31.8	33.1
13	32.6	34.6
14	33.2	36.0
15	33.6	37.5
16	33.9	39.1
17	34.4	40.8

especially skilled at exploring strengths and challenges to behavioral change related to a medical target such as overweight and obesity.

Comprehensive, Multidisciplinary Intervention. Stage three intervention goes beyond stage two by employing multidisciplinary childhood obesity treatment (e.g., with a behavioral specialist, nutritionist, and physical activity specialist) and a structured behavioral program (e.g., negotiating and reinforcing positive healthy behaviors). (For more information on multidisciplinary treatment and types of collaborators, see the listed collaborative terms.) Ideally, families are seen weekly for 8-12 weeks with additional follow-up services.

Family therapists included in multidisciplinary treatment teams typically utilize family-behavioral and family-centered treatments. Family-behavioral treatments have been documented to be an effective strategy for weight-loss in children (Edmonds et al., 2001; Young, Northern, Lister, Drummond, & O'Brien, 2007), and are listed in the expert recommendations (Barlow, 2007) for stages three and four (structured comprehensive multidisciplinary intervention and tertiary care intervention). In a recent meta-analysis of 16 studies, interventions that included a family-behavioral component produced larger effect sizes than interventions without a family-behavioral component (Young et al., 2007). Epstein et al. (1994) found that behavioral family-centered treatment, which emphasized reinforcement for child and parent behavior changes and weight loss, may have lasting effects into young adulthood. Issues such as readiness to change (see Table 1), parenting skills (e.g., use of praise, rewards, and discipline), and healthy role-modeling were all important components in family-centered childhood obesity treatment (Connolly, Gargiula, & Reeve, 2002).

Tertiary Care Intervention. Stage four is aimed at severely obese youth by utilizing treatments such as medications (e.g., Sibutramine or Orlistat), very-low calorie diets, and/or weight control surgery (i.e., gastric bypass or lap-band) in addition to behavioral treatment. Thus, the treatment of obesity can occur in traditional one-on-one medical encounters in a primary care context, or can evolve to multidisciplinary and collaborative care models (see terms for different types of collaborative models) to address biological complexities and diverse psychosocial issues, as well.

Typically in a tertiary care setting, providers with psychosocial expertise are co-located in the same office as the other healthcare providers. In tertiary care interventions, family therapists can be helpful in exploring issues such as depression, low self-esteem, teasing, perceived and actual social support, and other psychosocial related variables. Family therapists are well trained to assess and intervene at a systemic level and should position themselves in primary,

CHILDHOOD OBESITY & STIGMA

Regardless of the stage of treatment (i.e., prevention plus to tertiary care) the care of children who are overweight or obese is based first and foremost on provider and patient interaction and thus, the first factor to consider is the provider-patient relationship. Inherent in the dichotomy of the provider-patient relationship is the patient's past and present relationships and experiences (either negative or positive) with healthcare providers, teams, and settings. Therefore, in the clinical world it is essential to explore the potentially negative experiences that patients may have had in other healthcare contexts, specifically around weight bias (i.e., negative interactions that affect our interpersonal interactions in a harmful way) (Puhl & Latner, 2007) and stigmatization. Family therapists can help solicit illness stories from children and families who may have had negative experiences with healthcare related to weight bias and stigmatization.

The journal *Obesity* (November, 2008) devoted an entire issue to weight bias, with six articles focusing on youth. Children are specifically identified as being vulnerable to the effects of weight bias (Puhl & Latner, 2007). Unfortunately there are only a few researchers who have published on weight bias across the lifespan (2008), making it difficult to predict what biases a family (and the individuals who make up a family) has experienced prior to current treatment.

Parents of obese children reported feeling blamed for their child's weight and dismissed by their healthcare providers (Edmunds, 2005). Weight bias against patients has been documented among physicians (Campbell, Engel, Timperio, Cooper, & Crawford, 2000; Hebl & Xu, 2001; Kristeller & Hoerr, 1997), medical students (Keane, 1990; Wigton & McGaghie, 2001), dietitians (Berryman, Dubale, Manchester, & Mittelstaedt, 2006; McArthur & Ross, 1997), nurses (Bagley, Conklin, Isherwood, Pechiulis, & Watson, 1989; Hoppe & Ogden, 1997; Maroney & Golub, 1992), and psychologists (Davis-Coelho, Waltz, & Davis-Coelho, 2000). In their initial interactions, healthcare providers' sensitivity with patients may assist in building a trusting patient-provider relationship, whereby care is well received at any stage of treatment.

Patient's initial interactions may be eased by providers being mindful of certain "setting" concerns. In the waiting room, furniture should be weight-friendly with armless chairs or chairs that can hold wider body frames. It is important for reading material to be sensitive to children who may be potentially struggling with body image, so it's best not to provide magazines promoting an unrealistic body size expectation. Additionally, healthcare settings should have appropriate medical equipment for children with larger bodies (i.e., extra large blood pressure cuff size, scales that can weight over 300 pounds, and examination tables that can hold heavy bodies).

Some important questions for providers to consider about their own potential biases around weight are (Brownell & Puhl, 2007):

- Do I make assumptions based on weight regarding character, intelligence, personal success, health status, or lifestyle behaviors?
- Am I comfortable working with people of all shapes and sizes?
- Do I give appropriate feedback to encourage healthful behavior change?
- Am I sensitive to the needs and concerns of obese individuals?
- Do I treat the individual or the condition?

Other questions for providers to consider when working from a biopsychosocial framework include:

- How is beauty viewed by different ethnicities?
- How is weight spoken about in the patient's family?
- How does religion/spiritual practices influence feeding and meals?
- How do family members feel about weight loss?
- What kind of culture-specific foods are most commonly consumed in the family?

secondary, and tertiary care contexts where pediatric obesity is being treated. Ideally, in tertiary care, an integrated care model would be utilized where all healthcare providers would collaborate regarding patient encounters, treatment plans, and documentation in health records.

PEDIATRIC OBESITY CASE EXAMPLE: AMY

(Pratt, Lazorick, & Collier, 2011)

Amy, age 12, attended the Pediatric Healthy Weight Research and Treatment Center (PHWRTC) in spring of 2004 after she was referred by her pediatrician. She had a Body Mass Index (BMI) of 32.3 kg/m2, weighed 183.5 pounds, and complained she could not find clothes that fit.

Amy lived part-time with her father, who lived alone, and part-time with her mother, stepfather, and younger brother. During her evaluation, Amy reported "feeling blue" and admitted to thoughts of suicide. She was referred to a psychologist after a screening tool suggested she was at-risk for depression, anxiety, and suicidal ideation.

Amy attended four appointments at the center over 8 months, remained depressed, and continued to gain weight. Her diet at her mother's and father's houses was dramatically different, and Amy was expected to cook, clean, and perform other household duties at her dad's. The differences in households made it difficult for Amy to maintain an aggressive academic course-load while trying to make healthy changes such as increased activity and healthy food choices. She stopped coming to the center in December 2004.

Three years later, at age 16, Amy returned to the clinic ready to make changes. The center itself had evolved and psychosocial, medical, and nutrition services were now all located within the clinic. Now, when Amy visited the clinic, a family therapy intern accompanied her as she met with the physician. During her follow-up appointment two months later, her quality of life and depression inventories revealed suicidal ideation and her mother disclosed that Amy had recently taken a small overdose of over-the-counter sleeping pills. Her team of providers immediately collaborated on a care plan. Given the obvious signs of depression, priority was given to addressing her mental health needs before tackling diet- and activity-related lifestyle changes.

A family therapist evaluated Amy's risk of suicide, and formal psychotherapy began four days later with a medical family therapist specializing in treatment of obesity and diabetes. Amy attended weekly sessions that focused on self-esteem, body image, communication in her family, and integrating healthy lifestyle choices into her daily routines in her two households.

Since her integrated care visits and family therapy appointments, Amy has lost a few pounds and has maintained weight loss for the first time in her life. During therapy, she has suggested past sexual abuse, teasing at school, and substance abuse by family members. She is now working to prioritize her mental and physical health needs while managing the stressors in her life. Additionally, her mother and stepfather have begun couples therapy and they continue to frequent Amy's sessions as well.

Amy has also increased her activity level and has started to experience positive effects from her lifestyle changes. The team approach integrated care model has benefited Amy and her family members. They are all beginning to make changes so Amy can reach goals that were never accessible before.

CHILD-FOCUSED INTERVENTION RECOMMENDATIONS

Behavioral interventions have been seen as the "first line treatment" for weight loss since at least 1987 (Mellin, Slinkard, & Irwin, 1987). Whitlock, O'Connor, Williams, Beil, and Lutz (2008) published for the AHRQ the evidence from existing systematic reviews focused on behavioral, pharmacological, and surgical weight management interventions for overweight and/or obese children and adolescents in clinical and nonclinical community settings. Whitlock et al. defined behavioral interventions as including the modification of food consumption (e.g., limiting high-calorie, low-nutrient foods and beverages), increasing physical activity, frequent involvement of the child's family members, and optimally cognitive and behavioral therapy. Stated simply, behavioral interventions are currently delineated as physical activity, dietary, family, and behavioral treatments.

In the most recent Cochran review entitled, "Interventions for treating obesity in children," 64 studies were examined, 54 included lifestyle interventions (with a focus on diet, physical activity or behavior change) and 10 studies were on drug treatment (Oude Luttikhuis et al., 2009). The lifestyle intervention programs were reported to reduce children's weight at six and twelve months after beginning the program (Oude Luttikhuis et al., 2009). In moderate to severely obese adolescents, a reduction in weight was found when either of the drugs Orlistat or Sibutramine were given in addition to a lifestyle intervention (Oude Luttikhuis et al., 2009).

The working group on National Heart Lung and Blood Institute (NHLBI) Future Research Directions in Childhood Obesity Prevention and Treatment (2007) highlighted three main recommendations for behavioral and lifestyle interventions to treat obese children: "1) identify family dynamics which predict success of certain interventions and changes in family dynamics and relationships that are associated with favorable treatment outcomes; 2) identify utility of and methods for promoting self-monitoring of target behaviors by parents and children; and 3) investigate strategies to effectively recruit families into family-centered interventions" (p. 7). Therefore behavioral treatment for childhood obesity in and of itself may not be enough; as guidelines have shifted to include the family in treatment as well.

FAMILY-CENTERED INTERVENTION RECOMMENDATIONS

There are inherent benefits to treating a family rather than a child in isolation. For example, Epstein, Rocco, Roemmich and Beecher (2007) noted that, "Obesity runs in families, it has been hypothesized that targeting eating and activity change in the child and parent, along with teaching parents behavioral skills to facilitate child behavior changes, could mobilize family resources to improve the efficacy of childhood obesity treatments" (p. 381). The benefits of treating children and family members simultaneously may also create positive relationships between the child and parents' weight change (Wrotniak, Epstein, Paluch, & Roemmich, 2004, 2005), including parental nutrition and physical activity behaviors.

In the second half of the twentieth century, a family-centered approach to pediatric obesity care began to emerge (AAP, 2007). Edmunds, Waters, and Elliot (2001) stated that the family has proven to be the most appropriate environment for the treatment and prevention of childhood obesity. Providers who used family-centered childhood obesity treatment tended to view the family as the identified patient and thus included them in goals and treatment plans. In addition, family-behavioral treatments have been documented to be an effective strategy for weight-loss in children (Edmunds et al., 2001; Young, Northern, Lister, Drummond, & O'Brien, 2007).

Epstein et al. (1994) found that behavior family-centered treatment that emphasized reinforcement for child and parent behavior changes and weight loss may have lasting effects into young adulthood. Issues such as readiness to change, parenting skills (including praise, rewards, and discipline), and healthy role-modeling are important components to include in family-centered childhood obesity treatment (Connolly, Gargiula, & Reeve, 2002). Because each member of a family formulates his or her own perspective on illness and disease, it is important for treatment to include a comprehensive picture of the family's health. One way to accomplish this is to utilize inventories that not only address BPS issues (e.g., fatigue or depression) for the identified patient (the child) but also address different family members' perspectives on BPS issues present in the patient and the family.

FAMILY THERAPY AS A DOCUMENTED INTERVENTION FOR CHILDHOOD OBESITY

Literature that includes family therapy as a documented intervention for childhood obesity is scarce. There have been several studies that highlight family therapy as effective, but it is unclear in these studies if it is a trained family therapist conducting such interventions. Family therapy has been found to be effective in preventing pediatric obesity (Glenny & O'Meara, 1997). In fact, the effect of intervention and treatment on families is more significant than in individual therapy for childhood obesity (Flodmark et al., 1993). Flodmark et al. found family therapy to be effective in preventing the progression to severe obesity if the treatment started when the child was 10 to 11 years old. Additionally, at a one-year follow-up, these researchers found that those receiving family therapy interventions had significantly reduced their skinfold thickness and increased their physical fitness. Although they documented the impact family therapy may have on biological systems in an overweight child and his or her family, improvements in psychosocial states were not documented.

ABOUT THE AUTHORS

Keeley Pratt, PhD, LMFT, post-doctoral fellow, is currently working at Research Triangle Institute International (RTI International) researching different facets of childhood obesity including biomarkers, chemical exposures, family relationships, and treatment models. She is also teaching and supervising undergraduate and master's students in the Department of Child Development and Family Relations and the Marriage and Family Therapy Program at East Carolina University. Pratt is active at the Pediatric Healthy Weight Research and Treatment Center in Greenville, NC, where she supervises clinical interns who work as part of an integrated treatment team in the care of overweight children and their families. She has completed over 50 professional presentations and several publications related to childhood obesity, and is part of a pediatric obesity treatment team that was awarded recognition by the Agency for Healthcare Research and Quality (AHRQ), as well as the National Initiative for Children's Healthcare Quality (NICHQ). Pratt is a Clinical Member of the AAMFT.

Angela Lamson, PhD, LMFT, CFLE, is the program director for the marriage and family therapy master's program and medical family therapy doctoral program and associate professor at East Carolina University. She serves as the medical family therapy consultant at Pitt County Memorial Children's Hospital. Lamson is a Clinical Member and Approved Supervisor of the AAMFT.

RESOURCES FOR PRACTITIONERS

ORGANIZATIONS

Centers for Disease Control and Prevention
www.cdc.org
Informative site for child BMI and overview of physical activity and nutrition information.

National Initiative for Children's Healthcare Quality (NICHQ)
http://www.nichq.org
Provides childhood obesity tools for prevention, management, and treatment.

American Academy of Pediatrics (AAP)
www.aap.org
Contains the latest recommendations for childhood obesity care.

Agency for Healthcare Research Quality (AHRQ)
www.ahrq.org
Geared toward research developments and innovations.

American Obesity Association (AOA)
http://obesity1.tempdomainname.com/subs/childhood/

TERMINOLOGY

COLLABORATIVE CARE TERMS

Collaborative Care: A team with at least one medical and one behavioral health provider. Collaboration is based on an understanding that improvements in patient care are achieved more efficiently by working together and focusing on systems than they would be by working independently and focusing on individuals (Blount et al., 2007; Kilo, 1999).

Family Centered Care: An approach to prevention, assessment, and treatment that considers not only the child as the identified patient but the family with whom the child is in consistent contact (AAP, 2007).

Integrated Care: Collaborative patient care often with joint treatment plans between medical and behavioral health professionals (Blount, 2003). Often in an integrated care setting, a medical and behavioral health provider will provide side-by-side services for a patient (Patterson et al., 2002). Integrated care may involve more than a medical and behavioral health provider; as is the case with childhood obesity where often a physical therapist, case manager, and nutritionist or dietitian is included as well. In an integrated care consult, a physician and behavioral health professionals may see a patient together in the same physical space at the same time.

Multidisciplinary Care: Includes the expertise of several different disciplines (e.g., medical, nutrition, endocrine, family therapy, exercise physiology).

CHILDHOOD OBESITY LABORATORY TERMS

(NICHQ, 2007; Barlow, 2007)

Fasting Glucose (Blood Sugar): < 100, recheck every two years; ≥ 100 and < 126, pre-diabetes, provide counseling, consider oral glucose tolerance test, HbA1c, recheck yearly; ≥ 126, diabetes, refer to endocrine.

Fasting Cholesterol Levels:

LDL: < 110, repeat every five years; ≥ 110 and < 130, repeat in one year; ≥ 130 and < 160, obtain a complete family history, provide low-cholesterol diet, recheck in one year; ≥ 160 with risks or any LDL ≥ 190, refer to cardiology.

HDL: ≥ 40, routine care, recheck every two years, more frequently if weight gain continues or accelerates; < 40, increase omega-3 intake, decrease saturated fat and sugar, recheck in one year.

Blood Pressure (ages 3-19): For reliability a blood pressure measure should be conducted three separate times. Then blood pressure should be plotted on a table that includes gender-specific blood pressure levels by age and height percentile (< 90th percentile, routine care, recheck annually; ≥ 90th and < 95th percentile and ≥ 120/80 at any age (pre-hypertension),; ≥ 95th and < 99th percentile and has 5 mm Hg (Stage 1 hypertension) refer to cardiology or nephrology (especially if pre-pubertal), consider pharmacotherapy, recheck in one month; ≥ 99th percentile and 5 mm Hg (Stage 2 hypertension), all procedures above with additional referral to cardiology or nephrology, recheck within one week.

Body Mass Index (BMI):
Formula:
Kilograms and meters:
Pounds and inches:
weight (kg) / [height (m)]2
weight (lb) / [height (in)]2 x 703

The mission is to promote research, education, and advocacy to better understand, prevent, and treat *obesity* and improve the lives of those affected.

RECOMMENDED READINGS

Speiser, P., Rudolf, M., Anhalt, H., Camacho-Hubner, C., Chiarelli, F., Eliakim, A., et al. (2005). Consensus statement: Childhood obesity. *Journal of Clinical Endocrinology & Metabolism, 90,* 1871-1887.

TERMINOLOGY (continued)

(A normal BMI = 18.5-24.9; overweight = 25.0-29.9; obese = 30 or greater; and morbidly obese = 40 or greater.)

To calculate BMI for late adolescents and young adults (over the age of 18): Multiply your weight in pounds by 705; divide by your height in inches; divide this number by your height in inches a second time. A normal BMI = 18.5-24.9; overweight = 25.0-29.9; obese = 30 or greater; and morbidly obese = 40 or greater.

BMI 99th percentile cut-points for children under 18:

For children and adolescents, the BMI value is plotted on growth charts to determine the corresponding BMI-for-age percentile. See Table 2 for weight category classifications and Table 3 for adjusted BMI at the 99th percentile cut-points for boys and girls, who are at an increased risk for additional medical complications.

HIGHER ACCURACY BODY COMPOSITION PROCEDURES

Dual-energy X-ray Absorptiometry (DEXA): a four-compartment measure of total body bone mass, fat mass, lean tissue mass, and fat free mass (lean tissue [skeletal and organ tissue mass] and bone bass), conducted by x-ray technology.

Hydrodensitometry Weighing (underwater weighing): a two-compartment measure of fat mass and fat free mass involving underwater weighing in a stainless steel tank in a chair mounted on an underwater scale suspended from a diving board over a pool or hot tub.

Bioelectrical Impedance Analysis (BIA): a two-compartment measure of fat mass and fat free mass, resulting in a total percent of body fat, conducted by electrical currents going through body tissue

COMORBIDITIES ASSOCIATED WITH CHILDHOOD OBESITY TERMS

(Hassink, 2007; pp. 4-6)

Obstructive Sleep Apnea: a disorder of breathing during sleep characterized by prolonged partial upper airway obstruction or intermittent complete obstruction that disrupts normal sleep patterns. Patients need to have a nighttime polysomnography (i.e., sleep study) procedure done to diagnose the condition.

Metabolic Syndrome: condition characterized by insulin resistance. Components include obesity, elevated blood pressure and triglyceride levels, decreased high-density HDL cholesterol, increased low-density lipoprotein cholesterol, and impaired glucose tolerance.

Acanthosis Nigricans: characterized by hyperpigmentation and velvety thickening that occurs in the neck, axillae, and groin. Often associated with metabolic syndrome, insulin resistance, and type 2 diabetes.

Polycystic Ovarian Syndrome: may occur in adolescence and is characterized by insulin resistance in the presence of elevated androgens. Symptoms include oligomenorrhea or amenorrhea, hirsutism, acne, polycystic ovaries, and obesity.

Type 2 Diabetes: occurs when the diagnosis of hyperglycemia is made in the presence of insulin resistance and an elevated insulin level.

A recent statement geared toward healthcare providers working in medical settings in the treatment of childhood obesity.

Adolescent obesity and weight loss surgery: Special report. Consumer Guide to Bariatric Surgery. Available at http://www.yourbariatricsurgeryguide.com/obesity-teens.
This site outlines the appropriateness for surgery, testing, procedures/protocols, risks, and post-surgery expectations.

BOOKS

Satter, E. (2005). *Your child's weight: Helping without harming (birth through adolescence)*. Madison, WI: Kelcy Press.
The author (a family therapist) applies feeding dynamic principles and child and adolescent development to overweight and obesity in children.

Hassink, S. (Eds.) (2007). *Pediatric obesity: Prevention, intervention, and treatment strategies for primary care*. Elk Grove Village, IL: American Academy of Pediatrics.
This text provides up-to-date pediatric obesity tools and recommendations from the American Academy of Pediatrics.

REFERENCES

Achenback, T. (1991). *Manual for the child behavior checklist*. Burlington, VT: University of Vermont.

American Academy of Pediatrics (2007). Family-centered care and the pediatrician's role: *Pediatrics, 120,* 683-684.

Bagley, C., Conklin, D., Isherwood, R., Pechiulis, D., & Watson, L. (1989). Attitudes of nurses toward obesity and obese patients. *Perceptive Motor Skills, 68,* 954.

Barlow, S., & the Expert Committee. (2007). Expert committee recommendations regarding the prevention, assessment, and treatment of child and adolescent overweight and obesity: Summary Report. *Pediatrics, 120* (Supplement 4), S164-192.

Berryman, D., Dubale, G., Manchester, D., & Mittelstaedt, R. (2006). Dietetic students possess negative attitudes toward obesity similar to nondietetic students. *Journal of American Dietetic Association, 106,* 1678-1682.

Blount, A. (2003). Integrated primary care: Organizing the evidence. *Families, Systems & Health, 21,* 121-134.

Blount, A., Schoenbaum, M., Kathol, R., Rollman, B. L., Marshall, T., & O'Donohue, W. (2007). The economics of behavioral health services in medical settings: A summary of the evidence. *Professional Psychology Research and Practice, 38,* 290-297.

Britz B, Siegfried W, Ziegler A, et al. (2000). Rates of psychiatric disorders in a clinical study group of adolescents with extreme obesity and in obese adolescents ascertained via a population based study. *International Journal of Obesity. 24,* 1707-1714.

Brownell, K., Puhl, R. (2007). Weight bias in healthcare settings. *NAASO Obesity Society*. Retrieved March 1, 2009, from http://www.obesityonline.org.

Campbell, K., Engel, H., Timperio, A., Cooper, C., & Crawford, D. (2000). Obesity management: Australian general practitioners' attitudes and practices. *Obesity Research, 8,* 459-466.

Centers for Disease Control and Prevention. *Children's BMI*. Retrieved February 21, 2009, from http://www.cdc.gov/healthyweight/assessing/bmi/childrens_BMI/about_childrens_BMI.html#What%20is%20BMI%20percentile.

Chan, K., Mangione-Smith, R., Burwinkle, T., Rosen, M., & Varni, J. (2005). The PedsQL reliability and validity of the short-form generic core scales and asthma module. *Medical Care, 43,* 256-265.

Connolly, J., Gargiula, L., & Reeve, D. (2002). Selections from current literature: Treatment issues in childhood obesity. *Family Practice, 19,* 304-309.

Davis-Coelho, K., Waltz, J., & Davis-Coelho, B. (2000). Awareness and prevention of bias against fat clients in psychotherapy. *Professional Psychology Research and Practice, 31,* 682-694.

Davison, K., & Birch, L. (2001). Weight status, parent reaction, and self-concept in five-year-old girls. *Pediatrics, 107,* 46-53.

Dietz, W. (1998). Health consequences of obesity in youth: Childhood predictors of adult obesity. *Pediatrics, 101,* 518-525.

Doherty, B. & Harkaway, J. (1990). Obesity and family systems: A family FIRO approach to assessment and treatment planning. *Journal of Marital and Family Therapy, 16,* 287-298.

Dolan, K., Creighton, L., Hopkins, G., Fielding, G. (2003). Laparoscopic gastric banding in morbidly obese adolescents. *Obesity Surgery, 13,* 101-104.

Edmunds, L., Waters, E., & Elliott, E. (2001). Evidence based management of childhood obesity. *British Medical Journal, 323,* 916-919.

Edmunds, L. (2005). Parents' perceptions of health professionals' responses when seeking help for their overweight children. *Family Practice, 22,* 287-292.

Engel, G. (1977). The need for a new medical model: A challenge for biomedicine. *Science, 196,* 129-136.

Epstein, L., Rocco, A., Roemmich, J., & Beecher, M. (2007). Family-based obesity treatment, then and now: Twenty-five years of pediatric obesity treatment. *Health Psychology, 26,* 381-391.

Epstein, L., Valoski, A., Wing, R., & McCurley, J. (1994). Ten-year outcomes of behavioral, family-based treatment for childhood obesity. *Health Psychology, 13,* 373-383.

Epstein L, Roemmich, J., Raynor, H. (2001). Behavioral therapy in the treatment of pediatric obesity. *Pediatric Clinics of North America, 48,* 981-993.

Epstein, L., Paluch, R., Gordy, C., Saelens, B., & Ernst, M. (2000). Problem solving in the treatment of childhood obesity. *Journal of Counseling and Clinical Psychology, 68,* 717-721.

Epstein, L., Valoski, A., Wing, R., & McCurley, J. (1994). Ten-year outcomes of behavioral, family-based treatment for childhood obesity. *Health Psychology, 13,* 373-383.

Federal Interagency Forum on Child and Family Statistics. (2007). America's Children: Key National Indicators of Well-Being, 2007. Federal Interagency Forum on Child and Family Statistics, Washington, DC: U.S. Government Printing Office.

Flodmark, C. E., Lissau, I., Moreno, L. A., Pietrobelli, A., & Widhalm, K. (2004). New insights into the field of children and adolescents' obesity: The European perspective. *International Journal of Obesity, 28*(10), 1189-1196.

Freedman, D., Dhan, L., Serdula, M., Ogden, C., & Dietz, W. (2006). Racial and ethnic differences in secular trends for childhood BMI, weight, and height. *Obesity, 14,* 301-308.

Glenny, A., & O'Meara, S. (1997). *Systematic review of interventions in the treatment and prevention of obesity.* City, England: University of York.

Golan, M., Fainaru, M., & Weizman, A. (1998). Role of behavior modification in the treatment of childhood obesity with the parents as the exclusive agents of change. *International Journal of Obesity, 22,* 1217-1224.

Gordon, H. H., & Hill, L. F. (1957). Obesity. Pediatrics, *20,* 540-546.

Griffiths, L., Wolke, D., Page, A., Horwood, J., & Team, A. (2006). Obesity and bullying: Different effects for boys and girls. *Archives of Disease in Childhood, 91,* 121-155.

Harkaway, J. (1986). Structural assessment of families with obese adolescent girls. *Journal of Marital and Family Therapy, 12,* 199-201.

Hassink, S. (Ed.) (2007). *Pediatric obesity: Prevention, intervention, and treatment strategies for primary care.* Elk Grove Village, IL: American Academy of Pediatrics.

Hebl, M., & Xu, J. (2001). Weighing the care: Physicians reactions to the size of a patient. *International Journal of Obesity Related Metabolism Diseases, 25,* 1246-1252.

Hedley, A., Ogden, C., Johnson, C., Carroll, M., Curtin, L., & Flegal, K. (2004). Prevalence of overweight and obesity among U.S. children, adolescents and adults, 1999-2002. *JAMA, 291,* 2847-2850.

Hoot, J., & Lynn-Garbe, C. (2005). *Weighing in on the issue of childhood obesity. Childhood Education, 81,* 70-76.

Hoppe, R., & Ogden, J. (1997). Practice nurses' beliefs about obesity and weight related interventions in primary care. *International Journal of Obesity, 21,* 141-146.

Inge, T., Garcia, V., Guice, K., Albanese, C., Hammer, L., Harmon, C., Kane, T., Oldham, K., Helmrath, M., Daniels, S. (2004). Bariatric surgery for severely obese adolescents: Concerns and recommendations. *Pediatrics, 114,* 217-223.

Institute of Medicine (2005). Childhood obesity in the United States: Facts and figures. *Preventing Childhood Obesity: Health in the Balance.* Retrieved March 1, 2009, from www.iom.edu.

Janicke, D. (2007). Impact of psychosocial factors on quality of life in overweight youth. *Obesity, 15,* 1799-1807.

Janssen, I., Craig, W., Boyce, W. & Pickett, W. (2004). Associations between overweight and obesity with bullying behaviors in school-aged children. *Pediatrics, 113,* 1187-1194.

Keane, M. (1990). Contemporary beliefs about mental illness among medical students: Implications for education and practice. *Academic Psychiatry, 14,* 172-177.

Kiess, W., Reich, A., Muller, G., Meyer, K., Galler, A., Bennek, J., et al. (2001). Clinical aspects of obesity in childhood and adolescence—diagnosis, treatment and prevention. *International Journal of Obesity, 25* (Suppl 1), 575-579.

Kilo, C. (1999). Improving care through collaboration. *Pediatrics, 103,* 384-393.

Krebs, N. F., Himes, J. H., Jacobson, D., Nicklas, T. A., Guilday, P., Styne, D. Assessment of child and adolescent overweight and obesity. *Pediatrics.* 2007;120 (suppl 4):S193-S228.

Kristeller, J., & Hoerr, R. (1997). Physician attitudes toward managing obesity: Differences among six specialty groups. *American Journal of Preventative Medicine, 26,* 542-549.

Latner, J., & Stunkard, A. (2003). Getting worse: The stigmatization of obese children. *Obese Research, 11,* 452-456.

Latner, J., Stunkard, A., & Wilson, G. (2005). *Stigmatized students: Age, sex, and ethnicity effects in the stigmatization of obesity. 13,* 1226-1231.

Maroney, D., & Golub, S. (1992). Nurses' attitudes toward obese persons and certain ethnic groups. *Perceptive Motor Skills, 75,* 387-391.

McArthur, L., & Ross, J. (1997). Attitudes of registered dietitians toward personal overweight and overweight clients. *Journal of American Dietetic Association, 97,* 63-66.

Mellin, L., Slinkard, L., & Irwin, C. (1987). Adolescent obesity intervention: Validation of the SHAPEDOWN program. *Journal of the American Dietetic Association, 87,* 333-338.

National Center for Health Statistics. *Health, United States, 2007 with chart book on trends in the health of Americans.* Hyattsville, MD: 2007.

National Initiative for Children's Health Care Quality. (2007). *Expert Committee Recommendations on the Assessment, Prevention and Treatment of Child and Adolescent Overweight and Obesity: An implementation guide from the Childhood Obesity Action Network.* Retrieved March 1, 2009, from http://www.nichq. org or www.ihs.gov/nonmedicalprograms/dirinitiatives/documents/coan%20 implementation%20guide%20dr.%20scott%20gee.doc.

National Institute for Health Care Management. (2005). *Health plans emerging as pragmatic partners in fight against obesity.* Retrieved November 2, 2008, from http://www.nihcm.org/pdf/ObesityReport.pdf.

National Heart Lung & Blood Institute. (2007). *Working group on future research directions in childhood obesity prevention and treatment.* Retrieved September 2, 2008, from http://www.nhlbi.nih.gov/meetings/workshops/child-obesity/ index.htm.

Oude Luttikhuis, H., Baur, L., Jansen, H., Shrewsbury, V.A., O'Malley, C., Stolk, R.P., Summerbell, C.D. (2009). Interventions for treating obesity in children. *Cochrane Database of Systematic Reviews, 1.* Art. No.: CD001872. DOI:10.1002/14651858.CD001872.pub2.

Ogden, C., Carroll, M., & Flegal, K. (2008). High body mass index for age among U.S. children and adolescents, 2003-2006. *JAMA, 299,* 2401-2405.

Ogden, C., Flegal, K., Carroll, M., & Johnson, C. (2002). Prevalence and trends in overweight among U.S. children and adolescents, 1999-2000. *JAMA, 288,* 1728-1732.

Ogden, C.L., Carroll, M.D., Curtin, L.R., Lamb, M.M., Flegal, K.M. (2010). Prevalence of high body mass index in US children and adolescents, 2007 – 2008. *JAMA, 303,* 242-249.

Pinhas-Hamiel, O., Singer, S., Pilpel, N., Fradkin, A., Modan, D., & Reichman, B. (2006). Health-related quality of life among children and adolescents: Associations with obesity. *International Journal of Obesity, 30,* 267-272.

Pratt, K., Lazorick, S., Collier, D. (2011). *Online case example.* Retrieved June 1, 2011, from http://www.ahrq.org.

Pratt, K., Lamson, A., Lazorick, S., Swanson, M., Cravens, J., & Collier, D. (2011). A Biopsychosocial Pilot Study of Overweight Youth and Care Providers' Perceptions of Quality of Life. *Journal of Pediatric Nursing.* (In Press)

Pratt, K., Lamson, A., Swanson, M., Lazorick, S., & Collier, D. (2010). The Importance of Assessing for Depression with HRQOL in Treatment Seeking Obese Youth and their Caregivers. *Quality of Life Research.* (Under Review)

Prevalence of overweight among children and adolescents: United States. (1999-2000). Centers for Disease Control and Prevention.

Price, J., Desmond, S., Krol, R., Snyder, F., & O'Connell, J. (1987). Family practice physicians' beliefs, attitudes, and practices regarding obesity. *American Journal of Preventative Medicine, 3,* 339-345.

Puhl, R., & Latner, J. (2007). Obesity, stigma, and the health of the nation's children. *Psychological Bulletin, 133,* 557-580.

Puhl, R., & Latner, J. (2008). Weight bias: New science on a significant social problem. *Obesity, 16* (supl 2), 1-2.

Ravens-Sieberer, U., Redegeld, M., & Bullinger, M. (2001). Quality of life after inpatient rehabilitation in children with obesity, *International Journal of Obesity and Related Metabolic Disorders, 25,* 63-65.

Rosenbaum, S., Wilensky, S., Cox, M., & Wright, D. B. (2005). Reducing obesity risks during childhood: The role of public and private health insurance. Washington: George Washington University Center for Health Services Research and Policy. Retrieved October 5, 2008, from http://www.gwumc.edu/sphhs/departments/healthpolicy/chsrp/downloads/Obesity%20Report%20Final.pdf.

Russell-Mayhew, S. (2007). Eating disorders and obesity as social justice issues: Implications for research and practice. *Journal for Social Action in Counseling Psychology, 1,* 1-13.

Schwimmer, J., Burwinkle, T., & Varni, J. (2003). Health-related quality of life of severely   obese children and adolescents. *JAMA, 289,* 1813.

Spear, B. A., Barlow, S. E., Ervin, C., Ludwig, D. S., Saelens, B. E., Schetzina, K. E., et al. (2007). Recommendations for treatment of child and adolescent overweight and obesity. *Pediatrics, 120* (Supplement 4), S254-288.

Speiser, P., Rudolf, M., Camacho-Hubner, C., Chiarelli, F., Eliakim, A., Freemark, M., et al. (2005). Consensus statement: Childhood obesity. *Journal of Clinical Endocrinology and Metabolism, 90.*

Sugerman, H., Sugerman, E., DeMaria, E., et al. (2003). Bariatric surgery for severely obese adolescents. *Journal of Gastrointestinal Surgery, 7,* 102-108.

Swallen, K., Reither, E., Haas, S., & Meier, A. (2005). Overweight, obesity and health-related quality of life among adolescents: The national longitudinal study of adolescent health. *Pediatrics, 115,* 340-347.

U.S. Census Bureau. (2007). *2007 Population Estimates.* Retrieved March 1, 2009, from http://www.census.gov/popest/estimates.php.

U.S. Department of Health and Human Services, Health Resources and Services Administration, Maternal and Child Health Bureau. (2005). *The National Survey of Children's Health 2005.* Rockville, MD: U.S. Department of Health and Human Services.

Varni, J. (1999). Measurement model for the Pediatric Quality of Life Inventory. *Medical Care, 37,* 126-139.

Varni, J. (2001). Reliability and validity of the pediatric quality of life inventory version 4.0 generic core scales in healthy and patient populations. *Medical Care, 39,* 800-812.

Varni, J. (2002). The PedsQL4.0 Generic Core Scales: Sensitivity, responsiveness, and impact on clinical decision-making. *Journal of Behavioral Medicine, 25,* 175-193.

Varni, J. (2003). The PedsQL4.0 as a pediatric population health measure: Feasibility, reliability, and validity. *Ambulatory Pediatrics, 3,* 329-341.

Varni, J. (1998-2008). The Pediatric quality of life inventory 4.0.

Whitaker, R., Wright, J., Pepe, M., Siedel, K., & Dietz, W. (1997). Predicting obesity in young adulthood from childhood and parental obesity. *New England Journal of Medicine, 37,* 869-873.

Whitlock, E., O'Connor, E., Williams, S., Beil, T., & Lutz, K. (2008). Effectiveness of weight management programs in children and adolescents. Rockville, MD: Agency for Healthcare Research and Quality.

Wigton, R., & McGaghie, W. (2001). The effect of obesity on medical students' approach to patients with abdominal pain. *Journal of General Internal Medicine,16*, 262-265.

Williams, J., Wake, M., Hesketh, K., Maher, E., & Waters, E. (2005). Health-related quality of life of overweight and obese children. *JAMA, 283*, 70-76.

Wrotniak, B., Epstein, L. H., Paluch, R. A., & Roemmich, J. N. (2004). Parent weight change as a predictor of child weight change in family-based behavioral obesity treatment. *Archives of Pediatric and Adolescent Medicine, 97*, 354-362.

Wrotniak, B., Epstein, L. H., Paluch, R. A., & Roemmich, J. N. (2005). The relationship between parent and child self-reported adherence and weight loss. *Obesity Research, 13*, 1089-1096.

Young, K. M., Northern, J. J., Lister, K. M., Drummond, J. A., & O'Brien, W. H. (2007). A meta-analysis of family-behavioral weight-loss treatments for children. *Clinical Psychology Review, 27*, 240-249.

Zeller, M., & Modi, A. (2006). Predictors of health-related quality of life in obese youth. Obesity, 14, 122-130.

Zeller, M., Roehrig, H., Modi, A., Daniels, S., & Inge, T. (2006). Health-related quality of life and depressive symptoms in adolescents with extreme obesity presenting for bariatric surgery. *Pediatrics, 117*, 1155-1161.

Diabetes

Tai Mendenhall, PhD

Originally published as Clinical Update in Family Therapy Magazine
November-December 2009

THE DIABETES EPIDEMIC

"Diabetes" represents a class of chronic illnesses that includes several types of endocrine disorders, including immune mediated diabetes mellitus (Type 1), insulin resistant diabetes mellitus (Type 2), and gestational diabetes mellitus. The common thread across these disorders is that patients' bodies are not able to produce or use insulin properly. Insulin is a hormone produced by the pancreas that enables our cells to absorb glucose (sugar) from the blood and use it for energy (American Diabetes Association [ADA], 2009; National Institute of Diabetes and Digestive and Kidney Diseases [NIDDK], 2008).

Highly correlated with the United States' ever-rising obesity epidemic across both child and adult cohorts, diabetes is now one of the most widespread chronic diseases in the country. Prevalence estimates have steadily risen since the 1950s (increasing more than six-fold), and have skyrocketed over the last decade. More than 2,500 cases of diabetes are diagnosed each day in this country, with current estimates of those afflicted at over 23 million. Almost eight percent of the population is affected, and racial and ethnic minorities are disproportionately affected: Hispanic and African Americans are two to four times more likely to be diagnosed than Caucasians and non-Hispanic whites. American Indians are 3-10 times more likely to be diagnosed, depending on age (ADA, 2009; Buse, 2006; Indian Health Service, 2006; NIDDK, 2008).

These trends are further alarming in light of the myriad of health-related pathologies that diabetes can bring, including—but not limited to—cardiovascular disease (which represents the most common cause of death and disability in the United States), hyperlipidemia, neuropathy, retinopathy, dental disease, kidney failure, and sexual and urologic dysfunctions (ADA, 2009; Brown et al., 2003; Cavanaugh, Taylor, Keim, Clutter, & Geraghty, 2008; Dirks et al.,

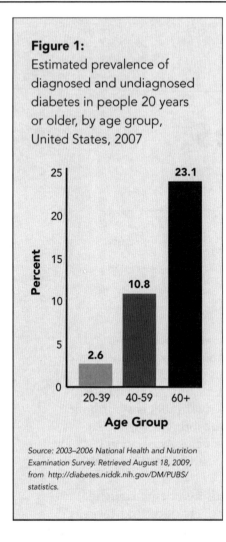

Figure 1:
Estimated prevalence of diagnosed and undiagnosed diabetes in people 20 years or older, by age group, United States, 2007

Source: 2003–2006 National Health and Nutrition Examination Survey. Retrieved August 18, 2009, from http://diabetes.niddk.nih.gov/DM/PUBS/statistics.

2005; NIDDK, 2008; Rhoades et al., 2006). In the arenas of mental health, patients with diabetes are more likely than their non-diabetic counterparts to struggle with a variety of psychological presentations, including depression and anxiety (Goldney, Phillips, Fisher, Hons, & Wilson, 2004; Kolbasovsky, 2004; Schram, Baan, & Pouwer, 2009).

Total annual economic costs of diabetes in the U.S. now exceed $174 billion. Medical expenditures for disease care and managing its complications cost approximately $85 billion per year, alongside $31 billion in general medical costs. One out of every five healthcare dollars spent in the U.S. today is for patients with diabetes, and a per capita annual cost for said patients is almost $12,000/year. Annual indirect costs of diabetes (e.g., work absenteeism, reduced productivity, unemployment and disability) are estimated at almost $60 billion (ADA, 2007).

The role(s) of patients' relationships and family contexts are important to consider in diabetes care, insofar as effective disease management extends far beyond straightforward biomedical interventions like injecting insulin to control blood sugar, or taking oral medications that target cardiovascular health. Living with diabetes encompasses a complex set of behaviors and lifestyle sequences in diet, exercise and physical activity, and everyday routines. If patients and their families work together in co-ownership of the disease and its management, a variety of positive effects in health will generally follow (e.g., improved perceptions of illness manageability, reductions in stress, weight loss, better compliance with medical regimens) (Fisher, 2006; Wysocki, Greco, Harris, Bubb, & White, 2001). However, this is oftentimes easier said than done, as family members try to balance being supportive versus being a "nag," as patients struggle with a sense of lost autonomy, and as everyone adjusts to an illness for which there is no known cure (Lewin et al., 2006; Trief, 2005).

DIAGNOSIS AND ASSESSMENT

As outlined previously, diabetes is actually a group of diseases that are characterized by defects in the body's production of insulin by the pancreas, receptivity to insulin, or both. Normally, when blood glucose elevates (after consuming food, for example), insulin is released from the pancreas to allow cells to absorb the energy. In patients with diabetes, the absence or insufficient production of insulin causes hyperglycemia (i.e., too much sugar in the blood), while at the same time starving the body's cells. Diabetes is a chronic medical condition; while it can be effectively managed, its course is permanent and there is no cure (ADA, 2008; NIDDK, 2008).

DIABETES SUBTYPES

Type 1 Diabetes. Type 1 diabetes (formerly called "Type I diabetes," with a Roman numeral, "juvenile diabetes," "insulin-dependent diabetes," and/or "IDDM") is usually diagnosed in children, adolescents, and young adults (under 30 years old). Patients struggling with this disease are not able to produce insulin because their body's immune systems have attacked and destroyed the pancreatic beta cells specialized to make it. Patients who are not overweight and have no family history of the illness are most likely to be diagnosed with this disease subtype—which is estimated to comprise 5 to 10 percent of all cases (ADA, 2008; Centers for Disease Control [CDC], 2009a; NIDDK, 2009).

Type 2 Diabetes. Type 2 diabetes (formerly called "Type II diabetes," "adult-onset diabetes," "noninsulin-dependent diabetes mellitus," and/or "NIDDM") is the most common type of this disease. While most often diagnosed during adulthood, Type 2 diabetes can develop at any age. This form of diabetes usually begins with insulin "resistance," which is a condition wherein muscle, liver, and fat cells do not use insulin as efficiently as they are supposed to. Consequently, the body needs more and more insulin to help glucose enter its cells. The pancreas initially keeps up with this added demand for insulin, but not forever—eventually losing its ability to secrete enough of the hormone in response to the body's needs. Patients who are overweight and have a family history of diabetes, obesity and/or cardiovascular problems (e.g., heart attack, high blood pressure) are most likely to be diagnosed with disease subtype (ADA, 2009; CDC, 2009a; NIDDK, 2008).

Gestational Diabetes. This type of diabetes first occurs in women during pregnancy. When pregnant, these patients' need for insulin appears to increase in much the same manner as with patients who have Type 2 diabetes. And while this form of diabetes generally resolves after the baby is born, women experiencing gestational diabetes are more likely to develop Type 2 diabetes later in life (ADA, 2008; NIDDK, 2009).

Other Diabetes subtypes. Several other types of diabetes exist, but are relatively rare and outside the scope of this Update. They include those caused by latent autoimmune diabetes in adults (LADA) (Leslie, Williams, & Pozzilli, 2006), maturity-onset diabetes of the young (MODY) (Winckler et al., 2007), genetic defects in insulin action (e.g., leprechaunism) (Luzi et al., 2007), diseases of the pancreas and rare autoimmune disorders (NIDDK, 2008). See NIDDK (2008) for a full review.

DIAGNOSING DIABETES

Common symptoms associated with diabetes are often not recognized at first as indicative of something more problematic because, in and of themselves, they can appear ephemeral or mundane. These symptoms include: frequent urination, excessive thirst, extreme hunger, increased fatigue, and unusual changes in weight. Irritability and blurry vision are also frequently noted in patients who are later diagnosed. Any person who experiences these symptoms (or combination of symptoms) should follow-up with his or her healthcare provider immediately, as early detection and treatment is highly correlated with reductions in disease severity and related complications (ADA, 2009; Fonseca, 2006; NIDDK, 2008).

The three most common tests used to diagnose diabetes are the fasting plasma glucose test, the oral glucose tolerance test, and the random plasma glucose test.

Fasting Plasma Glucose Test (FPG). This **test** measures blood glucose in a person who has not eaten anything for at least eight hours, and the most reliable assays are conducted in the morning. While not as sensitive as the oral glucose tolerance test, the FPG is the most preferred measure for diagnosing diabetes because of its low cost and ease of administration. People with a fasting glucose level of 100-125 milligrams per deciliter (mg/dL) are diagnosed as having "pre-diabetes"—which places them at risk of later developing Type 2 diabetes. Patients scoring 126 mg/dL or higher are then tested again on another day, and if the follow-up assay remains high, an official diagnosis of diabetes is made (ADA, 2009; NIDDK, 2008).

Oral Glucose Tolerance Test (OGTT). This **test** also requires that a person fasts at least eight hours, measuring plasma glucose levels immediately before and two hours after drinking a liquid containing 75 grams of glucose dissolved in water. If the blood glucose level is between 140-199 mg/dL two hours after drinking the liquid, the patient is diagnosed as having pre-diabetes. Having impaired glucose tolerance, like having impaired fasting glucose, means that a person has an increased risk of later developing Type 2 diabetes. Patients scoring 200 mg/dL or higher are then tested again on another day, and if the follow-up assay remains high, an official diagnosis of diabetes is made (ADA, 2009; NIDDK, 2008).

Random Plasma Glucose Test. This test measures blood glucose without regard to when the person being tested last ate (i.e., no fasting is necessary). If a patient's blood glucose level is scored at 200 mg/dL or higher at the same time that other common and aforementioned symptoms of diabetes are present, a provisional diabetes diagnosis is made. Follow-up testing FPG, or OGTT testing, is then carried out to confirm the diagnosis (ADA, 2009; NIDDK, 2008).

DIFFERENTIATING DIABETES SUBTYPES

Patients evidencing high levels of blood glucose through any of the above measures can then be followed-up with a C-peptide assay, which will determine if endogenous insulin production in the patient's body is present. If it is not, this means that beta-cell failure has occurred—and signifies that a diagnosis of Type 1 diabetes is indicated. A simple laboratory test for ketones (acid) in the blood or urine can also be employed; those who evidence high levels of ketones are usually diagnosed with Type 1 diabetes, whereas those who do not are usually diagnosed with Type 2 diabetes (ADA, 2009; NIDDK, 2008; Plodkowski & Shane, 2003).

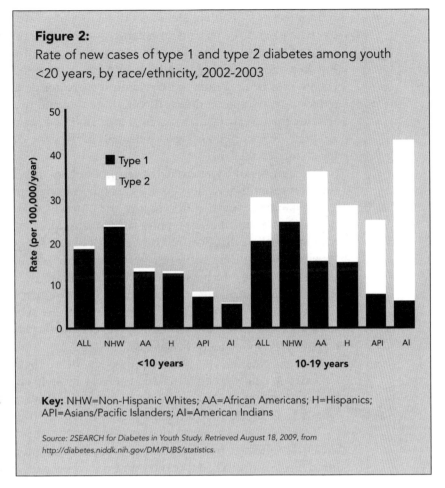

Figure 2:

Rate of new cases of type 1 and type 2 diabetes among youth <20 years, by race/ethnicity, 2002-2003

Key: NHW=Non-Hispanic Whites; AA=African Americans; H=Hispanics; API=Asians/Pacific Islanders; AI=American Indians

Source: 2SEARCH for Diabetes in Youth Study. Retrieved August 18, 2009, from http://diabetes.niddk.nih.gov/DM/PUBS/statistics.

It is also common for patients with Type 1 diabetes to initially present as having had a very rapid and severe onset of aforementioned symptoms (e.g., losing 30 pounds in a few weeks' time, acute onset of remarkable thirst), thus being very sick and seeking/needing emergency medical attention. Patients with Type 2 diabetes are usually diagnosed through routine testing and physical examinations (ADA, 2009; CDC, 2009a; NIDDK, 2008).

PATIENT AND FAMILY REACTIONS TO THE DIAGNOSIS

Patients' and their families' reactions to the diabetes diagnosis vary widely, from downplaying the importance of the disease, to communicating confident plans to manage it, to an emotional devastation secondary to the experience of coming to understand that one has a serious physical disease that will never go away (Eborall, Davies, Kinmonth, Griffin, & Lawton, 2007; Peel, Parry, Douglas, & Lawton, 2004).

A diagnosis of Type 1 diabetes is more likely to be made in context(s) of an acute and even life-threatening health crisis (e.g., ketoacidosis), more often involves children, and carries with it a care regimen that requires lifelong insulin injections. This constellation of factors translates into a great deal of fear by patients and/or parents of patients for the patient's life and/or a strong sense of burden vis-à-vis lifestyle and treatment routines that must last forever. Further, the psychology of adjusting to managing an illness via shots (i.e., insulin injections) tends to carry with it a greater deal of adjustment as compared to managing an illness through lifestyle and dietary behaviors alone. It is for these reasons that patients and families adjusting to Type 1 diabetes generally report higher levels of distress at the time of diagnosis (ADA, 2009; Delahanty et al., 2007).

A diagnosis of Type 2 diabetes is more likely to be met with mixed reactions by patients and their families. Sometimes patients have struggled with a longstanding worry of developing the illness (secondary to a strong family history of obesity, diabetes, and/or heart disease, for example), and ultimately respond to their diagnosis with a sense of defeat or apathy secondary to the "curse" that has long been pursuing them (Mendenhall et al., under review; Peel et al., 2004). Others have feared the disease and worked hard to avoid it through active engagement in healthy lifestyle behaviors—only to develop diabetes anyway, despite all of their efforts. These patients often report a sense of anger alongside struggling with having no clear "villain" to hold culpable (Peres, Franco, & Santos, 2008; Yi, Yi, Vitaliano, & Weinger, 2008). Sometimes patients and their families view being diagnosed with diabetes as a "wake-up call" to begin making the very lifestyle changes that they have known for a long time that they need to make (Eborall et al., 2007; Haslam, Sattar, & Lean, 2006; Mendenhall & Doherty, 2007b).

Patients with all types of diabetes frequently report a great deal of worry about their future, frustration or confusion with and regarding their treatment plans and goals, depression and weariness with managing the day-to-day challenges and requirements of managing their illness effectively (ADA, 2009; Delahanty et al., 2007; Goldney, Phillips, Fisher, & Wilson, 2004).

Mental health providers should work closely with biomedical providers, patients and their families as diabetes diagnoses are made to normalize, make space to process and work through these commonplace and varied reactions. Balancing sensitivity to this difficult time with the need to quickly impart information (but not too much information so as to be further overwhelming) is a challenge for treatment teams, and one that mental health providers who are familiar with the disease are well-equipped to assist with effectively (Delahanty et al., 2007; Peel et al., 2004; Peres, Franco, & Santos, 2008).

STANDARD RECOMMENDATIONS FOR DIABETES TESTING

Standard recommendations today are that adults ages 45 years or older be tested for pre-diabetes and Type 2 diabetes. People who are younger than 45 should consider testing if their Body Mass Index (BMI) score falls into the overweight, obese, or extremely obese categories, and if they have one or more established risk factors for the disease. BMI is easily calculated via weight-by-height ratios that are available though the National Institutes for

Health (e.g., see http://www.nhlbisupport.com/bmi). Established risk factors for diabetes include: being physically inactive; having a family member (e.g., parent or sibling) with diabetes; being a member of an ethnic or racial minority group (e.g., African American, American Indian, Alaska Native, Asian American, Hispanic/Latino, Pacific Islander); giving birth to a baby > 9 pounds; having been diagnosed with gestational diabetes; having (or being treated for) high blood pressure; and poor cholesterol levels (e.g., HDL > 35 mg/dL, triglyceride > 250mg/dL). Other risk factors include having polycystic ovary syndrome (PCOS); impaired glucose tolerance (IGT) or impaired fasting glucose (IFG); acanthosis nigricans (characterized by a dark, velvety rash around the neck or armpits); and/or any history of cardiovascular disease. If results of diabetes testing are normal, follow-up assays should be repeated at least every three years. For those diagnosed with pre-diabetes, immediate steps in disease management should commence and follow-up tests carried out again in one to two years (ADA, 2009; CDC, 2009a; NIDDK, 2008).

BIOMEDICAL TREATMENTS

Biomedical treatment for diabetes is highly individualized, depending on the patient's overall health and presence (or absence) of diabetes-related conditions and co-morbid diseases. Principal foci generally include controlling blood sugar through the administration of insulin, oral medications, and/or lifestyle changes in diet and physical activity. Antihypertensives, lipid-lowering drugs, and angiotensin-converting enzyme (ACE) inhibitors are also common within a diabetic patient's biomedical care (ADA, 2009; Fonseca, 2006; Nathan et al., 2009; NIDDK, 2008; Spann et al., 2006).

Patients with Type 1 diabetes are usually prescribed daily combinations of short-acting insulin (e.g., Humalog, Novolog) and longer-acting insulin (e.g., glargine, detemir). These insulins are generally self-administered via syringe injections, but some patients have their insulin administered by continuous infusion pumps (which look similar to an electronic pager). Eating a consistently healthy diet and getting an appropriate amount of physical exercise are also important, insofar as patients cannot rely on insulin injections alone to maintain indicated blood glucose levels and good overall health (ADA, 2009; Karmeen & Richard, 2006; NIDDK, 2008).

Patients with Type 2 diabetes are usually encouraged to begin controlling their blood glucose levels through weight loss via dietary and exercise regimens, unless it is determined that their glycosylated hemoglobin (A1c)—which represents patients' average metabolic control over the previous two to three months—is dangerously high. If the patient is not successful over the next three to six months, he or she is generally started on an oral medication (e.g., sulfonylurea, biguanide) to help control blood sugar levels. Combination treatments of injected insulin and oral medications may be indicated later if a patient's disease continues to progress and worsen (ADA, 2009; NIDDK, 2008; Spann et al., 2006).

DIABETES AND DISASTER PREPAREDNESS

Over the last 10 years, attention to multidisciplinary fieldwork in response to natural and man-made disasters has increased dramatically (Freedy & Simpson, 2007; Mendenhall & Berge, in press; Wieling & Mittal, 2008). These efforts have encompassed a combination of preparing providers (e.g., psychologists, marriage and family therapists, family physicians, emergency medical technicians) and public service workers (e.g., fire and rescue personnel, public health administrators, health educators) in the appropriate provision of emergency mental health and biomedical services in the field, and in assisting the lay public in general disaster preparedness, such as family emergency plans and emergency kits.

In emergency or disaster situations, persons with diabetes are presented with challenges unique to their disease that place them at considerably higher health risk. Providers are encouraged to discuss with their patients how to best prepare for these scenarios, as doing so could help circumvent a serious diabetic-related event or death.

First, it is important to encourage patients to store 3 to 7 days' worth of diabetes supplies in an easy-to-identify container stored in an easy-to-access location. The exact contents of this container will depend on the patient's unique biomedical care regimen, and could include any of the following (ADA, 2009; CDC, 2009):

- Insulin and insulin delivery supplies
- Lancets
- Back-up blood glucose meter (and extra batteries)
- Oral medication(s)
- Fast-acting glucose sources (glucose tablets, regular cola)
- Glucagon emergency kit
- List of emergency contact numbers
- Print out of a physician's orders

Patients with diabetes should also be encouraged to quickly identify themselves as having the disease to providers and organizers offering assistance in emergency or evacuee situations, and to consider wearing medical alert bracelets if/when the diabetic is not verbally able to communicate. It is also important to remember to drink a lot of fluids (which is easy to forget in the context of a disaster or crisis) to prevent dehydration, and to be especially careful about wounds and wound care (because people with diabetes are more prone to infections) (ADA, 2009; CDC, 2009; NIDDK, 2008).

Mental health professionals working with patients and families who live with diabetes must be familiar with these key and basic biomedical aspects of the disease and its treatment. A working understanding of the respective physiological processes of Type 1, Type 2, gestational and other subtypes of diabetes sets a framework and foundation for collaborating with any other provider(s) on the care team, and in effectively integrating attention to psychological, relational, and other contextual struggles with which patients are dealing. Mental health professionals should know goal ranges for patients' daily blood sugar levels, overall metabolic control, body-mass-index, blood pressure, lipid profiles, and other medical data that represent everyday facets of diabetes care. They should be fluent in terminology related to these data and familiar with short- and long-term goals as they relate to patients' physical health across these foci.

For a complete list of biomedical interventions for patients with diabetes (all types), mental health providers should visit the American Diabetes Association's (ADA) (www.diabetes.org) and the National Diabetes Information Clearinghouse (http://diabetes.niddk.nih.gov), which is sponsored by the National Institute of Diabetes and Digestive and Kidney Diseases (NIDDK).

PSYCHOSOCIAL TREATMENTS

In synchrony with attention to the physiological aspects of biomedical care, psychosocial treatments for diabetes focus on patients' psychological and relational well-being, and encompass attention to patients'/families' adjustment to: living with a chronic disease; depressive, anxiety, and stress-related symptoms often associated with (and exacerbating of) diabetes; and family and loved ones' involvement and support (or not) of patients' efforts in adopting or maintaining a healthy lifestyle. This is important because the majority of the work essential to effective diabetes management takes place outside of the healthcare professional's office; that is, in the day-to-day lives of patient's psychosocial worlds of home, school/work, family and friends (Beverly, Penrod, & Wray, 2007; Duke et al., 2008; Lewin et al., 2006; Mendenhall & Doherty, 2007a, 2007b).

Individual Therapy and Psychoeducation. Broad literature is available regarding diabetes management that is used to describe secondary prevention efforts focused on individual patients. Conventional treatment regimens generally encompass patients meeting with a primary care provider, diabetes educator, or nutritionist wherein specific health behaviors are taught and advocated en route to the ultimate goal of maintaining blood sugar levels within an indicated and normal range. These behaviors include meal planning (e.g., custom tailored to the patient's activity level and weight, with food intake sequenced and coordinated to when insulin's blood sugar lowering action is most effective), exercise (to reduce body-mass-index and lower blood sugar levels), and active blood sugar testing and record-keeping in order to monitor metabolic control (usually by a combination of fingertip capillary blood sample tests scheduled throughout the day before and/or after meals and at waking and/or bedtime) (Fisher et al., 1998; Fonseca, 2006; Karmeen & Richard, 2006; Keller, 2000; Padgett, Mumford, Hynes, & Carter, 1988).

It is important for mental health professionals working in these contexts to understand the well-established and reciprocal relationships between patients' mental health and disease management and outcomes. Effective therapists are skilled in clinical and psychoeducation interventions that attend to how psychological symptoms common in diabetes (e.g., depressive symptoms, anxiety symptoms) influence behaviors that work for or against the good disease management behaviors that biomedical members of the treatment team are advocating (e.g., dietary adherence, motivation to exercise), as well as how such symptoms can influence disease outcomes (e.g., blood sugar, blood pressure) even when patients are "doing everything right."

While better in comparison to control groups receiving no care and/ or standard medical care only, individual therapy and psychoeducation approaches are beginning to lose ground as the field increasingly recognizes the relationship and contextual complexities of effective disease management (Fisher, 2006; Leonard, Jang, Savik, & Plumbo, 2005). Put simply, patients do not live in a vacuum. Attending to one person's mental health functioning vis-à-vis a chronic illness and instituting changes in that person's lifestyle are more often than not going to influence the lives of others with whom he or she is connected, and it is thereby indicated to include these "others" in clinical endeavors targeting health improvement.

Couples Therapy and Psychoeducation. While only more recently integrated into practice, researchers have known for some time that there is a powerful and reciprocal link between the health of intimate relationships (e.g., marriages, domestic partnerships) and the respective physical health of the two people who inhabit the intimate relationship (Burman & Margolin, 1992; House, Landus, & Umberson, 1988). For example, we know that marital stability and quality affect immune functioning, endocrine stress hormones, development of illnesses such as hypertension, and even survival from serious illnesses (Coyne et al., 2001; Fisher, 2006; Kiecolt-Glaser & Newton, 2001; Robles & Kiecolt-Glaser, 2003; Trief, Ploutz-Snyder, Britton & Weinstock, 2004; Umberson, Williams, Powers, Liu, & Needham, 2006; Wickrama et al., 2001).

While work with couples struggling with diabetes still trails the far more established research base regarding parents and their young or adolescent aged children diagnosed with the disease, we know that marital quality and dyadic support are predictive of compliance with indicated self-care and dietary and exercise regimens (Cole & Chesla, 2006; Fisher, 2006; Trief et al., 2004). Beverly, Miller, and Wray (2008), for example, have connected spousal support to self-control regarding food choices and consumption, co-ownership of knowledge regarding the components of a healthy diet (called dietary competence), and a sense of teamwork in everyday relationship functioning and disease management. Beverly and Wray (2008) found similar dyadic processes in the arenas of exercise adherence in diabetes management, noting that: 1) spouses who perceived themselves as "being in this together" (collective support) were better able to communicate about diabetes and balance being supportive versus being a "nag"; 2) spouses who shared similar beliefs regarding health behaviors (collective motivation) were more likely to participate in physical activity and exercise together; and 3) spouses who shared a sense of collective responsibility for each other's health were more likely to stick to the physical activity regimens in which they were engaging.

Couples work also provides a forum to normalize and communicate about a variety of stressors and strains that partners are feeling in the context of living with a chronic illness. Feelings of vulnerability and fear (e.g., worries about one's own and/or partner's health), burden and resentment (e.g., related to caretaking or having to make lifestyle changes that are neither wanted nor welcome), and loss (e.g., of spontaneity in recreational activities, dietary choices, and/or daily routines) are commonplace, and represent critical issues equally important to attend to in diabetes interventions as teaching information about food portion sizes or helping motivate couples to go walking together in the evenings after work (Beverly, Penrod, & Wray, 2007; Pereira, Berg-Cross, Almeida, & Machado, 2008). Also important for some couples is how their sense of spirituality plays into coping with diabetes. Cattich and Knudson-Martin (2009), for example, have identified a variety of couple spiritual coping styles, ranging from those who view diabetes as an opportunity for growth and collaborative dyadic problem-solving, to those who see themselves as victims sans hope. Mental health providers should work to help patients and their spouses share, honor, tap, and even challenge these perceptions—as doing so can empower couples toward beneficent and shared change.

Family Therapy and Psychoeducation. Investigators who have included a family component in diabetes interventions are also driven by a growing awareness that patients' family contexts influence patients' physical health. Frequent references to literature that have identified strong relationships between diabetes patient outcomes (e.g., metabolic control, compliance with indicated self-care regimens, weight loss) and family characteristics (e.g., supportive versus unsupportive co-ownership of illness responsibilities, high versus low conflict and communication skills) illustrate this, and are put forth by researchers as logical grounding for addressing family issues while intervening with almost any physiological illness (Cameron et al., 2008; Gilden, Hendryx, Casia, & Singh, 1989; Trief, 2005; Trief, Grant, & Elbert, 1998; Trief, Himes, Orendorff, & Weinstock, 2001).

Mental health professionals working in diabetes care should endeavor to integrate this knowledge into the care that they provide. Whether this is working with families (spouses, children, parents, etc.) to better understand basic diabetes information alongside patients, or to take active roles in co-owning the disease with the patient, attention to patients' family contexts is essential. Many therapists engaged in these efforts work to empower patients and spouses to exercise together. They work with whichever family member is most "in charge" of grocery shopping and meal preparation (instead of only the patient, who might not be the one who shops for or prepares the family's food) to do so in a manner that is both appetizing and diabetes-sensitive. They help negotiate and resolve conflicts/struggles related to disease management (e.g., fights over whose food preferences are given priority, transportation inconveniences related to medical visits and/or participation in community education/support forums), loss (e.g., loss of previous spontaneity to eat whatever is desired, or to go to any restaurant at anytime), and fatigue (e.g., patients or family members not wanting to "deal with" diabetes anymore).

Patients and family members participating in family-oriented diabetes interventions tend to report significant increases in the quality of their relationships, as defined by greater cohesiveness, increased inter-member collaboration and involvement in diabetes care, improved communication and problem-solving competencies, and reductions in family conflict (Auslander,

Bubb, Rogge, & Santiago, 1993; Dougherty, Schiffrin, White, Soderstrom, & Sufrategui, 1999; Galatzer, Amir, Gil, Karp, & Laron, 1982; Fisher, 2006; Gilden et al., 1989; Harris, 1989; Wysocki et al., 1997; Wysocki et al., 1999; Wysocki et al., 2000). Patients' psychological adjustment is also benefited through family-based interventions: researches have demonstrated superior influence in reducing denial and increasing acceptance of the illness, improving perceptions that the illness is manageable, reducing subjective reports of stress, reducing the frequency of diabetic emergencies (e.g., diabetic ketoacidosis), improving body image and self esteem, and increasing overall perceptions of life quality (Geffken et al., 2008; Gilden, Hendryx, Casia & Singh, 1989; Satin, La Greca, Zigo, & Skyler, 1989; Thomas-Dobersen, Butler-Simon, & Fleshner, 1993; Wysocki et al., 1997; Wysocki et al., 1999; Wysocki, Greco, Harris, Bubb & White, 2001). Further, family-based interventions have demonstrated superiority over individually-oriented approaches in improving patients' compliance with indicated medical regimens (e.g., insulin injections, blood sugar monitoring, dietary constituents and schedule) and increased overall self care (Anderson, Wolf, Burkhart, Cornell, & Bacon, 1989; Delameter et al., 1990; Gilden et al., 1989; McNabb, Quinn, Murphy, Thorp, & Cook, 1994; Ryden et al., 1994; Thomas-Dobersen et al., 1993; Wing, Marcus, Epstein, & Jawad, 1991; Wysocki et al., 2000; Harris, Greco, Wysocki, & White, 2001).

While these findings are encouraging because they have been linked to physical outcomes in the general diabetes literature, current research has not unequivocally demonstrated that family-based interventions are superior in influencing patients' physical well being. Using hemoglobin A1c as a standard benchmark, some investigators maintain that participants in family-based interventions had better A1c levels at follow-up than compared to standard care and conventional treatment (Andersen et al., 1989; Cole & Chesla, 2006; Delamater et al., 1990; Gliden et al., 1989; Satin et al., 1989; Wing et al., 1987). However, other investigators have found no significant differences in patients' A1c change (Dougherty et al., 1999; Thomas-Dobersen, Butler-Simon & Fleshner, 1993; Wing et al., 1991; Wysocki et al., 2000). Efforts continue, however, to further refine and improve the influence of family-based interventions on patients' physical health (Nansel et al., 2009; Wysocki et al., 2007)

Social/Community Interventions. Interventions designed to elicit peer and social support positively influence a variety of health outcomes (Fitch & Nielsen, 1998; Mendenhall & Doherty, 2005; Stewart & Tilden, 1995; Toljamo & Hentinen, 2001; Waxler-Morrison, Hislop, Mears, & Kan, 1991). With diabetes, social support has been linked to better adherence with dietary recommendations (Skinner, John, & Hampson, 2000), fewer diabetic emergencies (Wagner et al., 2001), better metabolic control (Skinner, White, Johnston, & Hixenbaugh, 1999), less depression and anxiety (Cole & Chesla, 2006; Chernoff, Ireys, DeVet & Kim; 2002; Ireys, Chernoff, Devet & Kim, 2001), lower perceptions of family disruption (Sullivan-Bolyai et al., 2004) and better overall disease management (Barrera, Toobert, Angell, Glasgow,

& MacKinnon, 2006; La Greca et al., 1995). Additionally, some researchers have noted that when interventions are carried out in groups of diabetes patients (which promote the spontaneous development of supportive relationships), significant changes in A1c—as compared to non-systemic, patient-by-patient approaches—are achieved (Brown, 1992; Mendenhall et al., under review; van Dam et al., 2005). This fact highlights the importance of social pressures and support to comply with indicated behaviors in diabetes management (Mendenhall & Doherty, 2007; Rubin & Peyrot, 1992).

Employing interventions wherein patients are able to connect with other patients, and family members of diabetes patients are able to connect with other family members of different patients, enables communities of patients and families to tap a resource often overlooked in conventional healthcare: personal, lived experience. Veteran spouses can share with spouses of patients who have recently been diagnosed how they have achieved a balance between being supportive and being a "nag." Veteran patients can share with newly diagnosed patients how they were able to adjust their dietary intake in a manner that was not entirely unsatisfying or impossible to adhere to. Patients who are struggling with staying motivated to maintain arduous self-care routines can learn from other patients who have "been there" about different strategies that have proven successful. The utility of connecting patients and families with other patients and families in these types of ways has only begun to gain momentum in the field, but investigative efforts regarding the utility of doing so are likely to push this momentum into the mainstream over the next decade (Berge, Mendenhall, & Doherty, in-press; Cole & Chesla, 2006; Horowitz et al., 2008; Mendenhall & Doherty, 2005).

ABOUT THE AUTHOR

Tai Mendenhall, PhD, LMFT, is an assistant professor in the Department of Family Medicine and Community Health at the University of Minnesota (UMN) Medical School. He earned his doctoral degree from the UMN, specializing in marriage and family therapy, and completed an intensive clinical internship in medical family therapy at Wake Forest University School of Medicine. He is also the coordinator of behavioral medicine education at the UMN's St. John's Family Medicine Residency Program, and the clinical director of the UMN Medical Reserve Corps' Mental Health Trauma-Response Team. He co-facilitates a large community-based participatory research project oriented to diabetes management in the Twin Cities' American Indian community, and is working actively with providers and community members to develop new methods of outreach and engagement with young families and local school systems. Mendenhall has published several journal articles and book chapters, and has delivered numerous national and international presentations on these and related topics. He is a Clinical Member of the AAMFT, an Approved Supervisor, and a long-time board member of the Collaborative Family Healthcare Association.

RESOURCES FOR PRACTITIONERS

ONLINE

American Diabetes Association
http://www.diabetes.org
Offers information about diabetes (symptoms, diagnoses), conventional treatment strategies, and community programs and advocacy. This site also offers links to professional and scientific research and literature.

Centers for Disease Control
http://www.cdc.gov/diabetes
Offers information for both laypersons and professionals about diabetes, including research, statistics, and educational resources and publications.

National Diabetes Information Clearinghouse
http://diabetes.niddk.nih.gov
Offers terms and information regarding diabetes; overviews of diabetes symptoms and diagnostic foci; synopses of different treatment strategies; discussions regarding disease complications; and up-to-date statistics.

WebMD Diabetes Health Center
http://diabetes.webmd.com
Offers up-to-date information regarding diabetes facts, symptoms and types; diagnoses and tests; treatments; and patient support/resources.

BOOKS

Cole, I., & Chesla, C. (2006). Interventions for the family with diabetes. *Nursing Clinics of North America, 41,* 625-639.
Highlights key findings from research on families and diabetes across the lifespan, from parents/children to couples/families living with the disease.

Fisher, L. (2006). Family relationships and diabetes care during the adult years. *Diabetes Spectrum, 19,* 71-74.
Summarizes current literature regarding family factors linked to diabetes management and outcomes, health risks to partners that people with diabetes pose, and what we currently know about couple/family interventions. Proposed ways to push the field forward in the study of interventions that include patients' partners and attention to relationship foci.

Fonseca, V. (Ed.) (2006). *Clinical diabetes: Translating research into practice.* Philadelphia, PA: Elsevier.
Provides a comprehensive review of diabetes pathophysiology, complications, lifestyle management, pharmacologic therapies, and disease management approaches.

TERMINOLOGY

Beta cells: Cells in the pancreas that make and release insulin.

Blood glucose (aka "blood sugar"): The body's principal source of fuel, which is derived primarily from food. In diabetes, the body cannot effectively move blood glucose out of the blood and into its cells.

Blood glucose meter: A hand-held device that measures blood glucose levels. Assays are conducted using small drops of blood from a finger-prick (via lancet), which are placed on a test strip and inserted into the meter.

Body Mass Index (aka "BMI"): A measurement comparing weight and height to determine a person's overall fitness level.

C-peptide: Half of the precursor molecule to insulin that is split off when the body produces insulin. If C-peptides are low, Type 1 diabetes is likely.

Endogenous insulin: Insulin that is produced naturally by the body.

Glycosylated hemoglobin (aka "Hemoglobin A1c," "HbA1c," or "A1c"): Hemoglobin is a molecule found in red blood cells. Across all blood glucose levels, small proportions of hemoglobin molecules attach themselves to glucose and become "glycosylated." In people without diabetes, about 5% of hemoglobin is glycosylated. But as blood glucose levels rise, so too does glycosylated hemoglobin. In people with poorly controlled diabetes, it can rise as high as 12 to 13 percent. A simple blood test to determine a person's glycosylated hemoglobin level provides a snapshot of average blood-glucose control during the previous 2-3 months.

Hyperglycemia: High blood glucose (> 140 mg/dL); symptoms include increased thirst, frequent urination, and weight loss. Complications of untreated hyperglycemia include retinopathy, nephropathy, cardiovascular disease, and neuropathy.

Hypoglycemia: Low blood glucose (< 70 mg/dL); symptoms include numbness in the arms and hands, moodiness/irritability, dizziness/light-headedness, confusion, and sudden loss of consciousness.

Insulin: A hormone produced by the pancreas that enables the body's cells to absorb glucose from the blood. In Type 1 diabetes, a person's body does not produce insulin. In Type 2 diabetes, a person's body does not respond to or use insulin properly.

Ketoacidosis: An acute and dangerous complication caused by a lack of insulin in the blood. Without insulin, the body's cells aggressively break down fat for energy (so they do not starve). Metabolizing fat in this way introduces high levels of ketones into the blood and urine, which can lead to difficulty breathing, coma, and/or death.

Ketones: An acid (found in the blood and urine) that is produced as a by-product of fat-burning processes in the body.

Lancet: The small sharp device used to prick the skin for blood-glucose testing.

Neuropathy: Damage to the body's nerves and nervous system. Peripheral neuropathy affects the motor nerves that direct ambulation. Sensory neuropathy impairs the nerves that control pain perception, touch, and sight. Autonomic neuropathy affects the nerves that control involuntary functions (e.g., perspiration, heart rate).

Retinopathy: Damage to the small blood vessels in the eye. In background retinopathy, blood vessels leak fluid into the retina and cause blurred vision. In proliferative retinopathy, new abnormal blood vessels grow in the retina and can cause blindness.

REFERENCES

American Diabetes Association (2009). *ADA homepage: All about diabetes.* Retrieved August 1, 2009, from www.diabetes.org/about-diabetes.jsp.

American Diabetes Association (2007). Economic costs of diabetes in the U.S. in 2007. *Diabetes Care, 31,* 596-615.

Anderson, B., Wolf, F., Burkhart, M., Cornell, R., & Bacon, G. (1989). Effects of peer-group intervention on metabolic control of adolescents with IDDM: A randomized outpatient study. *Diabetes Care, 12,* 179-183.

Auslander, W., Bubb, J., Rogge, M., & Santiago, J. (1993). Family stress and resources: Potential areas of intervention in children recently diagnosed with diabetes. *Health and Social Work, 18,* 101-114.

Barrera, M., Toobert, D., Angell, K., Glasgow, R., & MacKinnon, D. (2006). Social support and social-ecological resources as mediators of lifestyle intervention effects for type 2 diabetes. *Journal of Health Psychology, 11,* 483–495.

Beverly, E., Miller, C., & Wray, L. (2008). Spousal support and food-related behavior change in middle-aged and older adults living with Type 2 diabetes. *Health Education & Behavior, 35,* 707-720.

Beverly, E., Penrod, J., & Wray, L. (2007). Living with Type 2 diabetes: Marital perspectives of middle-aged and older couples. *Journal of Psychosocial Nursing, 45,* 25-32.

Beverly, E., & Wray, L. (2008). The role of collective efficacy in exercise adherence: A Qualitative study of spousal support and Type 2 diabetes management. Retrieved on August 4, 2009, from http://her.oxfordjournals.org/cgi/content/abstract/ cyn032v1.

Burman, B., & Margolin, G. (1992). Analysis of the association between marital relationships and health problems: An interactional perspective. *Psychological Bulletin, 112,* 39-63.

Brown, W., Collins, A., Chen, S., King, K., Molony, D., Gannon, M. et al. (2003). Identification of persons at high risk for kidney disease via targeted screening: The NKF kidney early evaluation program. *Kidney International, 63,* S50-S55.

Buse, J. (2006). Scope of the problem: The diabetes and metabolic syndrome epidemic. In V. Fonseca (Ed.), *Clinical diabetes* (pp. 1-5), Philadelphia, PA: Elsevier.

Cameron, F., Skinner, C., de Beaufort, C., Hoey, H., Swift, P., Aanstoot, H., et. al. (2008). Are family factors universally related to metabolic outcomes in adolescents with Type 1 diabetes? *Diabetic Medicine, 25,* 463-468.

Cattich, J., & Knudson-Martin, C. (2009). Spirituality and relationship: A holistic analysis of how couples cope with diabetes. *Journal of Marital and Family Therapy, 35,* 111-124.

Cavanaugh, C., Taylor, C., Keim, K., Clutter, J., & Geraghty, M. (2008). Cultural perceptions of health and diabetes among Native American men. *Journal of Health Care for the Poor and Underserved, 19,* 1029-1043.

Centers for Disease Control (2009a). Diabetes public health resource. Retrieved on August 7, 2009, from http://www.cdc.gov/diabetes.

Centers for Disease Control (2009b). Diabetes care during natural disasters, emergencies, and hazards. Retrieved on August 6, 2009, from http://www.cdc.gov/diabetes/news/docs/disasters.htm.

Chernoff, R., Ireys, H., DeVet, K., & Kim, Y. (2002). A randomized, controlled trial of a community-based support program for families of children with chronic illness: Pediatric outcomes. *Archives of Pediatrics and Adolescent Medicine, 156,* 533-539.

Cole, I., & Chesla, C. (2006). Interventions for the family with diabetes. *Nursing Clinics of North America, 41,* 625-639.

Coyne, J., Rohrbaugh, M., Shoham, V., Sonnega, J., Nicklas, J., & Canford, J. (2001). Prognostic importance of marital quality for survival of congestive heart failure. *American Journal of Cardiology, 88,* 526-529.

Delahanty, L., Grant, R., Wittenberg, E., Bosch, J., Wexler, D., Cagliero, D., & Meigs, J. (2007). Association of diabetes-related emotional distress with diabetes treatment in primary care patients with type 2 diabetes. *Diabetic Medicine, 24,* 48-54.

Delameter, A., Bubb, J., Davis, S., Smith, J., Schmidt, L., White, N. et al. (1990). Randomized prospective study of self management training with newly diagnosed diabetic children. *Diabetes Care, 13,* 492-498.

Dirks, J., Zeeuw, D., Agarwal, S., Atkins, R., Correa-Rotter, R., D'Amico, G. et al. (2005). Prevention of chronic kidney and fascular disease: Toward global health equity. *Kidney International, 68,* S1-S6.

Doherty, W., Mendenhall, T., & Berge, J. (in press). The Families and Democracy and Citizen Health Care project. *Journal of Marital and Family Therapy, 36,* 389-402.

Dougherty, G., Schiffrin, A., White, D., Soderstrom, L., & Sufrategui, M. (1999). Home-based management can achieve intensification cost-effectively in type 1 diabetes. *Pediatrics, 103,* 122-128.

Duke, D., Geffken, G., Lewin, A., Williams, L., Storch, E., & Silverstein, J. (2008). Glycemic control in youth with Type 1 diabetes: Family predictors and mediators. Journal of Pediatric *Psychology, 33,* 719-727.

Eborall, H., Davies, R., Kinmonth, A., Griffin, S., & Lawton, J. (2007). Patients' experiences of screening for type 2 diabetes: Prospective qualitative study embedded in the ADDITION randomised controlled trial. *British Medical Journal, 335,* 457-458.

Fisher, L. (2006). Family relationships and diabetes care during the adult years. *Diabetes Spectrum, 19,* 71-74.

Fisher, L., Chesla, C., Bartz, R., Gillis, C., Skaff, M., Sabogal, F. et al. (1998). The family and type 2 diabetes: A framework for intervention. *Diabetes Educator, 24,* 599-607.

Fonseca, V. (Ed.) (2006). *Clinical diabetes: Translating research into practice.* Philadelphia, PA: Elsevier.

Freedy, J., & Simpson, W. (2007). *Disaster-related physical and mental health: A role for the family physician.* Retrieved on August 6, 2009, from http://www.aafp.org/afp/20070315/841.pdf.

Geffken, G., Lehmkuhl, H., Walker, K., Storch, E., Heidgerken, A., Lewin, A., Williams, L., Silverstein, J. (2008). Family functioning processes and diabetic ketoacidosis in youths with Type 1 diabetes. *Rehabilitation Psychology, 53,* 231-237.

Gilden, J., Hendryx, M., Casia, C., & Singh, S. (1989). The effectiveness of diabetes education programs for older patients and their spouses. *Journal of the American Geriatrics Society, 37,* 1023-1030.

Goldney, R., Phillips, P., Fisher, L., Hons, B., & Wilson, D. (2004). Diabetes, depression, and quality of life: A population study. *Diabetes Care, 27,* 1066-1070.

Haslam, D., Sattar, N., & Lean, M. (2006). Obesity—time to wake up. *British Medical Journal, 333,* 640-642.

Harris, S. (1989). What works? Success stories in type 2 diabetes mellitus. *Diabetic Medicine, 15,* S20-S23.

Harris, M., Greco, P., Wysocki, T., & White, N. (2001). Family therapy with adolescents with diabetes: A litmus test for clinically meaningful change. *Families, Systems & Health, 19,* 159-168.

House, J., Landus, K., & Umberson, D. (1988). Social relationships and health. Science, 29, 540-545.

Horowitz, C., Goldfinger, J., Muller, S., Pulichino, R., Vance, T., Arniella, G. & Lancaster, K. (2008). A model for using community-based participatory research to address the diabetes epidemic in East Harlem. *Mount Sinai Journal of Medicine, 75,* 13-21.

Indian Health Service. (2006). Facts on Indian health disparaties. Indian Health Service. Retrieved August 4, 2009, from http://info.ihs.gov/Files/Disparities-Facts- Jan2006.pdf.

Ireys, H., Chernoff, R., Devet, K., & Kim, Y. (2001). Maternal outcomes of a randomized controlled trial of a community-based support program for families of children with chronic illnesses. *Archives of Pediatrics and Adolescent Medicine, 155,* 771-777.

Karmeen, K., & Richard, B. (2006). Medical nutrition therapy for Type 1 and Type 2 diabetes. In V. Fonseca (Ed.), *Clinical diabetes* (pp. 252-262), Philadelphia, PA: Elsevier.

Keller, L. (2000). *Public health principles, or How do you know a public health program when you see one?* Saint Paul, MN: Minnesota Department of Health.

Kiecolt-Glaser, J. & Newton, T. (2001). Marriage and health: His and hers. *Psychological Bulletin, 127,* 472-503.

Kolbasovsky, A. (2004). Anger and mental health in type 2 diabetes. *Diabetes and Primary Care. 6,* 44-48.

Leonard, B., Jang, Y., Savik, K., & Plumbo, M. (2005). Adolescents with Type 1 diabetes: Family functioning and metabolic control. *Journal of Family Nursing, 11,* 102-121.

Leslie, R., Williams, R., & Pozzilli, P. (2006). Type 1 diabetes and latent autoimmune diabetes in adults: One end of the rainbow. *Journal of Clinical Endocrinology & Metabolism, 91,* 1654-1659.

Lewin, A., Heidgerken, A., Geffken, G., Williams, L., Storch, E., Gelfand, K., & Silverstein, J. (2006). The relation between family factors and metabolic control: The role of diabetes adherence. *Journal of Pediatric Psychology, 31,* 174-183.

Luzi, L., Zoppini, G., Targher, G., Battezzati, A., Muggeo, M., & Bonora, E. (2007). Insulin effect on serum potassium and auto-inhibition of insulin secretion is intact in a patient with leprechaunism despite severe impairment of substrates metabolism. *Diabetes/Metabolism Research and Reviews, 24,* 205-210.

McNabb, W., Quinn, M., Murphy, D., Thorp, F., & Cook, S. (1994). Increasing children's responsibility for diabetes self-care: The in-control study. *Diabetes Educator, 20,* 121-124.

Mendenhall, T., & Berge, J. (in press). Family therapists in trauma-response teams: Bringing systems thinking into interdisciplinary fieldwork. *Journal of Family Therapy.*

Mendenhall, T., Berge, J., Harper, P., GreenCrow, B., LittleWalker, N., WhiteEagle, S., Believeau, M., & BrownBear, S. (under review). *The Family Education Diabetes Series (FEDS). Community-based participatory research in the American Indian Community.*

Mendenhall, T., & Doherty, W. (2007a). The ANGELS (A Neighbor Giving Encouragement, Love, and Support): A collaborative project for teens with diabetes. In D. Linville and K. Hertlein (Eds.), *The therapist's notebook for family healthcare* (pp. 91-101). New York: Haworth Press.

Mendenhall, T., & Doherty, W. (2007b). Partners in diabetes: A community-based participatory research project in a family practice context. *Action Research, 5,* 378-406.

Mendenhall, T. J., & Doherty, W. J. (2005). Action research methods in family therapy. In F. Piercy, D. Sprenkle (Eds.), *Research methods in family therapy* (2nd ed., pp. 100-118), New York: Guilford.

Nansel, T., Anderson, B., Laffel, L., Simons-Morton, B., Weissberg-Benchell, J., Wysocki, T., Lannotti, R., Holmbeck, G., Hood, K., Lochrie, A. (2009). A multisite trial of a clinic-integrated intervention for promoting family management of pediatric type 1 diabetes: Feasibility and design. *Pediatric Diabetes. 10,* 105-115.

Nathan, D., Buse, J., Davidson, M., Ferrannini, E., Holman, R., Sherwin, R., & Zinman, B. (2009). Medical management of hyperglycemia in Type 2 diabetes: A consensus algorithm for the initiation and adjustment of therapy. *Diabetes Care, 32,* 193-203.

National Institute of Diabetes and Digestive and Kidney Diseases (NIDDK). (2008). National Diabetes Information Clearinghouse. Retrieved July 15, 2009, from http://diabetes.niddk.nih.gov.

Padgett, D., Mumford, E., Hynes, M., & Carter, R. (1988). Meta-analysis of the effect of educational and psychosocial interventions on management of diabetes mellitus. *Journal of Clinical Epidemiology, 41,* 1007-30.

Peel, E., Parry, O., Douglas, M., & Lawton, J. (2004). Diagnosis of type 2 diabetes: A qualitative analysis of patients' emotional reactions and views about information provision. *Patient Education and Counseling, 53,* 269-275.

Pereira, M., Berg-Cross, L., Almeida, P., & Machado, J. (2008). Impact of family environment and support on adherence, metabolic control, and quality of life in adolescents with diabetes. *International Journal of Behavioral Medicine, 15,* 187-193.

Peres, D., Franco, L., & Santos, M. (2008). Feelings of women after the diagnosis of type 2 diabetes. *Revista Latino-Americana de Enfermagem, 16,* 101-108.

Rhoades, D., Welty, T., Wang, W., Yeh, F., Cevereux, R., Fabsitz, R. et al. (2006). Aging and the prevalence of cardiovascular disease risk factors in older American Indians: The strong heart study. *Journal of the American Geriatrics Society, 55,* 87-94.

Plodkowski, R., & Shane, S. (2003). *Differentiating between type 1 and type 2 diabetes.* Retrieved August 18, 2009, from http://www.medscape.com/viewarticle/449804.

Robles, T., & Kiecolt-Glaser, J. (2003). The physiology of marriage: Pathways to health. *Integrative Physiological and Behavioral Science, 79,* 409-416.

Ryden, O., Nevander, L., Johnson, P., Hansson, K., Kronvall, P., Sjoblad, S. et al. (1994). Family therapy in poorly controlled juvenile IDDM: Effects on diabetic control, self-evaluation and behavioral symptoms. *Acta Paediatrica, 83,* 285-291.

Satin, W., La Greca, M., Zigo, M., & Skyler, J. (1989). Diabetes in adolescence: Effects of multifamily group intervention and parent simulation of diabetes. Journal of Pediatric *Psychology, 14,* 259-275.

Schram, M., Baan, C., & Pouwer, F. (2009). Depression and quality of life in patients with diabetes: A systematic review from the European Depression in Diabetes (EDID) Research Consortium. *Current Diabetes Reviews, 5,* 112-119.

Spann, S., Nutting, P., Galliher, J., Peterson, K., Pavlik, V., Dickinson, L., & Volk, R. (2006). Management of Type 2 diabetes in the primary care setting: A practice-based research network study. *Annals of Family Medicine, 4,* 23-31.

Sullivan-Bolyai, S., Grey, M., Deatrick, J., Gruppuso, P., Giraitis, P., & Tamborlane, W. (2004). Helping other mothers effectively work at raising young children with Type 1 diabetes. *The Diabetes Educator, 30,* 476-484.

Thomas-Dobersen, D., Butler-Simon, N., & Fleshner, M. (1993). Evaluation of a weight management intervention program in adolescents with insulin-dependent diabetes mellitus. *Journal of the American Dietetic Association, 93,* 535-540.

Trief, P. (2005). *Diabetes and your marriage: Making things work.* Retrieved August 4, 2009, from http://www.diabetesselfmanagement.com/Articles/Emotional-Health/diabetes_and_your_marriage.

Trief, P., Grant, W., & Elbert, K. (1998). Family environment, glycemic control, and the psychosocial adaptation of adults with diabetes. *Diabetes Care, 21,* 241-245.

Trief, P., Himes, C., Orendorff, R., & Weinstock, R. (2001). The marital relationship and psychosocial adaptation and glycemic control of individuals with diabetes. *Diabetes Care, 24,* 1384-1389.

Trief, P., Ploutz-Snyder, R., Britton, K., Weinstock, R. (2004). The relationship between marital quality and adherence to the diabetes care regimen. *Annals of Behavioral Medicine, 27,* 148-154.

van Dam, H., van der Horst, F., Knoops, L., Ryckman, R., Crebolder, H., & van den Borne. (2005). Social support in diabetes: A systematic review of controlled intervention studies. *Patient Education and Counseling, 59,* 1-12.

Umberson, D., Williams, K., Powers, D., Liu, H., & Needham, B. (2006). You make me sick: Marital quality and health over the life course. *Journal of Health and Social Behavior, 47,* 1-16.

Wickrama, A., Frederick, L., Wallace, L., Peiris, L., Conger, R., & Elder, G. (2001). Family influence on physical health during the middle years: The case of onset of hypertension. *Journal of Marital and Family Therapy, 63,* 527-539.

Wieling, E., & Mittal, M. (2008). JMFT special section on mass trauma. *Journal of Marital & Family Therapy, 34,* 127-131.

Winckler, W., Weedon, M., Graham, R., McCarroll, S., Purcell, S., Almgren, P. et al. (2007). Evaluation of common variants in the six known maturity-onset diabetes of the young (MODY) genes for association with type 2 diabetes. *Diabetes, 56,* 685-693.

Wing, R., Marcus, M., Epstein, L., & Jawad, A. (1991). A "family-based" approach to the treatment of obese Type 2 diabetic patients. Journal of Consulting and Clinical Psychology, 59, 156-162.

Wysocki, T., Greco, P., Harris, M., Bubb, J., & White, N. (2001). Behavior therapy for families of adolescents with diabetes: Maintenance of treatment effects. *Diabetes Care, 24,* 441-446.

Wysocki, T., Harris, M., Buckloh, L., Mertlich, D., Lochrie, A., Mauras, N., & White (2007). Randomized trial of behavioral family systems therapy for diabetes: Maintenance of effects on diabetes outcomes in adolescents. *Diabetes Care, 30,* 555-560.

Wysocki, T., Harris, M., Greco, P., Bubb, J., Danda, C., Harvey, L. et al. (2000).

Randomized, controlled trial of behavior therapy for families of adolescents with insulin-dependent diabetes mellitus. *Journal of Pediatric Psychology, 25,* 23-33.

Wysocki, T., McDonnell, K., Harris, M., Danda, C., Greco, P., Bubb, J. et al. (1997). Social validity of support group and behavior therapy interventions for families of adolescents with insulin-dependent diabetes mellitus. *Journal of Pediatric Psychology, 22,* 635-649.

Wysocki, T., Miller, K., Greco, P., Harris, M., Harvey, L., Taylor, A. et al. (1999). Behavior therapy for families of adolescents with diabetes: Effects on directly observed family interactions. *Behavior Therapy, 30,* 507-525.

Yi, J.P., Yi, J.C., Vitaliano, P., & Weinger, K. (2008). How does anger coping style affect glycemic control in diabetes patients? *International Journal of Behavioral Medicine, 15,* 167-172.

Parkinson's Disease

Jennifer Hodgson, PhD & Kristy Larson

*Originally published as Clinical Update in Family Therapy Magazine
May-June 2009 • Revised by authors June 2011*

PREVALENCE AND FAMILIAL IMPACT OF PARKINSON'S DISEASE

No face, no predictable path, and no known cure: living with Parkinson's disease (PD) is only for the most courageous patients and families. Each year in the United States, 60,000 new cases of PD are diagnosed adding to the 1.5 million Americans who currently have this disease (National Parkinson's Foundation [NPF], 2011). Although, 10 percent of those diagnosed are under the age of 40.3, PD more typically appears after age 65 (NPF, 2011). It is a disease that has no age, race, sex, or socioeconomic boundaries and is largely idiopathic. The younger one is at the time of diagnosis, the more aggressive a path PD appears to follow. According to the NPF, in less than one percent of cases, PD is clearly familial. Exposure to chemical and/or environmental toxins has been alleged to be causative by numerous activist groups and some researchers, but nothing conclusive has been found. In fact, the Michael J Fox Foundation for Parkinson's Research (MJFF) reported that a majority of scientists whose work they reviewed point to an interaction between environmental and genetic factors as causes for PD (2011).

According to Rose-Itkoff (1987), when a chronic illness such as PD enters the family, it initially takes a central role; requiring that families organize around it and adapt accordingly. However, excessive centrality of an illness may lead families to become "stuck" in patterns appropriate for short-term use but not for long-term effectiveness. Families may also organize around a certain belief or explanation of the illness (Phipps & Lazzarini, 1987). For example, some believe that their illness has been a blessing because it brought their family closer together. Their illness may promote group identity and interaction, determining how they address, resolve, or avoid conflict. Some have seen PD as an opportunity to try new talents together, like dancing, painting, and gardening as their former hobbies become more of a challenge. Others, like Michael J. Fox and his family, have used it as kindle for hope and a reason to push aggressively for a cure.

In the wake of a chronic illness diagnosis, and in spite of their optimism, families have to negotiate new role definitions, coping methods, and loss of or added responsibilities (Papadopoulos, 1995). Continual role changes may emerge as an illness progresses and "deeply held notions about relationships and obligations are suddenly subject to reevaluation and alteration" (Rose-Itkoff, 1987, p. 313). Patients with PD slowly become increasingly dependent on others for help with the instrumental and non-instrumental activities of daily living. Families and spouses grieve the loss of role definitions, physical functioning, responsibilities, dreams, and the prospect of a long life for their ill member (Papadopoulos, 1995; Roland, Jenkins, & Johnson, 2010). Adaptations to the demands of a chronic illness may far exceed a family's expectation for what life should be like at this stage.

With progressive chronic illnesses, "families must be prepared to keep re-forming … to keep pace with the changing picture of illness" (Rolland, 1994, p. 25). Flexibility and willingness to seek help from outside resources become crucial. With chronic progressive diseases, it is possible for families to run out of physical, emotional, financial stamina, and lose their ability to adapt and change. PD is a disease marked by biomedical and psychological symptoms and riddled with social ramifications.

DIAGNOSIS AND ASSESSMENT OF PARKINSON'S DISEASE

Parkinson's disease is a chronic, progressive neurodegenerative disease that was first diagnosed in 1817 by James Parkinson (American Parkinson Disease Association [APDA], 2011). Thought of as a disease marked by a tremor, PD is sundry in its presentation and progression. There is no biological marker that confirms its diagnosis, so the rate of misdiagnosis can be relatively high (MJFF, 2011). PD is most notable for its classic set of four major motor signs: resting tremors (shaking with the limb at rest), bradykinesia (slowness of movement), rigidity or muscle stiffness, and postural instability or imbalance (NPF, 2011). Symptoms typically begin unilaterally and then migrate bilaterally over time. While there are no definite diagnostic measures for PD, the presence of two of the above characteristics (Marjama-Lyons & Koller, 2001), as well as a positive response to the drug "levodopa" (Young, 1999), typically confirm its diagnosis.

Just as there are obvious motor symptoms that characterize this disease, there are also non-motor problems, or "dopamine-non-responsive" symptoms that can emerge. Non-motor symptoms may appear even before the classic major motor signs (see table 1). Regardless of how the disease manifests, dopamine plays a central role in its development. What happens is that cells of the substantia nigra degenerate, and therefore can no longer produce adequate dopamine. When this occurs, neurons elsewhere in the brain are no longer well regulated and do not behave normally. This results in loss of controlled movements, leading to slowed movements, tremor, and rigidity (ADPA, 2011). People do not die directly from PD, but rather from compli-

TABLE 1. SYMPTOMS OF PARKINSON'S DISEASE

Motor Symptoms	Nonmotor Symptoms
Akathisia (inability to sit still)	Anxiety
Bradykinesia (slowness in movement execution)	Cognitive Impairment (mild memory difficulties to dementia)
Decreased arm swing when walking	Depression
Difficulty arising from a chair	Digestion issues and Constipation
Difficulty turning in bed	Diminished sense of smell
Dyskinesias (difficulty or abnormality in performing voluntary muscular movements)	Drooling
Dystonias (sustained muscle contractions, resulting in repetitive, involuntary, twisting, or writhing movements and unusual postures or positioning)	Increased sweating
	Low blood pressure when standing
	Male erectile dysfunction
	Painful foot cramps and other unexplained pains
Lack of facial expression	Sleep disturbance
Micrographia (small handwriting)	Speech (low voice volume and muffled speech) and swallowing problems
Postural instability	
Resting Tremor	Urinary frequency/urgency
Rigidity and freezing in place	Note: These symptoms are neither in a particular order nor universal for all patients who develop Parkinson's. Adopted from www.apdaparkinson.org.
Stooped, shuffling gait	

cations associated with it (e.g., choking, falls).

In spite of all that is known about PD, its emergence is neither universal nor easy to diagnose. In fact, several other disorders with similar features are sometimes mistaken. These include: essential tremor (tremor is the only symptom), progressive supranuclear palsy (characterized by inability to look downward), multiple system atrophy (characterized by early and prominent autonomic symptoms), vascular parkinsonism (caused by multiple small strokes), and poisoning by carbon monoxide, manganese, or certain pesticides. For these reasons, and more, confirmation of this diagnosis from a neurologist who specializes in PD is recommended.

Two rating tools that neurologists commonly use to diagnose and identify the severity of PD include the Hoehn and Yahr Staging of Parkinson's Disease (Hoehn & Yahr, 1967) and the Unified Parkinson's Disease Rating Scale (UPDRS) (Fahn et al., 1987). The UPDRS is the more commonly used tool for following the longitudinal course of PD and alerting providers to challenges. For example, worse UPDRS scores were associated with mood disorders, higher physical fatigue scores (Havlikova et al., 2005) and lower health-related quality of life (Kleiner-Fisman, Stern, & Fisman, 2010). Mental health clinicians would benefit from familiarizing themselves with these rating tools (www.parkinson.org) as the providers and patients may reference them in communication and treatment plan formation.

In addition to the hardwired biology inherent to the illness, PD patients have to learn to psychosocially adjust and reorient their lives to achieve a new sense of themselves (Anderson, 1999). According to Reijnders, Ehrt, Weber et al. (2008), 40-50 percent of PD patients experience depression, which is associated with a wide variety of poor outcomes for patients and their families. Often times, depression may be overlooked because of the overlapping symptoms that PD and depression share (Cote, 1999; Ferreri et al., 2006; Frisina et al., 2008; Sawabini & Watts, 2004). The reverse may also be true, especially for younger patients who languish for years with a missed or incomplete diagnosis of solely depression (Hodgson et al., 2004). Menza, Dobkin, Marin et al. (2009) found that successfully treating depression in PD with antidepressants (nortriptylene superior to paroxetine) lead to less relapse and better sustained outcomes.

Depression is a serious and common co-morbid disorder among PD patients and their caregivers (Ehmann et al., 1990), which is why both parties warrant careful diagnosis and tracking. Psychomotor slowing, concentration, diminished appetite, sexual desire, sleeping difficulties, and social isolation due to the patient being uncomfortable with his or her appearance, tremors, or dyskinesia are some non-motor parkinsonian symptoms that may mimic depression (Ferreri et al., 2006). Pain has also been linked with depression among PD patients with those who reported more severe pain also having reported more severe depression (Ehrt, Larson, & Asrsland, 2009). Martinez-Martin et al. (2008) found that unlike the pattern for motor symptoms, non-motor symptoms in patients with PD could also be linked to several different types of strain and depression reported by caregivers. Moore and Seeney (2007) found that gross motor impairment, blaming oneself, avoidance, symptom severity, and recreational intimacy were strong predictors of depressive mood among patients, explaining 64 percent of the variance.

Patients with the highest degree of depression were reported to be in unstable relationships, followed by single patients, and then those in a stable partnership (Ellgring et al., 1993). Despite the challenges of certain family dynamics that may contribute to the psychosocial problems, family members are an important source of support. Ehmann et al. (1990) documented that social support and the perception of supportive relationships may protect people from becoming depressed in times of stress and may have a positive effect on mental well-being. Their inclusion in the treatment process is not optional.

According to Pontone, Williams, and Anderson et al. (2009), over 40 percent of PD patients may also experience anxiety, a secondary symptom of the disease. Anxiety is often viewed as an indirect consequence of the motor symptoms. It is sometimes overlooked as a symptom and underdiagnosed as an illness because physicians see it as a normal response to the progressively more challenging physical symptoms. The most common form of anxiety in PD patients is social anxiety and panic. Ellgring et al. stated that patients are often afraid of being negatively viewed in public and lose self-confidence. Many have had the experience of being mistaken for someone who is intoxicated. Panic may ensue when one feels frozen in place or worries about suddenly being unable to move. Both depression and anxiety not only complicate and exacerbate the stress of the physical symptoms, but they also place enormous pressure on the family to help manage the illness.

Lastly, patients with PD may experience dementia and prospective memory impairments related to the advancement of their disease. The Diagnostic and Statistical Manual of Mental Disorders, Fourth Edition, Text Revision (American Psychiatric Association, 2000) defines PD dementia (PDD) as cognitive impairments that include cognitive and motor slowing, executive dysfunction, and impaired memory retrieval. Although James Parkinson did not believe that cognitive decline was a part of this disease, Charcot and researchers after him noted that cognitive declines and personality changes were part of the symptomatology (Gibb, 1986; Gibb & Poewe, 1986; Pollack & Hornebrook, 1966). According to Aarsland et al. (2005), only 30 percent of patients experience cognitive impairment and dementia.

Patients who develop dementia during their disease course are often more likely to report visual hallucinations consisting of nonthreatening animals or people (Galvin et al., 2006), have more severe motor symptoms, and be at an advanced age (Aarsland et al., 2007; Giladi, et al., 2000; Hughes et al., 2000). Unfortunately, those diagnosed with dementia have a higher mortality rate (Levy et al., 2002), health care burden (Spottke et al., 2005), and frequency of institutionalization (Parashos et al., 2002; Tison et al., 1995). In addition, those who suffer with dementia, as well as their family members, face a reduced quality of life (Aarsland et al., 1999; Martinez-Martin et al., 2005). Therefore, treatment of PD should follow a biopsychosocial course with full consideration on both the impact of the disease on the patient, as well as, his or her family.

TREATMENT OPTIONS AND BIOMEDICAL ISSUES

Case Study. Carol and Doug were a couple in their mid 60s when Doug was diagnosed with PD. He had been a relatively healthy man until about five years prior when Carol noticed that he started slowing down and showing signs of depression. Doug refused to see the doctor, and this placed a great strain on their marriage. Carol actually contemplated leaving Doug, which is how they wound up in therapy. Their therapist was educated enough to ask Doug to go for a full physical to rule out anything that could be wrong that therapy alone could not fix. He hesitated, because he grew up believing that if you go to the doctor, he will find something wrong with you and make you take a pill for it. After some coaxing by his therapist and wife, he made an appointment. After a careful review of his symptoms, his primary care provider referred him to a local neurologist for further study. It was then revealed that the underlying cause of his increasingly fatigued and depressed state was PD. At that time, he had a barely noticeable resting tremor in his right index finger and interestingly did not swing his arms when he walked, another characteristic common to the disease.

IMPULSIVE BEHAVIOR IN PARKINSON'S PATIENTS

Impulsive behaviors have been found to occur after the diagnosis of PD and/or start of Dopamine Regulatory Therapy (DRT) (also referred to as Dopaminergic Agents [DA]). General features include behaviors motivated by the prospect of pleasure or gratification, including increased sexual activity (hypersexuality), gambling, and abuse of antiparkinsonian medications (Marsh & Callahan, 2005). Ondo and Lai (2008) found 19.7 percent of 300 patients taking a DA for either PD or restless leg syndrome reported struggling with gambling, spending, hypersexuality or wanton traveling. Increased impulsivity among PD patients appeared to correlate with younger age and larger doses of DA. Interestingly, 6-12 percent had no known pre-existing gambling addictions until the onset of PD and treatment (Avanzi et al., 2006; Voon et al., 2006).

Impulse Control disorders occur in 13.6 percent of PD patients (Weintraub, Koester, Potenza, et al., 2010). Researchers reported that dopamine agonists may cause the brain to have an unconscious bias toward risky choices in susceptible individuals (Voon, Gao, Brezing, et al., 2009). This may be a side effect of the medication rather than disease progression. Therapeutic interventions may depend upon the type of impulse control disorder. Clinicians treating impulse control disorders are encouraged to begin with awareness training (Radomsky et al., 2007) and incorporate the whole family into the treatment process. This involves identification of the problematic behavior, its function (i.e., positive and negative reinforcing consequences such as bodily sensations, emotions, or social interaction), and recording its antecedents, or warning signs, such as particular sensations, rising urges, or the presence or absence of identifiable triggers. Another treatment strategy such as Motivational Interviewing (Miller & Rollnick, 2002) has been recommended as a useful approach to working with sexual compulsivity (Del Giudice & Kutinsky, 2007) and substance abuse. The current trend in treating pathological gambling is with pharmacotherapy (SSRIs, opioid receptor antagonists, mood stabilizers, and anti-addiction drugs) (Iancu et al., 2008). While CBT has long been heralded as the treatment of choice for many impulse control disorders, Grant and Potenza (2007) noted limited treatment studies for others (i.e., kleptomania, intermittent explosive disorder). They also warned that while many providers prefer a pharmacotherapy route for treatment, the long-term benefits have not been adequately tested. It is imperative that clinicians pay attention to onset and progression of impulsive behaviors and address addiction issues in collaboration with the treating physicians who are monitoring and adjusting medications.

At first, the medication the neurologist prescribed, levadopa, seemed to be a miracle cure. He had never felt better, but over time, the effects started to wear off and the dosage was increased. Both Doug and Carol were aware that this would mean an eventual maxing out of the therapeutic dosage and then consideration of other interventions would be essential (e.g., brain surgery). Over the years, Doug got involved in physical therapy to help strengthen his muscles, elongate his gait, and learn how to cross different thresholds to help prevent falls. Doug had trouble with freezing in place when he would attempt to transition from a seated position to standing, exit a tile floored room to one with carpeting, or get out of bed. He fell numerous times and once even hit his head so hard that he knocked himself unconscious. When Doug started having dyskinesias, it was the mental health provider who alerted them to talk with their neurologist that perhaps the medication needed to be adjusted. Doug only saw his neurologist once every six months and saw his mental health provider once every two weeks. To complicate matters, Doug developed a heart problem and the medication he had to take on top of his PD medication led to some important and challenging conversations between all of his providers to avoid drug interaction effects. His therapist was at the helm of many of those conversations, encouraging everyone to talk together to help Doug better regulate his symptoms and medications.

Through couples therapy and the use of narrative therapy (Freedman & Combs, 2002), the couple learned to unite with one another against the PD and co-create a new narrative of empowerment over the illness. As Doug's voice softened and became less audible, Carol had to learn to temper her frustrations and insist that all conversations take place face to face. No longer could they talk to one another when in separate rooms and the days of Doug being the person who answered the phone slowly ended. To further compli-cate things, Doug started having visual hallucinations, seeing elephants pass through their living room and tigers run gleefully through their kitchen. They could giggle some about it, but this meant another medication, an antipsy-chotic, and the recognition that dementia was possibly beginning to set in as a part of his disease.

Explaining all of this to their children and grandchildren was not easy. Their mental health provider helped by having family sessions where they all would talk about the disease and their family resources as a unit. One by one the children accepted the disease, although one refused to believe it to be incurable. He was always researching new clinical trials and complementary treatments and would e-mail them to his mother. After not seeing any results, Doug and Carol grew tired of trying new things and just wanted to have faith in their existing treatment team. Although they added a speech patholo-gist and occupational therapist to it over time, there was a point where they needed to draw the line. Their mental health provider helped them to have that conversation too with their family and providers.

The last and probably more important resource that Doug and Carol added to their treatment team was the local PD support group. The group consisted of patients evidencing all stages of the disease. At first it was a bit intimidating for them to see how the disease could progress, but later it was a main source of comfort, support, and up to date information. The group took care of one another as they celebrated successes and mourned losses. Doug died from cardiac failure 15 years after being diagnosed with PD. The demands of caregiving took their toll on Carol as well and she too spent some time on an anti-depressant and in her own individual therapy subsequent to his death. In spite of the tragic ending, the one thing that maintained their marriage was their unification against the disease and hope for a cure. If PD patients and their families have anything in common, it is hope.

The main point of the vignette is to illustrate that the treatment of PD is not something that only a mental health provider can and should manage. It is a collective responsibility of a team of trained professionals in collaboration with the patient and his or her family. In a study done by Hodgson et al. (2004) with couples where one partner was diagnosed with PD, the couples reported on their preference for a multidisciplinary treatment team with providers who were knowledgeable about one another, the treatment options, and how to communicate with each other on a regular basis.

BIOMEDICAL TREATMENT OPTIONS

The medication treatments available to PD patients are relegated to levadopa and dopamine agonists. Levodopa is the usual treatment of choice in the elderly patient, because of its lower risk for psychiatric complications compared to dopamine agonists. A dopamine agonist may be preferable in the younger patient, who is likely to be more tolerant of its side effects, and for whom delaying motor complications is an important goal, given the longer treatment horizon. Dopamine Replacement Therapies (e.g., Levodopa/Carbidopa), Dopamine Agonists (e.g., Pramipexole, Ropinerole, Bromocriptine), MAO-Inhibitors (e.g., Selegiline, Rasagilene), COMT-Inhibitors (e.g., Entacapone, Tolcapone), and Other Pharmacological Approaches commonly used in conjunction with Levodopa/Carbidopa and dopamine agonists (e.g., Amantadine, Anti-Cholinergics) may also be appropriate initial treatment for mild to advanced symptoms, provided the side effects can be tolerated (MJFF, 2011).

Of course no medication regimen is complete without careful consideration of the impact of nutrition on the metabolism of medications. For example, patients who are placed on levadopa therapy should restrict protein intake and consume protein only in the evenings (Barichella et al., 2006). Protein appears to interfere with the metabolism of the levadopa and leads to impairments in mobility in the afternoons that are much better tolerated in the evenings when patients are less active. A registered dietitian/nutritionist who specializes in PD is a critical addition to the treatment team.

Surgical interventions such as deep brain stimulation and lesioning (e.g., pallidotomy or thalamotomy) are available toward the later-stages of the disease and may extend temporary relief and help assuage the symptoms, but they are not a cure. In the United States, deep brain stimulation (DBS) is the preferred surgical intervention (APDA, 2011). A pace maker-like device is inserted inside the surface of the chest and is connected to electrodes that lead to the area of the brain that is affected. According to the NPF (2011), concerns with surgical interventions that involve the brain include bleeding that can lead to stroke (2 percent chance) and a serious risk of infection (4 percent chance). A recent randomized controlled trial with 255 patients diagnosed with PD resulted in confirmation that DBS was more effective than best medication therapy, resulting in removal of dyskinesias, improvement in motor functioning, and an increase in quality of life at 6 months (Weaver et al.,

2009). However, they also found an increase in risk for adverse side effects.

Another category of biomedical therapy that is currently only experimental is called "restorative." This includes procedures such as transplantation of fetal cells or stem cells, growth factors, or gene therapy. The goal of these procedures is to increase dopamine production and correct the basic chemical defect of PD (NPF, 2011). For a full list of biomedical interventions for patients with PD, mental health providers should visit APDA (www.apdaparkinson.org), NPF (www.parkinson.org), and the MJFF (www.michaeljfox.org).

PSYCHOSOCIAL TREATMENT OPTIONS

Patients and their families may choose to get help with any denial, depression, and anxiety prior to initiating biomedical intervention. It may be the spouse coming in first for treatment, because the patient is in denial, experiencing depression or showing signs of anxiety, or sometimes vice versa. According to the NPF (2011) website, it is not uncommon for patients when first diagnosed to deny their illness. They may go for numerous opinions, delay treatment, and hide their symptoms for years.

Mental health providers can assist clients in the transition between the mindset of a well person to one who has a progressive illness. For example, Patterson (2001) developed the Shifting Perspectives Model of Chronic Illness designed to assist clinicians in supporting patients and families in allowing illness to come to the foreground or retreat to the background, depending on people's needs and situations. She embraced the idea that some people use denial as a positive construct, allowing them to hold the burden of the disease in the background so that they may sustain the sense of well-being that allows them to live. They view their symptoms as opportunities for transformation rather than as losses or limitations. Therapists can help clients and families to create space for a grieving process to occur and the re-discovery of a new narrative that includes hope, ability, and independence redefined. The goal is to help persons with PD to be functional and have a good quality of life. Until a cure is found, a return to one's pre-diagnosis state is not realistic.

For some, the label of PD or the label that comes with no longer being able to work and needing to go on disability may be an extreme hurdle to jump. Mental health providers working with individuals, couples, and families around issues of PD may want to encourage the family to externalize and name the illness something unique, something associated with empowerment. They may also help the family to identify sources of bibliotherapy and support groups where they can gain knowledge so that when and/or if a certain symptom or loss of ability occurs, there is a pre-existing plan on how everyone will handle it. The best resources for locating the closest support groups are the patient's neurologist and the NPF and APDA websites.

In the previous case example, one thing that was not mentioned was how Carol and Doug dealt with Doug's loss of independence. It took two minor car accidents and a scare with freezing at a traffic light to coax him into surrendering his license. While they will both admit this was not the best way to transition Doug into no longer driving, it was their way. For some families, this struggle requires the primary care provider or specialist to talk to the patient personally about it. If that is unsuccessful, the provider may need to make a call to the Department of Motor Vehicles to report the patient as being no longer safe behind the wheel. This loss of independence also occurs around decisions regarding retirement from work, changing of leisure activities, cooking, managing the finances, being home alone, taking medications, cutting up of food, and even dressing to some extent. Mental health providers should be part of helping the patient and family to have a plan in place for each of these milestones so there is a sense of control and input on the part of the patient along the way.

Communication with the patient's provider is best done in collaboration with the patient and family. Many individuals, particularly older adults and mainly men, tend to underreport the severity of symptoms and complications. Working with clients on how to discuss the progression of the disease and address any denial about the illness is an important place to start in therapy. Practicing conversations that the client could have with his provider about the disease is also beneficial, as many fear that being open will lead to more medications, worse side effects, and unfortunate verification of the disease's progression. Approaches such as Cognitive Behavioral Therapy (CBT) (Beck, 1979) allow for the client-therapist team to transform alarming/negative thoughts into more reassuring/positive ones. It is used to help clients change the way they think to feel/act better, even if the situation does not change.

INDIVIDUAL THERAPY

As it is largely under-diagnosed and detected, research is constantly underway to improve the screening of cognitive and affective dysfunctions among patients with PD. In a 2005 review of the literature on PD and depression, the authors concluded that "Given the effectiveness of techniques such as CBT in other chronically medically ill populations, the lack of research specific to the psychotherapeutic treatment of depression in PD patients is surprising" (Veazey et al., p. 321). However, that same year a pilot study was published using CBT as an intervention specific with PD (Feeney et al., 2005). They found that CBT was effective in treating anxiety and depression with gains maintained at one month follow up.

Assessing for dementia and mood disorders is also a bit challenging, as they tend to be more common in later life as well as in PD. Therefore, instruments sensitive to patients with PD are needed. Recently, one group has developed an instrument to screen for dementia specifically in patients with PD. The Parkinson neuropsychometric dementia assessment (PANDA; Kalbe et al., 2008) has five cognitive tasks and offers a short depression questionnaire. In initial testing PANDA showed high sensitivity and specificity for cognitive and affective dysfunctions.

While individual therapy is one method of treatment, the mental health provider should also be skilled in assessing for medication side effects and treating relational issues common to a diagnosis of PD. Mental health providers need to own a Physicians Desk Reference (2009) when working with PD patients noting any problematic or dangerous medication side effects and any worsening of symptoms that may warrant obtaining a release to communicate with the patient's medical provider.

COUPLE THERAPY

Parkinson's disease, like many other chronic conditions, changes the dynamics of the couple relationship. Greene and Griffin (1998) uncovered a relationship between marital quality and the exacerbation of PD symptoms. They found that heightened levels of marital distress lead to decreased control of PD patients over orofacial movements. This tied together the possibility that PD does not rest solely within the patient: it is a disease with a bidirectional influence between the patient and his or her support system.

According to Rolland (1994), the presence of a serious illness in a couple's relationship may upset the roles and preexisting boundaries that once served as the structure to their relationship. Hodgson et al. (2004) found that it was not the patients who reported feeling less supported in the marital relationship, it was the caregiving partners. This response may be due to the increased amount of caregiving required as the disease progresses. A few theories may explain this phenomenon. First, according to Lieberman and Williams (1993), there is a tendency for friends and family to withdraw as the disease takes up more and more of the caregiver's time. This lack of interaction and help may leave caregivers feeling alone in the process. Second, the progression of a long term health problem, such as PD, may lead some patients to stop taking active steps to change their overall situation (Folkman & Lazarus, 1988; Lazarus, 1993). With the patients not being perceived by the caregivers as doing their part, the caregivers may feel unsupported by them as well. Lastly, Sanders (1999) reported that the more patients tried to problem-solve for themselves the lower the caregiver adjustment. She speculated that patients may challenge caregivers' strategies for managing tasks. Ultimately, this effort may leave the caregivers feeling as if their partners are not appreciating or respecting their efforts. Spouse-caregivers in the Hodgson et al. (2004) study reported inevitably experiencing some sort of health related impact (e.g., headaches, depression, and anxiety) that they attributed to PD. Not only can the challenges of PD threaten a couple's emotional intimacy and individual health, but may also interfere with their sexual relationship.

For individuals with PD, sexual function and performance can be difficult and painful (Mecco, Rubino, Caravona, & Valente, 2008). Muscle rigidity and tremors contribute to difficulties that can cause increasing physical discomfort during sexual intercourse. As the disease progresses, the PD partner will become more dependent on the other partner and feelings of resentment, preoccupation with daily medical care and financial strains can take over the minds of both partners. Sexual relations are no longer seen as the fun and exciting endeavors they once were. Health professionals need to address sexual issues and make them a part of their assessment and treatment planning process.

In a study done by Koller et al. (1990), 80 percent of males and 79 percent of females stated that their current sexual frequency was less than before they had PD. Forty four percent of males and seventy one percent of females experienced a decrease in sexual interest. Fifty four percent of males were unable to achieve an erection and thirty eight percent of women were unable to achieve orgasm. Similar findings were reported by Lipe, Longstreth, Bird, and Linde (1990) when comparing sexual functioning in Arthritis and PD in married men. Increased age, severity of illness, and depression were associated with reduced sexual functioning.

Sex therapy techniques (e.g., Sensate Focus; Kaplan, 1974) can help enhance the intimacy of the relationship and encourage the couple to find new ways of being intimate with and without using sexual touch. Therapists need to work slowly with the couple on what feels good and how to modify sexual intimacy to accommodate a decrease in flexibility/range of motion, libido (possibly due to medications) and fear on the part of the partner concerned that he or she will hurt the patient. There are also reports that some patients with PD become hypersexual and this is also a concern to the partner who does not share that same level of enthusiasm or interest in the frequency of sex (see sidebar on Impulse Control). There is a need for future research, particularly in how sexuality is addressed in treatment plans for PD patients and couples, if at all.

As the disease progresses, the mental health provider will play a critical role in working with the couple on patient issues of high anxiety, intrusive thoughts, body self-absorption, hypersensitivity, social withdrawal, inability to tolerate frustration, anger, and depression (NPF, 2011). Patients with PD will often overdo it on a good day, soaking in as much activity and sense of accomplishment as possible, which can then be followed by several days or weeks of bad days where their disease is a constant intrusion. This creates an intense focus on the patient and his or her body that may lead to all of the issues noted earlier; each impacting the caregiver as well and the social system surrounding them. Helping patients to have a plan for what they can handle on a "good" day and learning not to overdo it are important for the mental health provider to address. Helping the partner to have patience as the patient deals with the aforementioned issues is another important area of work.

FAMILY THERAPY

It is not only the spouse or partner that wonders about the uncertainties of the disease, the children are affected too. Schrag et al. (2004) indicated that more than half (53.9 percent) of children, aged 12 to 48, with a parent who has PD, felt that they did not have enough information about the disease. Half of the participants felt that more information would decrease their feelings of uncertainty. Only a small percentage (30 percent) reported that they had enough support from local services and 44 percent had absolutely no help

TERMINOLOGY

Dopamine: Neurotransmitter that controls movement and balance and is essential to the proper functioning of the central nervous system (CNS)

Dopamine Agonists (DAs): combine with dopamine receptors to mimic dopamine actions. Such medications stimulate dopamine receptors and produce dopamine-like effects

Hoehn and Yahr Rating Scale: Scale used for the broad classification of patients with PD; lacks detail and ability to follow patients with motor fluctuations

Idiopathic: of unknown origin

Levodopa: Levodopa is a drug used to treat PD. It is also called L-dopa and, in the United States, is sold as Sinemet® in combination with Carbidopa or as a generic drug. Levodopa crosses the blood-brain barrier and is converted by the body to dopamine. A loss of dopamine-producing nerve cells in the part of the brain that controls movements leads to the symptoms of Parkinson's Disease

Lewy bodies: pink-staining spheres found in nerve cells, considered to be a pathological marker for Parkinson disease

Resting tremor: characteristic tremor that occurs as one of the primary symptoms of Parkinson's Disease, typically present in arm, leg, lips, chin or tongue. Occurs or exacerbates when at rest; decreases with active motions

Substantia nigra: (literally meaning black substance) is a small region in the brain stem, just above the spinal cord. It is one of the centers that help control movements. Cells within the substantia nigra (SN) produce and release the neurotransmitter dopamine

Unified Parkinson Disease Rating Scale (UPDRS): The UPDRS is the most commonly used tool to rate the symptoms of PD. This scale is intended to be used to follow the course of PD in patients over a period of time. It is made up of four parts: (1) mentation (the process of thinking), behavior, and mood; (2) activities of daily living; (3) motor symptoms, and (4) complications of therapy. A lower score shows that the person is having fewer problems related to their PD

Wearing-off phenomena: waning of the effects of a dose of levodopa prior to the scheduled time for the next dose, resulting in decreased motor performance

beyond the home. Younger children reported a higher burden of needing to provide daily help and greater impact on their social lives versus older children who expressed concerns about its greater impairment on family functioning. Depression was detected among 20 percent of the participants, ranging from mild to moderate. The children who reported being better adjusted were those who were able to balance autonomy with being close as a family and spending time together. They also had an extended support network and the availability of good service providers to help manage the situation.

It is important to keep the family's lines of communication open about the disease, especially with children. Being honest about current and future affects of the disease is important for the child's understanding and coping. Increasing the amount of resources that children can look to for answers and support will help them to feel more secure. Incorporation of a child life specialist to help younger children understand the disease is a wonderful resource, particularly for clinicians who are not accustomed to working with young children in therapy. Mental health providers can help by talking to young and adult children with their parents together and individually, providing age appropriate resources such as books, reputable Internet sites, and referrals to support groups that welcome family member involvement of all ages.

In a recent study on adult children's experience of a parent with PD, Blanchard et al. (2009) reported that some participants found it hard to watch a parent be so vulnerable to his or her disease. Others noted the stress and strain that it placed upon the caregiving spouse and sibling relationships. Challenges with the lack of geographic proximity at times caused rifts between family members. However, there were reports of an essential positivism that held the family together in fighting for a better quality of life and a cure. Some participants even noted the respect and appreciation they had for their own spouses who stepped up to help while the adult child had to work. Mental health providers should not reduce therapy to just the patient and partner. As evidenced by research, the children need to be included and informed. Because of their unique skill in working with systems, family therapists are the recommended providers for opening up lines of communication between patients, patients' family members, and members of the patient's treatment team. More specifically, family therapists who are trained in medical family therapy would be most suited for this role.

ABOUT THE AUTHORS

Jennifer Hodgson, PhD, LMFT, is an associate professor in the Departments of Child Development and Family Relations and Family Medicine at East Carolina University. She received her doctoral degree from Iowa State University, specializing in marriage and family therapy, and completed a fellowship in medical family therapy at the University of Rochester, New York. She co-authored the nation's first doctoral program in medical family therapy. She is a Clinical Member of the AAMFT, an AAMFT Approved Supervisor, COAMFTE Commissioner, and a long time member of the Collaborative Family Healthcare Association. She co-facilitates a local Parkinson's support group and has published in several journals and has given several presentations locally and nationally on the topic. She serves as a reviewer for several journals and as a co-editor for the "Collaboration in Action" department in the journal of Families, Systems, and Health.

Kristy Larson, BS, is a master's student in the marriage and family therapy program at East Carolina University with clinical and research interests in families coping with chronic illness and family violence intervention/prevention.

RESOURCES FOR PRACTITIONERS

American Parkinson Disease Association, Inc.
www.apdaparkinson.org
Informative site for clients, family members, researchers, and providers interested in the latest developments in PD.

National Parkinson Foundation
www.parkinson.org
Offers information and resources for those impacted by PD and for those wanting to learn more about it.

The Michael J. Fox Foundation for Parkinson's Research
www.michaeljfox.org
Geared toward developments in research, the site also offers information for patients, family members, and providers.

Parkinson's Disease Foundation
www.pdf.org
The mission of the Parkinson's Disease Foundation is not only to pursue the cure for Parkinson's but also to provide assistance to the people who live with the disease.

Sharma, N., & Richman, E. (2008). *Parkinson's disease and the family: A new guide.* Cambridge, MA: Harvard University Press. Provides a thorough review of the etiology, diagnosis, and current treatment of Parkinson's, with special consideration given to the effect on family dynamics and routines—including the often neglected topics of long-term care and sexual function. The authors also review the pros and cons of various alternative therapies, including nutritional supplements, massage therapy, and traditional Chinese medicine.

Graboys, T., & Zheutlin, P. (2008). *Life in the balance: A physician's memoir of life, love, and loss with Parkinson's disease and dementia.* New York: Union Square Press. Written from the perspective of a physician, the lead author shares a personal memoir of his experience living with PD.

Jenkins, K. (2008). *Who is pee dee? Explaining Parkinson's disease to a child.* New York: UCB Publishing. Written for use with a young child, this book gives parents and grandparents a tool to talk about Parkinson's.

Ali, R., & Ali, M. (2005). *I'll hold your hand so you won't fall: A child's guide to Parkinson's disease.* Jupiter, FL: Merit Publishing International. Written for children in grades 2-4, this book demystifies some of the more obvious symptoms, like shaking, trouble walking, and slurred speech, and also explains more puzzling or unseen symptoms such as sleep disorders, depression, and masked face, in which the patient cannot display expressions.

REFERENCES

Aarsland, D., Kvaløy, J. T., Andersen, K., Larsen, J. P., Tang, M. X., Lolk, A., et al. (2007). The effect of age of onset of PD on risk of dementia. *Journal of Neurology, 254,* 38-45.

Aarsland, D., Larsen, J. P., Karlsen, K., Lim, N. G., & Tandberg, E. (1999). Mental symptoms in Parkinson's disease are important contributors to caregiver distress. *International Journal of Geriatric Psychiatry, 14,* 866-874.

Aarsland, D., Zaccai, J., & Brayne, C. (2005). A systematic review of prevalence studies of dementia in Parkinson's disease. *Movement Disorders, 20,* 1255-1263.

American Parkinson Disease Association, Inc. (2009). Retrieved January 9, 2009, from http://www.apdaparkinson.org.

American Psychiatric Association. (2000). *Diagnostic and statistical manual of mental disorders DSM-IV-TR fourth edition.* Washington, DC: American Psychiatric Association.

Avanzi, M., Baratti, M., Cabrini, S., Uber, E., Brighetti, G., & Bonfà, F. (2006). Prevalence of pathological gambling in patients with Parkinson's disease. *Movement Disorders, 21,* 2068-2072.

Barichella, M., Marczewska, A., De Notaris, R., Vairo, A., Baldo, C., Mauri, A., et al. (2006). Special low-protein foods ameliorate postprandial in patients with advanced Parkinson's disease. *Movement Disorders, 21,* 1682-1687.

Beck, A. (1979). *Cognitive therapy and the emotional disorders.* New York: Penguin Group, Inc.

Blanchard, A., Hodgson, J., Lamson, A., Dosser, D., & McClenahan, E. (2009). Lived experiences of adult children who have a parent diagnosed with Parkinson's. *Qualitative Report* (In Press).

Cote, L. (1999). Depression: Impact and management by the patient and family. *Neurology, 52*(7), S7-S9.

Del Giudice, M., & Kutinsky, J. (2007). Applying motivational interviewing to the treatment of sexual compulsivity and addiction. *Sexual Addiction & Compulsivity, 14,* 303-319.

Ehmann, T. S., Beninger, R. J., Gawel, M. J., & Riopelle, R. J. (1990). Coping, social support, and depressive symptoms in Parkinson's disease. *Journal of Geriatric Psychiatry and Neurology, 3,* 85-90.

Ehrt, U., Larson, J. P., & Asrsland, D. (2009). Pain and its relationship to depression and Parkinson's disease. *American Journal of Geriatric Psychiatry, 17,* 269-275.

Ellgring, H., Seiler, S., Perleth, B., Frings, W., Gasser, T., & Gertel, W. (1993). Psychosocial aspects of Parkinson's disease. *Neurology, 43,* 41-44.

Fahn, S., Elton, R. L., & Members, U. P. (1987). Unified parkinson's disease rating scale. In S. Fahn, C. D. Marsden, M. Goldstein & D. B. Calne (Eds.), *Recent developments in Parkinson's disease vol. 2* (pp. 153-163). Florham Park, NJ: Macmillan Healthcare Information.

Feeney, F., Egan, S., & Gasson, N. (2005). Treatment of depression and anxiety in Parkinson's Disease: A pilot study using group cognitive behavioural therapy. *Clinical Psychologist, 9,* 31-38.

Ferreri, F., Agbokou, C., & Gauthier, S. (2006). Recognition and management of neuropsychiatric complications in Parkinson's disease. *Canadian Medical Association Journal, 175,* 1545-1552.

Folkman, S., & Lazarus, R.S. (1988). The relationship between coping and emotion: Implications for theory and research. *Social Science and Medicine, 26,* 309-317.

Freedman, J., & Combs, G. (2002). *Narrative therapy with couples and a whole lot more!: A collection of papers, essays and exercises.* Adelaide: Dulwich Centre Publications.

Frisina, P. G., Borod, J. C., Foldi, N. S., & Tenenbaum, H. R. (2008). Depression in Parkinson's disease: Health risks, etiology, and treatment options. *Neuropsychiatric Disease and Treatment, 4,* 81-91.

Galvin, J. E., Pollack, J., & Morris, J. C. (2006). Clinical phenotype of Parkinson disease dementia. *Neurology, 67,* 1605-1611.

Gibb, W. R. (1986). Idiopathic Parkinson's disease and the Lewy body disorders. *Neuropathology and Applied Neurobiology, 12*(3), 223-234.

Gibb, W. R., & Poewe, W. (1986). The centenary of Friederich H. Lewy 1885-1950. Neuropathology and Applied Neurobiology, 12(3), 217-222.

Giladi, N., Treves, T. A., Paleacu, D., Shabtai, H., Orlov, Y., Kandinov, B., et al. (2000). Risk factors for dementia, depression and psychosis in long-standing Parkinson's disease. *Journal of Neural Transmission, 107,* 59-71.

Grant, J. E., Potenza, M. N., Nathan, P. E., & Gorman, J. M. (2007). Treatments for pathological gambling and other impulse control disorders. In *A guide to treatments that work (3rd ed.).* (pp. 561-577). New York: Oxford University Press.

Greene, S. M., & Griffin, W. A. (1998). Symptom study in context: Effects of marital quality on signs of Parkinson's disease during patient-spouse interaction. *Psychiatry: Interpersonal and Biological Processes, 61,* 35-45.

Havlikova, E., Rosenbergerb, J., Nagyovab, I., et al. (2008). Clinical and psychosocial factors associated with fatigue in patients with Parkinson's disease. *Parkinsonism and Related Disorders, 14,* 187–192.

Hodgson, J., Garcia, R., & Tyndall, L. (2004). Parkinson's disease and the couple relationship: A qualitative analysis. *Families, Systems, & Health, 22,* 101-118.

Hoehn, M. M., & Yahr, M. D. (1967). Parkinsonism: onset, progression and mortality. *Neurology, 17,* 427-442.

Hughes, T. A., Ross, H. F., Musa, S., Bhattacherjee, S., Nathan, R. N., Mindham, R. H. S., et al. (2000). A 10-year study of the incidence of and factors predicting dementia in Parkinson's disease. *Neurology, 54,* 1596-1603.

Iancu, I., Lowengrub, K., Dembinsky, Y., Kotler, M., & Dannon, P. (2008). Pathological gambling: An update on neuropathophysiology and pharmacotherapy. *CNS Drugs, 22,* 123-138.

Kalbe, E., Pasquale, C., Kohn, N., Rudiger, H., Riedel, O., Wittchen, H.-U., et al. (2008). Screening for cognitive deficits in Parkinson's disease with the Parkinson Neuropsychometric Dementia Assessment (PANDA) instrument. *Parkinsonism & Related Disorders, 14,* 93-101.

Kaplan, H. S. (1974). *The new sex therapy: Active treatment of sexual dysfunctions.* Oxford England: Brunner/Mazel.

Kleiner-Fisman, G., Stern, M. B., & Fisman, D. N. (2010). Health-related quality of life in Parkinson disease: Correlation between Health Utilities Index III and Unified Parkinson's Disease Rating Scale (UPDRS) in U.S. male veterans. *Health and Quality of Life Outcomes, 8,* 91-100.

Koller, W. C., Vetere-Overfield, B., Williamson, A., & Busenbark, K. (1990). Sexual dysfunction in Parkinson's disease. Clinical Neuropharmacology, 13, 461-463.

Lazarus, R. S. (1993). Coping theory and research: Past, present, and future. *Psychosomatic Medicine, 55,* 234-247.

Levy, G., Tang, M. X., Louis, E. D., Cote, L. J., Alfaro, B., Mejia, H., et al. (2002).

The association of incident dementia with mortality in PD. *Neurology, 59,* 1708-1713.

Lieberman, A. N., & Williams, F. L. (1993). *Parkinson's disease: The complete guide for patients and caregivers.* New York: Simon & Schuster.

Lipe, H., Longstreth, W. T., Bird, T. D., & Linde, M. (1990). Sexual function in married men with Parkinson's disease compared to married men with arthritis. *Neurology, 40,* 1347-1349.

Marsh, L., & Callahan, P. (2005). Gambling, sex, and Parkinson's disease? *Parkinson's Disease Foundation.* Retrieved November 17, 2008, from http://www.pdf.org/en/spring05_Gambling_Sex.

Marjama-Lyons, J. M., & Koller, W. C. (2001). Parkinson's disease. *Geriatrics, 56,* 24-35.

Martinez-Martin, P., Arroyo, S., Rojo-Abuin, J., Rodriguez-Blazquez, C., Frades, B., de Pedro Cuesta, J., et al. (2008). Burden, perceived health status, and mood among caregivers of Parkinson's disease patients. *Movement Disorders, 23,* 1673-1680.

Martínez-Martín, P., Benito-León, J., Alonso, F., Catalán, M. J., Pondal, M., Zamarbide, I., et al. (2005). Quality of life of caregivers in Parkinson's disease. *Quality of Life Research, 14,* 463-472.

Mecca, G., Rubina, A., Caravona, N., & Valente, M. (2008). Sexual dysfunction in Parkinson's disease. *Parkinsonism & Movement Related Disorders, 14,* 451-456.

Menza, M., Dobkin, R. D., Marin, H., Mark, M. H., Gara, M., Buyske, S., Bienfate, K., & Dicke, A. (2009). A controlled trial of antidepressants in patients with Parkinson's disease and depression. *Neurology, 72,* 886-892.

Micheal J. Fox Foundation for Parkinson's Research. (2011). Retrieved May 31, 2011, from http://www.michaeljfox.org.

Miller, W. R., & Rollnick, S. (2002). *Motivational Interviewing: Preparing people for change.* New York: The Guilford Press.

Moore, K. A., & Seeney, F. (2007). Biopsychosocial predictors of depressive mood in people with Parkinson's disease. *Behavioral Medicine, 33,* 29-37.

National Parkinson Foundation. (2011). Retrieved May 31, 2011, from http://www.parkinson.org.

Ondo, W. G., & Lai, D. (2008). Predictors of impulsivity and reward seeking behavior with dopamine agonists. P*arkinsonism & Related Disorders, 14,* 28-32.

Papadopoulos, L. (1995). The impact of illness on the family and the family's impact on illness. *Counseling Psychology Quarterly, 8,* 27-35.

Parashos, S. A., Maraganore, D. M., O'Brien, P. C., & Rocca, W. A. (2002). Medical services utilization and prognosis in Parkinson disease: A population-based study. *Mayo Clinic Proceedings, 77,* 918-925.

Patterson, B. L. (2001). The shifting perspectives model of chronic illness. *Journal of Nursing Scholarship, 33,* 21-26.

Phipps, E., & Lazzarini, A. (1987). Fighting dragons: The construction of explanatory systems in genetic disease. *Family Systems Medicine, 5,* 304-311.

Physicians' Desk Reference. (2008). Physicians' Desk Reference 2009 (63rd edition). New York: Thomson Reuters.

Pollock, M., & Hornabrook, R. W. (1966). The Prevalence, Natural history and dementia of Parkinson's disease *Brain, 89,* 429-448.

Pontone, G. M., Williams, J. R., Anderson, K. E., Chase, G., Goldstein, S. A., Grill, S., Hirsh, E. S., Lehmann, S., Little, J. T., Margolis, R. L., Rabins, P. V., Weiss, H. D., & Marsh, L. (2009). Prevalence of anxiety disorders an anxiety subtypes in patients with Parkinson's disease. *Movement Disorders, 24,* 1333-1338.

Radomsky, A. S., Bohne, A., O'Connor, K. P., Antony, M. M., & Summerfeldt, L. J. (2007). Treating comorbid presentations: Obsessive-compulsive disorder and disorders of impulse control. In *Psychological treatment of obsessive-compulsive disorder: Fundamentals and beyond.* (pp. 295-309). Washington, DC: American Psychological Association.

Reijnders, M. A, Ehrt U., Weber W. E., Aarsland D.,& Leentjens A. F. (2008). A systematic review of prevalence studies of depression in Parkinson's disease. *Movement Disorders, 23,* 183-189.

Rolland, J. (1994). Families, illness, and disability: An integrative treatment model. New York: Basic Books.

Rolland, K. P., Jenkins, M. E., & Johnson, A. M. (2010). An exploration of the burden experienced by spousal caregivers of individuals with Parkinson's Disease. *Movement Disorders, 25,* 189-193.

Rose-Itkoff, C. (1987). Lupus: An interactional approach. *Family Systems Medicine, 5,* 313-321.

Sanders, N. E. (1999). An assessment of coping and adjustment in individuals with Parkinson's disease. (Doctoral dissertation, Oklahoma State University, 1998). *Dissertation Abstracts International, 60*(2-B), 0842.

Sawabini, K. A., & Watts, R. L. (2004). Treatment of depression in Parkinson's disease. *Parkinsonism & Related Disorders, 10,* S37.

Schrag, A., Morley, D., Quinn, N., & Jahanshahi, M. (2004). Impact of Parkinson's disease on patients' adolescent and adult children. *Parkinsonism & Related Disorders, 10,* 391-397.

Spottke, A. E., Reuter, M., Machat, O., Bornschein, B., von Campenhausen, S., Berger, K., et al. (2005). Cost of illness and its predictors for Parkinson's disease in Germany. *PharmacoEconomics, 23,* 817-836.

Tison, F., Dartigues, J. F., Auriacombe, S., Letenneur, L., Boller, F., & Alperovitch, A. (1995). Dementia in Parkinson's disease: a population-based study in ambulatory and institutionalized individuals. *Neurology, 45,* 705-708.

Veazey, C., Ozlem Erden Aki, S., Cook, K., Lai, E. C., & Kunik, M. E. (2005). Prevalence and Treatment of Depression in Parkinson's Disease. Journal of Neuropsychiatry and Clinical Neuroscience, 17, 310-323.

Voon, V., Hassan, K., Zurowski, M., de Souza, M., Thomsen, T., Fox, S., et al. (2006). Prevalence of repetitive and reward-seeking behaviors in Parkinson disease. *Neurology, 67,* 1118-1119.

Voon, V., Gao, J., Brezing, C., Symmonds, M., Ekanayake, V., Fernandez, H., Dolan, R., & Hallett, M. (2009). Dopamine agonists and risk: impulse control disorders in Parkinson's disease. *Brain, 134,* 1438-1446.

Weaver, F. M., Follett, K., Stern, M., Hur, K., Harris, C., Marks, W. J., Jr., et al. (2009). Bilateral deep brain stimulation vs. best medical therapy for patients with advanced Parkinson disease: A randomized controlled trial. *JAMA, 301,* 63-73.

Weintraub, D., Koester, J., Potenza, M., Siderowf, A. D., Stacy, M., Voon, V., Wehtteckey, J.,Wunderlich, G. R., & Lang, A. E. (2010). Impulse control disorders in Parkinson's disease. *Archives of Neurology, 67,* 589-595.

Young, R. (1999). Update on Parkinson's disease. *American Family Physician, 59,* 2155-2181.

Pregnancy and Delivery

Angela Lamson, PhD & Kenneth W. Phelps, PhD

Originally published as Clinical Update in Family Therapy Magazine
July-August 2010

LABOR AND DELIVERY

*Y*ou are pregnant. No matter if the pregnancy was planned or unexpected, or if the woman was told by a medical provider or by a pregnancy test, most women who have had this experience can remember precisely when they found out they were pregnant, especially the first time. From there, the story becomes as unique as the woman. This update will focus on the divergent experiences of pregnancy and delivery, including the many women, men, and families who have shared hundreds of stories with us pertaining to pregnancy loss, infertility, miscarriage, and stillbirth. We will highlight some possible areas for clinical attention during pregnancy, delivery, and/or shortly thereafter. Minimal discussion of adoption and postpartum depression are included as these important areas have been addressed in other *Clinical Updates*. Family therapists have a unique skill set to offer families navigating this stage of the life cycle. Approaching families and multidisciplinary colleagues from a systemic lens allows maneuverability to challenge maladaptive patterns, identify strengths, and create a safe space for transformation to occur.

On average, over four million births occur in one year across the United States (Centers for Disease Control [CDC], 2010). While the majority of pregnancies and births result in little or no complications, all new parents will experience changes in their couple or family dynamics. Certainly a number of psychosocial issues (across a continuum of severity) may come to the attention of a family therapist anytime during a pregnancy or delivery. For instance, some mothers are required to be hospitalized on bed rest to improve their chances of having a healthy mother-and-baby outcome at delivery. The extended hospital stay and inability to see individuals who may otherwise provide support can create psychosocial strain for mothers and their families. Additionally, a multitude of families are presented with the need for a non-emergency based cesarean section (c-section), which may create anxiety for expecting parents.

Other common areas that have been addressed by family therapists related to pregnancy and childbearing include: coping with infertility, questions related to parenting styles, paternity, conflicts in parental or intergenerational communication, child safety, sudden infant death syndrome, experiences with changes in birth plans, how to manage when a parent is absent (from lack of commitment to the child or from job-related expectations, such as military deployment), anxiety related to life change, questions related to sibling adjustment, and sensitivity for lesbian, gay, bisexual, or transgender (LGBT) couple experiences, interracial, inter-religion partnerships, or between partners and extended family or community members.

DIAGNOSIS AND ASSESSMENT

For families preparing for a new addition, psychosocial stress often begins long before their arrival to the labor and delivery unit. In one study, 78 percent of mothers reported low to moderate antenatal psychosocial stress, while 6 percent reported high antenatal psychosocial stress (Woods, Melville, Guo, Fan, & Gavin, 2010). A number of constructs were significantly associated with high psychosocial stress within this investigation, including depression, panic disorder, domestic violence, drug use, and having more than two medical comorbidities. Of note, these researchers found, consistent with prior research, that stress scores tend to decrease when reassessed throughout the pregnancy. While psychosocial stress may decline over the length of the pregnancy for many women, it continues to be linked to adverse pregnancy outcomes such as preterm birth and low birth weight (Hobel, Goldstein, & Barrett, 2008). Stress has been documented as chronic and cumulative, in some cases, through life experiences of "low socioeconomic status, experiences of racism, exposure to violence, negative health behaviors, loss/trauma, and lack of social support" (Hobel et al., 2008, p. 337). Whether acute or chronic, psychosocial stress may also influence quality of life during pregnancy. For instance, significant associations have been found between depression and/or anxiety and increased nausea and vomiting, prolonged sick leave during pregnancy, and increased number of visits to the obstetrician (Andersson, 2004). Andersson also reported that increased visits to the obstetrician were most closely linked to fear of childbirth. Goebert, Onoye, and Matsu (2007) sought to understand the psychosocial adaptation of healthy pregnant women in a study of 84 pregnant women in Hawaii who were assessed for perinatal mental health issues, ethnic differences, and comorbidity. Interestingly, 61 percent of the women who participated in this study screened positive for at least one mental health issue.

The presence of psychosocial stress calls for adequate screening and treatment of individual and family difficulties. In fact, the American College of Obstetricians and Gynecologists (ACOG, 2006) advocated for psychosocial screening in a recently released committee opinion. Marriage and family therapists should be well-versed in established assessments for psychosocial stress, which may assist in guiding treatment plans and stimulating effective collaboration among colleagues. Sieber, Germann, Barbir, and Ehlert (2006) highlighted the importance of assessing psychosocial issues early in pregnancy to reduce the chances of negative outcomes during delivery or postpartum. Hobel et al. outlined a number of valuable instruments with established validity, reliability, and scientific consensus for assessing psychosocial stress including: Life Events Inventory (Conchrane & Robertson, 1973), State-Trait Anxiety Inventory (Spielberger, Gorusch, & Lushene, 1970), Center for Epidemiologic Studies Depression Scale (Radloff, 1977), and Perceived Stress Scale (Cohen, Kamarck, & Mermelstein, 1983). Family therapists may find these brief measures particularly useful since they can easily be administered within the inpatient or outpatient context.

While assessing psychological well-being during pregnancy is imperative, clinicians should also assess depression in mothers (and other family members) in the postnatal period. Researchers (Hobel et al., 2008) suggested the use of the Edinburgh Postnatal Depression Scale (Cox, Holden, & Sagovsky, 1987) due to its established validity, reliability, and widespread use. Additionally, a relatively uncharted area of exploration, depression among expectant and new fathers, has recently surfaced in the literature as an important area of assessment and treatment. In fact, Paulson and Bazemore (2010) documented approximately 10 percent of fathers experienced prenatal and postpartum depression, which was moderately positively correlated to maternal depression in their recent meta-analysis. Certainly, assessment of mental health symptoms and diagnoses would also apply to partners within LGBT relationships and key family members and/or friends who are adjusting to the new pregnancy or birth. Social support is a crucial construct to assess, especially since when unavailable, women tend to be more susceptible to psychosocial stress (Glazier, Elgar, Goel, & Holzapfel, 2004). One final area for comprehensive assessment and clinical attention pertains to the loss experiences after a miscarriage or stillbirth. These experiences can quickly reverberate through the family system, challenging expectations and beliefs. In response to a controversial article on whether to hold or not hold one's baby after a stillbirth experience, Reynolds (2003) stated that the greatest injustice in the psychosocial management of stillbirth is the lack of a thorough psychosocial and psychiatric assessment prior to the introduction of postnatal care options for the stillborn child. Marriage and family therapists located in an inpatient or outpatient setting can likely best assist families by providing a context for processing the loss experience using a number of psychosocial treatment options discussed in this clinical update.

BIOMEDICAL ISSUES

There are a variety of complications that can occur during pregnancy. Again, the majority of patients treated through labor and delivery are healthy babies born to mothers with little to no risk factors during their pregnancy. However, the most common risk factors for women during pregnancy include: ectopic pregnancy, placenta previa, placental abruption, preeclampsia, sexually transmitted infections (STIs), thromboembolic disease, and others.

An *ectopic pregnancy,* also referred to as a mislocated pregnancy, involves symptoms of unexpected vaginal bleeding and cramping. The fetus may grow enough to rupture the fallopian tube (typically after about 6 to 8 weeks), after which the woman usually feels severe pain in the lower abdomen. If the tube ruptures later (after about 12 to 16 weeks), the risk of death for the woman is increased, because the fetus and placenta are larger and lead to an increased loss of blood. In most women, the fetus and placenta from an ectopic pregnancy are diagnosed early enough to be treated through the use of medication (e.g., methotrexate), however in some cases surgery may be necessary.

The complication of *placenta previa* occurs in one of every 200 deliveries when the placenta is mostly or completely covering the cervix, in the lower, rather than upper part of the uterus. Placenta previa can cause painless bleeding (i.e., a sentinel bleed) from the vagina that often begins suddenly in the second trimester of pregnancy (Sakornbut, Leeman, & Fontaine, 2007). A *placental abruption* is the premature detachment of a normally positioned placenta from the wall of the uterus. Detachment of the placenta occurs in 0.4 to 3.5 percent of all deliveries. This complication is more common among women who have high blood pressure (including preeclampsia) and among women who use cocaine (Hoyme et al., 1990).

Preeclampsia occurs in about five percent of pregnant women, which is an increase in blood pressure, accompanied by protein in the urine (proteinuria). Preeclampsia usually develops between the 20th week of pregnancy and the end of the first week after delivery. In one of 200 women who have preeclampsia, blood pressure becomes high enough to cause seizures; this condition is called eclampsia. One fourth of the cases of eclampsia occur after delivery, usually in the first two to four days. If not treated promptly, eclampsia may be fatal (less than one percent for mothers and about 12 percent for the baby) (Fugate & Chow, 2007).

Preterm premature rupture of membranes is the rupture of membranes during pregnancy before 37 weeks gestation and is related to about one-third of all preterm deliveries. This diagnosis occurs in three percent of pregnancies and can result in neonatal sepsis, umbilical cord prolapse, placental abruption, and fetal death (Medina & Hill, 2006).

Another complicating factor can be STIs, as some women may not know that they are carrying an STI during their pregnancy or at the time of delivery. Certainly some STIs are more dangerous for the fetus than others, especially when considering vaginal deliveries. For example, if Herpes lesions are preset at the time of labor, the baby will need to be born by Cesarean Section. Some hospitals are using rapid human immunodeficiency virus (HIV) testing during labor and delivery for pregnant women who were not tested previously during pregnancy. If a woman is found to be HIV-infected, providers are then able to begin antiretroviral therapy immediately to prevent perinatal transmission.

In the United States, *thromboembolic disease* is the leading cause of death in pregnant women and occurs when blood clots form in blood vessels that travel through the woman's bloodstream and block an artery. This disease most commonly occurs six to eight weeks after delivery. The risk is much greater after a cesarean section than after vaginal delivery (Block, 2003).

Additional hurdles may include women who are currently struggling with *substance or domestic abuse* (mental health providers are typically called in this situation) as children may not be safe to leave the medical context with the mother. Social service agencies must step in when there are identified child safety concerns. Mothers who weren't currently abusing substances at time of delivery but had used substances in the past should receive education about the passage of such drugs through breast milk. Domestic violence (including child maltreatment) is another complicating factor that can be elevated in circumstances where a child is born with a special need (Hibbard & Desch, 2007), finances are strained for the parent(s) (Frederick & Goddard, 2007), or the child is a result of an unwanted pregnancy (Coleman, Maxey, Rue, & Coyle, 2005).

Sometimes a pregnancy may feel normal to the expectant mother, yet complications exist for the fetus or newborn child. Three types of loss experiences that may occur among expectant or new parents: miscarriage, stillbirth, or neonatal death. Approximately one out of every four women who becomes pregnant will miscarry at some point in her life. A *miscarriage* is considered any fetal loss that occurs prior to 20 weeks gestation. About 15 to 20 percent of all pregnancies end in a miscarriage, typically within the first trimester or sometimes into the early second trimester (Puscheck, 2010).When a baby dies after 20 weeks gestation, this is known as a *stillbirth*. A specific cause of death can only be determined in about half of all stillbirth autopsies. Of those that are determined, most common causes include: problems with the placenta or umbilical cord (Silver et al., 2007), maternal medical conditions (including illness or preeclampsia), and birth defects (ACOG, 2009). Stillbirths do not typically occur during labor. Instead, most children pass hours or even weeks prior to labor and delivery. Stillbirths occur in about one percent of all pregnancies. A *neonatal death* is any death that occurs in the first 28 days of a child's life. Matthews et al. (2005) found that approximately 19,000 babies died in 2002 during their first month of life. The babies most at risk for neonatal death are those that are born prematurely (i.e., those born before 37 weeks gestation or 12 percent of all babies) (Martin, 2005). About 20 to 35 percent of babies born at 23 weeks of pregnancy survive and approximately 50 to 70 percent of babies born at 24 to 25 weeks, and more than 90 percent born at 26 to 27 weeks, survive (Alexander, 2003).

Many of the babies born prematurely that do not survive had at least one birth defect. Specifically, heart defects are the most common birth defect related to infant death. Approximately one-third of all neonatal deaths involving a birth defect were heart related. Chromosomal abnormalities are another common cause of neonatal deaths. Most of these deaths occur prior to the 23rd week of pregnancy (March of Dimes, 2010).

TREATMENT OPTIONS

Whether issues surrounding the pregnancy are biomedical or psychosocial, family therapists would benefit from using an interdisciplinary, systemic

SKILLS OF THE FAMILY THERAPIST

While family therapists are beginning to assume distinctive roles in labor and delivery units, the majority continue to act as consultants or referral sources for the family or provider faced with challenging situations. The skill set for family therapists who work with labor and delivery patients and providers will be diverse; however, every provider should have knowledge of the most common developmental processes and concerns that can occur throughout a pregnancy, delivery, and post-delivery experience. While medical providers are trained to give bad news, many are not comfortable with how to manage such situations once they arise. It is necessary for family therapists to develop appropriate techniques to support both providers and patients during typical deliveries and those with unexpected challenges. An initial list of necessary skills, including ways to manage healthy pregnancies and deliveries, pregnancy complications, and fetal/neonatal deaths are described below.

Healthy pregnancies and deliveries:

- Understand what providers/collaborators will be present, how to support one or both parents (natural and/or adoptive) prior to and following the delivery, and when to refer patients to other medical professionals.

- Gain awareness of mental health issues, such as anxiety and depression, that may influence post-discharge relationships between parents, parent(s) and child, or parent(s) and extended family/friends.

- Utilize theories to recognize and normalize family life cycle changes.

- Assess for safety including suicidal ideation, child maltreatment, homicidal ideation, domestic violence, and any concerns related to current or future substance abuse.

- Recognize that there may be unmet needs by one or both parents or disappointment with regard to expectations associated with prepared birth plans that had to change during the delivery process or complications with breastfeeding, etc.

Pregnancy complications:

- Appreciate specific psychosocial trends (guilt, blame, depression, etc.) amongst families navigating complications.

- Explore ways to assist parent(s) so that they may make difficult choices by facilitating discussions using effective communication techniques.

- Collaborate with chaplains, pastors, or priests for families with a strong religious or spiritual faith, since decisions may have implications for neonatal death or later disability.

- Provide therapy, psychoeducation, or support for one or both parents, a provider, or to the healthcare team in order to process the best outcome given a troubling situation.

Fetal/neonatal death:

- Within the hospital: flag patient charts with a unique symbol to let current and future providers know that a death of a child has occurred; using a symbol to attach to the door in labor and delivery units to signify that the baby died is a helpful indicator for a provider and serves to prepare each person for entering these rooms, reducing habitual greetings that can be invalidating.

- Encourage interaction with the baby, including picture taking or other helpful items in the memorialization of the child.

- Conduct small process groups to reduce compassion fatigue among providers.

- Recognize that there will be many unique challenges for the parent(s):

    - *Biological implications:* the mother's

SKILLS (continued)

breast milk will come in without a baby to feed, inability to sleep, loss of appetite, or overeating as a coping technique, and the physical healing process of having a child (e.g., exhaustion from labor, tearing from delivery, muscle pain from caesarian section).

- *Psychological implications:* anxiety, depression, nightmares, phobias, and post partum depression.

- *Social implications:* friends, family members, co-workers, etc., will respond to the parent(s) in diverse ways. Common occurrences: 1) parent(s) are requested to talk about their experience repeatedly; 2) people will say things out of their own discomfort about loss such as, "you are young and can have plenty more children," and; 3) conversely, others will share their loss experiences. These stories are sometimes very helpful, as they can let a parent know that others have faced similar pains. Sadly, this exchange of stories can also be damaging as family secrets become unraveled and unhealthy coping techniques are shared. Another significant issue is that of financial matters. These families are often times paying thousands of dollars for the regular check-ups from the pregnancy, for a delivery or cesarean section, and for a funeral (if the family chooses to have one for the baby).

- *Spiritual implications:* others often use religion to assist the parents with their coping, yet this may not be well received. Comments such as "this was God's will" have been shared with grieving parents who then consider turning away from their religion, spirituality, or religious/spiritual community rather than saying something such as, "you and your family will remain in my prayers." We have found that after a loss, people either turn toward their religion or spirituality, or they turn away from their belief system. Some feel as though they can rely on their higher power to soothe their pain, while others are reluctant to use their higher power and perhaps may push blame in the direction of a higher power for taking an innocent child away from his or her parents.

- A general skill set for any provider would be to have a strong understanding of cultural differences and competence in knowing about common childbirth rituals and practices for racial, ethnic, and religious groups present in one's community. A common complicating factor is the amount of information shared with new parents in paper form, given the number of patients that may be able to speak their native language, yet are illiterate. Another concern is the lack of bilingual or multilingual providers present for the labor and delivery process, including medical and mental health professionals. Certainly, a provider must learn many idiosyncratic elements related to patient care, including philosophy on childbirth, labor, delivery, roles of family members and providers, rituals related to childbirth or death, etc.

approach. Forming collaborative relationships with physicians, nurses, social workers, among others can ensure other providers are also aware of the unique stressors within the family system. Therapists can develop this rapport by phoning/e-mailing through a secured electronic health record to providers when sharing a family's care, sending thank you letters for referrals, offering inpatient didactics on psychosocial aspects of pregnancy, co-locating care within an outpatient clinic, and starting a community support group to address loss or postpartum depression. Collaboration should extend beyond colleagues through the inclusion of family during the pregnancy, labor, delivery, or a fetal loss experience. Others have also emphasized approaches and interventions that involve family throughout different stages of treatment to reduce risks for postpartum depression (Gruen, 1990). Researchers and clinicians must respond to these requests via an interdisciplinary approach to promote a better understanding of developmental processes, measurements, and interventions to prevent negative long-term implications on individuals, couples, and families. When taking a collaborative stance with colleagues, the patient, and family members, a biopsychosocial-spiritual approach emerges, leading to comprehensive, family-centered care.

Collaboration among professionals and inclusion of family members is only a first step in delivering quality care. Since acute and chronic stress can often lead to low birth weight or preterm birth, researchers in a recent review recommended teaching physical relaxation (meditation, yoga, etc.) and offering assessment and education (Hobel et al., 2008). These researchers further emphasized the role of social support for the pregnant woman often leading to less problematic outcomes. Thus, family therapists who work to build on relational strengths, reduce cut-offs or discord, and encourage respectful communication may also improve outcomes. For example, Dankoski (2001) used an emotionally focused approach to address this life cycle transition, which may be especially valuable when secondary emotions of anger emerge as attachment bonds are reorganized.

Specific attention should be given to systemic treatment of pregnancy loss. In their landmark *Medical Family Therapy* text, McDaniel, Hepworth, and Doherty (1992) recommended acknowledging and normalizing the loss, offering education, assessing biopsychosocial health, encouraging self-care, and exploring how family members have coped with past losses. These authors also recommend delaying another pregnancy to allow time for grieving. A number of short-term and long-term goals should be addressed in treatment and many are discussed in the following case example.

CASE EXAMPLE

Tom (28) and Samantha (29) unexpectedly lost their first baby at 34 weeks gestation. At a follow-up obstetrician visit, the couple reported an intense amount of grief and communication difficulties within the marriage. Their physician invited the co-located or onsite marriage and family therapist to meet the couple during this visit and introduce the idea of brief therapy. During the "warm-hand off" visit (i.e., introduction and meeting during the medical follow-up appointment), the family therapist normalized the parental grief and allowed a few moments for the couple to tearfully describe the isolation they felt after the stillbirth. Subsequently, an intake visit was scheduled with the couple to further address the unanticipated loss. Over a number of sessions, the therapy proceeded in three phases, averaging five to eight sessions in each phase. Phase one involved facilitating discussions of how to manage acute stressors, including physical changes, a prepared nursery in their home, and comments from family or friends. Phase two involved exploration of their different coping styles, development of rituals to remember the loss, and encouragement of communication to develop stronger attachment bonds between the couple. After a six-month break from therapy, the couple returned when they learned Samantha was pregnant yet again, since this news led to feelings of excitement, uncertainty, and fear. Thus, phase three involved accessing worries, encouragement of self-care, discussing the way they want to remember their first child (as the anniversary was approaching), and close partnership between medical and mental health providers. Collaboratively, the therapist and obstetrician were able to schedule a trip to the labor and delivery unit prior to their next birthing experience where the therapist coached the couple on mindfulness-based stress reduction strategies to lower anticipatory anxiety. This experience occurred in-vivo or in the stressful context to enhance the intervention's effectiveness and prepare them for the upcoming delivery process. Development of a birthing plan, including who the couple wanted in the delivery room, ways Tom could support Samantha, and coping strategies when difficult thoughts or emotions were activated, also occurred within this stage of therapy. A couple months after ending therapy, Tom and Samantha welcomed a healthy baby boy at 39 weeks. The marriage and family therapist intermittently met with Samantha for several sessions after the birth, due to some symptoms of postpartum depression. Tom attended many of these appointments to hear Samantha's needs for support and mutually discuss parenting responsibilities. The marriage and family therapist also obtained a release and spoke on a few occasions with Samantha's psychiatrist to ensure cohesive care. Samantha's depression eventually remitted and the couple ended mental health services with plans to try for another child in a few years. They continue to conceptualize their experience with pregnancy and delivery as profoundly important to their growth as a couple.

COLLABORATORS ON THE CARE TEAM

The care team can include a diverse group of collaborators depending on the birthing context, the wishes of the parent(s), and the complexity of the labor and delivery.

- **Adoption Services** – adoption agencies or facilitators that are invited by the mother or both parents (when adoption is a preferred choice for the future of the child) to be present during or shortly after the delivery of the child. Collaboration has typically taken place prior to the delivery process between the agency/facilitator and expecting parent(s)
- **Anesthesiologist or Nurse Anesthetist** – physician or nurse specializing in administering anesthesia and managing the medical care of patients before, during, and after surgeries
- **Certified Lactation Consultant** – teaches breastfeeding classes, coun-

sels parents through challenges in breastfeeding, provides breastfeeding supplies, identifies problems that may need to be referred to a physician or midwife

- **Chaplain** – offers pastoral care, spiritual support, and crisis intervention for patients, family, or staff
- **Child Life Specialists** – use developmentally-appropriate activities to help siblings of an unborn or newborn child to help them adjust to the hospital environment, prepare for a new sibling in the family, or cope with hospitalization, illness, or death of a sibling or mother
- **Doula** – provide physical, emotional and informational support during prenatal, childbirth, or post partum care
- **Neonatal Intensive Care Providers/Team** – a neonatologist is a pediatrician specializing in caring for babies requiring intensive care after birth. The neonatologist, in collaboration with nurses, pharmacists, and others, determines and coordinates the daily plan of care for premature infants
- **Nurses** – provide care in a variety of roles, including antepartum (complications), circulating (operating room during cesarean), labor and delivery (labor without complicated deliveries), postpartum (recently delivered), and scrub (directly with surgeon during cesarean)
- **Obstetrician or Certified Nurse Midwife** – physician or advanced practice nurse specializing in pregnancy and childbirth
- **Parent(s)** – biological, adoptive, or non-biological (partner to the mother or guardian)
- **Parent-to-parent support** – individuals who are trained to help a family who is facing something similar to the situation they previously managed in their own life, providing empathy, help in adjusting to the hospital environment, and preparing the family for the sights, sounds, and atmosphere of a neonatal intensive care unit. The trained individuals must show an understanding of boundaries and how to effectively support another family by listening and not add to the stress
- **Partner/Coach of Mother** – father of the child, another family member, friend, selected medical professional, or paid coach such as a doula
- **Pediatrician**- physician specializing in the medical care of infants, children, and adolescents
- **Perinatologists** – obstetrician specializing in high risk pregnancies or deliveries
- **Records Personnel** – collect information from the parents toward birth certificates or discharge planning
- **Recreational Therapist** – utilizes games, arts, crafts, or music to help patients build confidence and redirect their attention to activities rather than the stressful experience (often for mothers on hospital bed rest)
- **Social Workers** – collaborates with the family in case management (community referrals, shelters, adoption agencies, child protective services)

Angela Lamson, PhD, LMFT, CFLE, is currently an associate professor in the Department of Child Development and Family Relations at East Carolina University. She is the program director for the MFT masters program and MedFT doctoral program, clinic director for the ECU Family Therapy Clinic, board member for the Family Support Network of Eastern North Carolina, and director of the HUGS team within the Children's Hospital of Pitt County Memorial Hospital. Lamson is a Clinical Member and Approved Supervisor of the AAMFT.

Kenneth W. Phelps, PhD, LMFT, is currently an Assistant Clinical Professor of Neuropsychiatry and Behavioral Science at the University of South Carolina. He previously interned through the Family Support Network of Eastern North Carolina within the Neonatal Intensive Care, Pediatric Intensive Care, and Labor and Delivery Units. Phelps is a Clinical Member of the AAMFT.

PROFESSIONAL RESOURCES

ORGANIZATIONS

American Academy of Pediatrics (AAP)
www.aap.org
Information on medication, assessment, and pregnancy and neonatal treatments.

American Congress of Obstetricians and Gynecologists (ACOG)
www.acog.org
Information on women's and child health.

National Initiative for Children's Healthcare Quality (NICHQ)
www.nichq.org
Includes a Neonatal Improvement Project.

BOOKS

Gabbe, S. G., Niebyl, J. R., Simpson, J. L. Galan, H., Goetzl, L., Landon, M. Jauniaux, E. R. M., (Eds). (2007). *Obstetrics: Normal and problem pregnancies.* Philadelphia, PA: Churchill Livingstone Elsevier.

Ilse, S. (2002) *Empty arms: Coping with miscarriage, stillbirth and infant death.* Maple Plain, MN: Wintergreen Press.

Lederman, R., & Weis, K. (Eds). (2009). *Psychosocial adaptation to pregnancy: Seven dimensions of maternal role development (3rd ed).* Springer.

REFERENCES

Alexander, G. (2003). U.S. birth weight/gestational age-specific neonatal mortality: 1995-1997 rates for whites, Hispanics, and blacks. *Pediatrics, 111,* 61-66.

American College of Obstetricians and Gynecologists. (2006). ACOG committee opinion no. 343. Psychosocial risk factors: perinatal screening and intervention.

Obstetrics & Gynecology, 108, 469-477.

American College of Obstetricians and Gynecologists. (2009). Evaluation of still-births and neonatal deaths. *ACOG Committee Opinion, 383*

Andersson, L. (2004). Implications of antenatal depression and anxiety for obstetric outcome. *Obstetrics & Gynecology, 104,* 467-476.

Block, W. A. (2003). Thromboembolism prophylaxis and cesarean section. *Southern Medical Journal, 96,* 121.

Center for Disease Control. Births and Natality. Retrieved May 8, 2010, from http://www.cdc.gov/nchs/fastats/births.htm.

Cochrane, R., & Robertson, A. (1973). The life events inventory: A measure of the relative severity of psychosocial stressors. *Journal of Psychosomatic Research, 17,* 135-139.

Cohen, S., Kamarck, T., & Mermelstein, R. (1983). A global measure of perceived stress. *Journal of Health and Social Behavior, 24,* 385-396.

Coleman, P. K., Maxey, C. D., Rue, V. M., & Coyle, C. T. (2005). Associations between voluntary and involuntary forms of perinatal loss and child maltreatment among low income mothers. *Acta Paediatrica, 94,* 1476-1483.

Cox, J. L., Holden, J. M., & Sagovsky, R. (1987). Detection of postnatal depression: Development of the 10-Item Edinburgh Postnatal Depression Scale. *The British Journal of Psychiatry, 150,* 782-786.

Dankoski, M. E. (2001). Pulling on the heart strings: An emotionally focused approach to family life cycle transitions. *Journal of Marital and Family Therapy, 27,* 177-187.

Fugate, S. R., & Chow, G. E. Eclampsia. *Emedicine.* Retrieved July 7, 2007, from http://www.emedicine.com/med/topic633.htm.

Frederick, J., & Goddard, C. (2007) Exploring the relationship between poverty, childhood adversity and child abuse from the perspective of adulthood. *Child Abuse Review 16,* 323-341.

Glazier, R. H., Elgar, R. J., Goel, V., & Holzapfel, S. (2004). Stress, social support, and emotional distress in a community sample of pregnancy women. *Journal of Psychosomatic Obstetrics & Gynecology, 25,* 247-255.

Goebert ,D., Onoye, J., & Matsu, C. (2007). Mental health during pregnancy: A study comparing Asian, Caucasian, and native Hawaiian women. *Maternal and Child Health, 11,* 249-255.

Gruen, D. S. (1990). Postpartum depression: A debilitating yet often unassessed problem *Health & Social Work, 15,* 261-270.

Hibbard, R. A., & Desch L. W. (2007). Maltreatment of children with disabilities. *Pediatrics, 119,* 1018-1025.

Hobel, C. J., Goldstein, A., & Barrett, E. S. (2008). Psychosocial stress and pregnancy outcome. *Clinical Obstetrics and Gynecology, 51,* 333-348.

Hoyme, H. E., Jones K. L., Dixon S. D., Jewett, T., Hanson, J. W., & Robinson, L. K., et al. (1990). Prenatal cocaine exposure and fetal vascular disruption. *Pediatrics, 85,* 743-747.

March of Dimes. Professionals and researchers: Quick reference and fact sheet. Retrieved May 7, 2010, from http://www.marchofdimes.com.

Martin, J. A., Hamilton, B. E., Sutton, P. D., Ventura, S. J., Menacker, P. H., & Munson, M. L. (2005). *Births: Final data for 2003. National Vital Statistics Reports, 54,* 1-116.

McDaniel, S. H., Hepworth, J., & Doherty, W. J. (1992) Pregnancy loss, infertility, and reproductive technology. *Medical family therapy: A biopsychosocial approach to families with health problems* (pp. 152-183). New York: Basic Books.

McGoldrick, M., & Carter, B. (2003). The family life cycle. In F. Walsh (Ed.), *Normal family processes: Growing diversity and complexity* (pp. 375-398). New York: Guilford.

Medina, T. M., & Hill, D. A. (2006). Preterm premature rupture of membranes: diagnosis and management. *American Family Physician, 73(4),* 659-664.

Paulson, J. F., & Bazemore, S. D. (2010). Prenatal and postpartum depression in fathers and its association with maternal depression: A meta-analysis. *Journal of the American Medical Association, 303,* 1961-1969.

Puscheck, E. (2010). Early pregnancy loss. *E-medicine.* Retrieved May 7, 2010, from http://emedicine.medscape.com/article/266317-overview.

Radloff, L. A. (1977). The CES-D scale: A self-report depression scale for research in the general population. *Applied Psychological Measures, 1,* 385-401.

Reynolds, J. (2003). Stillbirth: To hold or not to hold. *Omega: Journal of Death and Dying, 48,* 85-88.

Sakornbut, E., Leeman, L., & Fontaine, P. (2007). Late pregnancy bleeding. *American Family Physician, 75,* 1199-1206.

Sieber, S., Germann, N., Barbir, A., & Ehlert, U. (2006). Emotional well-being and predictors of birth-anxiety, self-efficacy, and psychosocial adaptation in healthy pregnant women. *Acta Obstetricia et Gynecologica Scandinavica, 85,* 1200-1207.

Silver, R. M., Varner, M. W., Ruddy, U., et al. (2007). Work-up of stillbirth: A review of the evidence. *American Journal of Obstetrics and Gynecology, 196(5),* 433-444.

Spielberger, C. D., Gorush, T. C., & Lushene, R. E. (1970). *The State Trait Anxiety Inventory.* Palo Alto, CA: Consulting Psychologists Press.

Woods, S. M., Melville, J. L., Guo, Y., Fan, M. Y., & Gavin, A. (2010). Psychosocial stress during pregnancy. *American Journal of Obstetrics & Gynecology, 6,* e1-e6.

Psychogenic Non-Epileptic Attacks (PNEA)

William H. Watson, PhD & John T. Langfitt, PhD

*Originally published as Clinical Update in Family Therapy Magazine
September-October 2010*

FROM MYSTERY AND STIGMA TOWARD ACCEPTANCE AND UNDERSTANDING

Psychogenic non-epileptic attacks (PNEA) are paroxysmal behaviors that resemble epileptic seizures, but are caused by underlying psychological factors rather than by neurological or biomedical ones. They differ from other non-epileptic events that are commonly mistaken for seizures (e.g., syncope, hyperventilation, hypoglycemia, migraine, transient ischemic attacks) in that a thorough medical work-up has failed to reveal an organic cause. PNEA can be as variable as epileptic seizures themselves. They can involve convulsive movements, tremor, blacking out, clouded consciousness, loss of awareness, staring, unresponsiveness and amnesia for events during the attack. Like epileptic seizures, they typically occur at random, but may be more likely to occur in particularly stressful situations. PNEA have also been called pseudoseizures, psychogenic seizures, non-electrical seizures, conversion or stress seizures, hysterical fits, spells, events, or episodes. We prefer the term "psychogenic attacks" (i.e., generated from the psyche) rather than "pseudoseizures," as it avoids the implication that the events are being faked, or not really happening, and underscores the psychological basis of the symptom. Using the terms "non-epileptic" and "attack," rather than "seizure," also reduces confusion about the cause (Benbadis, 2010).

Management of psychogenic, non-epileptic attacks can be very challenging. Many therapists are not familiar with this relatively uncommon somatoform symptom. They may be uncomfortable working with a client who appears to have a significant neurologic condition. Patients may refuse to engage in psychotherapy when they believe their symptoms are caused by an underlying physical problem that their doctors are trying to pass off as "all in my head." However, with timely and accurate diagnosis and adoption of a comprehensive biopsychosocial perspective, these symptoms can become less mysterious and more amenable to treatment. This Clinical Update is based on information from a review of recent literature and the authors' combined 30 years of experience diagnosing and treating PNEA at the Strong Epilepsy Center in the Department of Neurology at the University of Rochester Medical Center.

PNEA are involuntary, physical manifestations of psychological distress in a psychologically vulnerable client who has been unable to express or manage this distress by other means. PNEA develop out of a complex interplay of predisposing, precipitating and maintaining biological, psychological and social factors (Reuber, 2009). Assessing the nature of the patient's "PNEA risk factors" is the main focus of the psychological evaluation. These risk factors provide a framework for understanding the patient's unique predicament and developing a treatment plan.

Epidemiology. The population incidence and prevalence of PNEA are not well-established. Most of what is known about the nature, diagnosis, assessment and treatment of PNEA comes from patients evaluated on specialized, epilepsy inpatient monitoring units. PNEA patients represent ~ 25-35 percent of patients evaluated on such units, leading to rough prevalence estimates of 2-33/100,000. PNEA typically first occur between the ages of 20 and 30 years, although cases have been diagnosed as young as age four and as old as age 70. They occur most commonly in women (~ 75 percent). Concurrent or past epileptic seizures have been documented in 10-50 percent of patients, further complicating diagnosis and treatment (Reuber & Elger, 2003).

DIAGNOSIS & ASSESSMENT OF PNEA

Accurate and timely diagnosis of PNEA is crucial to ensure appropriate care and to avoid unnecessary and potentially dangerous treatments. Unfortunately, definitive diagnosis is often delayed—by an average of seven years in one study (Reuber, Fernandez, Bauer, Helmstaedter, & Elger, 2002). During this time, patients are typically prescribed anti-epilepsy drugs (AEDs), which are ineffective with PNEA and often have significant side effects. Approximately a quarter of PNEA patients will have an unnecessary and potentially dangerous ICU admission as a result of a prolonged attack at some point during their illness (Reuber et al., 2003). Patients often lose driving privileges, lose their jobs, and find their activities restricted—e.g., no swimming, climbing, operating power tools—anything where a sudden loss of physical control or consciousness would be dangerous. Correct diagnosis is critical. In one study, healthcare costs were reduced by 85 percent in the six months following definitive diagnosis of PNEA, including a 97 percent reduction of emergency room services (Martin, Gilliam, Kilgore, Faught, & Kuzniecky, 1998).

MEDICAL EVALUATION

Differential Diagnosis. Evaluation begins with a thorough medical and neurologic examination to assess neurologic and other physical causes of the seizures. One aspect of the evaluation is obtaining a description or video of the seizures themselves, as seizure semiology (appearance) is clinically relevant. Clinical characteristics more commonly seen in psychogenic than in epileptic events include closed eyes (and resistance to others' attempts to open them), asynchronous limb movement, side-to-side head movement, pelvic thrusting, repeated waxing and waning in the intensity of motor activity, absence of a tonic (stiffening) phase, convulsive activity lasting more than two minutes, absence of cyanosis (turning blue), vocalization during convulsions, or rapid return of normal cognitive function with cessation of the event (Reuber et al., 2003). Injuries are rare with PNEA and typically are limited to bruises or minor lacerations, though more serious injuries can occur.

Long Term Monitoring. Such observations and other clinical data (e.g., a normal outpatient EEG) may strongly suggest PNEA, but exceptions occur frequently enough that such signs cannot be counted upon to provide a definitive diagnosis. For example, frontal lobe seizures share many behavioral characteristics with PNEA, leading some to refer to them as "pseudo-pseudo-seizures." One of our patients with video-EEG-documented frontal lobe epilepsy and a history of drug abuse had been repeatedly barred from the local emergency room by staff and was allegedly assaulted by police, all of whom mistook his seizures for malingering to obtain drugs. Occurrence of severe falls and injuries does not rule out PNEA, as these can occur, for example, in patients with a history of severe physical abuse in which the patient "relives" the abuse during the attack (we have had patients who have broken arms and teeth during their PNEA. One such patient had a childhood history of intentionally breaking her own hand and leg with a hammer or bat on multiple occasions in an effort to deal with severe family dysfunction and abuse). Even EEG data is equivocal: Individuals with epilepsy can have normal outpatient EEGs, and abnormal EEGs can sometimes be observed in people with no seizure disorder.

The gold-standard for definitive diagnosis of PNEA is concurrent video-EEG recording of events. This is accomplished through a Video/EEG Long Term Monitoring admission, which consists of admission to a specialized inpatient unit where patients (on video) and their EEG are continuously recorded, 24 hours a day, for several days or up to two weeks until one or more of their typical events occur. If the patient has a normal EEG during the event, then the event can be conclusively diagnosed as non-epileptic. With the elimination of any other biomedical cause—e.g., migraine, cardiovascular syncope with abnormal movements due to cerebral hypoxia—and especially in the presence of corresponding clinical characteristics and psychogenic risk factors, the non-epileptic episode is diagnosed as psychogenic.

Though the accuracy is quite high with such an evaluation, false positives and false negatives can occur, making close collaboration between treating therapist and the neurologists vital, especially in the face of the presentation of new symptom manifestations. Neurologists are generally quite open to re-evaluation (or clarification of diagnostic considerations) when significant clinical uncertainties remain or new ones develop. Such collaboration can be instrumental in providing treating therapists with the necessary confidence in the diagnosis to press on with therapy in the face of doubts that may arise about the psychological nature of the symptoms for even the most experienced clinician (including these authors).

PSYCHOLOGICAL EVALUATION

Psychogenic Risk Factors. A psychological evaluation is typically conducted either as part of a workup when a psychogenic etiology is suspected or after biomedical causes have been ruled out. Key to the evaluation is assessment of psychogenic risk factors, i.e., aspects of the presentation that are suggestive of a psychogenic etiology. One such risk factor is the correlation of the initial event and subsequent relapses with significant life events or emotional distress (Binzer, Stone, & Sharpe, 2004), including finding oneself in an unacceptable or intolerable situation with no escape (Griffith, Polles, Griffith, 1998). However, many patients with PNEA deny that stress is a trigger for their events, possibly due to minimization, denial, or alexithymia (literally, having no words for feelings). One such patient was a bright, verbal mother of three children under age five with an oft-absent husband and a conflictual relationship with her "helpful" mother-in-law. She calmly reported that her life was free of stress!

Other risk factors include a history of trauma, abuse, or bullying in childhood or young adulthood (Alper, Devinsky, Perrine, Vazquez, & Luciano, 1993; Holman, Kirkby, Duncan, & Brown, 2008; Bakvis et al., 2010); difficulty controlling anger or having grown up in an anger-engendering or anger-prohibiting household (true for men especially); the presence of secondary gain; prior exposure to seizures in others or oneself; a history of other medically unexplained symptoms or psychological diagnosis or treatment; coming from a somatizing family (Wood, McDaniel, Burchfiel, & Erba, 1998); psychological features such as an internalizing or counter-dependent (i.e., overfunctioning in the caretaking of others and resistance to being taken care of) or avoidant personality style, or dissociative or somatizing tendencies; neurological comorbidity (Howlett & Reuber, 2009); and, in children, a history of high functioning and hyper-compliance in the absence of a history of trauma (see sidebar). As with medical evaluation discussed above, none of these risk factors is diagnostically definitive, and care must be taken to conclusively rule out neurological etiology before reaching the diagnosis of PNEA.

Family and the Assessment Process. Family members should be included during the psychological evaluation whenever possible. They often can provide critical details about patient's history and the nature, timing and precipitants of attacks that the patient may omit or may not be aware of. Families are the fundamental context in which illness is experienced and responded to (McDaniel, Campbell, Hepworth & Lorenz, 2004). Families are often a vital source of support to patients as they deal with their symptoms. Much can be learned about the family context through inclusion of family, both from what they report and from how they relate to one another and how they respond to the patient's symptoms—whether anxious and distraught, overly solicitous and indulgent, appropriately supportive and encouraging, or critical and blaming. Finally, families typically are as anxious about the symptom as the patient—often more so. They have often had to stand by helplessly as the patient, contending with terrifying symptoms, has been given conflicting or confusing diagnoses and ineffective treatments. Active inclusion of the family in the assessment process gives them a chance to have their observations, fears, and concerns fully heard. Responsive inclusion of the family can be critical to lowering the anxiety of the whole system and to fostering trust in the medical team.

Diagnostic Considerations. In the DSM-IV, PNEA are considered a symptom, not a psychiatric diagnosis per se. PNEA can occur in the context of a number of different disorders including, most commonly, conversion disorder, as well as somatization disorder, PTSD, dissociative disorders, anxiety disorders, and others. In a recent prospective series of 27 patients, the distribution of diagnoses was: conversion disorder (63 percent), somatization disorder (19 percent), dissociative disorder NOS (7 percent), post-traumatic stress disorder (7 percent) and undifferentiated somatoform disorder (Marchetti et al., 2008). Other smaller series have reported prevalence of PTSD diagnoses in 22-100 percent of PNEA patients (Fiszman, ves-Leon, Nunes, D'Andrea, & Figueira, 2004).

It is critical to understand that vast majority of PNEA patients are not producing their symptoms voluntarily. PNEA is rarely a result of Malingering or Factitious disorder. These diagnoses should be suspected only when there is a strong external incentive (injury compensation, avoidance of responsibility) or other evidence that strongly suggests deliberate attempts to deceive (e.g., inconsistencies in the history provided, give-way weakness on motor testing, below-chance performance on symptom validity testing, tampering with test specimens). On rare occasions, children have reluctantly admitted to manufacturing attacks to draw attention to abuse or neglect. One child with confirmed epilepsy confessed in a session with his grandmother that he would sometimes also fake a seizure to escape punishment or chores. He then obliged us with a demonstration, to his grandmother's amazement and chagrin.

TREATMENT OPTIONS AND BIOMEDICAL ISSUES

Accepting the Diagnosis. The first hurdle to be overcome in the treatment of PNEA is acceptance of the diagnosis (Bowman & Markand, 2005). It is difficult to work through the underlying sources of emotional distress that are giving rise to the symptoms if one remains convinced that the real cause is a biomedical one that has yet to be discovered, or if one feels blamed for having the symptom in the first place. Yet the debilitating and often dramatic nature of the symptoms can make acceptance of their unconscious psychological origins difficult (Carton et al., 2003). This is true not only for patients and family members but also for providers, who may harbor overt or subtle skepticism about the involuntary nature of mind-body symptoms. Under such circumstances, it is easy for providers to become inpatient, dismissive, or blaming, and for patients and family members in turn to become hurt, angry, and defensive.

Presenting the Diagnosis. Outcome is better for patients who understand and accept the PNEA diagnosis. Given these challenges, it is important for clinicians to have a specific approach to discussing the psychogenic nature of the symptoms that is positive, non-blaming, respectful, and affirms both the psychological origin of the symptoms as well as their involuntary nature in terms that are common-sense and intuitive. At our epilepsy center, we have developed an approach to presenting the diagnosis that is applicable to virtually any mind-body or somatoform symptom. The goal is to lower defensiveness, promote understanding, elicit curiosity, facilitate exploration, and encourage pursuit of treatment.

Our approach to discussing a psychogenic diagnosis can be broken down into eight steps, presented below in the language we typically use with patients and their families:

1. Work as a team: It is important to have all the relevant providers on the same page, even if they practice independently. This reduces splitting and triangulation and lowers the anxiety of providers.
2. Highlight the positive: "Your tests are normal, indicating that your brain is healthy and side-effect-prone seizure medications are unnecessary."
3. Validate the reality: "Your symptoms are real; you are not making them up, faking them, or lying about them."
4. Connect the somatic to the psychological: "We understand these symptoms as representing your body's way of telling you that something is troubling you—something you may not even be fully aware of. Do you have any idea what that might be?"
5. Validate the patient's integrity: "This does not mean you are crazy or lazy, weird or bizarre."
6. Normalize: "These kinds of problems are actually quite common. We see them in a third of our patients presenting with intractable seizures."
7. Provide a framework for understanding the involuntary nature of mind-body symptoms as a more extreme variant of a very common aspect of human experience: the embodiment of emotional process (below).
8. Provide a non-blaming way to understand the relationship between symptom development and common PNEA personality styles: positive connotation of internalization, minimization, denial, dissociation, and counterdependency.

The Involuntary Nature of Mind-body Symptoms. A particularly intuitive and easily-understood way to frame this oft-misunderstood issue is by describing what the first author has called the embodiment of emotional process (Watson, 2007). Bodily expression of emotional states is automatic, involuntary, and not under one's direct conscious control, and when expressing negative affect, virtually always undesired and unwelcome. "Psychological in origin" does not mean consciously produced nor easily controlled. Even bodily expressions of emotion that we think of as voluntary are often not as subject to conscious control as we might expect. For example, when you see an old friend or loved one, your face smiles. The smile is not something you do on purpose but is automatic. Indeed, attempting to fully control a smile can prove nearly impossible, as any poker player can attest. Is that smile something that "you are just doing to yourself," or is "all in your head?" No. Such questions come out of a failure to understand the close interconnection of mind and body. Rather than being all in one's head, these symptoms are in both head AND body. It is how body and mind work together.

> ## TERMINOLOGY
>
> **EEG:** electroencephalogram; a graphical record of the electrical activity of the brain.
>
> **Epilepsy:** a neurological disorder characterized by periodic electrical seizures. A single seizure does not mean one has epilepsy. In half of the cases of epilepsy, no cause can be found.
>
> **Epileptiform:** when referring to an EEG, showing brain waves consistent with epilepsy
>
> **Ictal:** of or relating to a seizure or convulsion
>
> **Interictal:** between seizures, i.e., when a seizure is not occurring.
>
> **Paroxysmal:** relating to any sudden, violent outburst; a fit of violent action or emotion.
>
> **Seizure:** uncontrolled electrical firing of nerve cells in the brain at a rate up to 4 times higher than normal, which causes an "electrical storm" in the brain and can produce a convulsion or other physical (or emotional) manifestation.

Other examples of involuntary somatic expression of emotional process are plentiful: Blushing when embarrassed occurs not because one is having an allergic reaction but because of an emotion. Awareness of the emotional source of the "symptom" in no way means you can therefore control it. In fact, may intensify the process. A well-known actor throws up before every performance, fully aware that this symptom is psychological in origin. However, it does not follow that the actor therefore does this on purpose, wants to be doing it, or can directly control it. The same goes for many other common emotionally-driven experiences expressed somatically including fear of flying, or other phobias, panic attacks, insomnia generated by anxiety, nervous stomach, tension headaches, feeling weak physically when grief stricken or terrified, feeling dizzy, tired, short of breath when emotionally overwhelmed or avoiding uncomfortable affect.

This is not to say that we have no control whatsoever over our body's expression of emotional states, but rather that such control is much more indirect than we commonly appreciate; it is not as simple as merely lifting our finger to scratch our nose. In fact, direct attempts to control bodily expressions of emotions can sometimes make them worse, as any insomniac knows. Control is often possible, but is usually indirect and requires experimentation, openness, and patience—as in learning to distract oneself sufficiently to permit the bodily relaxation to occur that allows sleep to come.

Symptom Development and Personality Style. Patients understandably want to know how these "stress-related" symptoms can be happening to them, especially given the (apparent) lack of stress in their lives. Others conclude that to eliminate these symptoms, they need to eliminate all stress from their lives. Others worry about how abuse from long ago can be causing such huge problems in the present, especially if they've addressed the abuse in previous therapy.

To counter such misunderstandings, we find it helpful to provide patients with a positively connoted, strength-oriented description of the etiology of somatoform symptoms as often developing in strong individuals who are more inclined to worry about others than themselves and who prefer not to talk about (or even notice) their own problems or concerns. In this way, we touch on psychological processes often seen in somatoform patients: internalizing, minimizing, dissociation, counter-dependency, and alexithymia. We explain that how they manage stress is far more germane to their symptoms than stress itself. The most important stressors to understand are not necessarily external but internal ones, perhaps distress they have long ago ceased to notice. Even small external circumstances can then trigger strong reactions that come apparently out of the blue. So the issue is not, for example, early abuse, per se, but the process of disconnection from self that abuse (or other family factors) sets in motion, resulting in a pattern of responding to one's own emotional pain by numbing it rather than dealing with it effectively. Such strength and self-sacrifice is even admirable but can lead to problems when distress accumulates beyond a certain point and finally something gives—and symptoms develop.

In our experience, patients and families respond very positively to this way of framing the diagnosis and underlying dynamics, often nodding in recognition. In fact, on several occasions we have had families come to us for second opinions from major epilepsy centers in other parts of the country, in each case angry and resentful about having received a PNEA diagnosis of a family member. In each case, our workups confirmed the PNEA diagnosis and after presenting it with the above framework we have seen resistance turn to acceptance, and hostility to appreciation.

It is not unusual for symptoms to significantly decrease or cease altogether following presentation of the diagnosis without additional treatment, though there is little evidence about the length of such remissions (Farias, Thieman, Alsaadi, 2003).

Treatment. There are reports in the literature of successful treatment of PNEA using a wide variety of approaches, including insight-oriented, CBT, biofeedback, neurofeedback (i.e., EEG-based biofeedback), hypnosis, and group therapy. Overall, however, there is a dearth of well-designed studies clearly demonstrating the effectiveness of psychotherapeutic treatment of PNEA (Baker, Brooks, Goodfellow, Bodde, & Aldenkamp, 2007) and virtually no evidence about which approach is most effective. Nonetheless, psychotherapy remains the consensus treatment of choice (LaFrance & Barry, 2005). Medication generally has not been found to be useful in the treatment

SPECIAL PRESENTATIONS OF PNEA

Two scenarios are worth particular mention because they involve otherwise healthy and high functioning persons in whom typical PNEA risk factors are often absent. Ford (1977) described the development of conversion symptoms in historically very physically and psychologically healthy, action-oriented, emotionally unsophisticated men. Symptoms developed following an injury or organic illness that initially appeared life-threatening but was ultimately self-limiting or manageable. Yet PNEA with significant functional disability persists despite the resolution of the initial stressor. The onset of the PNEA can be understood as an expression of the patient's overwhelming fear of dependency and loss of function in the face of the initial threat. The attacks are then reinforced by solicitous family members or by the prospect of relief from responsibilities via disability status. Once the organic problem has resolved, symptoms can persist if there continues to be fear of recurrence of organic problems or if social reinforcers persist. Ford dubbed this 'Humpty-Dumpty syndrome', reflecting the notion that these formerly high-functioning patients had a sudden "fall" and couldn't be put back to together again.

Kozlowska (2001, 2003) describes a puzzling pattern of "good children" presenting with conversion disorder. With no history of abuse, and with high-functioning, if subtly intimidating, parents, these children are notably well-behaved, even 'hyper-compliant,' often described as happy, healthy, bright, active, talented, uncomplaining, and accomplished (a number of our cases literally have been cheerleaders). So what could be wrong? Kozlowska proposes that such children have an insecure attachment style, typically as a result of early parental ambivalence about the child. These children adopt a "compulsive compliant strategy" early on to minimize hostility and facilitate closeness with the attachment figure, suppressing awareness of their own dependency needs. Conversion symptoms appear when the child cannot perform or meet the parents' standards any longer or when events threaten to undermine already insecure attachments and they fear losing parental approval and love. Examples of precipitating events in such children from our practice include loss of a source of achievement or emotional outlet through injury or illness, impending or actual separation (e.g., going off to college), or impending or actual initiation of sexual activity or other activity that puts them at sharp odds with parental values. Successful treatment results in a child who is symptom-free though often much more outspoken, even unpleasant at times, but much more successful in negotiating age-appropriate compromise between their needs and needs of others.

of PNEA except when the attacks are exacerbated by other emotional conditions such as PTSD, OCD, major depression, or panic disorder, in which case SSRIs have proved helpful (Bowman and Markand, 2005).

Therapy for PNEA generally focuses on understanding the emotional triggers for events, developing problem-solving skills to address the issues relating to the triggering events, encouraging verbalization for patients who may avoid or have difficulty expressing their inner world and who need to decrease anxious over-attentiveness to others and improve self-care skills (Bowman and

Markand, 2005). Some patients may need help recognizing and interrupting dissociative processes and learn skills to stay grounded in the here-and-now. Patients dealing with significant trauma need to develop distress tolerance skills in advance of the trauma work lest symptoms grow worse as the patient confronts traumatic memories with no effective way to manage the resulting overwhelming affect.

Family therapy or other systems interventions are indicated when family members unwittingly reinforce the symptoms through being overly indulgent or solicitous, overreacting (e.g., encouraging unnecessary emergency room visits with each attack); overanxious hovering (Watson & McDaniel, 2000); when family members provoke attacks through negative attention, criticism, or abuse; when the symptom serves as an attempt to express or solve a problem in the family system; or when wider system interventions are indicated, as when health care providers are split over the diagnosis, or school systems are in a panic about a child's attacks at school, which can lead to contagion if not intercepted (Langfitt, 2007).

Somatoform symptoms typically present first, and often only, in medical settings and thus are well suited to a medical family therapy approach. Mc-Daniel and colleagues describe an approach to the treatment of somatoform symptoms in a primary care context that emphasizes early involvement of the family in treatment, helping the patient link the somatic with the emotional, collaboration with patient and all providers, looking for triggering psycho-social events/stressors, focus on strengths and competence, adaptive coping, focus on improvement in daily functioning and quality of life over symptom improvement, openness to the possible development of biomedical illness, and slow, gradual termination (McDaniel, Hepworth, & Doherty, 1995; Mc-Daniel, Campbell, Hepworth & Lorenz, 2004).

Evidence. A randomized controlled trial conducted by Goldstein et al., (2010) found evidence that CBT is more effective than standard medical care in the treatment of PNEA. LaFrance et al., (2009) obtained promising results in a prospective clinical trial of a 12-session CBT intervention designed specifically for PNEA, with substantial improvement in 11 of 17 patients, though no follow-up data is reported.

Several authors argue that PNEA patients differ significantly from one another and require differing approaches to treatment based on type. For example, Rush et al., report 100 percent improvement in (including 80 percent PNEA free) in a cohort of 26 patients divided into 6 subgroups based on their psychosocial history and PNEA etiology with targeted treatment approaches for each—anxious (relaxation training), abused with personality disturbance (a DBT-style treatment), abused with PTSD (exposure), somatizing (insight-oriented and psychoeducation), depressed (CBT, distress tolerance skills), and low IQ (reinforcement schedules to encourage appropriate behavior and extinguish PNEA) (Rush, Morris, Allen, & Lathrop, 2001).

An integrative psychodynamically-based approach is presented in detail by Howlett & Reuber (2009), along with three case examples. Their approach augments psychodynamic interpersonal therapy with CBT, somatic trauma therapy, and family involvement to target changes in unhealthy relational patterns and more effective processing of emotions. They report preliminary findings of improvement in 50 percent of their cases on at least one outcome measure.

Outcome. This is variable though generally poor without treatment, with high rates of ongoing disability. Poor outcome is associated with anger at the diagnosis, chronicity of the symptoms, ongoing abuse, important secondary gains (including litigation), personality disorder, and a somatization disorder diagnosis. Better outcome is associated with a conversion disorder diagnosis, younger age, shorter duration of illness, higher education, having many friends currently or in childhood, acceptance of the diagnosis, and psychotherapy. Full symptom remission rates for patients who pursue treatment range from approximately 30 to 80 percent, while general improvement ranges up to 100 percent. (Carton, Thompson, & Duncan, 2003; Ettinger, Dhoon, Weisbrot, & Devinsky, 1999; Reuber et al., 2003; Thompson, Osorio, & Hunter, 2005).

ABOUT THE AUTHORS

William H. Watson, PhD, is associate professor of psychiatry (psychology) and neurology, a member of the senior training faculty of the University of Rochester Institute for the Family and a family psychologist with the Strong Epilepsy Center in the Department of Neurology. He is an AAMFT Clinical Member and Approved Supervisor, a past president of the Society of Family Psychology/APA Division 43, and APA's 2009 Family Psychologist of the Year. His area of interests include a family systems understanding of mind/body problems, spirituality in family therapy, family systems in the workplace, and couples therapy.

John T. Langfitt, PhD, ABPP, is associate professor of Neurology and Psychiatry at the University of Rochester School of Medicine. He has been the clinical neuropsychologist and coordinator of psychosocial services at the Strong Epilepsy Center since 1991. His clinical, research and teaching career has focused on the psychosocial effects of seizure disorders and their treatments.

RESOURCES FOR PRACTITIONERS

Barsky, A. J. & Deans, E. C. (2006). *Stop being your symptoms and start being yourself: A 6-week mind-body program to ease your chronic symptoms.* New York: Collins. A Harvard professor of Psychiatry presents a program for overcoming medically intractable chronic symptoms of all kinds by reducing obsession with negative feelings and somatic preoccupations, and focusing on living well.

Griffith, J. L., & Griffith, M. E. (1994). *The body speaks: Therapeutic dialogues for mind–body problems.* New York: Basic Books. Presents a narrative approach to the treatment of mind-body problems with specific focus on PNEA. Mind-body problems often arise from struggling with an "unspeakable dilemma" (damned if you do, damned if you don't, and damned if you talk about it). Treatment involves helping client and family to speak the unspeakable and escape the influences of binding self-narratives.

Sarno, J. E. (2006) *The divided mind: The epidemic of mindbody disorders.* New York: HarperCollins. A noted expert on mind-body problems, Sarno traces the history of psychosomatic medicine, including Freud's important contribution, and describes the dynamics that give rise to psychosomatic illness.

Schachter, S.C. & LaFrance, W.C. (Eds.). (2010). *Gates and Rowan's Nonepileptic Seizures with DVD (Cambridge Medicine)*(3rd Ed). New York: Cambridge University Press. A comprehensive multidisciplinary textbook on the subject, focusing in particular on management and treatment, including family therapy approaches and collaborative healthcare. Includes seizure videos on dvd.

Schubiner, H. (2010). *Unlearn your pain: A 28 day process to reprogram your brain.* Pleasant Ridge, MI: Mind Body Publishing. Presents a 4-week journaling- and meditation-based intervention for psychogenic pain that shows promise for mind-body problems in general, including PNEA, especially given reports of coexisting chronic pain or fibromyalgia in up to 75% of PNEA patients (Benbadis, 2005). Schubiner reports an 80% success rate for patients completing his program.

Woolfolk, R.L. & Allen, L.A. (2007). *Treating somatization: A cognitive-behavioral approach.* New York: Guilford. Includes both a comprehensive framework for understanding mind-body problems and a 10-session treatment manual for clinicians.

REFERENCES

Alper, K., Devinsky, O., Perrine, K., Vazquez, B., & Luciano, D. (1993). Nonepileptic seizures and childhood sexual and physical abuse. *Neurology, 43*(10), 1950-1953.

Baker, G. A., Brooks, J. L., Goodfellow, L., Bodde, N., & Aldenkamp, A. (2007). Behavioural treatments for non-epileptic attack disorder. *Cochrane database of systematic reviews.* Retrieved August 25, 2010, from http://www.cochrane.org/reviews/en/ab006370.html

Bakvis, P., Spinhoven, P., Giltay, E. J., Kuyk, J., Edelbroek, P. M., Zitman, F. G. et al., (2010). Basal hypercortisolism and trauma in patients with psychogenic nonepileptic seizures. *Epilepsia, 51*(5), 752-759.

Benbadis, S. R. M. (2010). Psychogenic nonepileptic "seizures" or "attacks"?: It's not just semantics: Attacks. *Neurology, 75,* 84-86.

Benbandis, S. R. M. (2005). A spell in the epilepsy clinic and a history of "chronic

pain" or "fibromyalgia" independently predict a diagnosis of psychogenic seizures. *Epilepsy & Behavior, 6,* 264-265.

Binzer, M., Stone, J., & Sharpe, M. (2004). Recent onset pseudoseizures—clues to
aetiology. *Seizure, 13*(3), 146-155.

Bowman, E. S., & Markand, O. N. (2005). The diagnosis and treatment of pseudoseizures. Psychiatric annals, 35(4), 306-317.

Carton, S., Thompson, P. J., & Duncan, J. S. (2003). Non-epileptic seizures: Patients' understanding and reaction to the diagnosis and impact on outcome.
Seizure, 12, 287-294.

Ettinger A. B., Dhoon A., Weisbrot D. M., Devinsky O., (1999) Predictive factors
for outcome of nonepileptic seizures after diagnosis. *The journal of neuropsychiatry and clinical neuroscience, 11,* 458-463.

Farias S. T., Thieman C., Alsaadi T. M., (2003) Psychogenic nonepileptic seizures:
acute change in event frequency after presentation of the diagnosis. *Epilepsy &
behavior, 4*(4), 424-429.

Fiszman, A., ves-Leon, S. V., Nunes, R. G., D'Andrea, I., & Figueira, I. (2004).
Traumatic events and posttraumatic stress disorder in patients with psychogenic
nonepileptic seizures: A critical review. *Epilepsy & behavior, 5*(6), 818-825.

Ford, C. V. (1977). A type of disability neurosis: The humpty dumpty syndrome.
International Journal of psychiatry in medicine, 8, 285-294.

Goldstein, L.H., Chalder, T, Chigwedere, C., Khondoker, M.R., Moriarty, J., Toone,
B.K., & Mellers, J.D.C. (2010). Cognitive-behavioral therapy for psychogenic
nonepileptic seizures. *Neurology, 74,* 1986-1994.

Griffith, J., Polles, A., Griffith, M. E., (1998) Pseudoseizures, families, and unspeakable dilemmas. Psychosomatics: *Journal of consultation liaison psychiatry, 39*(2),
144-153.

Griffith, J. L., & Griffith, M. E. (1994). *The body speaks: Therapeutic dialogues for
mind–body problems.* New York: Basic Books.

Holman, N., Kirkby, A., Duncan, S., & Brown, R. J. (2008). Adult attachment style
and childhood interpersonal trauma in non-epileptic attack disorder. *Epilepsy
research, 79*(1), 84-89.

Howlett, S., & Reuber, M. (2009). An augmented model of brief psychodynamic interpersonal therapy for patients with nonepileptic seizures. *Psychotherapy: Theory,
research, practice, training, 46*(1), 125–138.

Kozlowska, K. (2001). Good children presenting with conversion disorder. *Clinical
child psychology and psychiatry, 6*(4), 575-591.

Kozlowska, K. (2003). Good Children with Conversion Disorder: Breaking the
Silence *Clinical child psychology and psychiatry, 8*(1), 1359–1045.

LaFrance, W. C., & Barry, J. J. (2005). Update on treatments of psychological non-
epileptic seizures. *Epilepsy & behavior, 7,* 364-374.

LaFrance, W. C., Miller, I. W., Ryan, C. E.; Blum, A., Solomon, D. A.; Kelley, J.E.,
& Keitner, G. I. (2009). Cognitive behavioral therapy for psychogenic nonepileptic seizures. *Epilepsy & behavior, 14*(4), 591-596.

Langfitt, J. T. (2007). A systems perspective on mind–body disorders: A case example
of psychogenic non-epileptic attacks (PNEA), *The family psychologist, 23*(1), 4-6.

Marchetti, R. L., Kurcgant, D., Neto, J. G., von Bismark, M. A., Marchetti, L. B., &
Fiore, L. A. (2008). Psychiatric diagnoses of patients with psychogenic non-
epileptic seizures. *Seizure, 17*(3), 247-253.

Martin, R. C., Gilliam, F. G., Kilgore, M., Faught, E., & Kuzniecky, R. (1998). Improved health care resource utilization following video-EEG-confirmed diagno-

sis of nonepileptic psychogenic seizures. *Seizure, 7*(5), 385-390.

McDaniel, S. H., Campbell, T. L., Hepworth, J. & Lorenz, A. (2004). Chapter 2: How families affect illness: Research on the family's influence on health. In *Family-oriented primary care: A manual for medical providers* (2nd Ed.)(pp. 16-27). New York, Springer.

McDaniel, S. H., Campbell, T. L., Hepworth, J. & Lorenz, A. (2004). Chapter 19: Integrating the mind-body split: A biopsychosocial approach to somatic fixation. In S.H. McDaniel, T.L. Campbell, J. Hepworth, & A. Lorenz (Eds.), *Family-oriented primary care: A manual for medical providers* (2nd Ed.)(pp. 326-345). New York: Springer-Verlag.

McDaniel, S. H., Hepworth, J., Doherty, W. (1995). Medical family therapy with somatizing patients: The co-creation of therapeutic stories. In D. D. Lusterman, S. H. McDaniel, & R. H. Mikesell, (Eds.), *Integrating family therapy: Handbook of family psychology and systems therapy* (pp. 377-388). Washington, DC: American Psychological Association.

Reuber, M. (2009). The etiology of psychogenic non-epileptic seizures: Toward a biopsychosocial model. *Neurologic Clinics, 27*(4), 909-924.

Reuber, M. & Elger, C. E. (2003). Psychogenic nonepileptic seizures: Review and update. *Epilepsy & behavior, 4*(3), 205-216.

Reuber, M., Fernandez, G., Bauer, J., Helmstaedter, C., & Elger, C. E. (2002). Diagnostic delay in psychogenic nonepileptic seizures. *Neurology, 58*(3), 493-495.

Reuber, M., Pukrop, R., Bauer, J., Helmstaedter, C., Tessendorf,N., & Elger, C. E. (2003). Outcome in psychogenic nonepileptic seizures: 1 to 10-year follow-up in 164 patients. *Annals of neurology, 53*(3), 305-311.

Rush, M. D., Morris, G. L., Allen, L., & Lathrop, L. (2001). Psychological treatment of nonepileptic events. *Epilepsy & Behavior, 2*, 277-283.

Thompson, N. C., Osorio, I., Hunter, E. E. (2005). Nonepileptic seizures: reframing the diagnosis. *Perspectives in psychiatric care, 41*(2), 71-78.

Watson, W. (2007). Bridging the mind–body split: Towards an integrative framework for thinking about somatoform symptoms. *The family psychologist, 23*(1), 1, 30-33.

Watson, W. & McDaniel, S. (2000). Rational therapy in medical settings: Working with somatizing patients and their families. *JCLP/In session: Psychotherapy in practice, 56*(8), 1065-1082.

Wood, B. L., McDaniel, S., Burchfiel, K., & Erba, G. (1998). Factors distinguishing families of patients with psychogenic seizures from families of patients with epilepsy, *Epilepsia, 39*(4), 432-437.

Sexual Health

Katherine M. Hertlein, PhD & Gerald R. Weeks, PhD

Originally published as Clinical Update in Family Therapy Magazine
March-April 2009

THE BIRDS AND BEES OF SEXUAL HEALTH

Sexual health is an important concept that directly and indirectly affects the lives of individuals, couples, and families. Those described as "sexually healthy" are considered to have a physically and emotionally enjoyable sexual life. The World Health Organization (2006) defined sexual health as: "the integration of the physical, emotional, intellectual and social aspects of sexual being, in ways that are positively enriching and that enhance personality, communication and love." Contained in this definition is the concept that sexual health affects and is affected by several aspects of a person's life, such as sexual development, sexual functioning, physiology, emotions, relationship satisfaction, intimacy, and love.

Although sexual health affects many areas of one's life, clients and marriage and family therapists (MFTs) may not make sexual health a priority. Some therapists believe they have limited knowledge to discuss concerns related to sexual health. This could be due to the fact that many MFTs do not receive specialized training in sex therapy during the course of their graduate work; likewise, sex therapy training may not include detailed education on how to provide couples therapy (Hertlein, Weeks, & Gambescia, 2008; Weeks, 2005). Further, as the treatment of sexual problems becomes more medicalized (Hertlein et al., 2008; Lieblum, 2007), MFTs may not feel that they have the adequate medical training to pursue medical options or obtain information regarding physiological etiology and treatment of a particular problem. Finally, couples may have fears that impair their ability to put sexual health at the forefront. These include fears of intimacy, anger, abandonment, and other feelings (Hertlein, Weeks, & Sendak, 2009). With a fear of intimacy, for example, the couple's overall sexual health is compromised because attempts to move toward sexual interaction would increase the likelihood of the feared object: intimacy.

MFTs and other systemically-trained therapists are capable of addressing the complex interaction of physical, emotional, intellectual, and social aspects in the promotion of sexual health. For example, MFTs can assist adolescents who have misguided notions regarding contraception, which can directly influence their decision-making regarding sexual health behaviors. MFTs can also help some couples understand the extent to which imbalances in the couple's power dynamic or fears of intimacy limit their ability to achieve overall sexual health.

There are several approaches/treatment models that are designed to help a couple achieve optimal sexual health. Treating sexual dysfunctions was originally handled from a psychoanalytic perspective, because it was believed that sexual symptomatology was derived from an underlying problem, which required long-term, intensive individual treatment (Wiederman, 1998). As the behavioral models began to take prominence in the late 1960s and early 1970s, treatment for sexual dysfunction followed suit. Kaplan's (1974) approach is primarily behavioral and in many ways was similar to that of Masters and Johnson (1966), in terms of the individually-oriented thinking that pervaded the Masters and Johnson approach. Kaplan did offer a psychodynamic overlay in her approach and was, therefore, exploring the problems from a depth perspective, similar to that of the early sex therapists. It was often difficult, however, to understand how the psychodynamic perspective added to her behavioral emphasis or created greater change (Kaplan, 1974).

Cognitive behavioral therapies (CBT) have also been utilized in the treatment of sexual problems. McCabe (2001) found that a CBT approach to treatment improves attitudes about sex, believed sex was more enjoyable than prior to treatment, and experienced improvement in the dysfunction. Some elements of the cognitive behavioral approach include communication training (including verbalization of feelings, active versus passive listening, and effectively managing conflict), reducing performance anxiety, and prescribing sensate focus activities (see, for example, McCabe, 2008).

Trepper, Treyger, Yalowitz, and Ford (2008) outlined a solution-focused sex therapy approach. In this framework, the therapist helps the client focus on small steps leading to big changes, using "solution-talk," focusing on the present and future, and the search for exceptions and emphasis on solutions. This approach can be very powerful with sex therapy clients because of the overwhelming sense of negativity and failure they experience. Many of these couples chastise themselves for not being able to do what they perceive comes naturally to others. This negative belief about themselves, paired with unsuccessful sexual interactions, creates a heavily problem-saturated environment around the sexual problem, burdening the couple and making movement toward resolution extremely difficult.

Finally, there are approaches that integrate cognitive, behavioral, psychodynamic, and couple components. The Intersystems Approach is one such approach and incorporates the variety of contexts in which the individual and couple are embedded. Conceptualized as a vulnerability model (i.e., assessing several areas of vulnerability to sexual problems) (see, for example, Trepper

& Barrett, 1989) and grounded in the Intersystems approach developed by Weeks (1994) and outlined in detail by Hertlein et al. (2008), helping couples attain optimal sexual health includes assessment and treatment across five dimensions: individual-psychological, individual-biological, dyadic, family-of-origin, and sociocultural. In this approach, these domains help clients develop and maintain a positive, respectful approach to sex and sexuality. The Intersystems Approach grew out of the early theoretical thinking of Weeks (1977) and was refined over many years. The approach was first applied to sex therapy by Weeks and Hof and later in books by Weeks and Gambescia (2000; 2002). The Intersystems Approach moves beyond technical eclecticism to a comprehensive theory, which can embrace multiple theoretical perspectives. While the approach itself has not been empirically validated, the factors contributing to each component of the theory (i.e., individual biology, individual psychology, etc.) has at least one supporting piece of research (see Hertlein et al., 2008, for specific references). Thus, if you examine the individual, interactional, and intergenerational aspects of each system, you will find there is research that supports each component. Logically, it would follow that if a problem is maintained by several factors that are determined during assessment, then the treatment of each of those factors would be essential to recovery or improvement.

Though there are many clinical models, there are few empirically validated approaches to treatment (Heiman & Meston, 1997a). Of the studies reviewed by Heiman and Meston, some approached validation, but not had any long-term data and the short-term data showed a high relapse rate. This is likely due to several reasons:

- The youth of the field of sex therapy (Wiederman, 1998)
- Few certified sex therapists (approximately 444 certified sex therapists in the U.S., per www.aasect.com, most of which are in practice
- Treatment manuals are uncommon (Heiman & Meston, 1997a)
- Lack of control groups (Heiman & Meston, 1997a)
- Limited research funding (Heiman & Meston, 1997a)

These factors make it virtually impossible to research the effectiveness of sex therapy. As usual, clinical practice runs ahead of the science or empirical validation.

DIAGNOSIS AND ASSESSMENT

Because sexual health encompasses both physical and emotional well being, MFTs have a distinct advantage in forming a diagnostic impression from a systemic perspective, including how individual, interpersonal, and contextual dimensions contribute to sexual health concerns. The traditional view of treating sexual problems is individualistic and behavioral, whereas our perspective is clearly systemic, resulting in a comprehensive assessment and treatment experience. The DSM-IV-TR (APA, 2000) based its definition of problematic sexual behavior on the Masters and Johnson (1966) human sexual response cycle. The sexual dysfunctions listed in the DSM-IV-TR are "characterized by a disturbance in the processes that characterize the sexual response cycle or by pain associated with sexual intercourse" (APA, 2000, p. 535). Sexual dysfunctions are classified as being in one of four categories (see Table 1).

One way to identify the extent to which the sexual health problem stems

TABLE 1

Disorder	DSM Code	Diagnosis (from DSM-IV-TR) "Persistent or recurrent..."
Sexual Aversion Disorder	302.79	Extreme aversion to, and avoidance of, all (or almost all) genital sexual contact with a sexual partner
Hypoactive Sexual Desire Disorder	302.71	Deficient (or absent) sexual fantasies and desire for sexual activity.
Female Sexual Arousal Disorder	302.72	Inability to attain, or to maintain until completion of sexual activity, an ad equate lubrication-swelling response of sexual excitement
Male Erectile Disorder	302.72	Inability to attain, or maintain until completion of sexual activity, an adequate erection.
Female Orgasmic Disorder	302.73	Delay in, or absence of, orgasm following a normal sexual excitement phase.
Male Orgasmic Disorder	302.74	Delay in, or absence of, orgasm following a normal sexual excitement phase during sexual activity that the clinician, taking into account the person's age, judges to be adequate in focus, intensity and duration
Premature Ejaculation	302.75	Ejaculation with minimal sexual stimulation before, on, or shortly after penetration and before the person wishes it.
Dyspareunia	302.76	Genital pain associated with sexual intercourse in either a male or a female.
Vaginismus	306.51	Involuntary spasm of the musculature of the outer third of the vagina that interferes with sexual intercourse.

from organic or psychological factors is through using the specifiers as outlined in the DSM-IV-TR (APA, 2000). Sexual dysfunctions identified as "lifelong" are those that the client describes as being present since her earliest sexual activity. For example, some clients may report they have never experienced an orgasm in any context or with any partner. Such a case might suggest that the sexual dysfunction may be associated with a longer-term health issue or physiological characteristic. Similarly, cases where the sexual dysfunction seems to occur in every situation (generalized) may point to a different etiology than a situational specifier. For example, one of our clients found himself to be unable to obtain an erection with his wife, but could with his affair partner. This suggests that the erectile problem was situational and that treatment could focus more heavily on issues pertaining to his relationship with his wife.

Other Diagnostic Considerations. One of the challenges about sexual dysfunction and diagnosis of sexual health problems is the extent to which the symptomatology meets the DSM-IV-TR (APA, 2000) diagnostic criteria. One diagnostic item is that the condition results in "marked distress" (APA, 2000, p. 541). This is an important consideration for those cases where the symptomatology does not meet the criteria for a diagnosis with the existing DSM-IV-TR (APA, 2000) categories, but still produces distress for the client (Nathan, 2003). Specifically, the DSM-IV-TR focuses on the more traditional sexual dysfunctions rather than problems such as too little foreplay, little affection, afterplay, variety, etc. One early research team showed that minor problems produced more marital distress than some of the major problems (Frank, Anderson, & Rubenstein, 1978). Our theory about why this might be true is that the major problems are perceived as out of the person's control. For example, a couple might believe one partner strongly desires to have an erection, but is unable to because of health reasons or medication. The "minor problems" such as choosing an inconvenient time or too little foreplay are usually perceived as being under voluntary control. In one case, a wife told her husband many times she was not a "morning person" and did not want to have sex in the morning. He only approached her in the mornings for sex and never at night. This type of problem does not require a sex therapist but is an ideal problem for an MFT to treat. MFTs should review the presenting sexual problems that may not qualify as an Axis I dysfunction, but do produce similar levels of distress (i.e., varying levels of sexual desire or different ideas about turn-ons). Some options for diagnosis in this factor are discussed later.

In many cases, the distress is not individual or intrapsychic, but interpersonal. In fact, in our experience, many couples present with sexual problems because it is the partner without the "problem" who is upset. This can occur when there are different expectations of the sexual relationship or sexual behavior, different learning histories, role changes, or others. It is incumbent upon the therapist to identify to what extent, if any, there is a discrepancy in the couple's report regarding the problem and identify whether the distress is experienced by the individual or couple.

Comorbidity. Frequently, sexual health concerns also co-occur with chronic illness, physical conditions, mental health problems, mood/anxiety disorders, and/or substance abuse problems. Depression can contribute to a variety of sexual problems, including hypoactive sexual desire disorder (HSD), dyspareunia, and erectile dysfunction, to name a few. Other sexual problems such as painful intercourse and erectile dysfunction may increase the likelihood of the development of HSD (Weeks, Hertlein, & Gambescia, 2008). A classic example involves a couple experiencing an erectile problem. A husband, significantly older than his wife, was taking multiple heart medications. He found that when he tried to have intercourse, he failed to obtain an erection and consequently began to avoid sexual interactions in order to avoid the feeling of failure and of disappointing his partner. His wife's interpretation of his hesitation to engage in sexual activity, however, was that he simply lacked desire for her (not an uncommon interpretation in couples). A single therapy session cleared up this misinterpretation and initiated the process of how to have sex more effectively. In this case, the wife was convinced that his erection problem demonstrated he was losing sexual interest in her. It was critical that she be educated on the following: (1) erections and desire are not necessarily the same; (2) given her partner's age, medical problems, medications, and rapidly increasing performance anxiety to please her, it was very likely he would demonstrate some erectile problem. The therapist worked with the man to help him understand that it was essential that he verbalize his desire for her and to take enough Viagra to overcome his medical condition. The most important element of this session, however, was that they both knew the other still felt strong desire, which for them was equated with love and commitment.

Men with a unique physiological composition or illnesses such as diabetes, epilepsy, and multiple sclerosis may be more vulnerable to erectile dysfunction, but negative cognitions and performance anxiety also contribute (Betchen, 2008). Patients with certain types of cancer may be more prone to arousal and desire problems for both physical reasons (e.g., damage to sexual organs) (Seagraves & Balon, 2003) or psychological reasons (e.g., body image concerns) (Waldman & Eliasof, 1997). Therefore, MFTs need to conceptualize and treat the problem within the entire client context and research how sexual problems stem from or contribute to other issues. There may be a reciprocal relationship between the level of relationship satisfaction and sexual problems. For an overview of the individual biological and psychological factors related to each sexual dysfunction, see Hertlein et al. (2008).

Multiaxial Diagnosis from the Intersystems Perspective. In many cases, problems with one's sexual health are exacerbated by relationship difficulties, such as power imbalances, resentments, or communication concerns. With this etiology, traditional behavioral non-systemic prescriptions will not change the sexual problem. Our preference is to treat the couple problems first and then move on, or begin to phase in, the treatment of sexual problems (Guay et al., 2003). A couple locked in conflict, or one that has intimacy problems, which are expressed via sex, will fail to respond to the traditional approach of giving sensual/sexual prescriptions. Once again, the systemically-oriented therapist

FIGURE 1

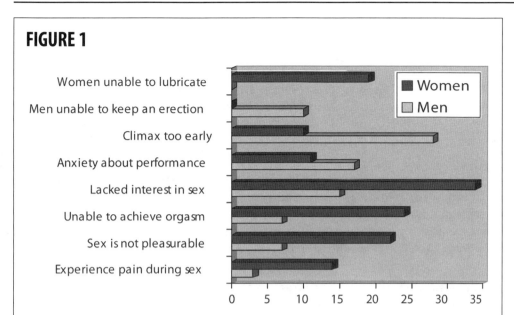

Percentage of population

Figure 1 shows the frequency of sexual dysfunction in the general population in the U.S. This study is fairly consistent with other studies that have been conducted. This research team and others have demonstrated that almost every couple coming to therapy has a high probability of having a major sexual problem.

Laumann, E. O., Gagnon, J. H., Michael, R. T., & Michaels, S. (1994). The social organization of sexuality: Sexual practices in the United States. Chicago: University of Chicago Press. (p. 369)

has the advantage over the behaviorally/individually-oriented therapist due to the more comprehensive perspective.

In same-sex relationships, there are other considerations. In addition to the assessment of how individual, interactional, and intergenerational factors play a part in the development and maintenance of a sexual problem, MFTs should attend to the problems of heteronormativity and internalized oppression (Hertlein et al., 2009) and recognize that heteronormativity underlies the diagnostic categories in the DSM. For example, the sexual pain disorders refer to pain during intercourse, which eliminates lesbian women who experience pain under other circumstances (Hertlein et al., 2009). Other factors specific to same-sex relationships that need to be considered are lack of education, HIV status discrepancies, and therapists should also be aware that their knowledge and any countertransference issues about same-sex relationships can affect the treatment process (Bettinger, 2004; Nichols, 1989).

There are several authors who outline how to conduct sex therapy for same-sex couples. Reece (1988), George and Behrendt (1987), and Carballo-Diéguez and Reimen (2001) identified specific interventions for working with same-sex couples, such as therapist education and awareness of own values,

WORKING WITH THE CHRONICALLY ILL

Therapists should be vigilant for clients who have been diagnosed with chronic illness and are experiencing sexual problems. There are several illnesses that affect sexual functioning, including (but not limited to): Parkinson 's disease (Yu, Roane, Miner, Fleming, & Rogers, 2004), Multiple Sclerosis (Smeltzer & Kelley, 1997), stroke (Monga & Kerrigan, 1997), cancer (Waldman & Eliasof, 1997), diabetes (Schover & Jensen, 1988), and cardiac concerns (Schover & Jensen, 1988).

Physical consequences of illness. Physical consequences of experiencing chronic illness can include a range of sexual issues, including loss of desire, arousal problems, orgasm problems, erectile dysfunction in men (Schover & Jensen, 1988; Tilton, 1997), and dyspareunia in women. For some illnesses such as cancer, women may experience lubrication difficulties (Schover & Jensen, 1988) and changes in genital sensation. There may be changes in the motor system that can make sexual acts more difficult (rigidity, tremors, etc). Another issue may be the greater occurrence of genitourinary infections.

Physical consequences of pharmacotherapy treatments. While pharmocological treatments for physical and mental illnesses frequently address the disorder and reduce symptomatology, these medications may have unintended sexual side effects. Seagraves and Balon (2003) reviewed the side effects of medications, and therapists should have this book on hand as a reference guide in order to understand how medications are impacting the sexual clinical picture. Heiman and Meston (1997b) noted that there are three principal ways medications affect sexual functioning: peripherally, centrally, and hormonally. Common consequences appear to be delayed/inhibited orgasm, impaired sexual desire (more common with SSRIs as opposed to MAOIs) (Heiman & Meston, 1997b). Further, some of the sexual side effects of antipsychotic medications include reduced desire and orgasm problems, though such effects could be related to the extrapyramidal side effects of antipsychotics and the likely lowered sexual functioning prior to the illness (Heiman & Meston, 1997b). Hormone therapy may also result in diminished desire and

addressing internalized homophobia, and specific sexual strategies. Further, Reece (1987), Hall (1987), and Bettinger (2004) each developed frameworks for treating same-sex couples with sexual problems. Bettinger's approach is systemic and was developed for gay male couples; Hall's approach is for lesbian couples and includes looking at the larger contexts in which the couple is embedded; Reece's (1987) framework is directed toward gay couples experiencing discrepancies in sexual desire.

The Intersystems approach provides a framework for therapists to consider both the physical as well as dyadic concerns, which are impairing a couple's sexual health. The severity of the relationship problem and the extent to which it impacts sexual health will be a critical component to the course of treatment (Hertlein et al., 2009) and therefore should be reflected in the multiaxial diagnosis. Relational diagnostic codes most frequently used by sex therapists include Partner Relational Problem or Physical/Sexual Abuse of an Adult (V61.1), Relational Problem Related to a Mental Disorder or General Medical Condition (V61.9), or Relational Problem (V62.89).

Because "sexual health" is an all-encompassing term relating to one's physical, social, and emotional well being, MFTs should account for each axis

---

WORKING WITH THE CHRONICALLY ILL (continued)

arousal for both men and women. For men, treatments for prostate cancer that involve reducing the testosterone level as low as possible frequently reduce desire and arousal. Retrograde ejaculation can be a side effect of some treatments. In cases where there is surgery because of damage to important nerves, there may be reduced sensation as well as impaired erectile ability for men and lubricating capacity for women. For women, healing from pelvic or genital surgery can cause scar tissue, reducing the size and shape of the vagina, and result in dyspareunia.

Psychological consequences. Psychosocial factors have been identified as contributing to sexual dysfunctions in populations discussed above with chronic illness, including relationship dissatisfaction, depression, and body image concerns (Waldman & Eliasof, 1997). After a period of suspended sexual activity, anticipatory anxiety can fuel the loss of desire, creating a self-fulfilling belief that spirals into further sexual difficulty. Pelvic or genital surgery can also have a psychological impact, in that patients may question their gender and sexual identities.

Treatment considerations. MFTs need to be vigilant about the presence of illness as a contributing factor of sexual problems for a couple by conducting a thorough history. For many clients, they need to be reassured that normal or near normal functioning will return, but they need to be patient and find other means of sexual expression until that time. For other clients who will not have the opportunity to return to normal functioning, the therapist and couple can develop alternate ways to demonstrate sexuality. This involves being creative about sexual behavior and their definition of intimacy. Further, MFTs need to be aware of the importance of collaboration between therapists and the primary care or specialist treating the patient for this concern. Many of our clients do not report their sexual health concerns to their physicians because of embarrassment and shame. Collaboration allows the most effective course of treatment to be implemented.

---

in their diagnosis. In order to promote sexual health, therapists should attend to all aspects which might be affecting one's sexual life. Assessment via the Intersystems Approach as described by Hertlein et al. (2008) and Hertlein et al. (2009) highlighted the manner in which relationship dynamics, emotional contracts, communication patterns, messages from family-of-origin, and sociocultural pressures all precipitate, contribute to, or exacerbate the sexual problem.

TREATMENT/BIOMEDICAL INTERVENTIONS

There are a wide variety of specific interventions, techniques, and resources that are used in sex therapy. Seasoned MFTs may be familiar with the more commonly utilized techniques, such as sensate focus (Lazarus, 1965), implementing relaxation strategies, using medications, teaching sexual skills, and others. The breadth of interventions can be classified into three categories: behavioral, biomedical, and systemic, and are outlined as follows.

Behavioral Treatments. Sex therapy has its roots in behavioral interventions. The names associated with the origin of sex therapy include Masters

---

and Johnson (1970), Heiman and LoPiccolo (1988), Kaplan (1974), and Rimm and Masters (1974), who based their treatment approach on the assumption that sexual problems are the result of several faulty conditionings, including: faulty learning, misinformation, lack of education, negative attitudes about sex, and limited sexual experience. Behavioral interventions include such activities as homework assignments (Leiblum & Rosen, 2000; Wincze & Carey, 1991), communication training, and education. In general, there was little appreciation of the numerous systemic factors that could precipitate and maintain sexual problems (Weeks, 2005). Frequently, the use of relational or psychodynamic techniques occurred when the behavioral interventions were not effective (Kaplan, 1974). As aforementioned, however, the paucity of research and empirical-based sex therapy treatment warrants further investigation to determine if relational treatment for sexual health concerns is still secondary to individually based care today.

Sensate focus is a behavioral intervention where a couple systematically becomes desensitized to sexual stimuli as a way to reduce anxiety surrounding intercourse (Lazarus, 1965). It was introduced by Masters and Johnson (1970) and refined by Kaplan (1974). In general, the therapist begins by working with the couple to identify any barriers toward engaging in sensate focus activities. Once any barriers have been removed, treatment focuses on moving the couple forward incrementally toward experiencing varying degrees of sexual pleasuring through non-anxious situations. Typically, couples are asked to participate in sensate focus-related homework activities three times per week, with a processing period after each activity to detail what was pleasurable and focus on how each partner communicated to the other. Eventually, the couple gradually moves from positive, non-genital touching experiences to intercourse. See Weeks and Gambescia (2008) for a further discussion of how to conduct systemic sensate focus work.

Biomedical Treatments. Recently, many pharmaceutical companies have worked to address the problem of sexual dysfunction through pharmacological treatments. The development of Viagra® (sildenafil) in 1998 dramatically shifted the sex therapy field toward a medical intervention orientation. Since its development, other companies began to develop comparable medications to stake their claim on this issue, such as Levitra® (vardenafil) and Cialis® (tadalafil) (Verhulst & Reynolds, 2008). In short, there are many pharmaceutical options to assist men with their erectile problems, and these problems are seen as strictly medical problems that can be corrected via pharmaceuticals rather than marriage and family therapy or systemic sex therapy (Ridley, 2008; Verhulst & Reynolds, 2008). Another treatment approach for men is testosterone replacement therapy, particularly if they suffer from a low level of the hormone. As a result of continued medical developments, individuals experiencing these sexual problems may pursue medical solutions rather than therapeutic approaches (Ridley, 2008; Weeks & Gambescia, 2000). However, this does not allow for an understanding of the sexual problem as something that may be caused by other problems.

Drug companies have been working to develop solutions to address the other factors in sexual health, including medications that are designed to treat low desire. For women, such medications tend to focus on adjusting hormone levels. Estrogen therapy helps women by improving vaginal tone and elasticity, and increasing vaginal blood flow and lubrication. Progestin therapy can increase desire and arousal when paired with estrogen therapy. Androgen therapy provides male hormones to women, though the treatment can be controversial since long-term effects are unknown. Other physiological treatments for women include strengthening pelvic muscles through Kegel exercises (Hertlein et al., 2008; VandeCreek, Peterson, & Bley, 2007), consultation with a physical therapist (Meana, 2008) and herbal supplements, such as Ginkgo biloba, which can improve circulation throughout the body. However, therapists should advise clients that there can be severe risks to any supplements taken (FDA, 2006) and that many of these supplements are not approved by the FDA. Further, while there are some studies that suggest Viagra® can be effective for women, most of the research fluctuates between being inconclusive or demonstrating it is not effective. Bancroft (2002) advised that therapists exercise caution when considering the use of Viagra® for women, particularly because of the differences in sexuality between men and women and the recognition that sexuality is a complex interplay of emotions, cognitions, and other factors.

PDE-5 inhibitors (like Viagra®) should not be viewed as the solution for returning to a satisfying sex life. When the sexual problem has some of its roots in communication problems, conflict, and other relationship issues, medications will not achieve the desired end. Additionally, medical intervention focuses on an individual rather than a couple, and treatment decisions are made by the symptomatic individual. Once erection can be achieved, it may be difficult for the couple to resume the same rhythm in the sexual relationship that they had previously, particularly if there was a significant amount of time where the couple was abstinent. MFTs are trained to consider how each system is working to contribute to the problem, and there is a demonstrated need to shift to a paradigm that encompasses the systemic case conceptualization of an MFT. The Intersystems approach fills this niche. The end result is that the couple realizes that sexual problems cannot be "cured" with a pill, etc. The therapist facilitates work that resolves the complex myriad of issues that may have produced the problem as well as the distress that the problem has created for the relationship. The key for MFTs is to understand that medical alternatives are available, but to encourage the couple to conceptualize the case from an Intersystems perspective in order to pursue a wide range of treatments (behavioral, relational, etc.) for the greatest chance of success. MFTs should bear in mind that, while the medical solution may be a tempting one, physicians often do not have the time or training to discuss potential relationship factors that are complicating the sexual problem for partners, and this information is typically not included in the medical evaluation (Leiblum, 2007).

Systemic Treatments: The Intersystems Approach. Because the field of sex therapy was based on behavioral and psychodynamic interventions, there are few truly systemic treatments. Wincze and Carey (2001) outlined a model that integrates biological and psychological factors in sexual dysfunction; Borrelli-Kerner and Bernell (1997) emphasized the importance of couples' treatment in sexual cases. Yet each of these approaches falls short in consistently and completely attending to the individual, interactional, and sociocultural factors in sexual functioning, as the Intersystems Approach does. Developed by Weeks (1977) and described in detail by Weeks and Cross (2004) and Hertlein et al. (2008), its roots are in systemic theories and represents a framework that incorporates the behavioral constructs, biomedical advances, and relational components impairing one's sexual health. This framework relies on conducting assessment and treatment across five dimensions: individual-biological, individual-psychological, dyadic, family-of-origin, and sociocultural factors. Our approach guides the therapist in addressing not only the individual biological issues, which may be contributing to the problem, but also systemically attends to the psychological, emotional, and cultural factors that surround the problem. Treatment is organized around individual, interactional, and intergenerational components of a client system. See Hertlein et al. (2008) for a detailed description of how to apply the model to the sexual dysfunctions.

IMPROVING SEXUAL HEALTH

Considering sexual health from a systemic perspective, there are several specific ways we have developed to improve sexual health for clients. The first step is to conduct an assessment addressing each of the dimensions outlined in the Intersystems approach. This includes a comprehensive sexual history attending to individual dynamics, relationship satisfaction, family-of-origin factors, and socialization factors. In conducting your assessment, attend to the physical, social, emotional, sociocultural, and intellectual factors that are contributing to the vulnerabilities in sexual health. The second step is to provide education to the clients. This can involve correcting the misinformation that the couple may have, as well as providing more alternatives to sexual interaction, as a way to redefine sexual health and intimacy. Bibliotherapy and education can be very powerful adjuncts to treatment in such cases where the problem is compounded by a lack of education. Couples may hold many myths about sexuality and sexual behavior, and bibliotherapy can be one manner of helping clients separate myth from reality. Effective bibliotherapy in sex cases can include videos, books, and use of the Internet. Specific suggestions are outlined in the Resources section of this Update as well as in Hertlein et al. (2009).

The proper maintenance of sexual health can be accomplished through the prevention and/or treatment of sexual issues. MFTs need to encourage their clients to talk about their sexual health, even if the therapist experiences discomfort doing so. Years of experience show that many couples are simply reluctant to bring up sexual problems until later in treatment, if at all. If the therapist asks general questions about sexual functioning, some couples will report that their sex life is satisfactory. At some point, after establishing a relationship, the therapist can suggest to the couple that little has been said about

TERMINOLOGY

Hypoactive sexual desire disorder: hypoactive means not active or limited activity. This term in sex treatment is usually associated with desire, hence the term "hypoactive sexual desire disorder."

Dyspareunia: difficult or painful sexual intercourse. This is commonly associated with women, though men can have it as well. To be diagnosed with dyspareunia, one must have persistent and recurrent pain during and after intercourse that is not associated with a lubrication problem.

Vaginismus: painful contraction or spasm of the vagina. It is a conditioned response of the pubococcygeus muscle that prevents insertion of an object, including tampons and sexual intercourse, making penetration difficult.

Genitourinary: relating to the genital or urinary organs. The term refers to the group of organs of the urinary system and the reproductive system.

Anejaculation: failure of ejaculation of semen. This means that there is no semen from the prostate or seminal ducts into the urethra. Causes of anejaculation can include medical illnesses, injury to the spinal cord, diabetes, medication, and surgery.

Desire: the desire to engage in sexual activity, including fantasies.

Excitement: subjective sense of sexual pleasure. Physiological changes also occur during this phase, including penile tumescence and erection for men, and vaginal lubrication and swelling of the external genitalia for women.

Orgasm: defined as the peak of a sexual experience. Includes the contraction of muscles such as the anal sphincter for both men and women. In women, the vagina walls contract and in men, ejaculation of semen.

Resolution: Termination of the sexual response characterized by muscle relaxation. Men are unable to obtain a further erection or ejaculation during this time, where women can resume the cycle at any point.

sex. The therapist can then ask specific questions such as:

- Are the two of you happy with how often sex occurs?
- Do you have any problems getting or keeping an erection? (men)
- Are you able to delay ejaculation long enough so that you are both satisfied? (both partners)
- Are you both able to have an orgasm? Would you like anything to change around your ability to have an orgasm?
- Is there any pain with intercourse?

A series of specific questions may be asked if the therapist expects to get a clear picture. The questions above are just a sample and can be worded differently to fit each couple.

In couples with no apparent sexual health concerns, create a treatment plan that will encourage them to maintain their sexual health. Include strategies such as:

- Providing education and recommend bibliotherapy
- Addressing fears

- Starting slowly
- Monitoring progress

Therapists who are best trained to attend to the sexual health of a client are knowledgeable about couple therapy, sex therapy, medical sex therapy, psychology, and larger systems. Effective treatment encompasses, at a minimum, assessment in each of these areas and hopefully intervention in whatever areas difficulties exist. Because of the perception by some clients that sexual dysfunction is easily treated with medications, it is incumbent upon the therapist to explain how each of the areas may be contributing to the sexual problem, and educate the couple on treatment options for the individual, interactional, and intergenerational components.

ABOUT THE AUTHORS

Katherine M. Hertlein, PhD, is an assistant professor in the Department of Marriage and Family Therapy at the University of Nevada–Las Vegas. She received her master's in marriage and family therapy from Purdue University Calumet and her doctorate in marriage and family therapy from Virginia Tech. She is a Clinical Member of the AAMFT and a member of AASECT. She has been published in several journals and serves as reviewer for several journals. She has co-edited a book on interventions in couples treatment, interventions for clients with health concerns, and a book on infidelity treatment. Recently, Hertlein co-editedr and co-authored Systemic Sex Therapy and co-authored A Clinician's Guide to Systemic Sex Therapy. She presents nationally and internationally on sex, technology, and couples.

Gerald R. Weeks, PhD, ABPP, is professor and chair of the Department of Marriage and Family Therapy at the University of Nevada–Las Vegas. He is a licensed psychologist, Fellow, Approved Supervisor, and Clinical Member of the American Association for Marriage and Family Therapy, and is Board-Certified by the American Board of Professional Psychology and the American Board of Sexology. He has published 18 books, including the major contemporary texts in the fields of sex, marital, and family therapy. Weeks is past president of the American Board of Family Psychology and has lectured extensively throughout North American and Europe on sex, couple, and psychotherapy. He has close to 30 years of experience in practicing and supervising sex, couple, and family therapy.

RESOURCES FOR PRACTITIONERS

American Association of Sexuality Educators, Counselors and Therapists (AASECT)
www.aasect.org
A resource for client referrals, ethics information, as well as job listings, and FAQ about human sexuality.

Hertlein, K. M., Weeks, G., & Sendak, S. (2008). *A clinician's guide to systemic sex therapy*. New York: Routledge. State of the art of sex therapy from a new paradigm: an integrative or systemic framework. The chapters explore the etiology, treatment, and case examples of dysfunction from the systemic perspective.

Society for Sex Therapy and Research (SSTAR)
www.starnet.org
Provides a communication forum, newsletters, sex therapist directory, and links to helpful resources.

Society for the Scientific Study of Sexuality (SSSS)
www.sexscience.org
SSSS is an interdisciplinary organization that values quality research as well as educational, clinical and social application of sexuality, providing people access to various publications, as well as information about awards and grants that are available.

Weeks, G., & Gambescia, N. (2002). *Hypoactive sexual desire: Integrating couple and sex therapy*. New York: W. W. Norton. Presents a comprehensive treatment model for HSD based on the integration of medical and psychological interventions.

Weeks, G., & Gambescia, N. (2000). *Erectile dysfunction: Integrating couple therapy, sex therapy, and medical treatment*. New York: W. W. Norton. Presents a comprehensive treatment model for ED based on the integration of medical and psychological interventions.

REFERENCES

APA (2000). *The diagnostic and statistical manual of mental disorders: Text revision (4th ed.)*. Washington, DC: American Psychiatric Association.

Bettinger, M. (2004). A systems approach to sex therapy with gay male couples. In J. J. Binger and J. L. Wetchler (Eds.) *Relationship therapy with same-sex couples*. New York: Hawthorn Press.

Bancroft, J. (2002). The medicalization of female sexual dysfunction: The need for caution. *Archives of Sexual Behavior, 31*(5), 451-455.

Betchen, S. J. (2008). Premature ejaculation: An integrative, intersystems approach for couples. In K. Hertlein, G. Weeks, & N. Gambescia (Eds.), *Systemic sex therapy* (pp. 131-152). New York: Routledge.

Borrelli-Kerner, S., & Bernell, B. (1997). Couple therapy of sexual disorders. In R. Charlton & I. Yalom (Eds.), *Treating sexual disorders* (pp. 165-199). San Fransisco: Jossey-Bass.

Carballo-Diéguez, A., & Reimine, R. H. (2001). Sex therapy with male couples of mixed-(serodiscordant-) HIV status. In P. J. Kleinplatz (Ed.), *New directions in sex therapy: Innovations and alternatives* (pp. 302-321). New York: Brunner-Routledge.

FDA (2006). FDA Warns Consumers About Dangerous Ingredients in "Dietary Supplements" Promoted for Sexual Enhancement. Retrieved December 14, 2008, from http://www.fda.gov/bbs/topics/NEWS/2006/NEW01409.html.

Frank, E., Anderson, C., & Rubenstein, D. (1978). Frequency of sexual dysfunction in "normal" couples. *New England Journal of Medicine, 299*(3), 111-115.

George, K. D., & Behrent, A. E. (1987). Therapy for male couples experiencing relationship problems and sexual problems. *Journal of Homosexuality, 14*(3-4), 77-88.

Guay, A. T., Spark, R. F., Bansal, S., Cunningham, G. R., Nankin, H. R., Petak, S. M., et al. (2003). American Association of Clinical Endocrinologists medical guidelines for clinical practice for the evaluation and treatment of male sexual dysfunction: A couple's problem–2003 update. *Endocrine Practice, 9*(1), 77-95.

Hall, M. (1987). Sex therapy with lesbians: A four-stage approach. *Journal of Homosexuality, 14*(1-2). 137-156.

Heiman, J. R., & LoPiccolo, J. (1988). *Becoming orgasmic: A sexual and personal growth program for women.* New York: Prentice Hall.

Heiman, J., & Meston, C. (1997a). Empirically validated treatment for sexual dysfunction. *Annual Review of Sex Research, 8,* 148-194.

Heiman, J., & Meston, C. (1997b). Evaluating sexual dysfunction in women. *Clinical Obstetrics and Gynecology, 40*(3), 616-629.

Hertlein, K. M., Weeks, G. R., & Gambescia, N. (2008). *Systemic sex therapy.* New York: Routledge.

Hertlein, K. M., Weeks, G. R., & Sendak, S. (2009). *A clinician's guide to systemic sex therapy.* New York: Routledge.

Kaplan, H. S. (1974). *The new sex therapy.* New York: Brunner/Mazel.

Lazarus, A. A. (1965). The treatment of a sexually inadequate man. In L. P. Ullmann and L. Krasner (Eds.) *Case studies in behavior modification.* New York: Holt.

Lieblum, S. R. (2007). Sex therapy today. In S. Lieblum (Ed.), *Principles and practice of sex therapy* (4th ed.). New York: Guilford Press.

Lieblum, S., & Rosen, R. (2000). *Principles and practice of sex therapy* (3rd ed.). New York: Guilford Press.

Masters, W., & Johnson, V. E. (1970). *Human sexual inadequacy.* New York: Bantam Books.

Masters, W., & Johnson, V. E. (1966). *Human sexual response.* New York: Bantam Books.

McCabe, M. P. (2008). Anorgasmia in women. In K. Hertlein, G. Weeks, & N. Gambescia (Eds.), *Systemic sex therapy* (pp. 211-236). New York: Routledge.

McCabe, M. P. (2001). Evaluation of a cognitive behavior therapy program for people with sexual dysfunction. *Journal of Sex & Marital Therapy, 27,* 259-71.

Meana, M. (2008). Painful intercourse: Dyspareunia and vaginismus. In K. Hertlein, G. Weeks, & N. Gambescia (Eds.), *Systemic sex therapy* (pp. 237-261). New York: Routledge.

Monga, T. N., & Kerrigan, A. J. (1997). Cerebrovascular accidents. In M. L. Sipski & C. J. Alexander (Eds.), *Sexual function in people with disability and chronic illness: A health professional's guide* (pp. 189-220). Gaithersburg, MD: Aspen.

Nathan, S. G. (2003). When do we say a woman's sexuality is dysfunctional? In S. B. Levine (Ed.), *Handbook of clinical sexuality* (pp. 95-110). New York: Brunner-Routledge.

Nichols, M. (1989). Sex therapy with lesbians, gay men, and bisexuals. In S. R. Leiblum and R. C. Rosen (Eds.), *Principles and practice of sex therapy: Updated for the 1990s* (2nd ed). (pp. 269-297). New York: Guilford Press.

Reece, R. (1988). Special issues in the etiology and treatments of sexual problems among gay men. *Journal of Homosexuality, 15*(1-2), 43-57.

Reece, R. (1987). Causes and treatments of sexual desire discrepancies in male couples. *Journal of Homosexuality, 14*(3-4), 157-172.

Ridley, J. (2008). What every sex therapist needs to know. In K. Hertlein, G. Weeks, & N. Gambescia (Eds.), *Systemic sex therapy* (pp. 1-20). New York: Routledge.

Rimm, D., & Masters, J. C. (1974). B*ehavior therapy: Techniques and empirical findings*. New York: Academic Press.

Schover, L. R., & Jensen, S. B. (1988). *Sexuality and chronic illness: A comprehensive approach*. New York: Guilford Press.

Seagraves, R. T., & Balon, R. (2003). *Sexual pharmacology: Fast facts*. New York: W. W. Norton & Company.

Smeltzer, S. C., & Kelley, C. L. (1997). Multiple sclerosis. In M. L. Sipski & C. J. Alexander (Eds.), *Sexual function in people with disability and chronic illness: A health professional's guide* (pp. 177-188). Gaithersburg, MD: Aspen.

Tilton, M. C. (1997). Diabetes and amputation. In M. L. Sipski & C. J. Alexander (Eds.), *Sexual function in people with disability and chronic illness: A health professional's guide* (pp. 279-302). New York: Guilford Press.

Trepper, T., & Barrett, M. J. (1989). *The systemic treatment of incest: A therapeutic handbook*. New York: Brunner/Mazel.

Trepper, T. S., Treyger, S., Yalowitz, J., Ford, J. J. (2008). Solution-focused brief therapy for the treatment of sexual disorders. In K. Hertlein, G. Weeks, & N. Gambescia (Eds.), *Systemic sex therapy* (pp. 363-386). New York: Routledge.

VandeCreek, L., Peterson, F., & Bley, J. (2007). *Innovations in clinical practice: Focus on sexual health.* Professional Resource Press, Sarasota, FL.

Verhulst, J., & Reynolds, J. K. (2008). Sexual pharmacology: Love potions, pills, and poisons. In K. Hertlein, G. Weeks, & N. Gambescia (Eds.), *Systemic sex therapy* (pp. 311-340). New York: Routledge.

Waldman, T. L., & Eliasof, B. (1997). Cancer. In M. L. Sipski & C. J. Alexander (Eds.), *Sexual function in people with disability and chronic illness: A health professional's guide* (pp. 337-354). New York: Guilford Press.

Weeks, G. (1977). Toward a dialectical approach to intervention. *Human Development, 20,* 277-292.

Weeks, G. (1994). The Intersystem Model: An integrative approach to treatment. In G. Weeks & L. Hof (Eds.), *The marital-relationship therapy casebook: Theory and application of the intersystem mode, 1,* (pp. 3-34). New York: Brunner/Mazel.

Weeks. G. R. (2005). The emergence of a new paradigm in sex therapy. *Sexual and Relationship Therapy, 20*(1), 89-105.

Weeks, G., & Cross, C. (2004). The intersystem model of psychotherapy: An integrated systems approach. *Guidance and Counselling, 19,* 57-64.

Weeks, G., & Gambescia, N. (2000). Erectile dysfunction: Integrating couple therapy, sex therapy, and medical treatment. New York: W. W. Norton.

Weeks, G., & Gambescia, N. (2002). *Hypoactive sexual desire: Integrating couple and sex therapy.* New York: W. W. Norton.

Weeks, G. R., & Gambescia, N. (2008). A systemic approach to sensate focus. In K. Hertlein, G. Weeks, & N. Gambescia (Eds.), *Systemic sex therapy* (pp. 341-362). New York: Routledge.

Weeks, G. R., Hertlein, K. M., & Gambescia, N. (2008). The treatment of hypoactive sexual desire disorder. In K. Hertlein, G. Weeks, & N. Gambescia (Eds.),

Systemic sex therapy (pp. 81-106). New York: Routledge.

Wiederman, M. W. (1998). The state of theory in sex therapy. *Journal of Sex Research, 35*(1), 88-99.

Wincze, J. P., & Carey, M. P. (1991). S*exual dysfunction: A guideline for assessment and treatment* (2nd ed). New York; Guilford.

World Health Organization (2006). *Defining sexual health. Report of a technical consultation on sexual health.* Retrieved December 9, 2008, from http://who.int/reproductive-health/publications/sexualhealth/index.html.

Yu, M., Roane, D. M., Miner, C. R., Fleming, M., & Rogers, J. D. (2004). Dimensions of sexual dysfunction in Parkinson's disease. *American Journal of Geriatric Psychiatry, 12,* 221–226.

Adult Attachment

Gail Palmer, MSW & Alison Lee, PhD

Originally published as Clinical Update in Family Therapy Magazine
March-April 2008

Marriage and family therapists (MFTs) are given the task of responding to and helping one of our most precious resources—that of our intimate adult relationships. In order to effectively understand and help the distressed couples who enter our offices, we need to be able to focus on the level of the relationship and gear our interventions toward modifying and changing the relationship dynamic. Attachment theory provides us with a clear, clinical conceptualization of adult love relationships and relationship-oriented therapeutic approaches to our couples' problems.

Adult attachment is defined as the bond that exists between individuals who are emotionally connected to one another and who have primary significance in each other's lives. John Bowlby began in 1958 to postulate that human beings, both as children and as adults, are biologically wired to seek and maintain a few intimate relationships. A secure attachment is created through an emotionally responsive and accessible attachment figure. This security provides the individual with both a safe haven to come home to, and a secure base from which to explore and provides a source of comfort, support, nurturance and love. There is mounting evidence that a secure attachment is optimal for physical and mental health, and is enriching to one's sense of self and well being (Mikulincer, Florian & Weller, 1993).

Bowlby also postulated that when an attachment bond is threatened, there is a predictable response to the separation distress, including angry protest, clinging, depression and despair, and if the attachment figure remains inaccessible, eventually detachment. How each individual responds to unresponsiveness of an attachment figure over time can be defined along two basic dimensions—anxiety and avoidance (Fraley & Waller, 1998). Therefore, one can either over activate proximity-seeking behaviors when the bond is threatened by anxious clinging, pursuit or anger, in an attempt to have the important other respond, or alternatively, especially if the hope for responsiveness is diminished, one could deactivate attachment behaviors and either avoid or limit emotional contact and suppress one's attachment needs.

A third way of responding is a combination of both anxiety and avoidance, and involves both seeking contact, but then rejecting the contact when it is offered. This strategy is referred to as fearful-avoidant (Bartholomew & Horowitz, 1991). These strategies for coping with unresponsiveness can develop into habitual styles of relating to others and become a way to approach relationships, influencing how one experiences oneself and the other in relationships.

Bowlby (1969; 1979; 1980) labeled these styles as being comprised of internal working models of self and other. Securely attached people believe that others are trustworthy and dependable and that they can expect that they will be loved and valued. Insecurely attached individuals have had recurring experiences teaching them others cannot be trusted, and that they will be hurt and that either others do not want to be as close as they would like (anxious attachment style) or they are uncomfortable being close (avoidant attachment style). One can imagine that insecure internal working models of self and other could be seen as a major factor in troubled relationships and that a distressed adult relationship would continue to reinforce and maintain these learned strategies. What is important for marriage and family therapists, however, is that these models can be modified through effective attachment-based intervention.

ASSESSMENT OF ATTACHMENT STRATEGIES

At the core of primary relationships lies the question: *Can I count on you to be there to understand me and respond to me when I need you?* (Johnson, 2003). In the context of managing a negative answer to this question, people develop different attachment strategies. Research indicates that these strategies, limited in number, cluster around two dimensions: anxiety and avoidance.

- Hyper-activating the attachment system by becoming preoccupied with the relationship, monitoring for signs confirming or disconfirming the availability of connection. These *preoccupied attachment* strategies can include jealous, blaming, critical and even coercive behaviors, and are typical of those with high scores on attachment-related anxiety.
- Attempting to de-activate the attachment system by numbing out or shutting down in order to invest less of oneself in the relationship. These more *dismissive* strategies involve taking a withdrawn position in the relationship, engaging in a cool, rational and dismissing manner. They are characteristic of individuals who achieve a high score on attachment avoidance.
- Alternating between each of the above strategies, as is typical of the coping of trauma survivors, who score high on both avoidance and anxiety. These people have been badly hurt in close relationships, yet seek them desperately (Johnson, 2002; Johnson, 2006).

Discussion regarding whether to continue to conceptualize attachment strategies as types or, more recently, as dimensions, is ongoing. For an in-depth review of assessment measures for attachment, and a discussion of related issues, the reader is referred to Mikulancer and Shaver (2007). Attachment strategies, types or dimensions, are not addressed as diagnostic categories in the most recent *Diagnostic and Statistical Manual of Mental Disorders* (DSM-IV-TR) (APA, 2005). The only reference to attachment is Reactive Attachment Disorder of Infancy or Early Childhood (2005).

Also according to Bowlby (1969), working models of the self (Am I lovable?) and of the other (Can I trust you?) are formed in the context of early attachment experiences. Attachment theory suggests that anxiety-related strategies are related to a negative model of self, whereas underlying more avoidant strategies lies a negative working model of other. Attachment strategies are assessed using interview data, behavioral observation, and self-report measures.

INTERVIEW DATA

Structured Interview: The Adult Attachment Interview (AAI). Main, Kaplan and Cassidy (1985) developed this procedure to assess how adults protect themselves from the perceived dangers of intimate relationships. This in-depth and comprehensive interview schedule systematically questions early attachment relationships, stability of family life, losses and other traumatic experiences. Participants are asked if they can recall feeling upset, emotional or hurt when they were little, or if they felt pushed away or ignored, and to identify what they did under such circumstances. The focus is on the *meaning* that the interviewee assigns to prior attachment-related experiences; thus also explores beliefs regarding the self and the other (working models of attachment). There is an important protocol for conducting the AAI, and it is accompanied by a precise coding and classification system. Training is necessary to ensure this procedure is carried out optimally.

Unstructured Interview. Attachment strategies can also be assessed via an unstructured approach as suggested by Johnson and colleagues (2005). Working from an emotionally focused therapy (EFT) approach, clinicians question each client about early attachment relationships, previous adult relationship experiences and experiences of loss and trauma (2005). Has this client experienced a secure attachment relationship before? Has this client learned to receive comfort and support in times of need? Does this client know how to provide support and comfort? Has she experienced trauma? Who was there to support her? In whom does he confide? The impressions the clinician gains from such questions are likely to converge with the picture of the client's attachment style, emerging from pencil-and-paper tests and behavioral observation.

OBSERVATION OF BEHAVIOR

In the session, as couples interact around difficult themes, the therapist can discover how partners might respond to each other in times of need or distress. As conflict arises between the couple, the attachment system of each partner is aroused and the attachment strategies frequently manifest before the therapist's eyes. For example, the Joneses arrive late for their appointment, and the wife is shrilly berating her husband because he arrived 20 minutes late to meet her outside her office to drive to the appointment. "You let me stand in traffic for 20 minutes. You never called to say you'd be late. Typical! I have important work to do. You never respect what matters to me." The therapist may see Mrs. Jones as protesting her experience that her husband does not respect, value, or even care about her needs. Mr. Jones remains calm and unflustered in the face of his wife's shrill attack, showing no emotion or even concern regarding his wife's protest. "Don't be so silly, dear," he tells her, "I was simply delayed in traffic; it's no big deal." Is Mr. Jones struggling to de-activate his attachment system in order to calm and placate his wife and perhaps regulate his emotions regarding her attack? This will be explored as therapy progresses. Understanding how partners manage their attachment needs gives the clinician a road map for identifying primary emotions, and working models of self and other.

Therapists take notice in the session what one partner does in response to the other partner. If he weeps, does she stare out of the window? If she reaches for him to take his hand, does he pull away? By being aware of one partner's reaction to emotional cues of the other, the therapist finds more data to help build the picture of partners' availability for emotional engagement and soothing responses to the partner.

PSYCHOMETRIC MEASURES

There are numerous self-report measures designed to assess attachment strategies in intimate relationships. Two valid and reliable self-report paper-and-pencil tests are the Experiences in Close Relationships scale (ECR) (Brennen, Clark, & Shaver, 1998; Fraley, Waller, & Brennen, 2000) and the Relationship Questionnaire (RQ) (Bartholomew & Horowitz, 1991). The ECR is a 36-item scale based on two dimensions (anxiety and avoidance), assessing general patterns of closeness and intimacy in romantic relationships. Secure attachment strategies are associated with positive marital outcome and insecure (anxious, avoidant or anxious-avoidant) strategies are related to lower levels of marital functioning. The RQ is brief and easy to use in clinical situations. Respondents are required to endorse one of four short descriptions of four different attachment types: secure, fearful, preoccupied and dismissing.

ASSESSING WORKING MODELS OF SELF AND OTHER

Although hypotheses can be made about working models early in therapy, from the testing, interview data and behavioral observations, typically, they are not explicitly seen, heard, or addressed until partners have achieved safety (with both their partner and the therapist) in sessions. When negative interactions are de-escalated, clients are more able to engage in primary emotion and discuss core vulnerabilities. The clinician then listens for phrases such as, "I feel so small, so unimportant...it is too hard to trust you could ever love me" and "I'm afraid. I am afraid to let you know what it's like."

TREATMENT OPTIONS

Couples who rely on insecure attachment strategies will generally experience decreased marital satisfaction (Feeney, 1994; Lussier, **Sabourin**, & Turgeon, 1997) and therefore will likely be the couples that look for therapy to help alleviate the distress. In session, partners will enact and evoke their attachment dance as conflict activates internal working models, and individuals will respond to relationship challenges differently depending upon their preferred attachment strategy (Feeney, 2004). Bowlby (1969) believed, however, that people are capable of changing their models of self and other. This has been supported in research as Davila and Cobb (2004) found that 30 percent of attachment studies reported the development of different attachment strategies over time, generally in the direction of greater security (Baldwin & Fehr, 1995; Davila, Burge, & Hammen, 1997). Marriage and family therapists possess the unique opportunity to provide a therapeutic experience that impacts the attachment security of couples and there is evidence to suggest that improving relationships can result in increasing attachment security (Johnson & Taliman, 1997).

Attachment theory is the ideal guide for treatment as it is systemic, linking the self with the system, and the system with the self. Therapy involves the connecting of the interactional patterns between partners and their internal models of self and other. Old working models are not linguistically coded and are preverbal, nonverbal or paraverbal, and therefore must be accessed experientially (Wallin, 2007). The therapist must be able to focus on the interaction between the couple, which generally is an enactment of the internal script, and on the emotional underpinnings of the couple's interaction. In session, the therapist creates a safe haven and intervenes with the couple to help them create emotionally supportive and accessible responses to one another. Change for couples comes from the creation of new dialogues that arise as a result of a reprocessing of the inner emotional experience, which is imbedded in each partner's internal working models (Johnson, 2006).

Emotionally focused therapy links all the critical elements integral to adult attachment and provides a powerful experientially-based therapy designed to strengthen the attachment bond. Outcome research has found that EFT produces positive results for 70-73 percent of couples with 90 percent reporting their relationships as being significantly improved (Johnson, Hunsley, Greenberg, & Schindler, 1999). Interventions are made on both the interpersonal and intrapsychic levels with the goals of: 1) de-escalation of negative cycles, such as attack/withdraw that tend to reinforce and maintain attachment insecurity; 2) creation of responsive and accessible interactions through specific change events—withdrawer reengagement and blamer softening—that promote attachment security; 3) consolidation of attachment rituals that continue

COUPLE ATTACHMENT: IN SICKNESS AND IN HEALTH

Serious chronic illness can bring couples closer together or pull them apart. Previous relationship security and attachment styles may provide some predictability as to which couples will be resilient in the face of chronic illness. However, as with other traumatic experiences, chronic illness may challenge even the most secure couple relationships. Illness introduces unknowns and heightens the vulnerability in both partners.

John Bowlby's original conceptualization of attachment theory was based on separation from attachment figures and coping with illness (Mikail, 2003). Illness and hospitalization heightened the fear of being alone and children were unable to derive comfort from an attachment figure at a time of increased vulnerability. Research now provides evidence that even for adults a positive close relationship predicts physical and mental health and longevity (Johnson, 2002). In turn, isolation is now recognized as more dangerous to our health than smoking (House, Landis, & Umberson, 1988). Further, emotional support is rated as the most helpful type of support and the strongest contributor to long-term adjustment when faced with serious illness (Helgeson & Cohen, 1996; Johnson, 2002).

Couple therapy can help maintain or create the safe haven needed by both partners to weather the storm of chronic illness and possible death. In the face of illness, both partners must ask the questions, "Am I still loveable?" and "Can I depend on my partner?" Lost is the previous reciprocity, or give and take, and a new balance needs to be found. Failure to do so creates greater risk of relationship distress which, in turn, has been shown to have an adverse effect on physical health and coping by both partners. Therapy interventions that provide a process to explore this new uncertainty and imbalance can play a key role in bringing couples closer together. Benefits of these interventions can be found even when illness results in the death of a partner as research shows that maintaining secure attachment is associated with better ability to grieve and cope with loss (van Doorn et al., 1998; Johnson, 2002).

Kathy Stiell, MSW, is an AAMFT Clinical Member and practices at the Ottawa Couple and Family Institute and the Aphasia Centre of Ottawa, which she co-founded in 1990. Stiell has expertise in working with couples and families living with chronic and progressive illness and has developed techniques to make EFT accessible to clients living with communication difficulties, such as aphasia.

to redefine the relationship as a safe haven (Johnson, 2003).

EFT utilizes attachment emotions as they arise in the interactional dance to begin to shape and prime soft and responsive interactions. Insecure strategies are ways for partners to protect themselves emotionally and to help regulate their emotions in an intimate relationship. Therefore, an individual with an avoidant attachment style might take a rational, cool stance with her partner, dismissing, ignoring or deflecting the lover's bids for connection.

For example, Rod, in response to his wife's request for affection, states that he really doesn't need "any of that stuff" and that really, all he is looking for from his wife is respect. As his wife dissolves in tears, the therapist explores with Rod the look of sadness on his face. Rod is able to express his feeling bad and wanting to comfort his wife, but also states, "I am so bad at this, I just do not know how to do it and I want to....but I don't know how." The therapist helps this individual engage and stay in contact with his attachment emotions, specifically his anxiety around failing his wife and his fear that in the end she would reject him. This softer, more accessible response allows his wife to see a different side of her husband and de-escalate her negative emotional reactions. Eventually, Rod will be helped to express his attachment needs to his partner and become a more fully emotionally-engaged, responsive and accessible partner. Looking at his wife, Rod slowly states, "I have such a hard time with this. I know you need me to show you more how I feel and I want to try. I just might get it wrong and I need you to understand and be patient."

For the partner who demonstrates a preoccupied attachment style, there are usually difficulties around differentiating and regulating emotions. An anxious partner may take a critical, blaming stance towards the partner as a protective measure, and as a means to ignite a response, using anger as a shield to more vulnerable attachment needs. Jill, with a raised and pitched voice, says, "You are never there for me—you look after number one—you are nothing but selfish and irresponsible. You are just like one of the kids." As the therapist helps validate and normalize the anger as a protest to disconnection, utilizing slow and reflective interventions, there begins an uncovering of softer, more vulnerable emotions. Jill is able to state, "I am just so tired and lonely. I feel all alone." This more open stance segues into the shaping of a change event in EFT where a previously blaming, critical spouse is able to ask for her attachment needs to be met from an emotionally vulnerable position.

It is at this juncture in therapy when fears relating to models of self and other are more directly experienced. As the therapist notes Jill's refusal to hear her partner's reach for her, she gently explores what is blocking the engagement, and Jill moves further and further into her emotional experience, helping her articulate that she knows "how" but does not know "what" (Wallin, 2007). The therapist helps reframe Jill's anger as a shield for her fear that no one will be there for her, a fear she learned a long time ago, when she needed to grow up quickly and look after herself. Jill then accesses the sadness and grief she feels about no one being there for her in her life, and her fear regarding trusting her partner's present response. "I don't know how—how could he be there—no one has ever been there." As the therapist gently encourages Jill to depend on her husband, she also touches her fear that if she really lets him in, he will find her unlovable and unworthy. The therapist then helps Jill communicate her attachment needs in a direct, yet soft manner. "I need you to take care of me," which allows her husband to respond, "Sure I can do that—it's been so long since you let me help you—I want to be there for you."

For couples, when one or both partners display fearful-avoidant attachment strategies, the therapy is slower, as interventions are smaller and graduated to the partner's ability to safely assimilate them. The cycles in these couples are often complex and disorganized, as there is both the desperate longing for closeness, immediately followed with an intense fear of this closeness, resulting in a "come here; go away" strategy in relationships. The therapist helps the partner with the difficult task of asking for closeness, in the face of believing one is bad or dirty, and eventually creates a more secure couple bond, which can become a healing place for the original childhood trauma (Johnson, 2003).

In EFT, reengaging the spouse who has been emotionally withdrawn and softening the more critical partner constitutes change events that are critical to the treatment success (Johnson, 2003). These events begin to redefine the relationship as secure, where partners can turn towards each other and be comforted, nurtured, supported and loved. Partners can then be intimate and interdependent with each other, and the creation of attachment rituals helps to reinforce and maintain attachment security. Acknowledging separations and reunions, spending time-sharing thoughts and feelings, celebrating special events and occasions, are all examples of daily expressions of the importance of the other and the relationship.

BEHAVIORAL APPROACHES

In behavioral approaches, couples are taught to give and receive support with each other, the assumption being that attachment insecurity arises because of a knowledge or skill deficit (Cobb & Bradbury, 2003; Davila, 2003). The creation of interactional patterns, where the partners experience each other as available, supportive and accepting, helps increase the feeling of security, and as a result, should impact positively the internal models of others. Likewise, when partners receive validation, empathy and comfort from their most significant other, the internal view of self should be positively shifted in the direction of feeling more worthy and lovable.

Davila has outlined four suggestions that address a couple's attachment issues for therapists utilizing behavioral interventions. These include: 1) Conducting an attachment-based assessment; 2) Understanding the controlling problem as an attachment issue; 3) Helping couples develop support skills, as well as conflict resolution skills; 4) Helping couples develop comfort with intimacy and reduce abandonment fears (2003).

Further long-term outcome research is needed to, in fact, prove whether changing a relationship from distressed to secure, does alter the underlying attachment models (Cobb & Bradbury, 2003).

FUTURE RESEARCH

The research on attachment is growing and future developments may help us understand more how attachment security affects certain elements of adult life including sexuality, cultural differences, adult trauma and illness. Also, understanding in more detail how the therapist can effectively intervene with specific client groups is needed; for example, gay and lesbian couples, or couples who belong to traditional and patriarchal religious or ethnic groups.

ABOUT THE AUTHORS

Gail Palmer, MSW, is a Founding Member of the Ottawa Couple and Family Institute. She maintains a private practice, is an EFT supervisor and trainer, and a family therapy professor at the School of Social Work at Carleton University, Ottawa. Palmer is a Clinical Member and an Approved Supervisor of the AAMFT.

Alison Lee, PhD, is a clinical psychologist, practicing individual and marital therapy in Ottawa, where she is vice president and co-founder of the Ottawa Couple and Family Institute. Lee is a practitioner, trainer and supervisor of EFT for couples.

PROFESSIONAL RESOURCE

ONLINE

International Centre for Excellence in Emotionally Focused Therapy (ICEEFT)
www.eft.ca/home.htm
Based in Ottawa, Ontario, Canada, this international organization provides Emotionally Focused Therapy for couples and families and conducts leading research and offers training to clinicians. The center has links to various EFT centers located across Canada and the U.S. that have similar goals and functions.

REFERENCES

American Psychiatric Association. (2005). *Diagnostic and statistical manual of mental disorders,* pp. 127-130. Washington, DC: APA.

Baldwin, M. W., & Fehr, B. (1995). On the instability of attachment style ratings. *Personal Relationships. 2,* 1269-1287.

Bartholomew, K. & Horowitz, L. (1991). Attachment styles among young adults. A test of a four-category model. *Journal of Personality and Social Psychology. 61,* 226-244.

Bowlby, J. (1969). *Attachment and loss. Vol. 1: Attachment.* London: Hogarth Press.

Bowlby, J. (1979). *The making and breaking of affectional bonds.* London: Tavistock.

Bowlby, J. (1980). *Attachment and loss: Vol. 3. Loss: sadness and depression.* New York: Basic Books.

Brennan, K. A., Clark, G. L., & Shaver, P. R. (1998). Self-report measure of adult attachment: An integrative review. In J. A. Simpson & W. S. Rhodes (Eds.), *Attachment theory and close relationships* (pp. 46-76). New York: Guildford Press.

Cobb & Bradbury. (2003). Implications of adult attachment for preventing adverse marital outcomes . In Johnson & Whiffen (Eds.), *Attachment processes in couple and family therapy* (pp. 258-280). New York: Guildford Press.

Davila, J., Bruge, D., & Hammen, C. (1997) Why does attachment style change? *Journal of Personality and Social Psychology. 73,* 826–838.

Davila, J. (2003). Attachment processes in couple therapy: Informing behavioral models. In Johnson & Whiffen (Eds.), *Attachment processes in couple and family therapy* (pp.124-143). New York: Guildford Press.

Davila, J., & Cobb, R. (2004). Predictors of change in attachment security in adulthood. In Rholes & Simpson (Eds.), *Adult attachment: Theory, research and clinical implications* (pp. 133–158). New York: Guildford Press.

Feeney, J. (1994). Attachment style, communication patterns and satisfaction across the life cycle of marriage. *Personal Relationships. 1* (pp. 333-348).

Feeney, J. (2004). Adult attachment relationship functioning under stressful conditions. In Rholes & Simpson (Eds.), *Adult attachment: Theory, research and clinical implications* (pp. 339-366). New York: Guildford Press.

Fraley, R. C., Waller, N. G., & Brennan, K. A. (2000). An item response theory analysis of self-report measures of adult attachment. *Journal of Personality and Social Psychology, 78*(2), 350, 365.

Fraley, R. C., & Waller, N. G. (1998). Adult attachment patterns: A test of the typological model. In J. A. Simpson & W. C. Rholes (Eds.) *Attachment theory and close relationships* (pp. 77-114). New York: Guildofrd Press.

Helgeson, V. S., & Cohen, S. (1996). Social support and adjustment to cancer: Reconciling descriptive, correlational, and intervention research. *Health Psychology, 15*, 135-148.

House, J., Landis, K., & Umberson, D. (1988). Social relationships and health. *Science 241* (pp. 540-545).

Johnson, S. M. (2006). *Attachment processes in couple and family therapy.* New York: Guilford.

Johnson, S. M., Bradley, B., Furrow, J., Lee, A., Palmer, G., Tilley, D., & Woolley, S. (2005). *Becoming an emotionally focused couple therapist: The workbook* (pp. 134-137). New York: Routledge.

Johnson, S. M. (2003). Introduction to attachment: A therapist's guide to primary relationships and their renewal. In Johnson & Whiffen (Eds.) *Attachment processes in couple and family therapy* (pp. 3- 17). New York: Guildford Press.

Johnson, S. M. (2003). Attachment theory: A guide for couple therapy. In Johnson & Whiffen (Eds.) *Attachment processes in couple and family therapy* (pp. 103-123). New York: Guildford Press.

Johnson, S. M. (2002). The trauma of physical illness. In *Emotionally focused couple therapy with trauma survivors.* New York: Guilford Press

Johnson, S. M., Hunsley, J., Greenberg, L., & Schlinder, D. (1999). Emotionally focused couples therapy: Status and challenges. *Clinical Psychology: Science and Practice. 6*, 67-79.

Johnson, S. M., & Taliman, E. (1997). Predictors of success in emotionally focused marital therapy. *Journal of Marital and Family Therapy. 23*, 135-152.

Lussier, Y., Sabourin, S., & Turgeon, C. (1997). Coping strategies as moderators of relationship between attachment and marital adjustment. *Journal of Social and personal Relationships. 14* (pp. 777- 791).

Main, M., Kaplan, N., & Cassidy, J. (1985). Security in infancy, childhood, and adulthood: A move to the level of representation. *Monographs of the Society for Research in Child Development, 50*(1-2, Serial No. 209), 66-104.

Mikail, S. F. (2003). Attachment and the experience of chronic pain. In *Attachment processes in couple and family therapy.* New York: Guilford Press.

Mikulincer, M. & Shaver, P. R. (2007). *Attachment in adulthood: Structure, dynamics and change* (pp. 81–113). New York: The Guildford Press.

Mikulincer, M., Floria, V., & Weller, A. (1993) Attachment styles, coping strategies and post-traumatic psychological distress. *Journal of Personality and Social Psychology, 64* (pp. 817-826).

van Doorn C., Kasl, S. V., Beery, L. C., Jacobs, S. C., Prigerson, H. G. (1998). The influence of marital quality and attachment styles on traumatic grief and depressive symptoms. *Journal of Nervous and Mental Disease, 186,* 566-573.

Wallin, D. J. (2007). *Attachment in psychotherapy.* New York: The Guilford Press.

Adult Attention Deficit Hyperactivity Disorder

Joel L. Young, MD & Jaime Saal, MA

Originally published as Clinical Update in Family Therapy Magazine
September-October 2008

ERASING THE STEREOTYPE OF ADHD

Attention Deficit Hyperactivity Disorder (ADHD) no longer has a "poster child"—not even a "poster *person*," for that matter. The image of ADHD in past decades has been the frenzied, elementary-aged boy dangling from the monkey bars, disrupting his class and disobeying all authority. This inexorable behavior drove his desperate parents and teachers to seek an understanding of his symptoms. As more has been learned, what was thought to be a disorder of childhood, of males, and of hyperactivity alone, has undergone significant revision.

ADHD is defined as a disorder of excessive inattention, distractibility, hyperactivity and impulsivity that begins in childhood and negatively impacts the individual's performance at school, work and home. ADHD is estimated to affect 6 to 8 percent of children, a prevalence seen throughout the world (American Academy of Pediatrics). ADHD symptoms persist into adulthood between 30 to 60 percent of the time, and 4 to 5 percent of American adults are afflicted. Although symptoms change in severity over time, they do not disappear and often remain, impairing daily life (Faraone et al., 2006).

ADHD symptoms do not follow the same trajectory in every individual. Whereas hyperactivity and behavioral disruption are the hallmark of childhood presentations, these symptoms generally decline with age (Biederman, 2000). In adults with ADHD, inattentive symptoms, poor focus, disorganization, and problems with motivation predominate. Millstein reports that over 90 percent of clinically-referred outpatient ADHD adults reported inattentive symptoms as their chief complaint (Millstein et al., 1999).

So what happened to the aforementioned boy on the monkey bars, if left untreated? Symptoms change through the life cycle. Childhood hyperactivity on the playground may, as an adult, look like an inability to sit through

---

a meeting. Disregarding a teachers command now manifests as an inability to listen to, or address, a spouse's or partner's concerns. He may now be a 30-something man who has difficulty waiting at a red light or in line at a restaurant. He may become bored so easily that his intimate relationships are in perpetual turmoil. These are the vexing issues that may motivate him to seek treatment.

FUNCTIONAL IMPAIRMENT IN ADULTS WITH ADHD

As a diagnosis that persists across the lifespan, there is a great deal for the family therapist to consider. The condition is more than an inconvenience; it adversely affects the individual's relationships, both with his workplace and his family. Individuals with untreated ADHD have a higher risk than their non-ADHD peers for divorce, car accidents, gambling and general money management issues, substance abuse, and legal difficulties (Barkley et al., 2008). Awareness of these public health and societal implications sheds new light on the importance of consistent identification of the disorder and efficacious treatment for the ADHD adult.

Cynics who question the validity of the ADHD diagnosis argue that it is over-diagnosed and of limited consequence. Recent research argues otherwise. In 2008, Barkley, Murphy and Fischer published a longitudinal study of individuals with ADHD and found that common areas of impairment were in educational and occupational achievement and family functioning. As these are central building blocks of self-esteem and fulfillment in adulthood, it is easy to understand why these patients pursue treatment.

It is understood that individuals with ADHD struggle academically. Barkley's study revealed that ADHD individuals have lower rates of high school and college completion than their non-ADHD peers (Barkley et al., 2008). As they age, this impairment shifts to the occupational arena. Another study found that only 34 percent of participants with an ADHD diagnosis were currently employed full-time, as compared to 59 percent of the non-ADHD control group (Biederman & Faraone, 2006). Countless others with ADHD are underemployed or encounter job related-conflict because of their tardiness, disorganization and other core ADHD symptoms.

The symptoms directly impact family life. Spouses and partners of ADHD individuals complain of poor follow-through and unmet promises. When the ADHD husband or wife has difficulty holding a job, the family's finances may suffer, bringing additional tension to the household. Partners may have limited tolerance with an overdrawn bank account or forgetting about carpool responsibilities.

Although this condition begins in childhood, the impact may be more evident as relationships evolve. Growing families bring additional responsibilities and the individual with ADHD, who was able to compensate for symptoms early in life, may be revealed under these pressures. The stress on a couple parenting an ADHD child is enormous. When gathering a family's story, the therapist cannot underemphasize the impact an individual's psychiatric diagnosis (ADHD, depression, etc.) may have on the entire family. For this reason, it is the prerogative of the family therapist to evaluate individual family members.

DIAGNOSIS AND ASSESSMENT

The process of diagnosing ADHD should consist of two parts: the clinical interview and psychological screening.

The Clinical Interview. As in any psychiatric intake, the clinician should identify the client's reason for presentation, his or her symptoms, physical and mental health history, family history, goals for treatment, previous medications and academic and professional history. It is important to pay particularly close attention to the timeline of reported symptoms. A current criterion for ADHD diagnosis is the presence of the symptoms prior to the age of seven (DSM-IV, APA, 1994), although it is expected that future DSM editions will eliminate the strict early age requirement and instead demand that symptoms be traceable to early adolescence.

Because the patient may not have an understanding of the various ADHD symptom presentations, clinicians must not rely on the patient to identify when their ADHD symptoms first started. Rather, the more appropriate method might be to explore what school was like for the patient as far back as they can remember. Accessing old report cards can be helpful.

Family history can be particularly instructive in screening for ADHD. Biederman and colleagues (1990) found that over 25 percent of the first-degree relatives of children with ADHD also had a diagnosis of ADHD, as compared to 5 percent incidence in the control groups. Whether a sibling, parent or child of the patient has an ADHD diagnosis, there is a higher probability of the diagnosis for the patient undergoing assessment.

Basic clinical observation represents another crucial aspect of the interview. A client's report may not be congruent with his or her body language. Does he or she fidget throughout the session? Is the client tangential in thoughts and/or speech? Is his or her presentation tearful or angry? Does the client interrupt the clinician? These behavioral observations can offer precious information that the client is not verbally offering.

During the diagnostic process, the clinician should explore how the family unit has been affected by the reported symptoms. Is there discord between the client and partner? Are there strained relationships with the children due to impatience or lack of follow-through? The client may have already described personal goals for treatment, but what are his or her goals for familial relationships? With the client's permission, this is an appropriate time to obtain collateral input from a partner. The client may not be aware of the impact his or her behavior has on the household.

Psychological Screening. Many useful tools exist to evaluate for ADHD. The Adult Self-Report Scale (World Health Organization) was recently adapted to capture the adult experience. The six-question version is more predictive than diagnostic in nature (Adler, 2004), but is quick, easy to administer and available without cost. A longer, 18-item version is also available.

The Brown Attention Deficit Disorder Scales (Brown, 2005); *Conner's Adult ADHD Rating Scales* (Conners, Erhardt, & Sparrow, 2005), and *Adult Attention Deficit Disorder Evaluation Scales* (McCarney, 2004) take anywhere from 10 to 40 minutes to administer and screen specifically for ADHD. As the individual's insight can be limited, versions of these scales are designed for partners or other family members. The screening tools are proprietary and have a nominal per cost usage fee.

It is difficult to develop an appropriate treatment plan without understanding the full scope of the individual's mental health. Given the high incidence of comorbidities, the screening process should include tools that assess for anxiety, mood disorders, sleep disorders, substance use, eating disorders and symptoms of impulse dyscontrol. To this end, the *Adult Self-Report Inventory* (Gadow, Sprafkin, & Weiss, 2008) can be effective. The ASRI is a multi-page screening tool that, upon scoring by the clinician, flags clusters of symptoms as a "low," "moderate," or "high" probability of a particular diagnosis or diagnostic category. It is imperative for diagnosticians to review the completed assessment and take note of which questions elevated the symptom clusters to "moderate" or "high," as some diagnoses are easily tripped.

Although most screening tools are designed to offer a quantitative assessment of an individual's symptoms, they do not typically *qualify* the symptoms. Therefore, it is often necessary for the diagnosing clinician to probe further. Are there patterns associated with the client's experience of a particular symptom? For example, does he or she indicate feeling often depressed? When questioned, he or she may indicate that his or her mood suffers when struggling at work, which is often. Perhaps the depression is situational, stemming from frustration over chronic ADHD symptoms. As the evaluation is conducted, the clinician should seek to differentiate between primary and secondary symptoms.

COMORBIDITY: AN IMPORTANT PIECE OF THE DIAGNOSTIC PUZZLE

Co-occurring conditions are the rule, not the exception, with adult ADHD. Females and males with ADHD were found to have a 52 percent and 46 percent lifetime incidence, respectively, of multiple anxiety disorders, as compared to 15 percent and 10 percent of females and males without an ADHD diagnosis. Similarly, the rate of diagnosis of major depression during the lifetime of females and males with ADHD was found to be 36 percent and 27 percent respectively. In contrast, the lifetime incidence of major depression in the control group was six percent for women and four percent for men (Biederman, 2004).

Psychiatric comorbidities, other than anxiety and depression, also need to be considered. The ADHD population has higher rates of substance use disorders, conduct disorder, oppositional defiant disorder, antisocial personality disorder, and dysthymia (Barkley et al., 2008).

ELIZABETH: A CASE STUDY OF ADHD

Elizabeth is a 41-year-old sales associate. She is athletic and charismatic; qualities which seem to bring her success on the job. Although she presents as "having it all," she reports having struggled with fatigue and depression for as long as she can remember. Elizabeth is constantly late to work and often loses her train of thought in meetings, making a promotion to management nearly impossible. Given her strong interpersonal abilities, her sales numbers are good, but her supervisor and co-workers are frequently disappointed by her lack of follow through. She, too, feels that she is capable of more.

Elizabeth's home life is also a significant source of stress. Household projects have been postponed for years; closets are stuffed, counters are piled high. On many days, Elizabeth avoids going home; her husband's impatience with her disorganization frequently culminates in shouting arguments. She has trouble organizing herself to go to bed at a scheduled time and her lack of sleep causes her to be exhausted in the morning. Given her persistent tardiness, professional stagnation, lack of productivity and marital discord, Elizabeth reports feeling anxious and depressed and endorses feelings of inadequacy, underperformance and low self-esteem.

After a particularly stressful week at work, and upon the urging of a friend, Elizabeth decides to seek help. She is skeptical of the process; previous trials of anti-depressant medications have yielded little benefit. After a comprehensive interview and diagnostic screening, Elizabeth is diagnosed with ADHD. It appears that she does not have a primary anxiety and mood disorder, but rather her ADHD is causing her intense frustration and despair. Her treatment plan will include a combination of ADHD medications and coaching. Hesitantly, Elizabeth agrees to this approach.

CASE STUDY: FOLLOW-UP

One month later, Elizabeth reports that her three appointments with her ADHD coach are teaching her to create a useful structure to her day. On the medication, Elizabeth reports that she is more alert and focused. She is able to leave her house in the morning without returning several times to retrieve forgotten items. On weekends, she feels motivated to organize her house and has sufficient energy to respond to her family's needs. At the second monthly appointment, she notes that her manager has complimented her on her increased productivity, and tensions with her husband have diminished. By month four, Elizabeth explains that the medication and the tools learned through the coaching process have made her more productive and consistent. As her mood and self-concept have improved, her anxiety has retreated. Although not symptom-free, Elizabeth is starting to feel more like the put-together person that she presents to the world.

Elizabeth's response is typical of many individuals who receive ADHD treatment. It is instructive on a number of fronts. Like many adults ultimately diagnosed with ADHD, Elizabeth initially was treated with antidepressant

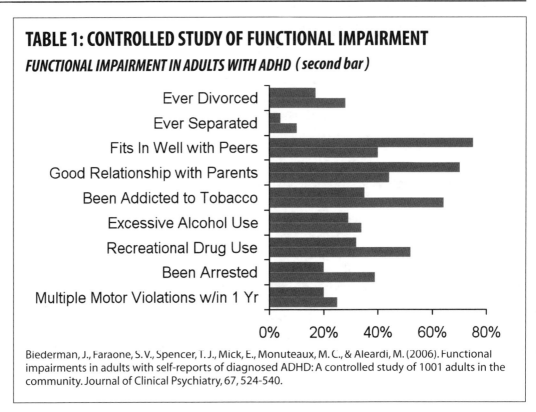

TABLE 1: CONTROLLED STUDY OF FUNCTIONAL IMPAIRMENT

FUNCTIONAL IMPAIRMENT IN ADULTS WITH ADHD (second bar)

Biederman, J., Faraone, S. V., Spencer, T. J., Mick, E., Monteaux, M. C., & Aleardi, M. (2006). Functional impairments in adults with self-reports of diagnosed ADHD: A controlled study of 1001 adults in the community. Journal of Clinical Psychiatry, 67, 524-540.

medication. Given the fact the diagnosis was ADHD and not major depression, it follows that her response to antidepressant medication was suboptimal. Furthermore, ADHD need not be a diagnosis of exclusion. If screening tests are performed at the initial visit, an ADHD diagnosis often becomes clear and integrated treatments of therapy and medications can be quickly instituted. Usually, in this situation, a favorable response is forthcoming.

ADHD AND BIPOLAR DISORDER: DIAGNOSTIC OVERLAP

Elizabeth's case demonstrates the need to distinguish ADHD and related frustration from anxiety and depression. Other common diagnoses also have overlapping symptoms. The hyperactivity of ADHD and manic phase of bipolar disorder are frequently confused. Hyperactive/impulsive features of ADHD can seem much like symptoms of bipolar mania. Overlapping symptoms include: excessive talking; being "on the go"; acting without thinking; racing thoughts; and mood swings (Young, 2007).

There are several pieces of information that the diagnosing clinician should consider in differentiating between the two diagnoses. ADHD symptoms date from childhood and are usually associated with educational problems. Cognitive compromise does not accompany bipolar disorder, and symptoms of mania and depression usually present in late adolescence or young adulthood. ADHD symptoms are chronic and unrelenting, whereas manic and depressive symptoms of bipolar disorder alternate and are episodic. Psychosis is not present in ADHD, but is a common feature of mania. Perhaps most importantly, the mood swings associated with ADHD are rapid and mild in contrast to the lengthy and severe episodes characteristic of the bipolar patient (Young, 2007).

ADHD AND SUBSTANCE USE DISORDERS

ADHD appears to be a risk factor for the development of substance use disorders. As with mood disorders noted previously, it is important to ferret out attentional issues in this population. Many adults with untreated ADHD report unrelenting anxiety. Unless the diagnosis is made and treatment is offered, many individuals with ADHD find marijuana and alcohol use to be a means of self-treatment. Treatment with conventional ADHD medications might offer some relief. A study by Biederman and his colleagues followed ADHD children for four years until early adolescence. At follow-up, he found that 75 percent of the untreated ADHD youth abused substances, in contrast to 25 percent of those treated with stimulant medications and 17 percent of the control group. They concluded that untreated ADHD was a significant risk factor for substance use disorder in adolescents (Biederman et al., 1999). It is essential that further research be conducted on the utility of ADHD treatment on adults actively abusing substances.

Due to the many complicated facets of the diagnostic process, all clients should be evaluated critically; particularly those with refractory depression, anxiety and substance use disorders. Awareness of symptom overlap among mental health disorders and a solid understanding of common comorbidities are crucial elements of successful diagnosis and treatment.

TREATMENT OPTIONS: MEDICATIONS AND THERAPY

The most efficacious treatment regimen is one that includes pharmacological treatment in combination with a psychotherapeutic approach (coaching or cognitive-behavioral therapy). All of the four approved medications for adult ADHD address core symptoms of ADHD. Stimulant medications include Focalin XR, Adderall XR, and Vyvanse. Focalin XR is d-methylphenidate, a molecule similar to Ritalin. Adderall XR is composed of four different amphetamine salts. Both of these medications are long-acting, usually between 8 and 12 hours in duration. Long-acting medications are far less likely to be abused or diverted in contrast to the older, shorter-acting stimulant formulations like Ritalin or Adderall. Vyvanse is a prodrug; its amphetamine base is activated only when the medication hits the gastrointestinal tract. No euphoria results if it is injected or snorted (Dennison Haines, 2005).

Strattera is the only non-stimulant medication currently approved for adult ADHD. It is the longest-acting ADHD medication. Although Strattera requires several weeks to take effect, it possesses anti-anxiety properties. It can re-regulate sleep cycles and has virtually no abuse potential. Some patients benefit from a combination of a stimulant medication *and* Strattera (Dennison Haines, 2005).

TERMINOLOGY: ATTENTION DEFICIT HYPERACTIVITY DISORDER

Although frequently referred to as ADD, officially no such condition exists. ADHD is composed of the three subtypes. Many are confused that the majority of patients with ADHD do not, in fact, have hyperactive symptoms. ADHD, predominately inattentive type, is often referred to informally as ADD. It is expected that the newer definition of the condition will eliminate the confusing nomenclature and rework criteria of the various subtypes (DSM-IV):

ADHD, Predominately Inattentive Type

- Fails to give close attention to details and makes careless mistakes
- Has difficulty sustaining attention
- Does not seem to listen
- Does not follow instructions
- Has difficulty organizing tasks
- Avoids tasks that require sustained mental effort
- Loses things
- Is easily distracted
- Is often forgetful

ADHD, Predominately Hyperactive/Impulsive Type

Hyperactivity

- Fidgets
- Has trouble remaining seated
- Subjective feeling of restlessness
- Has difficulty engaging in leisure activities quietly
- Is on the go
- Talks excessively

Impulsivity

- Blurts out answers to questions
- Impatient when waiting
- Interrupts others

ADHD, Combined Type

- Has symptoms of inattention, hyperactivity and impulsivity

Comorbidity: The coexistence of two or more disease processes.

Dysthymia: Generally experienced as a less severe, but more chronic form of major depression. Specifically, dysthymia is characterized by depressed mood experienced most of the time for at least two years.

Refractory: Unyielding to treatment.

Stimulant medication: These include methylphenidate and amphetamine-based medications. These medications work throughout the brain and increase levels of dopamine and norepinephrine, particularly in the locus ceruleus. Increases in brain dopamine level can be associated with physiological reinforcement and euphoria. For this reason, many ADHD medications are considered controlled substances. Newer stimulant medications that are not taken up slowly in the brain do not seem to have this physiological effect.

Non-stimulant medication: Currently, the only available non-stimulant ADHD medication is atomoxetine (Strattera). Compared to the stimulant medications, Strattera does not increase brain dopamine to the same levels as stimulants and stays clear of the locus ceruleus. In the near future, more non-stimulant options should be available for ADHD treatment.

NON-PHARMACOLOGICAL THERAPIES

Understanding Coaching. Most experts agree that medications play a paramount role in the treatment of ADHD. Although many of those diagnosed with ADHD want a "magic pill," they require additional assistance in learning to structure their day and organize their world. Adults with ADHD have functioned with these symptoms since childhood and a medication regimen alone tends not to be the most effective *long-term* solution (NIMH, 2007).

Coaching involves a specialized treatment plan tailored to assist the client in effectively coping with ADHD symptoms. The coach and client work together to address the symptoms that may be hindering the client's success in his or her academic, work or personal life. The coaching process focuses on the individual's strengths and works to create strategies to overcome weaknesses (Young & Giwerc, 2003).

Coaching is most effective for individuals who are motivated to change their behavior. The focus of coaching is tangible and pragmatic. Typically, a session will focus on a particular issue, i.e., organization. At this meeting, the client and coach might discuss the use of daily planners, breaking down complicated tasks into smaller steps, and the development of routines that ensure improved organizational skills. For example, adults rarely forget to brush their teeth, so encouraging the client to place their morning medication next to their toothbrush improves compliance. The coach assigns homework that would help the client implement these organizational strategies and follows up on the client's progress at the next scheduled meeting.

It is not uncommon for feelings of frustration or anger to surface as the client deals with the daunting task of re-working their behavioral patterns. This is where basic therapeutic techniques such as active listening and unconditional positive regard should be introduced into the coaching process. The relationship between client and coach is crucial, as it helps the ADHD individual feel validated. The coach may be one of the few people in the client's life who can understand the many difficult aspects of living with this disorder (Giwerc & Young, 2003).

Counseling the ADHD Individual. Therapy is recommended over coaching for the ADHD individual who is dealing with intra-psychic conflict or severe comorbid mental health conditions such as anxiety, depression or substance abuse. In such cases, the pragmatic focus of coaching may not be sufficiently comprehensive. Only when the comorbid conditions have been adequately treated and the patient is stabilized can the therapist and client move forward to address the impact of ADHD symptoms on the various aspects of their life.

Cognitive-behavioral techniques (CBT) have proven effective in challenging irrational belief systems the client has come to adopt. Common maladaptive thought patterns that can be addressed include over generalizing the negative (Barkley, 2008) and comparing themselves to non-ADHD peers. In these situations, the CBT therapist identifies the psychological schema and helps the client identify the irrationality of the belief. This technique is treacherous, but helpful when clients employ default behaviors like externalizing their deficits onto someone else in their life (Young, 2007). The title of Kate Kelly and Peggy Ramundo's, *You Mean I'm Not Lazy, Stupid or Crazy?!*, crystallizes the quandary that many ADHD individuals experience as they work with their therapists to understand their condition and gain insight into the cognitions and behaviors.

When a family or couple presents for therapy and an ADHD diagnosis has been identified, this diagnosis needs to be considered in the creation of the treatment plan for that family. First and foremost, the therapist may need to educate the family so they better understand their family member's behaviors in the proper context. The use of educational DVDs or web sites is helpful. With this knowledge in hand, the family is better able to work with the clinician to determine the most effective ways to support their loved one's positive change.

A TEAM APPROACH: COMBINING INDIVIDUAL ADHD TREATMENT WITH MARITAL AND FAMILY THERAPY

Individual and marital and family therapy interventions for the ADHD individual are not mutually exclusive. Therapy or coaching can help the individual communicate more effectively with family members and gain an awareness of how his or her behaviors may contribute to any destructive dynamics within the home environment.

Individuals with ADHD should be encouraged to work on their own personal goals so they are better equipped to handle family issues. With the permission of the client, communication between the coach and family therapist can be important. The therapist can offer insight into patterns of thoughts and feelings that drive the client's behaviors, as well as any underlying mental health diagnoses that may compound the picture. The coach can keep the therapist informed of the strategies and techniques being addressed. From here, the therapist may be able to enlist family members to provide support to the individual as these new behaviors are implemented. Both members of the treatment team can encourage medication compliance and offer their observations about the clinical effects of the medication to the prescribing physician.

Whatever combination of techniques is put together to treat the ADHD individual, it is clear that a multimodal approach to treatment proves to be the most effective (NIMH, 2007).

CONCLUSION

Any clinician practicing today can be certain that they will, at some point, work with an ADHD individual. We now know that, when it comes to the diagnosis of adult ADHD, the symptoms *themselves* are often just the tip of the iceberg. It is the patterns of behavior *born out of* these symptoms that can be especially destructive. The clinician must be comfortable identifying the underlying symptoms of ADHD and distinguishing them from other common psychiatric conditions. An emphasis should be placed on differential diagnosis and an appreciation of common ADHD comorbidities, including depression, substance use disorder and generalized anxiety. In order to optimize outcome, it is essential for the coach or individual therapist, the MFT, and the prescribing clinician to communicate openly. With consistent and effective treatment, adults with ADHD *and their families* can lead happier, more harmonious lives.

BUILDING AN ADHD PRACTICE

Although there has been an increasing interest in adult ADHD, mental health practitioners have not kept up with the demand. In many cities throughout the country, individuals with ADHD have few places to turn. In Internet blogs and national meetings, individuals with ADHD lament their lack of options. They know where to go if they need treatment for their asthma or acne. Most have access to any number of LASIK surgeons. Often times, ADHD treatment resources for adults are sparse.

This creates an opportunity for marriage and family therapists (MFTs). ADHD arouses passions in those who suffer from the disorder and those who treat the condition. Individuals with ADHD often feel alienated throughout their life, and if they learn that a local professional has developed a program, they will gather. The challenge to the MFT is how to construct an integrated program.

HOW TO GET STARTED

A firm understanding of the science and clinical practice of ADHD is essential. Read some of the classics about ADHD, including Hallowell and Ratey's *Driven to Distraction* (1995). Join CHADD and ADDA, both important advocacy groups for children, adolescents and adults with ADHD. Their annual national meetings are excellent places to obtain updates and meet like-minded professionals. Contact your regional CHADD group to meet local ADHD thought leaders. Professionals will generate referrals if they demonstrate an interest in counseling or advocating for those with the condition.

Pursue specialized training in ADHD coaching. According to David Giwerc, president of the ADD Coach Academy, many of the students in his 12-month telephone course are MFTs. The course offers a comprehensive understanding of the condition and updates the approach to coaching the adult with ADHD. Upon graduation, the title *Certified ADD Coach* adds a unique credential to the practitioner's portfolio. It is important to be a good diagnostician as well. Routinely screen patients for ADHD and other comorbidities. (Refer to our section on diagnostic approaches.) Do not fall into the trap of treating clients before they are accurately diagnosed. Linda Vanderpol, a marriage and family therapist in Toledo, OH, recently added a formal evaluation to her clinic, *Caring Counts* (www.caringcounts.com). Linda states, "It is so helpful to know exactly what I am dealing with before I develop a treatment plan for my clients."

ADHD is a huge field and every clinician will find aspects of the field particularly appealing. Clinicians with an interest in treating young children may focus on helping parents to manage their child's behavior. Therapists interested in adolescent issues need expertise with peer conflict, academic advising, and issues related to substance misuse. High school and college students with ADHD struggle with finding future direction and need professionals to help them identify their vocational and academic strengths and weaknesses. Therapists focused on the adult condition must be prepared to delve into occupational and marital issues. In addition, adults with ADHD are often raising children with this diagnosis and, for the MFT, this intensifies a complicated clinical situation.

In many ways, ADHD fits the quintessential biopsychosocial model of treatment. These chronic symptoms can cause impairment in several aspects of the client's psychological development. At its root, ADHD is a brain-based disorder that responds well to medications. In order to offer comprehensive care, the MFT will need to develop an alliance with a local psychiatrist or a primary care practitioner. Many non-psychiatric physicians (primary care physicians, for example) are amenable to prescribing ADHD medications but, often, do not have the time or background to undertake a comprehensive workup. They may, therefore, rely on marriage and family as well as individual therapists to help them in this regard.

ABOUT THE AUTHORS

Joel L. Young, MD, is the medical director of the Rochester Center for Behavioral Medicine outside of Detroit, and assistant clinical professor of psychiatry at Wayne State University School of Medicine. Dr. Young completed his psychiatric training at the University of Michigan Hospitals. He is certified by the American Board of Psychiatry and Neurology and holds added qualifications in geriatric and forensic psychiatry. In addition, he is a diplomate of the American Board of Adolescent Psychiatry. Dr. Young and his clinic have been primary investigators in a number of clinical trials involving antidepressant, ADHD, and bipolar medications. He lectures widely and is the author of many articles and textbook chapters. His book, *ADHD Grown Up: A Guide to Adolescent and Adult ADHD*, was published by W. W. Norton in 2007.

Jaime Saal, MA, LPC, NCC, is the executive director and a staff therapist at the Rochester Center for Behavioral Medicine in Rochester Hills, Michigan. Saal completed her undergraduate work in psychology at the University of Michigan and earned her master's degree in counseling at Indiana University, where she also completed a training program in functional family therapy. Saal is a licensed and nationally certified mental health counselor. She counsels couples, families, and individuals ranging from adolescents to older adults. Her particular areas of clinical interest include ADHD and related conditions, including stress management and relationship and self-esteem issues.

RESOURCES FOR PRACTITIONERS

ADD Coach Academy
www.addca.com
Informative Web site for anyone interested in becoming an ADHD coach or learning about the coaching process.

ADHD: Not Just a Child's Disorder, Video, 2003.
An informative video explaining the three types of ADHD, its symptoms, and treatment options. Also includes ADHD clients telling their stories. This video makes a great psychoeducational tool for ADHD individuals and their families.

Children and adults with Attention Deficit/Hyperactivity Disorder
www.chadd.org
Site offers articles, conference information, and support forums to individuals with ADHD and their families.

Hallowell, N., & Ratey, J. (1995). *Driven to Distraction: Recognizing and Coping with Attention Deficit Disorder from Childhood Through Adulthood.* New York, NY: Random House, Inc.

An in-depth look at ADHD and its ramifications, including vignettes of individuals with the diagnosis

Rief, S. (2003) *ADHD Book of Lists: A Practical Guide for Helping Children and Teens with Attention Deficit Disorders.* San Francisco, CA: Jossey Bass, Inc.
Helpful manual for anyone affected by ADHD. Covers a broad spectrum of topics relevant to the management and understanding of ADHD.

The Attention Deficit Disorder Association
www.add.org
Offers information and support to those impacted by ADHD.

Young, J. L. (2007). *ADHD Grown Up: A Guide to Adolescent and Adult ADHD.* New York, NY: W.W. Norton, Inc. A comprehensive guide to treating and understanding ADHD and its comorbidities.

REFERENCES

Adler, L. A. (2004). Clinical presentations of adult patients with ADHD. *Journal of Clinical Psychiatry, 65*(Suppl. 3): 8-11.

American Academy of Pediatrics (2000). Clinical practice guidelines: diagnosis and evaluation of the child with attention-deficit/hyperactivity disorder. *Pediatrics, 105* (5) 1158-1170.

American Psychiatric Association. (1994). *Diagnostic and statistical manual of mental disorders,* 4th ed. (DSM-IV). Washington, DC: American Psychiatric Publishing, Inc.

Barkley, R. A., Murphy, K. R., & Fischer, M. (2008). *ADHD in adults: What the science says.* New York, NY: The Guilford Press.

Biederman, J., Faraone, S. V., Spencer, T. J., Mick, E., Monuteaux, M. C., & Aleardi, M. (2006). Functional impairments in adults with self-reports of diagnosed ADHD: A controlled study of 1001 adults in the community. *Journal of Clinical Psychiatry, 67,* 524-540.

Biederman, J. (2004). Impact of comorbidity in adults with attention deficit/hyperactivity disorder. *Journal of Clinical Psychiatry, 65* (Suppl. 3), 3-7.

Biederman J., Mick, E., Faraone, S. V. (2000). Age-dependent decline of symptoms of attention deficit hyperactivity disorder: Impact of remission definition and symptom type. *American Journal of Psychiatry, 157,* 816-818.

Biederman, J., Faraone, S. V., Mick, E., Spencer, T., & Wilens, T. (1999). Pharmacotherapy of attention-deficit/hyperactivity disorder reduces risk for substance use disorder. *Pediatrics, 104:* E20.

Biederman, J., Faraone, S. V., Keenan, K., & Knee, E. (1990). Family-genetic and psychosocial risk factors in DSM-III attention deficit disorder. *Journal of the American Academy of Child and Adolescent Psychiatry, 29,* 526-533.

Brown, T. (2005). Brown ADD scale. Psychological Assessment Resources, Inc.

Conners, C. K., Erhardt, D., & Sparrow, E. (2005). Conner's adult ADHD rating scales. Psychological Assessment Resources, Inc.,

Dennison Haines, C. (2005). *Medical Treatment of ADHD.* Retrieved September 1, 2008, from http://www.webmd.com/add-adhd/adhd-medical-treatment.

Faraone, S. V., Biederman, J., Mick, E. (2006). The age-dependent decline of attention deficit hyperactivity disorder: a meta-analysis of follow-up studies. *Psychological Medicine, 6,* 159-165.

Gadow, K. D., Sprafkin, J., & Weiss, M. (2008). Adult self-report inventory 4. Checkmate Plus, Inc.

Goodman, D. (2005). In J. Biederman (Ed.), *ADHD across the lifespan: From research to clinical practice: An evidence-based understanding.* Hasbrouck Heights, NJ: Veritas, Inc.

Hallowell, E., & Ratey, J. *Tips on ADHD and couples.* Retrieved September 1, 2008, from www.addresources.org.

Hallowell, E., & Ratey, J. (2005). *Delivered from distraction: Getting the most out of life with attention deficit disorder.* New York, NY: Random House, Inc.

Kelly, K., & Ramundo, P. (1993). *You mean I'm not lazy, stupid or crazy? A self-help book for adults with attention deficit disorder.* New York, NY: Simon & Schuster, Inc.

Kessler, R. C., Adler, L., Barkley, R., Biederman, J., Connors, C. K., Demler, O., Faraone, S. V., Greenhill, L. L., Howes, M. J., Secnik, K., Spencer, T., Ustun, T. B., Walters, E. E., Zaslavsky, A. M. (2006). The prevalence and correlates of adult ADHD in the United States: Results from the National Comorbidity Survey Replication. *American Journal of Psychiatry, 163*(4), 716-723.

McCarney, S. B. (2004). *Attention deficit disorders evaluation scale, third edition (ADDES-3).* Hawthorne Educational Services, Inc.

Millstein, R., Willens, T., Biederman, J. & Spencer, T. (1999). Presenting ADHD symptoms and subtypes in clinically referred adults with ADHD. *Journal of Attention Disorders, 2*(3), 159-166.

NIMH. (**March, 2007**). *Improving long-term efficacy and effectiveness outcomes in ADHD: A treatment development workshop.* **Rockville, Maryland.**

World Health Organization. (2003). ASRS-V1.1 Screener.

Young, J. L., & Giwerc, D. (2003, December). Just what is coaching? *Attention Magazine,* 36-45.

Young, J. L. (2007). *ADHD grownup: A guide to adolescent and adult ADHD.* New York, NY: W.W. Norton.

Bullying

Anjali Pinjala, PhD & Jeremy Pierce, MA

Originally published as Clinical Update in Family Therapy Magazine
November-December 2010

A SYSTEMIC CONCEPTUALIZATION AND TREATMENT OF BULLYING

Although bullying has been a persistent thread interwoven within the fabric of the human experience, only recently has this topic been given much publicity. This publicity has mainly centered on suicides and homicides committed by children as young as nine years old who had been relentlessly bullied. It highlights the fact that bullying can have devastating behavioral, emotional and psychological consequences. The detrimental effects of bullying run the gamut from school avoidance and behavior problems to suicides and homicides. Although bullying occurs at all ages and in many contexts, for this article, the focus will be on bullying within schools. Bullying or peer harassment is antisocial behavior that encompasses physical assault or unwanted physical contact, extortion, threats and intimidation, vandalism and destruction of property, cruel teasing, shaming, spreading of rumors and gossiping. Bullying can be face to face or through electronic media such as texting, e-mailing, social networking or postings on the Internet. Bullying among children is widespread with a 20 percent victimization rate from 6th to 12th grade (Carlyle & Steinman, 2007). In addition, nearly 10 percent of bullies self-reported perpetrating Internet bullying (Williams & Guerra, 2007). Bullying behavior begins manifesting itself during preschool with a dramatic increase in middle school and a tapering off in high school (Carlyle & Steinman, 2007; Nansel et al., 2001). Bullying affects the entire system within which it is perpetuated. At school, while bullying affects the target, the bully and bystanders, it also creates a climate of fear and insecurity that is felt by the entire school population.

A common misconception is that bullying is a personality trait, but the reality is that it is simply a learned behavior. Early in life, by observation and adaptation of certain relational patterns, a child learns that bullying is a quick and easy way to get various needs met. The habit of using aggression to get needs met is a seductive and powerfully self-reinforcing behavior. Interestingly, families of bullies and targets tend to share common relational patterns of behavior, and a child who has learned these relational patterns may exhibit either bully or target behavior based on the context within which they are embedded at any particular time. For example, a child who observes bullying at home may in turn bully at school. Whether a child engages in bully or target behavior is based on three contextual and cognitive variables. These three variables are: (a) the bully must believe that there is an opportunity to bully with little or no reprisal; (b) both the target and the bully must believe that the target is weaker than the bully and the bully can successfully take advantage of the target; and (c) the bully has learned to use bullying to get certain needs met.

There are several signs and symptoms indicating that a child is being bullied: truancy, lowered academic performance and increased disruptive classroom behavior. The target feels a sense of shame and isolation and gradually becomes identified as a "loser." This reshaping of the target's identity also results in lowered self esteem, anxiety and depression; or in severe cases, suicide or homicide. In fact, a careful study of the many school shootings showed that the shooters felt that they were the targets of bullies.

The effect of bullying behaviors has far reaching consequences for the bully as well. Childhood bullying behaviors later morph into aggressive behaviors of domineering bosses, aggressive coworkers, abusive partners and child abusers. Studies show that youth who engage in bullying behaviors are five times more likely to be convicted of a felony by the time they are 30 years old and four times more likely to have at least one criminal conviction by the age of 24 (Olweus, 1993). If a child cultivates the habit of using bullying to get their needs met, they do not develop the crucial social skills of collaboration and cooperation. Since a bully does not consider the impact of their behavior on the target, empathy is not developed. Most devastating though, is, since bullying is a learned behavior, the cycle of violence jumps to another generation of bullies and targets.

From a school-wide perspective, when bullying is rampant on campus: (a) it creates a campus wide sense of being unsafe; (b) school staff, parents and students all share a sense of impotence to handle the situation; (c) bullying behaviors are observed by bystanders and are imitated, thus the intensity and frequency of bullying spirals upwards; (d) destructive and disruptive behaviors increase; and (e) academic performance is lowered while school refusal, truancy and dropout rates increase.

DIAGNOSIS AND ASSESSMENT

The DSM–IV-TR does not list bullying as a disorder and bullying is rarely the presenting problem in therapy. However, the presenting problems are usually symptoms of the bullying. Therapists who are not aware of the signs and symptoms of bullying may not recognize bullying as the underlying issue. Some of the symptoms of bullying are depressed mood, anxiety, truancy, school refusal or disruptive classroom behavior. In order to assess whether a child is being bullied, careful clinical interviews should be conducted with the caregiver and the child. A child will understand that they are being bullied but will not disclose this to adults due to fear of reprisal or shame. Therefore, first and foremost, the therapist must create rapport, trust and credibility with a child. While there are no DSM criteria for diagnosing bullying, there are several distinct behavioral, cognitive and emotional symptoms that a child will exhibit when they are the target of a bully. While not all of the following signs and symptoms will be present, the most prevalent symptoms are lowered academic performance and school avoidance. During the clinical assessment interview, the following should be explored:

Lowered school performance and school avoidance. A significant underlying cause for absences, school avoidance, school dropout or truancy is bullying. For bullied children, school is a scary, hostile, shaming and lonely place. Further, when they do go to school, the threat of bullying preoccupies and distracts from academics. Children will begin to lose interest in school work, resulting in lowered academic performance. This preoccupation is also manifested in behavioral, cognitive and emotional symptoms like anxiety and disruptive classroom behaviors. It is important that the therapist assess for bullying when presented with symptoms of ADHD and other behavioral disorders.

Isolation or few or no friends. There is self-imposed isolation when a target feels shamed. Alternatively, once someone is identified as a target, others stay away from them for fear of becoming targets themselves. Additionally, the target is seen as a "loser" and other students do not want to be associated with a "loser" (Due et al., 2005).

Reluctance to engage in activities. A child who may have been active in sports, clubs and other extracurricular activities may suddenly show a reluctance to continue these activities. The cause may be that they are being bullied while engaged in these activities. Alternatively, it may be a symptom of depression brought on by bullying.

Loss of possessions and destruction of properties. A bullied child may have their money, books, electronics or other possessions taken from them or damaged. Targets may also be made to buy their way out of being bullied.

Bruises and other signs of abuse. Frequent and unexplained bruises or other signs of physical abuse are often indications of bullying, as is torn clothing.

Emotionality. This is the number one presenting problem a therapist will encounter. Bullied children exhibit symptoms of sadness, anger, moodiness, irritability, depressed mood and crying spells.

Complaints of physical distress. Bullied children complain of frequent headaches, stomachaches, or other physical ailments which may be psychosomatic or it may be a sign of physical injury resulting from bullying (Kshirsagar, Agarwal, & Bavdekar, 2007; Due et al., 2005). Alternatively, the child may pretend to be ill to avoid school.

Has trouble sleeping or has frequent bad dreams. The distress of being bullied is sometimes manifested in nightmares, bad dreams or an inability to fall asleep or to stay asleep.

FIGURE 1: PERCENTAGE OF YOUTH SELF-REPORTING VERBAL, PHYSICAL, AND INTERNET BULLY PERPETRATION.

Type of bullying	5th Grade	8th Grade	11th Grade
Verbal	32.60%	78.50%	72.30%
Physical	34.80%	44.60%	37.80%
Internet	4.50%	12.90%	9.90%

(Williams & Guerra, 2007)

Experiences a loss of appetite. Anxiety about school and overwhelming emotions can also lead a child to lose his or her appetite or have drastic changes in appetite.

If the therapist suspects the child is being bullied and trust has been established, the next step is to assess the child's interactions with peers, friends and others in school to understand the dynamics of peer relationships. After this gathering of information, if the therapist determines that the child is a target of bullying, the therapist should employ a systemic treatment approach.

TREATMENT OPTIONS

Effective treatment of bullying must incorporate both intervention and prevention. Bullying is a systemic problem, so a systemic treatment approach is most effective. Because of their systemic orientation, family therapists are uniquely qualified to deal with bullying. While the therapist works to stop the targeting of a particular child, focus should also be on how to reduce bullying in the school system within which the child is embedded. This systemic approach is not only beneficial to the presenting client, but also to the entire school population (Young et al., 2009; Ross & Horner, 2009; Evers et al., 2007). Further, by working at a systemic level, the therapist will create opportunities to expand the scope of their practice and the family therapy profession in general.

As discussed earlier, in order for bullying to occur there must be: (a) an opportunity to bully without reprisal; (b) a perception by both the bully and target that the bully is more powerful than the target; and (c) the bully has learned that bullying is an easy way to get certain needs met. When any one of these three factors is disrupted, bullying will not occur. Effective intervention and prevention programs address all three factors.

When intervening in an ongoing case of bullying, the therapist must work with the target to reduce or eliminate the first two variables of bullying. In order to rectify the perception of an imbalance of power between the target and the bully, the therapist has to educate and empower the target. With understanding comes empowerment, so the therapist must create an understanding of the dynamics of bullying focusing on the specific behaviors that attract bullies. Additionally, the therapist must work to reduce the feeling of self blame and shame and increase the knowledge that the child has a right to be safe at school and that the bully is the transgressor. The therapist should then move on to identifying and addressing specific characteristics and behaviors that may advertise the perception that the child is either physically, emotionally or socially weak or can be bullied. Some bully attracting perceptions of the child are: (a) not fitting within the school norm (this could be because of the way they look or dress; they are perceived as too smart or not smart enough; their ethnicity, race, religion, sexual orien-

> **TERMINOLOGY**
>
> **Target:** person who is singled out to be bullied.
>
> **Bully:** the perpetrator of the bullying behavior.
>
> **Witness or Bystander:** those who witness or know of the bullying.
>
> **School avoidance:** When a child does not want to go to school or participate in school-related activities; usually a symptom of targets.
>
> **Truancy:** a number of unexcused absences from school.

tation or SES); (b) reacting emotionally, quickly and easily to teasing; (c) being shy and withdrawn; (d) exhibiting timid body language; (e) showing poor social skills; and (f) appearing anxious and insecure.

The therapist should address each of these behaviors or attributes with strategies and exercises to reduce them. The therapist should also include social skills training and an understanding of body language. When this personal awareness of bully attracting behavior is relayed to the child in a caring and non-judgmental manner, it further empowers the child. This understanding creates a sense of control and an understanding of the power they have in changing the bully-target dynamics. This sense of personal empowerment reduces the perception of power imbalance between the target and the bully.

Friends and peer groups are important deterrents to bullying. Children who are alone and isolated are easy targets for bullies. The family therapist therefore should educate the child on what constitutes a good friend and teach the child strategies and behaviors to find and maintain functional friendships. In addition, the therapist should assess the functionality of the child's present friendships and peer groups. Often, targets join particular peer groups to protect themselves from being bullied. Although this group does protect the target, the group may perceive the target as their personal target and thus the child may be bullied by members of their particular peer group.

A powerful tool that targets have is the ability to ask for help and to report to an adult that they are being targeted. However, this tool is often ignored because children have learned that not only is it ineffective to ask for help, but when they report being targeted they are labeled as a tattler and are further victimized. The therapist can help the child identify when to tell, how to tell and who to tell about being bullied. They can help the child identify a caring adult who will listen, act, monitor and take steps to protect the child from further harm.

The therapist should also work with the caregiver to help them support the child and provide tips on how to effectively work with the school to ensure that steps are taken to protect the child from further bullying. This could involve identifying the school staff in charge of dealing with this behavior and working with them to develop and implement a successful action plan. Often there is an adversarial and defensive dynamic between school staff and caregivers. The therapist should coach the caregiver on how to approach the school staff in a collaborative but assertive manner. The therapist can help caregivers identify the goals of the collaboration between school and caregiver. Basic actions that caregivers should expect from the school are: that the target is believed; the bully is identified; the bully has been informed that the bullying has been reported and the school does not tolerate bullying; the bully and any of the bully accomplices are made to commit to stop bullying the child; school staff has been informed of the bully behavior and will be on alert for further bullying behavior; the bully is informed of the school rules with clear, uniform and standardized consequences for bullies; and the parent has a contact person on the school staff.

Finally, the therapist should present themselves to the school as a resource to help the school create and implement procedures to ensure that no more bullying will occur between this particular target and the bully or the bully's friends and accomplices. The therapist should approach the school in a very collaborative manner, as the school may be leery of experts injecting themselves in school business.

While a therapist can effectively help a particular child overcome bullying, a more effective strategy is to deal with bullying in a systemic manner (Whitted & Dupper, 2005). As a member of the community and as a professional schooled in the systemic mindset, a family therapist can conduct workshops, trainings and seminars for school districts, caregivers and children to create awareness, understanding and effective programs to not only curb, but prevent bullying. Prevention programs focus on eliminating bullying opportunities. The systemic approach requires the collaboration of the decision makers, teachers, school staff, children, parents and the community.

A systemic prevention program should include education and awareness about the dynamics of bullying in the form of interactive trainings, workshops and seminars. This education and awareness should be given to schools, caregivers, children and members of the community. The following should be addressed: (a) an understanding of what bullying is; (b) debunking the myths of bullying; (c) creating an awareness that bullying occurs and the prevalence of such within the school district; (d) an understanding of the effects of bullying on the target, the bully, the bystander and the community at large; (e) an understanding of the difference between bullying and children "rough housing"; (f) debunking the misconception that bullying is a normal and harmless part of childhood; and (g) when, how, where, why, to whom and by whom bullying is perpetrated. Effective prevention programs strive to create a sense of shared ownership and responsibility of bully prevention among targets, bullies, bystanders, school staff, caregivers and the community.

BULLYCIDE

Bullycide is a relatively new term that refers to bullying that leads to suicide. The term was first introduced by journalist Neil Marr in the book *Bullycide: Death at Playtime*. It is important that clinicians and parents alike understand that now, more than ever, adolescents who are dealing with bullies at school are looking to make permanent escapes from life when their efforts to get help from those around them is futile or ineffective.

According to the CDC, suicide is the 11th overall cause of death in the U.S. It is the 3rd ranked cause of death in the 13-18 year old bracket. These statistics tell us that at the onset, we must be concerned with suicide and self-injury in general when working with an adolescent population. It is even more critical when working with an adolescent population that is being bullied, as the pervasiveness of the problem and lack of support seem overwhelming and often insurmountable.

Bullying can often lead to children feeling helpless, and this feeling of helplessness may be supported by the inactions of those who know of the child's situation and do nothing to ameliorate the problem. It is also important to remember that at this age, teenagers still operate at a more concrete rather than abstract cognitive level. Add to the mix typical adolescent impulsivity and it becomes a very dangerous situation.

Bullying steadily increases during elementary school, peaks during the middle school years (12-14), and slowly abates during the high school years. It is therefore prudent for those working with an upper elementary and middle school population to assess for risk of suicide. It should be noted however, that suicide attempts due to bullying have also been documented in the earlier elementary ages as well.

Assessment follows the standard suicide assessment protocol, including both careful observation and questioning. Threats should be taken seriously and school staff should be alert and receptive to information received about students in distress. Students should be encouraged to report to staff and parents if they have information or a suspicion that someone is suicidal or has threatened suicide. Parents should be educated to understand what to look for in their child to prevent bullying or bullicide. Look for behaviors that are out of the norm, such as giving away of possessions or a sudden calm after a period of great distress. Explore and co create with the client a list of people who can be relied on for support and do not be afraid to bring in outside help.

Together, standardized and clear policies and procedures must be created and implemented. These should incorporate a system to: (a) monitor bullying; (b) provide a clear understanding of what behaviors constitute bullying; (c) what to do and who to report to when a bullying incident is observed; (d) what steps are taken and by whom when a report is made; (e) what are the consequences of bullying and who administers the consequence; and (f) identify follow up procedures that are in place. The roles and responsibilities of target, bully, bystanders, school staff, caregivers and community members should all be standardized and clearly defined. When schools adopt a systemic prevention program with these components, the incident of bullying is reduced by 50 percent in the first year alone (Olweus, 1994). The old maxim, "what gets measured, gets done," is particularly applicable in impacting the success of any systemic program to reduce bullying in schools. Accordingly, the therapist should also work with the school system to develop appropriate metrics to measure and report on the performance of any implemented bullying reduction programs.

Bullying is a behavior that has been around for a long time. In fact, we are so familiar with this behavior that we often normalize it. However, bullying is not normal. Rather, it is a detrimental and dysfunctional manner of human interaction that should and can be curtailed. Due to their systemic orientation, family therapists are uniquely positioned and qualified to be a catalyst in curbing this behavior.

ABOUT THE AUTHORS

Anjali Pinjala, PhD, is the founder and executive director of the Texas Child & Family Institute. For the last 12 years, she has used a program which she created (*Stop Bullying!*) to help schools in Texas to reduce bullying. This program is systemic in orientation as it involves the parents, school staff and the students. She is a Clinical Member of the AAMFT and a Texas Approved Supervisor for family therapy. Pinjala is a board member of the Texas Marriage and Family Therapy Association and is currently the president of Houston Association of Marriage and Family Therapy. She is a board member for the Baytown Chamber of Commerce and sits on the Texas advisory committee for the Medicaid and CHIP programs.

Jeremy Pierce, MA, is a staff clinician at the Texas Child & Family Institute. He recently earned his MA in marriage and family therapy from the University of Houston–Clear Lake. He is a Student Member of the AAMFT, and a member of TAMFT and HAMFT. Jeremy has been actively involved in helping to shape and deliver the bully prevention program, *Stop Bullying!*

RESOURCES FOR PRACTITIONERS

Olweus, D. (1993). Bullying at school: What we know and what we can do. NY: Blackwell.

Olweus, D., Limber, S., & Mihalic, S. (1999). The Bullying Prevention Program: Blueprints for violence prevention. Boulder, CO: Center for the Study and Prevention of Violence.

U.S. Dept. of Health & Human Services, Health Resources & Services Administration website www.stopbullyingnow.hrsa.gov/kids

REFERENCES

Carlyle, K., & Steinman, K. (2007). Demographic differences in the prevalence, co-occurrence, and correlates of adolescent bullying at school. *Journal of School Health, 77*(9), 623-629.

Due, P., Holstein, B. E., Lynch, J., Diderichsen, F., Gabhain, S. N., Scheidt, P., et al. (2005). Bullying and symptoms among school-aged children: International comparative cross-sectional study in 28 countries. *European Journal of Public Health, 15*(2), 128-132.

Evers, K., Prochaska, J., Van Marter, D., Johnson, J., & Prochaska, J. (2007). Transtheoretical-based bullying prevention effectiveness trials in middle schools and high schools. *Educational Research, 49*(4), 397-414.

Kshirsagar, V. Y., Agarwal, R., & Bavdekar, S. (2007). Bullying in schools: Prevalence and short-term impact. *Indian Pediactrics, 44*(1), 25-28.

Nansel, T., Overpeck, M., Pilla, R., Ruan, W., Simons-Morton, B., & Scheidt, P. (2001). Bullying behaviors among US youth: Prevalence and association with psychosocial adjustment. *Journal of the American Medical Association, 285*(16), 2094-2100.

Olweus, D. (1993). Bullying at school: What we know and what we can do. NY: Blackwell.

Olweus, D. (1994). Bullying at school: Basic facts and effects of a school based intervention program. *Journal of Child Psychology and Psychiatry, and Allied Disciplines, 35*(7), 1171-1190.

Ross, S., & Horner, R. (2009). Bully prevention in positive behaivor support. *Journal of Applied Behavior Analysis, 42*(4), 747-759.

Whitted, K., & Dupper, D. (2005). Best practices for preventing or reducing bullying in schools. Children and Schools, 27(3), 167-175.

Williams, K., & Guerra, N. (2007). Prevalence and predictors of internet bullying. Journal of Adolescent Health, 41, S14-S21.

Young, A., Hardy, V., Hamilton, C., Biernesser, K., Sun, L., & Niebergall, S. (2009). Empowering students: Using data to transform a bulling prevention and intervention program. Professional School Counseling, 12(6), 413-420.

Families of Juvenile Sex Offenders

Richard Gillespie, MDiv

Originally published as Clinical Update in Family Therapy Magazine
March-April 2010 • Revised by author June 2011

CLINICAL ASSUMPTIONS ABOUT FAMILIES OF JUVENILE SEX OFFENDERS

There is an assumption among the public and some professionals that families of juvenile sex offenders are chaotic or abusive, and that these family systems share common characteristics. While there are some common traits involved, these families are diverse. Araji (as cited in Righthand & Welch, 2001) described past studies of families of juvenile sex offenders that indicated there were high rates of parental separation, substance abuse, domestic violence, parental histories of childhood abuse, poor parent-child relationships, unsatisfactory role models, and highly sexualized environments, with family interactions seen as a primary source of the problem. Pithers et al. (as cited in Righthand & Welch) found that the caregivers and their families experienced much stress due to poverty, and much effort was exhausted in meeting basic needs. The families were often disorganized and had a high rate of sex abuse histories. Most families in this study (72 percent) had at least one sex abuse victim in the family. Bischof, Stith, and Wilson (1992) indicated that research in this area is sparse, but concluded that families of juvenile sex offenders have greater family cohesion than other families, though juvenile sex offenders see their families as having less cohesion than non-problem families. There were no differences seen in family adaptability in the three kinds of families. Thornton et al. (2008) stated that families of intrafamilial adolescent sex offenders were characterized as disorganized, uncommunicative, and often adversarial. Tolan (as cited in Righthand & Welch) indicated that families of juvenile sex offenders could be classified as one of two family types: chaotic with role confusion, or rigid and enmeshed with strict rules and perfectionist parental role expectations. Graves et al. (1996) indicated constructs that were collapsed into four bipolar variables that included chaotic-rigid, separated-connected, flexible-structured, and disengaged-enmeshed. Research suggests a variety of types of family systems are involved in this group.

Another incorrect thought about the families of youth with sexual behavior problems is that denial of the youth's offense is the main area of clinical work. Ryan and Lane (1997) stated that a number of areas are worthy of family assessment, including enmeshment, isolation, intergenerational sexual and physical abuse, internal and external stresses, abuse of power, conflicting parental relationship styles, emotional deprivation, and impaired communication styles. The issue of family secrets also looms over the evaluation. It is important to understand the family member's perceptions of the abuse or disclosure of it, and to include the reaction of extended family and significant others. These families need a full assessment on regular systems issues (i.e., communication, openness, etc.) and also on the specific issues related to sex offending.

DIAGNOSIS & ASSESSMENT

Most research on the psychiatric condition of juvenile sex offenders has focused on the adolescent rather than the parents. Awad & Saunders (1991, as cited in Kemper & Kistner, 2007) stated that juvenile sex offenders vary in history of physical and sexual abuse. There is a division of opinion about how pedophilia develops. Some researchers feel that it mainly develops in adulthood, but can begin in a smaller number of adolescents. Others feel that it usually develops during adolescence.

Some juvenile sex offenders were sexually abused as children, some were neglected, others excessively punished, and others deprived of close relationships (Sawite & Kear, 2001; Berlin, 2001; Hewitt, 1995 as cited in Comer, 2004). Awad & Saunders (as cited in Graves et al., 1996) stated that research has only modestly addressed the parental psychiatric history in these cases. Parental psychiatric conditions have been conceptualized in general terms, and present findings contradict each other. It also may be a consequence of other factors involved in the larger system. Where specific disorders were mentioned, it was usually depression. Graves et al. stated that combined data of studies suggested that 20 percent of mothers and 12 percent of fathers of sexually offending youth were identified as having a psychiatric illness.

A review of the literature shows that conduct disorder diagnoses have been observed in juveniles who sexually offended, as stated by Miner, Siekert, and Ackland (as cited in Righthand and Welch, 2001). Kavoussi, Kaplan, and Becker (as cited in Righthand and Welch) found that conduct disorder was the most common DSM diagnosis in their sample of juvenile sex offenders, reported at 48 percent. Prentsky and Knight (as cited in Prentsky et al., 2000) found that impulsivity and life impulsivity have been associated with juvenile sex offending. Becker, Kaplan, and Tenke (as cited in Becker & Hunter, 1997) indicated that juvenile sex offenders have higher rates of depressive symptoms than the general juvenile population. Where these juveniles had a childhood history of physical or sexual victimization, as many as 29 percent appeared to be severely depressed. Becker, Kaplan, and Tenke (as cited in Becker and Hunter) emphasized the importance of evaluating whether juvenile sex offenders are depressed, especially if they were victims themselves. A thorough evaluation of depressive symptoms and appropriate treatment becomes very important to the overall success of treatment.

Most recent theory and research has focused on attachment as a salient factor in sexual assault (Ward, Hudson, & McCormack, 1997; as cited in Stirpe et al., 2006). Attachment issues, as seen in the study by Saunders, Awad, and White (1986, as cited in Barbaree, Marshall, & Hudson, 1993), were part of the report that sexually assaultive males came from disturbed family backgrounds where the parents lacked commitment to each other and had weak attachments to the children. Baker, Tabacoff, Tornusciolo, & Eisenstadt (2004) stated that families of juvenile sex offenders exhibited higher levels of secrecy and taboo behaviors than families of youth with other conduct disorders. Newman & Newman (1999) found that a lack of monitoring by adults and lack of opportunity to talk about sexuality can put youth at risk for early experiences that are abusive.

Assessment is applicable to the family system in several ways. First, it is helpful in understanding the problematic familial interaction style, as seen in four bipolar variables of flexible-structured, chaotic-rigid, separated-connected, and disengaged-enmeshed types (Graves et al., 1996). This evaluation should focus on the previously mentioned characteristics of isolation, enmeshment, external and internal stresses, abuse of power, emotional deprivation, intergenerational sexual and physical abuse, impaired communication, and conflicting parental relationship styles (Ryan & Lane, 1997). Assessment in these areas will provide valuable information to build rapport with the family and to develop a treatment plan.

There are a number of useful assessment tools that are helpful in gaining information about the family system, as well as the individual juvenile sexual offender. The first two of these are general (but beneficial) family assessment tools that give important information about the family system and interactions. One is the McMaster Family Assessment Device and the McMaster Structured Interview of Family Functioning (Ryan et al., 2005). This assessment is helpful in looking at areas of communication, problem solving, roles, affective responsiveness, affective involvement, behavior control, and general functioning. The structured interview looks at these same areas in a more conversational way. The other helpful assessment device is the Family Assessment Measure, III (Skinner, Steinhauer, & Santa-Barbara, 1995) which looks at strengths and problem areas for families in such areas as roles, communication, and values. Each family member can assess general ratings, as well as compare their relationship to another in the family. Several agencies use the FAM III to chart progress of the family in treatment over time.

There are several other assessment measures that indicate overall progress or risk to re-offend sexually and contain important family information. O'Neal et al. (2008) have developed a helpful new instrument that can be used by therapists called the Treatment Progress Inventory for Adolescents who Sexually Abuse. It measures treatment progress initially, and then for every three-month period. It measures a number of areas, including inappropriate sexual behavior, healthy sexuality, social competency, cognitions supportive of sexual abuse, attitudes supportive of sexual abuse, victim awareness, affective/behavior regulation, risk prevention awareness, and positive family caregiver dynamics. The latter section looks at family dynamics, including the knowledge the family caregivers have of the factors that are related to the sex abuse and the areas of high risk situations for future sexual abuse. It also looks at the family caregiver's ability to discipline, monitor, and give direction to the teenager in an appropriate way. It covers the health, or lack of health, in the parental-teenage relationship. A survey of therapy providers of therapy for juvenile sex offenders identified the parent's belief in the efficacy of/and willingness to participate in sex offender-specific assessment and treatment as positive factors related to the youth's amenability to treatment (Kimonis, 2011).

Another instrument in estimating the risk for sexual re-offense in adolescents is the Estimate of Risk of Adolescent Sexual Reoffense Recidivism Version 2.0, or ERASOR (Worling & Curwen, 2001). While it provides an overall assessment, it includes a number of family elements for assessment, including high stress family environment, problematic parent-offender relationships/parental rejection, and parents not supporting sexual offense-specific assessment and treatment. Also included is an assessment of whether the environment supports opportunities to re-offend sexually, which might or might not include the parents as supervisors of the home environment. The ERASOR is an instrument that uses empirically-guided, clinical judgment methodology to predict adolescent sexual recidivism. It estimates the risk of a sexual re-offense for those 12 to 18 who have previously committed a sex offense.

Each of these instruments can add information to the picture of the whole family system. Certainly, a thorough interview of family members is vital, which touches on family of origin issues in both immediate and extended family. Chaffin, Letourneau and Silovsky (2002) stated that clinical assessment should include child maltreatment history, social history, history of problem behavior, strength identification, reports of general psychological and social functioning, and analysis of comorbid impulse control problems.*

TREATMENT OPTIONS

Treatment for the juvenile sex offender will involve individual and group therapy with sex offender- specific treatment, such as the structured exercises suggested by Paige and Murphy (2007). This treatment will usually include a number of issues, such as relapse prevention planning (Murphy & Paige, 2000; as cited in Laws, Hudson, & Ward, 2000). The Association for Treatment of Sex Abuse (ATSA) recommends treatment standards with a rehabilitative focus for juvenile sex offenders (2000).

Ryan & Lane (1997) mentioned a series of treatment issues for parents that may include denial, minimization, and projection of blame. The family may at first react in disbelief, or be quick to blame others. They often mini-

LEGAL AND ETHICAL CHALLENGES

There are two issues that may arise when working with families of youth with sexual behavior problems. One is in how the confidentiality of the youth is handled in relation to family therapy. The preferred treatment for juvenile sex offenders is group treatment, along with the lesser use of individual therapy. Therapeutic issues that have been revealed in group or individual therapy may be important clinical problems to consider in family therapy (i.e., sexual development issues, the youth witnessing parental sexual activity due to parent's substance abuse, etc.). It is important to have the written consent of the adolescent before revealing such issues in terms of preserving his or her confidentiality and the therapeutic relationship. The AAMFT Code of Ethics (2001) in Subprinciple 2.2 states, "In the context of couple, family, or group treatment, the therapist may not reveal any individual confidences to others in the client unit without the prior written permission of that individual." However, this issue may be addressed by the therapist urging the adolescent to reveal this material on his or her own.

Another issue that occasionally comes up is when the youth reveals details of additional sexual offenses in family therapy. Most states have laws that require health professionals, including MFTs, to report suspected instances of child sexual and physical abuse and neglect. Marriage and family therapists disclose to clients as early as possible the nature of confidentiality, possible limitations to that right, and the specific circumstances where a legal report may have to occur, as stated in Subprinciple 2.1 of the AAMFT Code of Ethics (2001). If possible, the marriage and family therapist should have a signed release from the client to report this information or support the client in making the report on his own. Marriage and family therapists must comply with laws that apply in their state regarding the reporting of alleged unethical conduct as stated in Subprinciple 1.6 (AAMFT Code of Ethics, 2001).

mize the entire incident. Lack of empathy for the victim is a huge issue as the parents may be too involved in denial of the activity to see anything else. This may be true even when the victim is a sibling in the home, as the victim may be the family scapegoat and the sexually abusive youth the favored youth. Powerlessness may be an issue as the family may feel that they have no power with the legal system or perhaps no power over their child's behavior, which may have been antisocial in other areas. Anger and other strong feelings are often an issue for families, who act their feelings out rather than share or talk them out. The therapist's task becomes helping the family learn to express anger, sadness, and other emotions in appropriate, safe ways. Intergenerational abuse may be a part of the family history in physical and/or sexual abuse. Accountability becomes a huge issue here in terms of all family members needing to learn to protect and respect one another. I have worked with some families with as many as three or four generations of history of sexual abuse. Family secrets enter in and are used by families to prove loyalty, project power, and to protect family members from painful consequences, including dissolution of the family. Another issue is blurred role boundaries with parents behaving like children and children like parents in some families. To the surprise of some, there is often confusion about sexuality in these families and a need for good information about positive sexuality. Another issue becomes the importance of not forgetting the needs of other siblings in the family. Divided loyalties often enter into family therapy which may take the form of mixed feelings when one sibling offends another. Substance abuse and family mental health history may also be issues as these result in behaviors that impact the whole family.

Certainly treatment options can include traditional family therapy, as well as other forms. When there is a sibling who is the victim of sexual abuse, Trauma-focused Cognitive-Behavioral Therapy (Cohen, Mannarino, & Deblinger, 2006) has become recognized as an evidence-based treatment that is helpful to victims. It also makes strong use of involvement of the parents/ caretakers in the treatment.

In my experience, it is important that work between victims of sexual abuse and offenders not take place until each has completed his or her own therapeutic work. Victims should only take part in family therapy when the therapist feels they are ready. Also, the juvenile offender must have worked through the clarification process, have ended the denial of the offense, and be ready for family therapy in the opinion of the therapist. It also becomes very important to set up relapse prevention/safety plans for the family for when the juvenile offender may return from a residential or other setting. In my work through Tennessee Department of Children's Services, these plans must be approved by the juvenile court, therapist, and a regional psychologist, who is an important check and balance for family and public safety. The plan should be a safety one that can be monitored and changed over time as needed. This should include privacy rules and efforts to support the youth in self-control strategies. There should be no sexual material in the house, and the adults should dress modestly. The plan should allow the offender to be monitored in different situations and setting. Bathing and sleeping should be separate between victim and juvenile offender. Adult supervision should always be present when the two could be around each other. The juvenile is in need of a support network to talk out any sexual feelings that are problematic.

Paige (2009) mentioned the use of family education/support groups as having value in the treatment of families of juvenile sex offenders. There are various family materials found for family education/support groups on relapse prevention, like that of Steen (1999). Bennett & Marshall (2005) mentioned the importance in group work with parents of emphasizing strengths and positives in the family context and having a problem-focused approach to stressors. I have previous experience with this in helping create a family education and support group for parents at Mt. View Youth Development Center in Dandridge, TN. The group would meet Saturdays of every other month for three hours. There would be presentation of basic material about the nature and dynamics of sex offending, often using workbooks or other materials that were used in group treatment with the youth. These dealt with topics like the effects of sexual abuse on victims, reasons or causes of sex offending, cycles of offending, and the effects of sex offending on the families of the offenders, and ways to control sexual feelings. There would be a period for questions and answers for the parents. This would be followed by a time for parents to share their feelings about their youth being in a juvenile justice setting for this behavior.

Paige (2009) also mentioned the value of Multisystemic Therapy and Functional Family Therapy in the treatment of the families of juvenile sex offenders. Alexander (2009) noted that functional family therapy could be used to treat a variety of juvenile delinquency issues including sex offending. It involved the use of three phases of treatment including engagement, behavior change, and generalization with different techniques used in each phase. Relational analysis is used in each phase to look at the strengths of the family to be employed in the various issues that come up. Research on FFT spans 30 years and includes one randomized and two quasi-experimental studies. The first study initially was with 46 families who received FFT through the University of Utah, while 40 families received it with psychodynamic or no therapy. The group receiving FFT had less than 50 percent of the recidivism of the other three groups (Alexander & Parson, as cited in Sprenkle, 2002). In a replication study in Ohio, FFT was conducted for 16 sessions in homes with youth who had even more serious offenses resulting in a recidivism rate of 11 percent, compared to 67 percent in the non-treatment controls. This was a reduction of 80 percent of recidivism (Gordon, Aurbuthnot, Gustafson, & McGreen, as cited in Sprenkle, 2002). Overall, FFT has evidenced a significant reduction in recidivism when compared to treated and non-treated controls and outcomes that remain stable for up to five years (Gordon, as cited in Sprenkle, 2002). FFT works to reduce the self-defeating cycle and malevolent emotions when families enter therapy by helping delineate the family relational pattern (Sexton & Alexander, as cited in Sprenkle, 2002). FFT in in-session process evaluations shows improved family functioning, less silence, improved family interactions, and more equality of speech (Sprenkle, 2002). We have started making wide use of functional family therapy techniques in treatment of families of juvenile sex offenders in my own juvenile justice site.

Letourneau, Henggler, Borduin, Shewe, McCart, Chapman, and Saldana (2009) did a study of community-based interventions using multisystemic family therapy with juvenile sex offenders with services that were typical of those provided for juvenile sex offenders in the United States. Juveniles were randomized for MST or other typical treatments for juvenile sex offenders. The outcomes over a 12-month period looked at sexual behavior problems, out-of-home placements, substance abuse, and mental health functioning. The study showed that MST showed significant reductions in sexual behavior problems, out-of-home placements, substance abuse, delinquency, and externalizing symptoms. The findings suggest good promise for family and community-based interventions in handling the clinical needs and antisocial behavior of juvenile sex offenders. MST has been in development for some 25 years. A typical goal is to enhance caregivers' ability to monitor youth behavior and whereabouts and to give positive consequences for positive

TERMINOLOGY

Deviant sexual behavior: This is behavior that may be counter to our values or seem inexplicable. It may reflect the mores or customs of a specific culture or given time period of history. Another way that it is defined is a persistent preference for nongenital sexual outlets. It may be behavior that is abusive and damaging to others, in some cases.

Paraphilias: This involves sexual response to unusual stimuli, such as children or other non-consenting persons, pain or humiliation, or nonhuman objects. The person must have acted on the impulses, or be greatly distressed by them, to have the psychiatric diagnosis for paraphilia.

Pedophilia: A paraphilia where an adult has persistent or recurrent sexual attraction to children. Most are male. Pedophilia may have varied and complex origins that may include poor social skills or possibly a history of having been abused as a child. There is a lot of current research to understand this better.

Juvenile sex offender: A heterogeneous group of adolescents that may include some with long-term issues of attraction to children or other deviant behaviors. It also may include those involved in a one-time activity that has horrible effects on a victim. A more appropriate term would be "adolescents with sexual behavior problems."

Psychosexual evaluation: An evaluation of the juvenile's psychological condition, family history and patterns, and possible risk of sexual re-offense. It involves getting a detailed family and individual history, as well as standard testing instruments to look at risk, family, and psychological issues.

Thinking error: This is a distortion or excuse a juvenile uses to justify his or her sexual offending of another person. It is part of what juveniles must examine in treatment and be aware of to not be caught in a cycle of abuse of others.

HRS: These are high risk situations that a juvenile must be aware of that contributed to his or her past offense and can be a risk for possible sexual re-offense.

Grooming: This is how a juvenile "sets up" his or her victim for a sexual offense. It has been compared to flirting and trying to get the other person interested in sex, except that in this case it can involve those who cannot give consent. Grooming may be ritualistic and involve promises, bribes, games, rewards, threats and intimidation.

Mature and Immature Sexuality: This has become an area of research in recent years with the immature sexuality in teenagers seeming to come out of lack of supervision by parents and the mobility of our society. Also contributing to this is the fact that some parents do not spend time talking to their adolescents about sexuality. The results can range from a teenager becoming pregnant or having an STD, to youthful sexual offending that comes from experimentation or expressing feelings in inappropriate and destructive ways.

behavior and sanctions for behavior that is irresponsible (Sprenkle, 2002). MST has adapted specific interventions from other empirically-guided behavior interventions that have some empirical support. These include strategic family therapy (Haley, as cited in Sprenkle, 2002), and structural family therapy (Minuchin, as cited in Sprenkle, 2002), behavioral parent training (Munger, as cited in Sprenkle, 2002), and cognitive behavioral therapies (Kendall & Braswell, as cited in Sprenkel, 2002). Psychopharmacological treatments could also be added to psychosocial ones as the need presents itself. MST and FFT have promise and empirical backing for use as clinical interventions in this area.

In a number of families with an adolescent with sexual behavior problems, the sexual acting out behavior spreads out over several generations. This can be from two to four generations, in some cases. Sometimes, an adolescent who was sexually abused may abuse other children of his own age or may carry the behavior to his own children when he grows up. This raises the question about family patterns possibly repeating themselves. Miller, Anderson, and Keals (2004) suggest that there is substantial evidence that levels of individual and family functioning transmit over generations. A good example is a study showing that there is multigenerational transmission of violence (Alexander, Moore & Alexander, as cited in Miller, Anderson, and Keals, 2004). Bowen's theory of intergenerational transmission of behaviors and functioning is a good theoretical approach to examine juvenile sex offending. Most research in intergenerational transmission has ignored Bowen's theoretical viewpoint, so more research is needed with this perspective. I have used this theory in working with these families to examine family-of-origin issues in order to improve their understanding of family patterns and to develop behavior plans to break this cycle.

ABOUT THE AUTHOR

Richard Gillespie, MDiv, LMFT, is a Clinical Member and Approved Supervisor of the American Association for Marriage and Family Therapy, president-elect of the Tennessee Association for Marriage and Family Therapy, and a Clinical Member of the Association for Treatment of Sex Abuse. He is also an Approved Community Provider of the Tennessee Sex Offender Treatment Board. Gillespie is a therapist on the Juvenile Sex Offender Unit of Taft Youth Development Center of Tennessee Department of Children's Services in Pikeville, TN. He has presented on families of juvenile sex offenders at the state conference of TAMFT.

Note: I am greatly indebted to Dr. Jacque Paige and Dr. William Murphy of the University of Tennessee-Memphis for training and materials in this area.

RESOURCES FOR PRACTITIONERS

Association for Treatment of Sex Abuse
atsa.com
Information about research and public policy on sex offender treatment. Members receive current research newsletter.

National Center for Sexual Behavior of Youth
www.NCSBY.org.

Provides information about children and adolescents with illegal sexual behavior.

Sexual Abuse: A Journal of Research and Treatment
Springer Science + Business Media, Inc.
Resource for the latest information on research and treatment of sex offending.

Taylor, M. (1990). *Foy guys my age: A book about sexual abuse for young men.* Northville, MI: Hawthorne Center

The Safer Society Press (Brandon, VT)
www.safersociety.org
Provides workbooks, books, and videos for the use of practitioners in treatment of sex abuse.

You Have the Power (Nashville, TN)
yhtp.org
Provides training for groups and professionals and offers a video training program on the effects of sexual and physical abuse.

REFERENCES

ATSA Executive Board of Directors. (2000). The effective legal management of juvenile sex offenders.   Retrieved September 9, 2009, from www.atsa.com.

Baker, A. L.J., Tabacoff, R., Tornusciolo, G., & Eisenstadt, M. (2004). Family secrecy: A comparative study of juvenile sex offenders and youth with conduct disorders. *Family Process, Vol. 42, Issue 1,* 105-116.

Barbaree, H. E., Marshall, W. L., & Hudson, S. M. (1993). *The juvenile sex offender.* New York: Guildford Press.

Bennett, R. B. & Marshall, E. K. (2005). Group work with parents of adolescent sex offenders: Intervention guidelines. *Advances in Social Work, Vol. 6 No. 2,* 276-289.

Bischof, G. P., Stith, S. M., & Wilson, S. M. (1992). A comparison of the family systems of adolescent sexual offenders and nonsexual offending delinquents. *Family Relations, 41*(3), 318-323. Retrieved September 25, 2009, from JSTOR Family Relations.

Bonner, B. (2009). *Taking action: Support for families of adolescents with illegal behavior.* Brandon: Safer Society Press.

Chaffin, J.F., Letourneau, M. & Silkovsky, E. (2002). Adults, adolescents, and children who sexually abuse children: A developmental perspective. *The ASPAC Handbook on Child Maltreatment* (pp.205-232). Thousand Oaks: Sage Publications.

Cohen, J. A., Mannarino, A. P., & Deblinger, E. (2006). *Treating trauma and traumatic grief in children and adolescents.* New York: Guilford Press.

Comer, R. J. (2004). *Abnormal psychology.* New York: Worth Publishers.

Graves, R. B., Openshaw, D. K., Ascione, F. R., & Ericksen, S. L. (1996). Demographic and parental characteristics of youthful sexual offenders. *International*

Journal of Offender Therapy and Criminology, 40(4), 300-317.

Hunter, J. A., Figueredo, A. J., Malamuth, N. M., & Becker, J. V. (2003). Juvenile sex offenders: Toward the development of a typology. *Sexual Abuse: A Journal of Research and Treatment. 15*(1), 27-33.

Isaacs, A. (2007). The influence of family on adolescent sexual behavior. Retrieved September 23, 2009, from www.allacademic.com.

Kahn, T. J. (2002). *Pathways guide to parents.* Brandon: Safer Society Press.

Kimonis, E. R., Faniff, A., Borum, R., & Elliott, E. (2011). Clinician's perceptions of indicators of amenability to sex offender-specific treatment in juveniles. *Sexual Abuse: A Journal of Research and Treatment. 23*(2). 193-211.

Letourneau, E. J., Henggeler, S. W., Borduin, C. M., Schewe, P. A., McCart, M. R., Chapman, J. E., & Saldana, L. (2009). Multisystemic therapy for juvenile offenders: 1-year results from a randomized effectiveness trial. *Journal of Family Psychology, 23*(1), 89-102.

Newman, B. M. & Newman, P. M. (1999). *Development through life: A psychosocial approach.* Belmont: Brooks/Cole.

O'Neal, B. J., Burns, G. L., Kahn, T. J., Rich, P., & Worling, J. (2008). Initial psychometric properties of a treatment planning and progress inventory for adolescents who sexually abuse. *Sexual Abuse: A Journal of Research and Treatment, Vol.* 20, 161-187.

Our Children: Child Sexual Abuse: A Resource Guide to help Children, Parents, and Professionals. (2000). Nashville: You Have the Power.

Page, J., & Murphy, W. D. (2007). *Manual for structured group treatment with adolescent sex offenders.* Oklahoma City: Wood 'N' Barnes.

Page, J. (2009). Working with families of sexually abusive youth. Presentation at Tennessee Sex Offender Treatment Board Conference, Nashville, TN.

Rathus, S. A., Nevid, J. S., & Finchner-Rathus, L. (2005). *Human sexuality in a world of diversity.* Boston: Pearson.

Righthand, S., & Welch, C. (2001). *Juveniles who have sexually offended: A review of the professional literature.* Washington DC: Office of Juvenile Justice and Delinquency Prevention.

Ryan, C. E., Epstein, N. B., Keitner, G. I., Miller, I. W., & Bishop, D. S. (2005). *Evaluating and treating families: The McMaster Approach.* New York: Routledge.

Ryan, G., Lane, S. (Ed.). (1997). *Juvenile sex offending: Causes, consequences, and correction.* San Francisco: Jossey-Bass.

Skinner, H. A., Steinhauer, P. D., & Santa-Barbara, J. (2005). *Family assessment measure, Version III.* Retrieved September 10, 2009, from PAR, Inc.

Sprenkle, D. H. (Ed.). (2002). *Effectiveness research in marriage and family therapy.* Alexandria, VA: AAMFT.

Steen, C. (1993). *The relapse prevention workbook for youth in treatment.* Brandon: Safer Society Press.

Stirpe, T., Abracen, J., & Stermac, L. (2000). Sexual offenders' state-of-mind regarding child attachment: A controlled investigation. *Sexual Abuse: A Journal of Research and Treatment, 18,* 289-302.

Thornton, J. A., Stevens, G., Grant, J., Indermaur, D., Charmarette, C., & Halse, A. (2009). Intrafamilial adolescent sex offenders: Family functioning and treatment. *Journal of Family Studies, 14/2-3,* 362-375. Retrieved September 25, 2009, from Atypon.

User Guide to the AAMFT Code of Ethics. (2006). Alexandria, VA: AAMFT.

Worlin, J. R. (2004). The estimate of risk of adolescent sexual offense recidivism (ERASOR): Preliminary psychometric data. *Sexual Abuse: A Journal of Research and Treatment, 16*, 235-254.

Financial Strain on Families

Money Matters! in Marriage and Family Therapy

Sarah Stuchell, MA & Ruth Houston Barrett, MA

*Originally published as Clinical Update in Family Therapy Magazine
May-June 2010*

Since December 2007, this country has been facing the longest recession since the Great Depression of the 1930s (National Bureau of Economic Research, 2010). Hundreds of thousands of Americans have lost their jobs, health insurance, retirement savings, and even their homes. Across all demographic and socioeconomic groups, job loss and economic decline trigger a cascade of stressors, which create anxiety, depression, marital conflict, and adverse effects on children (Mistry, Biesanz, Taylor, Burchinal, & Cox, 2004).

The fewer buffers people have, such as second incomes or strong social support, the worse the impact of these stressors. However, higher income and social class do not in themselves inoculate against the negative effects of economic decline on families (Leinonen, Solantaus & Punamäki, 2002).

MFTs commonly see the critical role that money can play in couples and families. Financial distress adversely affects psychological, physical, and relational health of adults and children, including psycho-emotional outcomes of depression, anxiety, anger, and stress (Dakin & Wampler, 2008). Financial strain negatively impacts marital relationships, interactions, and satisfaction (Vinokur, Price & Caplan, 1996); parent/child relationships, parenting practices, and parenting satisfaction (Mistry, Vandewater, Huston & McLoyd, 2002); and child/adolescent behavior, academics, and mental, social, and physical development and health (Mistry et al., 2002; Gutman & Eccles, 1999; Duncan & Brooks-Gunn, 1997). Given these significant systemic impacts, clinicians who apply therapy time and emphasis to the often-somewhat-taboo subject of finances, may indeed find that *money matters*.

Serious family financial problems generally have more to do with the strain of *low income* than poor financial management (Kerkmann et al., 2000). *Job insecurity* also creates financial stress, with increased marital tension (Hughes & Galinsky, 1994) and decreased family functioning (Larson, Wilson, & Beley, 1994), exacerbated by depression (Barling & MacEwen, 1992) and psychosomatic symptoms (Mauno & Kinnunen, 1999). The greater the experience of job insecurity, the greater the experience of financial stress, loss of control stress, and stress expressions at home (Nolan et al., 2000).

For couples, money is the top-rated problem area, even before and early into marriage (Storaasli & Markman, 1990). It is the most commonly reported argument starter (Stanley, Markman, & Whitton, 2002) and topic of dissent (Goldberg, 1987; Oggins, 2003). Strongly associated with marital dissatisfaction and psychological distress (Dakin & Wampler, 2008), disagreements over finances rank among the top contributors to divorce (Lawrence, Thomasson, Wozniak, & Prawitz, 1993). Couples dissatisfied with their financial situation frequently consider their entire relationship to be a failure (Blumstein & Schwartz, 1983).

For families, economic hardship has significant harmful effects on parents' psychological health and children's cognitive, behavioral, emotional, and physical development (Duncan & Brooks-Gunn, 1997; McLoyd, 1998). Children from low-income families are at increased risk for academic problems, juvenile delinquency, and teenage pregnancy (Brody et al., 1994), and to suffer from socio-emotional problems like anxiety, depression, peer conflict, and conduct disorders (Bolger, Patterson, Thompson & Kupersmidt, 1995). Negative impacts on children seem to derive largely through the mediating effects of family processes, as postulated by the family economic stress model.

THEORETICAL LENS AND PREVIOUS FINDINGS

Family Economic Stress Model
The *family* economic stress model emerged from a longitudinal study of 500 European-American families in the 1980's rural Midwest, when thousands of families lost their farms or farm-related jobs (Iowa Youth and Families Project; Conger & Elder, 1994). Financial difficulties cause families to enter a complex, downward spiral. As income falls, families experience such pressures as being unable to pay their bills and having to scrimp on food, utilities, and healthcare. Some move in with other families, or relocate to look for work. As economic pressures mount, so does parents' emotional distress, in the form of depression, heightened anxiety, irritability, anger, and alienation. These symptoms create havoc in family relationships.

Perceived financial inadequacy significantly affects marital relationships, parenting, and children's outcomes, through a chain of mediating variables (e.g., Mistry, Vandewater, Huston & McLoyd, 2002; Conger, Rueter, & Conger, 2000; McLoyd, 1998):

Financial strain. Low income and negative financial events create the psychological experience of not being able to afford goods and services called *economic pressure* or *financial strain*.

Effects on couples. Financial strain manifests in several ways: mental health suffers, women commonly become depressed (Mayhew, 1998), and men become irritable and withdrawn; marital self-image experiences a serious blow, spousal hostility increases, and spousal warmth decreases (Freeman, Carlson

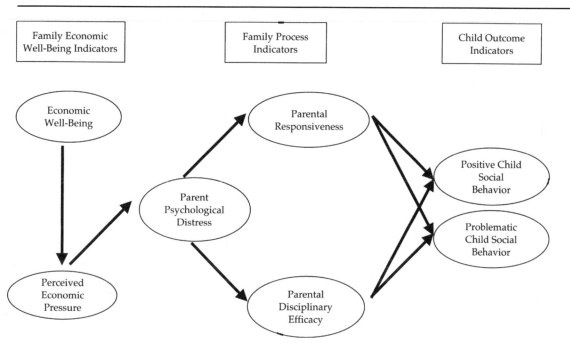

| Family Economic Well-Being Indicators | Family Process Indicators | Child Outcome Indicators |

The Family Economic Stress Model (Mistry, Vandewater, Huston & McLoyd, 2002)

& Sperry, 1993); marital satisfaction and stability decrease (Kerkmann, Lee, Lown, & Allgood, 2000; Robila & Krishnakumar, 2001).

Effects on parenting. Deteriorating parental mood and conflict lead to less positive parenting and more negative parenting (Brody, Arias & Fincham, 1996). Distressed parents exhibit diminished nurturance and sensitivity toward their children, less affection, rely less on reasoning and loss of privileges and more on aversive, coercive techniques (e.g., threats, derogatory statements, slaps), and feel less effective and capable in disciplining their children (Conger, McCarty, Yang, Lahey, & Kropp, 1984; McLoyd, 1990; Mistry, Vandewater, Huston & McLoyd, 2002). Parent-adolescent relations worsen (Gutman, McLoyd & Tokoyawa, 2005). Fathers become irritable, tense, and explosive, with increased tendency to be punitive and arbitrary in children's discipline (Elder, Liker, & Cross, 1984; Elder et al., 1985). Depressed mothers report parenting to be more difficult and less satisfying (McLoyd & Wilson, 1990).

Effects on children. In turn, poorer parenting leads to children's poorer socio-emotional adjustment, poorer academic achievement (Gutman & Eccles, 1999), and increased behavior problems (Duncan & Brooks-Gunn, 1997). Negative fathering predicts temper tantrums, irritability, and negativism in young children, especially boys, and moodiness, hypersensitivity, feelings of inadequacy, and lowered aspirations in adolescent girls (Elder et al., 1984; Elder et al., 1985). Mother's negative parenting increases cognitive distress and depression symptoms in adolescents (McLoyd & Jayaratne, 1994), and lower preschool ability in younger children (Jackson, Brooks-Gunn, Huang & Glassman, 2000). Poorer parent-adolescent relations predict more negative adjustment in adolescents (Gutman et al., 2005).

Empirical tests of the family economic stress model have reliably demonstrated these mediated relationships between income and family well-being (e.g., Mistry, Biesanz, Taylor, Burchinal, & Cox, 2004; Robila & Krishnakumar, 2001).

Further studies have shown that **the model extends to diverse populations**, in addition to the European-American, rural, two-parent families for which it was originally developed. These include families of:

- Various ethnicities, including African-American (Conger et al., 2002; Gutman, McLoyd & Tokoyawa, 2005; McLoyd & Jayaratne, 1994), Chinese-American (Bi & Herman, 2009), Korean-American (Moon, Blurton & McCluskey, 2008), and Hispanic (Mistry, Vandewater, Huston & McLoyd, 2002; Lopez Plunkett, 2003; Barrera et al., 2002).
- Differing geographical settings: urban (Conger et al., 2002), inner city (Gutman et al., 2005), and in the New Orleans area before and after Hurricane Katrina (Scaramella, Sohr-Preston, Callahan & Mirabile, 2008).
- Diverse *family* structures, including a variety of two-caregiver households (Conger et al., 2002) and single-parent households (Gutman & Eccles, 1999; Jackson, Brooks-Gunn, Huang & Glassman, 2000),
- Children of younger ages (Conger et al., 2002) and adolescents (Gutman et al., 1999; Mayhew, 1998; McLoyd et al., 1994).
- Both boys and girls (Mistry et al., 2002; Loukas, Prelow, Suizzo & Allua, 2008).
- Additionally, a number of mediating family processes have been explored.

Those that *mediate the impact of financial strain on child outcomes* include:
- Positive parenting practices (Bank, Forgatch, Patterson & Fetrow, 1993)
- Peer associations (Loukas et al., 2008)
- Family routines (Prelow, Loukas & Jordan-Green, 2007)
- Adolescent social competence (Prelow et al., 2007)
- Social support (via improvements in parental well-being and parenting behavior) (Taylor, 1997).
- Self-regulation in adolescents (Brody, Stoneman, & Flor, 1995)
- Adolescents' perceptions of the parent-child relationship (McLoyd et al., 1994; McLoyd & Wilson, 1990)
- Finance-related parent-child conflict (Conger et al., 1994)
- Maternal psychological well-being aspects such as depression, stress, and efficacy (Mistry, Lowe, Benner & Chien, 2008).

Other pieces include:
- Father-child relations suffer following economic loss if the child, prompted by the mother's interpretation of the economic crisis, blames the father and loses respect for him (Elder, 1974).

- Whereas financially stressed mothers reported feeling "okay" when they could keep abreast of basic needs, affording some nonessential extras is associated with feelings of pride and accomplishment (Mistry & Lowe, 2006).
- Partners' treatment of each other mediates the impact of financial stress on marital quality and stability (Conger & Elder, 1994), with couple interactions being stronger mediators than personal emotional distress (Gudmunson et al., 2007).

FINANCIAL DISTRESS AND GENDER CONSIDERATIONS

Men and women in couple relationships have traditionally responded differently to economic challenges. Husbands and wives often have had dramatically different perceptions about their income and assets (Zagorsky, 2003). Traditionally, husbands have been more likely to fill the provider role and thus to feel the greater brunt of financial strain (Crowley, 1998), to respond adversely to stressful *circumstances* (Conger et al., 1990), and to display dysfunctional social behavior in response (Leinonen, Solantus, & Punamaki, 2002). In contrast, wives have been more likely to respond adversely to stressful *relationships* (Conger et al., 1990) and to undergo emotional, internal changes, such as depression, as a consequence (Leinonen et al., 2002).

Women have cited poor money management as a primary cause for divorce (Amato & Rogers, 1997), yet financial concerns may be more important to husbands' marital satisfaction than to wives' (Aniol & Snyder, 1997). Currently, notions of "his" and "her" marriages may be changing: a recent, national study found little differences between the genders, with husbands and wives very much alike in assessing their financial situation and potential for divorce (Gudmunson et al., 2007). This may be due to changing societal norms regarding work and domestic life, which is evolving into the dual earner household. A second income can be a protective factor from financial strain (Gaunt & Benjamin, 2007), and generally wives' increased income increases marital satisfaction (Schaninger & Buss, 1986). Low-income couples are less likely than middle-income couples to have both spouses in full-time employment, adding to their felt economic pressure around job insecurity or loss (Dakin & Wampler, 2008).

Traditional men experience more job insecurity than traditional women, while egalitarian men and women exhibit similar degrees of job insecurity. It seems that centrality of family life, when felt by men or women, provides some buffering from unemployment stress (Gaunt & Benjamin, 2007).

CLINICAL IMPLICATIONS AND THERAPEUTIC TECHNIQUES

Research on family finances as a marital issue has had little impact on how couples therapy is conducted (Dakin & Wampler, 2008). Today's economic climate forces the issue to the forefront of clinician's work as so many families are forced into situations of financial hardship. Knowing the financial situation

THE "TRUE CURRENCY OF MONEY"*
WORKING WITH MEANING IN COUPLES THERAPY

The following questions can serve as a guide to exploring the history and emotional significance of money for each partner, taken from Shapiro et al. (2007):

(1) What are your earliest memories of money in your family? What is your best and worst memory regarding money? What feelings do these memories generate? Was money viewed as good, bad, scary, dirty, or neutral for you as a child? Did anyone help you to understand these feelings as a child? Were there any family stories about money?

(2) How did your parents talk about money between themselves and with the children? Was it easy to talk about, or was it treated like a secret? What kind of tone was used in the discussions? Did your parents fight about money, and if so, how?

(3) Did your parents agree about how to deal with money? Who was in charge of spending, and who was in charge of saving? Did working, or earning the bigger portion of the income, connect to control over money?

(4) How did your mother think and feel about, and deal with, money? How did her parents think and feel about, and deal with, money? Did your mother enjoy working (or staying home)? How did you know and what impact has this had on you? Repeat using father. How well off did you feel growing up? How did that change over the course of your growing up, if at all?

(5) What is your first memory of having an argument or disagreement about money in your family? What were your feelings regarding arguments about money, and how has this impacted you?

(6) If you have siblings, were different genders or different ages treated differently in regard to money? How are your attitudes and feelings about money different from or the same as those of your siblings?

(7) What is your first memory of making money of your own? How much control did you have over any money you made or received as a gift?

(8) Where else did you get messages or information about money while growing up? Other relatives, religion, peers, TV, culture? How did these messages influence you?

(9) What financial expectations did your parents and grandparents have of you? How was this communicated to you? What financial expectations do you have of your parents or grandparents?

(10) What would you like to do differently from your parents regarding money in your relationship? What would you like to do the same?

Stanley & Einhorn, 2007, p. 293

of clients can be helpful in assessing for psychological, behavioral, and relational problems, in planning interventions, and in being realistic about what is possible to change in the wider context. Without asking, clinicians might be unable to fully envision the range of difficulties a family may be facing—such as lack of transportation, healthcare, and child care (Dakin et al., 2008); utility, phone, and Internet cutoffs; debt collection, repossessions, and eviction notices; and the inability to properly feed, clothe, and maintain a home for the family.

Clinicians should help clients create and maintain adequate coping mechanisms to weather financial crises. A systemic approach can treat current symptoms of suffering, while also working to strengthen family resources and relationships that will buffer and protect the family from short- and long-term effects of financial strain. Therapy should involve multiple levels of assessment and treatment:

- *Financial health* issues, such as instrumental and psychoeducational interventions to aid job searching and financial management.
- *Mental health* issues, such as stress, anxiety, confidence and esteem loss, and depression, in adult and child family members.
- Behavior issues, academic issues, and issues of negative activities and peers, in *children and adolescents.*
- *Couples and marriage* issues, reducing financial strain effects on relationships.
- *Parent/child* relationship issues, parenting emotions and practices, understanding negative and positive parenting practices and effects.
- *Family* issues, including family counseling to reduce blame, to build resiliency, and activate family resources.
- *Community* issues, helping families to engage with community resources and increase social support.

In addressing these areas of financial strain's systemic impacts on individuals, marriages and families, the following research results may inform clinicians.

MFT: RESEARCH INFORMS CLINICAL WORK

Clinicians can make good use of research findings about what moderates adverse effects of financial strain on families.

Couples/marriage therapy. It is well established that couples who treat each other well in times of financial stress fare much better than those who resort to blaming, negative attributions, and conflictual couple interactions (e.g., Conger & Elder, 1994; Gudmunson et al., 2007). While some amount of argument about money is to be expected, *how* couples argue is important to relationship quality (Gottman, 1994), pointing to a need for couples to develop reliable methods to communicate safely and effectively. Couples therapy (such as narrative or emotion-focused therapy) aimed at reducing harmful interactions and negative meaning-making processes may be especially helpful to couples dealing with financial strain, working to help couples collaboratively partner, support, and care for each other through difficult times.

Family therapy and parenting. Evidence is clear that positive parenting practices and good parental relationships substantially buffer children from the serious negative impacts of financial strain in families (Mistry, Vandewater,

Huston & McLoyd, 2002). Family therapy in this area can go a long way in helping children. Clinicians may work with mothers and fathers to reduce irritability and stress expressed toward children, and to reduce negative parenting—aversive, punitive, arbitrary, coercive techniques (e.g., threats, derogatory statements, slaps)—and to build positive parenting (e.g., reasoning and loss of privileges) that is nurturing, affectionate, and sensitive to children's needs.

Research indicates that parents, as well as children, benefit when parents feel more effective and capable; parent/child relationships improve, and parenting feels less difficult and more satisfying. In turn, as parental well-being improves, so does children's (Mistry, Lowe, Benner & Chien, 2008).

Community and social support resources. Social support is known to improve parental well-being (e.g., Taylor, 1997), and enhancing client's social support can be a fruitful area for therapy. For example, research indicates that parents who maintain strong community ties do much better over time (Conger & Conger, 2002). Further, kids whose parents are connected to church, school, and civic organizations live their own lives accordingly, and their involvements predict successful outcomes as well. Encouraging clients to tap into community and social support resources is likely to increase well-being and improve long- and short-term outcomes.

Relational financial therapy. In relational family therapy, therapeutic interventions are designed to encourage empathy and understanding regarding each other's financial behaviors. Examples include: creating a spending diary, gathering and organizing financial documents, inviting couples to examine their family scripts for handling finances, discussing long-term goals, and teaching one's children financial literacy (Gale, Goetz, & Bermudez, 2009).

ISSUES THAT FAMILIES WITH FINANCIAL STRAIN COMMONLY FACE

Clinicians may expect to encounter the following themes and concerns common to families dealing with financial strain.

Grieving losses. Economic hardship and job loss create a series of losses. As families lose jobs, homes, and life dreams, grief can be crippling. Some of these may be ambiguous losses, which may never truly be resolved (Boss, 2006). In extreme cases, a family member may commit suicide as overwhelming losses may feel devastating and hopeless. Assisting clients through the grieving process takes on a central role. Helping families to adapt by recognizing and building upon strengths and resources is particularly important to family resilience (Walsh, 1998).

Confronting denial or unrealistic expectations. Helping clients gently accept harsh realities is necessary to moving forward. This may be a time for families to create new paradigms about their financial health and well-being, to create new relationships with finances and material possessions, and to develop new methods of money management. For example, as banks withhold lending, and consumer credit reports get tainted, the credit crunch forces families to rely on money-on-hand for products instead of lines of credit. They are forced to shift paradigms from one of "borrowing" to "saving" and living within

> ## TERMINOLOGY
>
> **Financial strain:** refers to attitudes of concern, worry, and stress associated with perceived financial problems.
>
> **Financial stressors:** are life events that impact a family unit that can produce changes in a family social system. Financial stressors come from three sources: personal, family, and financial situations.
>
> **Personal stressors:** include things such as, investment losses, injuries, disabilities, accidents, illnesses, and wage garnishments.
>
> **Family stressors:** include things such as, major life-cycle events, such as marriages, births, retirement, job loss, divorce, and death. These types of events often require substantial amounts of money to resolve, which can in itself, be a cause of serious financial problems.
>
> **Financial stressors:** include things such as personal consumer choice situations, such as, moving, paying for household and vehicle repairs, foreclosures, legal problems, bankruptcy, medical bills, and pre-existing excessive consumer debt. These type of stressors tend to increase total stress levels, as well as financial stress levels, which in turn, tend to lead to a lower level of financial satisfaction.
>
> **Job insecurity:** is characterized as a subjective experience, reflecting the individual's perceptions and interpretations of the situation and is considered a classic job stressor resulting in various types of strain.
>
> **The Family Stress Model** (Conger & Conger, 2002): describes a pattern whereby economic pressure leads to disruptions in individual emotional well-being, which in turn leads to poorer marital relations, including marital instability.
>
> **Gender Role Theory:** posits that family roles such as mother and spouse are more central to the identity of women, whereas work roles such as main breadwinner are more central to the identity of men. In this way, work roles are perceived as a significant source of self-esteem for men, whereas family roles are perceived as a significant source of self-esteem for women. Men's tendency to attach greater importance to their work, therefore, may cause them to be more vulnerable than women to employment-related stress, whereas women are relatively protected from this stress due to the centrality of home and family to their identity.
>
> **Gender Ideology:** suggests that women and men with traditional attitudes regarding gender will allocate roles along traditional lines, such that the man takes on the role of breadwinner and the woman is responsible for household labor and childcare. Couples with egalitarian, non-traditional attitudes will allocate the chores more equally, leading to a greater participation of the woman in breadwinning and the man in household labor.

their means—which now is significantly lower than before.

Symbolism and meaning creation. Working with financial issues means dealing with "the true currency of money" (Stanley & Einhorn, 2007, p. 293); that is, the underlying meanings that comprise money's symbolic value for couples. In fact, money is so imbued with meaning that it is one of the most powerful tools a therapist can use (Shapiro, 2007). What may appear to be a difference of opinion about how to manage finances may actually symbolize underlying issues of boundaries, families of origin, trust, commitment, and power (Shapiro, 2007). Thus, therapy should address these issues of couple identity, working out clear plans and mutual understanding, while focusing on what money represents. Narrative therapy that deconstructs old meanings and co-creates new, more helpful meanings around money may be especially helpful.

Restoring trust. Money, like sex, is an area in which one partner can make unilateral decisions that might devastate the other partner, which helps explain why money and sex are two of the most contentious issues for couples. Trust can be threatened around issues of debt, money spending, and financial management. Money is fertile ground for deceit and damaged trust, when, for complex reasons involving identity, shame, and fear of recrimination, people can be highly motivated to hide their financial behavior from their partners (Stanley & Einhorn, 2007). Restoring damaged trust, honesty, and trustworthiness are important areas of therapy.

Emotion regulation and couples skills development. The concrete, harsh reality of inadequate finances to sustain basic needs is real and overpowering, impacting relationships by making it harder to regulate emotions (Stanley & Einhorn, 2007). Interventions should include emotional support between partners, as well as reducing conflict, enhancing communication, and restoring commitment (Stanley et al., 2007).

Stress management. Stress management includes relaxation techniques, meditation, yoga, positive visualization, massage therapy, and stress-reducing hobbies like gardening and knitting. Healthy lifestyles are especially important during times of stress, yet maintaining healthy eating and exercise habits may become difficult as money constraints prevent families affording expensive healthy foods and gym memberships. Exploring options that fit within their new budgets is necessary, including exercise that can occur for free outdoors, and price-comparison shopping for groceries.

INSTRUMENTAL AND PSYCHOEDUCATIONAL INTERVENTIONS

In addition to the previous areas of treatment, clients facing financial and employment difficulties may benefit significantly from practical help. For instance, clinicians' partnering with or referring to financial planners to assist in monetary decisions can be helpful to clients (Gale, Goetz, & Bermudez, 2009). Also, consider job search therapy. Job search interventions include learning job search strategies, practical skills and confidence needed to find employment, interviewing skills, problem solving activities, coping with job-seeking stresses and setbacks, empowerment interventions to take risks and re-think themselves (Price, Van Ryn & Vinokur, 1992). In three major randomized trials, those who participated in these activities via a jobs program were less prone to distress and depression, gained confidence, engaged in effective job searches, got jobs faster, and secured higher paying jobs.

How families cope and adapt to economic hardship, such as planned budgeting, the use of savings and credit accounts, and price-comparison shopping to secure needed and desired expenditures makes a difference in how economic hardship impacts the family (Mistry, Lowe, Benner & Chien, 2008). Money management can be a major source of marital conflict (Aniol & Snyder, 1997), and couples who argue about money are really arguing about how to manage the money they have (Blumstein & Schwartz, 1983). However, frequently couples are not excellent in financial management behaviors and financial planning skills (Godwin & Carroll, 1986; Titus, Fanslow, & Hira, 1989). For instance, good management should include: formal budgeting, keeping written plans and records of expenditures, reviewing expenditures, and using a planning horizon of one year or more (Beutler & Mason, 1987).

ABOUT THE AUTHORS

Sarah Stuchell, MA, MFT, a licensed marriage and family therapist and Clinical Member of the AAMFT, is in private practice with office locations in Malibu and Newport Beach, CA. She is completing a doctorate in MFT at Loma Linda University, and specializes in substance abuse research and treatment, as well as issues of gender, power and equality.

Ruth Houston Barrett, MA, MFT, is a marriage and family therapist intern working with victims of crime in Inglewood, Compton and other inner city areas of Los Angeles, CA. She is completing a doctorate in MFT at Loma Linda University, and specializes in the effects of chronic illness on families, as well as issues of gender, power and equality. Houston Barrett has training and interest in employing advanced statistical techniques, such as structural equation modeling, and feels a strong imperative to work toward bridging research, policy, and clinical work.

The authors write the "Did You Know?" column for the AAMFT California Division Newsletter.

RESOURCES FOR PRACTITIONERS

BOOKS

Bach, D. (2002). *Smart couples finish rich.* New York: Broadway Books.

Gallen, R. (2002). *The money trap.* New York: HarperResource.

Hayden, R. (1999). *For richer, not poorer: The money book for couples.* Deerfield Beach, FL: Health Communications.

Klontz et al., (2008). *Facilitating financial health.*

Opdyke, J. D. (2004). *Love and money.* Hoboken, NJ: Wiley.

Orman, S. (1997). *The 9 steps to financial freedom*. New York: Crown.

Schwab-Pomerantz, C., & Schwab, C. (2002). *It pays to talk*. New York: Charles Schwab.

Spragins, E. (2002, July 2). Love & money. *New York Times*, p. 10.

Warren, E. (2005). *All your worth*. New York: Simon & Schuster.

FILM

Maxed Out. (2006). Directed by J. D. Scurlock.

FINANCIAL PLANNERS

Financial Planning Association (FPA)

www.plannersearch.org
The primary professional organization representing financial planners. This Web site can help identify financial planners in therapists' geographic locations. Those who hold professional designations of Certified Financial Planner (CFP) or Accredited Financial Counselor (AFC) are required to adhere to high ethical standards and act in the best interest of the client.

WEB SITES

Comptroller of the Currency Administrator of National Banks

HelpWithMyBank.gov
This site assists customers of national banks and helps them find answers to national banking questions.

Family and Consumer Sciences

www.fcs.uga.edu/ext/econ
Information for all audiences about the wise use of credit. Topics include credit reports, credit scores, avoiding credit pitfalls, getting out of debt and bankruptcy.

Institute for Financial Literacy

www.financiallit.org
The mission of the Institute is to make effective financial literacy education available for all American adults.

MyMoney.gov

www.mymoney.gov
The U.S. government's Web site dedicated to teaching all Americans the basics about financial education.

National Endowment for Financial Education
www.nefe.org
A site offering help in learning to manage money, no matter the financial challenge. Articles, tools and other resources are available.

REFERENCES

AAMFT. (2009). What are credit counseling agencies and how do they function? *Family Therapy. 8*(5), 25-30.

Amato, P. R., & Rogers, S. J. (1997). A longitudinal study of marital problems and subsequent divorce. *Journal of Marriage and the Family. 59*, 612-624.

Aniol, J. C., & Snyder, D. K. (1997). Differential assessment of financial and relationship distress: Implications for couples therapy. *Journal of Marital and Family Therapy, 23*(3), 347-352.

Bank, L., Forgatch, M. S., Patterson, G. R., & Fetrow, R. A. (1993). Parenting practices of single mothers: Mediators of negative contextual factors. *Journal of Marriage and the Family. 55*, 371–384.

Barling, J., & MacEwen, K. (1992). Linking work experiences to facets of marital functioning. *Journal of Organizational Behavior, 13*, 573-583.

Barrero, M., Jr., Prelow, H., Dumka, L., Gonzales, N., Knight, G., et al. (2002). Pathways from family economic conditions to adolescents' distress: Supportive parenting, stressors outside the family, and deviant peers. *Journal of Community Psychology, 30*(2), 135-152.

Beutler, I. F., & Mason, J. W. (1987). Family cash-flow budgeting. *Home Economics Research Journal, 16*, 3-12.

Bi, Y., & Herman, K. (2009). *Internalizing symptoms of Chinese children in low-income families.* Washington, District of Columbia, US: American Psychological Association, 2009. 4. [Conference Abstract].

Blumstein, P., & Schwartz, P. (1983). *American couples.* New York: William Morrow.

Bolger, K. E., Patterson, C. J., Thompson, W. W., & Kupersmidt, J. B. (1995). Psychosocial adjustment among children experiencing persistent and intermittent family hardship. *Child Development, 66*, 1107–1129.

Boss, P. (2006). *Loss, trauma, and resilience: Therapeutic work with ambiguous loss.* New York: W. W. Norton & Co.

Brody, G. H., Arias, I., & Fincham, F. D. (1996). Linking marital and child attributions to family processes and parent-child relationships. *Journal of Family Psychology, 10*, 408–421.

Brody, G. H., Stoneman, Z., Flor, D., McCrary, C., Hastings, L., & Conyers, O. (1994). Financial resources, parent psychological functioning, parent co-caregiving, and early adolescent competence in rural two-parent African-American families. *Child Development, 65*, 590–605.

Brody, G., Stoneman, Z., & Flor, D. (1995). Linking family processes and academic competence among rural African American youths. *Journal of Marriage & Family, 57*(3), 567-579.

Conger, R.D., & Conger, K.J. (2002). Resilience in Midwestern families: Selected findings from the first decade of a prospective, longitudinal study. *Journal of Marriage and Family, 64*, 361-373.

Conger, R., & Elder, G. (1994). *Families in troubled times: Adapting to change in rural America. Social Institutions and Social Change.*

Conger R. D., Elder, G. H., Lorenz, F. O., Conger, K. J., Simons, R. L., Whitbeck,

L. B., et al. (1990). Linking economic hardship to marital quality and instability. *Journal of Marriage and the Family. 52,* 643-656.

Conger, R. D., Ge, X., & Lorenz, F. O. (1994). Economic stress and marital relations. In R. D.Conger, G. H. Elder, F. O. Lorenz, R. L. Simons, & L. B. Whitbeck (Eds), *Families in troubled times: Adapting to change in rural America* (pp. 187-203). Hawthorne, NY: Aldine de Gruyter.

Conger, R. D., McCarty, J., Yang, R., Lahey, B., & Kropp, J. (1984). Perception of child, child rearing values, and emotional distress as mediating links between environmental stressors and observed maternal behavior. *Child Development, 54,* 2234-2247.

Conger, K. J., Reuter, M. A., & Conger, R. D. (2000). The role of economic pressure in the lives of parents, their adolescents: The family stress model. In L. J. Crockett, & R. K. Silbereisen (Eds.), *Negotiating adolescence in times of social change* (pp. 201-223). New York: Cambridge University Press.

Conger, R. D, Wallace, L., Sun, Y., Simons, R., McLoyd, V., & Brody, G. (2002). Economic pressure in African American families: A replication and extension of the family stress model. *Developmental Psychology, 38*(2), 179-193.

Crowley, M. S. (1998). Men's self-perceived adequacy as the family breadwinner: Implications for their psychological, marital and work-family well-being. *Journal of Family and Economic Issues, 19,* 7-23.

Dakin, J., & Wampler, R. (2008). Money doesn't buy happiness, but it helps: Marital satisfaction, psychological distress, and demographic differences between low- and middle-income clinic couples. *The American Journal of Family Therapy, 36,* 300-311.

Duncan, G., Yeung, W., Brooks-Gunn, J., & Smith, J. (1998). How much does childhood poverty affect the life chances of children? *American Sociological Review, 63*(3), 406-423.

Elder, G. H., Jr., (1974). Children of the Great Depression, Chicago: University of Chicago Press.

Elder, G., Liker, J., & Cross, C. (1984). Parent-child behavior in the Great Depression: Life course and intergenerational influences. In P. Baltes & O. Brim (Eds.), *Life-span development and behavior* (pp. 109—158). Orlando, FL: Academic Press.

Elder, C , Nguyen, T., & Caspi, A. (1985). Linking family hardship to children's lives. *Child Development. 56,* 361-375.

Freeman, C., Carlson, J., & Sperry, L. (1993). Adlerian marital therapy strategies with middle income couples facing financial stress. *The American Journal of Family Therapy, 21*(4), 324-332.

Gale, J., Goetz, J. & Bermudez, M. (2009). Relational financial therapy. *Family Therapy. 8*(5), 25-30.

Gaunt, R., & Benjamin, O. (2007). Job insecurity, stress and gender: The moderating role of gender ideology. *Community, Work and Family, 10*(3), 341-355.

Godwin, D. D., & Carroll, D. D. (1986). Financial management attitudes and behavior of husbands and wives. *Journal of Consumer Studies and Home Economics, 10,* 47-55.

Goldberg, M. (1987). Patterns of disagreement in marriage. *Medical Aspects of Human Sexuality, 21,* 42-52.

Gottman, J., & Carrère, S. (1994). Why can't men and women get along? Developmental roots and marital inequities. *Communication and relational maintenance* (pp. 203-229). San Diego, CA US: Academic Press.

Gudmunson, C., Beutler, I., Israelsen, C., Hill, E., & McCoy, J. (2007). Linking financial strain to marital instability: Examining the roles of emotional distress and marital interaction. *Journal of Family and Economic Issues, 28*(3), 357-376.

Gutman, L., & Eccles, J. (1999). Financial Strain, Parenting Behaviors, and Adolescents' Achievement: Testing Model Equivalence between African American and European American Single- and Two-Parent Families. *Child Development, 70* 1464-76.

Gutman, L., McLoyd, V., & Tokoyawa, T. (2005). Financial strain, neighborhood stress, parenting behaviors, and adolescent adjustment in urban African American families. *Journal of Research on Adolescence (Blackwell Publishing Limited), 15*(4), 425-449.

Hughes, D., & Galinsky, E. (1994). Work experiences and marital interactions: Elaborating the complexity of work. *Journal of Organizational Behavior, 15,* 423-438.

Jackson, A., Brooks-Gunn, J., Huang, C., & Glassman, M. (2000). Single mothers in low-wage jobs: Financial strain, parenting, and preschoolers' outcomes. *Child Development, 71*(5), 1409-1423.

Kerkmann, B. C., Lee, T. R., Lown, J. M., & Allgood, S. M. (2000). Financial management, financial problems and marital satisfaction among recently married university students. *The Journal of the Association for Financial Counseling and Planning Education, 11*(2), 55-64.

Larson, J.H., Wilson, S.M., & Beley, R. (1994). The impact of job insecurity on marital and family relationships. *Family Relations, 43,* 138-143.

Lawrence, F.C., Thomasson, R.H., Wozniak, P.J., & Prawitz, A.D. (1993). Factors relating to spousal financial arguments. *Financial Counseling and Planning, 4,* 85-93.

Leinonen, J.A., Solantus, T.X., & Punamaki, R. (2002). The specific mediating paths between economic hardship and the quality of parenting. *International Journal of Behavioral Development, 26,* 423-435.

Lopez Plunkett, L. (2003). Factors within the parent-child relationship most affected by poverty: A study of impoverished Latina mothers and their children. *Dissertation Abstracts International, 64.*

Loukas, A., Prelow, H., Suizzo, M., & Allua, S. (2008). Mothering and peer associations mediate cumulative risk effects for Latino Youth. *Journal of Marriage & Family, 70*(1), 76-85.

Mauno, S., & Kinnunen, U. (1999). Job insecurity and well-being: A longitudinal study among male and female employees in Finland. *Community, Work, and Family, 2,* 147-172.

Mayhew, K. (1998). Family financial strain and family relationship perceptions: Predictors of adolescent depressed mood. *Dissertation Abstracts International Section A,* 58.

McLoyd, V. C. (1990). The impact of economic hardship on black families and children: Psychological distress, parenting, and socioemotional development. *Child Development, 61,* 311-346.

McLoyd, V. C. (1998). Socioeconomic disadvantage and child development. *American Psychologist.* 53, 185-204.

McLoyd, V. C., & Jayaratne, T. (1994). Unemployment and work interruption among African American single mothers: Effects on parenting and adolescent socioemotional functioning. *Child Development, 65*(2), 562-589.

McLoyd, V.C., & Wilson, L. (1990). Maternal behavior, social support, and economic conditions as predictors of psychological distress in children. In V. C. McLoyd & C. Flanagan (Eds.), *New directions for child development: Vol. 46. Economic stress: Effects on family life and child development* (pp. 49-69). San Francisco: Jossey-Bass.

Mistry, R., Biesanz, J., Taylor, L., Burchinal, M., & Cox, M. (2004). Family income and its relation to preschool children's adjustment for families in the NICHD Study of Early Child Care. *Developmental Psychology, 40*(5), 727-745.

Mistry, R., & Lowe, E. (2006). What earnings and income buy: The "basics"' plus "a little extra": Implications for family and child well-being. *Making it work: Low-wage employment, family life, and child development* (pp. 173-205). New York: Russell Sage Foundation.

Mistry, R., Lowe, E., Benner, A., & Chien, N. (2008). Expanding the family economic stress model: Insights from a mixed-methods approach. *Journal of Marriage and Family, 70*(1), 196-209.

Mistry, R., Vandewater, E., Huston, A., & McLoyd, V. (2002). Economic well-being and children's social adjustment: The role of family process in an ethnically diverse low-income sample. *Child Development, 73*(3), 935.

Moon, B., Blurton, D., & McCluskey, J. (2008). General strain theory and delinquency: Focusing on the influences of key strain characteristics on delinquency. *Crime & Delinquency, 54*(4), 582-613.

National Bureau of Economic Research. (2010). Information on recessions and recoveries, the NBER Business Cycle Dating Committee, and related topics. Retrieved April 15, 2010, from http://www.nber.org/cycles/main.html.

Nolan, J. P., Wichert, I. C., & Burchell, B. J. (2000). *Workers on the edge: Job insecurity, psychological well-being and family life*. Cambridge: Economic Policy Inst.

Oggins, J. (2003). Topics of marital disagreement among African-American and Euro-American newlyweds. *Psychological Reports, 92*, 419-425.

Prelow, H., Loukas, A., & Jordan-Green, L. (2007). Socioenvironmental risk and adjustment in Latino youth: The mediating effects of family processes and social competence. *Journal of Youth & Adolescence, 36*(4), 465-476.

Price, R. H., Van Ryn, M., & Vinokur, A. D. (1992). Impact of a preventive job search intervention on the likelihood of depression among the unemployed. *Journal of Health and Social Behavior, 33*, 158-167.

Robila, M., & Krishnakumar, A. (2001). Impact of financial strain on children's psychological functioning: the mediating role of family processes. *Impact of financial strain on children's psychological functioning: the mediating role of family processes.*

Scaramella, L., Sohr-Preston, S., Callahan, K., & Mirabile, S. (2008). A test of the family stress model on toddler-aged children's adjustment among Hurricane Katrina impacted and nonimpacted low-income families. *Journal of Clinical Child & Adolescent Psychology, 37*(3), 530-541.

Schaninger, C. M., & Buss, W. C. (1986). A longitudinal comparison of consumption and finance handling between happily married and divorced couples. *Journal of Marriage and Family, 63*, 458-472.

Shapiro, M. (2007). Money: A therapeutic tool for couples therapy. *Family Process, 46*, 279-291.

Stanley, S. M., & Einhorn, L. A. (2007). Hitting pay dirt: Comment on "Money: A therapeutic tool for couples therapy." *Family Process, 46*(3), 293-299.

Stanley, S. M., Markman, H. J., & Whitton, S. (2002). Communication, conflict, and commitment: Insights on the foundations of relationship success from a national survey. *Family Process, 41,* 659-675.

Storaasli, R. D., & Markman, H. J. (1990). Relationship problems in the early stages of marriage: A longitudinal investigation. *Journal of Family Psychology, 4,* 80-98.

Taylor, R. (1997). The effects of economic and social stressors on parenting and adolescent adjustment in African-American families. *Social and emotional adjustment and family relations in ethnic minority families* (pp. 35-52). Mahwah, NJ: Lawrence Erlbaum Associates Publishers.

Titus, P. M., Fnaslow, A. M., & Hira, T. K. (1989). Net worth and financial satisfaction as a function of household money managers' competencies. *Home Economics Research Journal, 17,* 309-318.

Vinokur, A., Price, R., & Caplan, R. (1996). Hard times and hurtful partners: How financial strain affects depression and relationship satisfaction of unemployed persons and their spouses. *Journal of Personality and Social Psychology, 71*(1), 166-179.

Walsh, F. (1998). *Strengthening family resilience.* New York: The Guilford Press.

Zagorsky, J. L. (2003). Husbands' and wives' view of the family finances. *Journal of Socio-Economics, 32,* 127-146.

American Association for Marriage and Family Therapy

Grandparents Raising Grandchildren

Megan L. Dolbin-MacNab, PhD & Ryan M. Traylor, MS

Originally published as Clinical Update in Family Therapy Magazine
January-February 2008

Over the last 30 years, the number of American children being raised by a grandparent has more than doubled to 4.5 million, representing 6.3 percent of all U.S. children (Lugaila & Overturf, 2004). Grandparent caregivers number around 2.4 million (Simmons & Dye, 2003). Although grandparents assuming responsibility for the care of their grandchildren is not new (Uhlenberg & Kirby, 1998), in the last 15 years, the needs of these families have gained considerable public attention. In state and federal governments, there has been a notable increase in the development of legislation and the earmarking of funds to assist grandparents raising grandchildren (Beltran, 2000; Bryson & Casper, 1999). Within local communities, there has been a proliferation of mental health services for grandparent-headed families. Most of these services emphasize psychoeducation and social support (Cox, 1999; Minkler, Driver, Roe & Bedeian, 1993). However, as custodial grandparents frequently express a desire for more intensive intervention (Burnette, 1999; Landry-Meyer, 1999), therapists are increasingly encountering these families within their practices.

There are multiple explanations for the increase in grandparent-headed families. Central to these explanations is an escalation in social problems associated with the middle generation. These problems include substance abuse, child abuse and neglect, incarceration, HIV/AIDS, physical and mental illness, divorce, and death (Jendrek, 1994; Minkler, 1999; Roe & Minkler, 1998). Also contributing to the increase in grandparent-headed families are changes in state and federal policies that encourage or require foster children to be placed with relatives (Minkler & Fuller-Thomson, 2005). Cultural traditions, such as familism, may further encourage grandparent involvement in childrearing (Burnette, 1999; Goodman & Silverstein, 2005). Finally, some grandparents assume caregiving responsibilities in order to prevent their grandchildren from entering the foster care system, keep the family together, or assist during a family crisis (Hayslip & Kaminski, 2005).

DEMOGRAPHIC CHARACTERISTICS

Examinations of nationally representative data reveal that grandparent-headed families are extremely diverse and cut across racial, ethnic, socioeconomic, and geographic lines. As such, it is impossible to describe a typical grandparent-headed family. Nonetheless, there are certain socio-demographic characteristics that tend to be associated with these families. These demographic characteristics are significant, as they provide insight into the common needs and experiences of custodial grandparents and their grandchildren.

Structurally, approximately 20 percent of custodial grandparents report incomes that fall below the poverty line (Simmons & Dye, 2003). Approximately one-third of grandparent-headed families are skip generation families, in that they do not include either of the grandchild's parents (Bryson & Casper, 1999). Skip generation families are one of the fastest growing forms of grandparent-headed families (Bryson & Casper, 1999). Although estimates regarding grandparent relationship status vary widely, Census data suggest that approximately half of custodial grandparents are married (Bryson & Casper, 1999). Regardless of family structure, caregiving tends to be a long-term commitment, with 39 percent of grandparents providing 5 or more years of care to their grandchildren (Simmons & Dye, 2003).

A disproportionate number (63 percent) of custodial grandparents are female (Bryson & Casper, 1999; Simmons & Dye, 2003). Most grandparent caregivers are relatively young, with the highest percentage (35 percent) of grandparents being between the ages of 50 and 59 (Simmons & Dye, 2003). African American grandparents are more likely to assume caregiving responsibilities than their white or Latino counterparts (Fuller-Thomson, Minkler & Driver, 1997; Minkler & Fuller-Thomson, 2005; Simmons & Dye, 2003).

Compared to children being raised by parents, children being raised by grandparents are more likely to be African American, under the age of six, and poor (Bryson & Casper, 1999). Children living in grandmother-headed households, with no parents present, are especially likely to be poor (Bryson & Casper, 1999). Data also suggest that, when compared to other children, children living with custodial grandparents are less likely to have health insurance and more likely to be living in a household receiving public assistance (Bryson & Casper, 1999).

AREAS FOR ASSESSMENT

Assessment, within the context of custodial grandparenting, involves attending to numerous individual, relational, and contextual issues. Difficulties with any number of these issues could motivate a grandparent-headed family to seek therapy services. Because grandparent-headed families may come to therapy with multiple presenting problems, therapists must conduct a comprehensive and ongoing assessment in order to gain a clear understanding of all the relevant issues. Although there may be some commonalities in the issues that bring custodial grandparents and grandchildren to therapy, the great diversity within these families means that therapists should be careful to avoid making generalizations. Also, if the assessment identifies needs that are beyond the scope of therapy (e.g., financial, physical, or legal problems), therapists should be prepared to make an appropriate referral.

GRANDPARENTS

The assumption of caregiving responsibilities impacts all facets of grandparents' lives. There are positive aspects of caregiving, such as a greater sense of purpose (Jendrek, 1993), a second chance at successful parenting (Ehrle & Day, 1994), and a close emotional relationship with the grandchild (Dolbin-MacNab & Keiley, 2005). However, as custodial grandparenting is more often associated with multiple physical, social, emotional, and structural stressors, therapists should attend to grandparents' personal experiences with stress and coping.

Custodial grandparenting has been called an "off-time" role in that grandparents are entering the parenting role at a time in their lives when they did not expect to be parenting (Jendrek, 1993; 1994). As such, custodial grandparents often report feelings of anger, shame, and resentment about their new role and the inability of their adult child to function as a parent. They may also experience grief and loss associated with declines in time for themselves, changes in their future plans, and increased social isolation (Jendrek, 1994).

Grandparents may also experience stress related to legal issues such as establishing guardianship, enrolling grandchildren in school, and obtaining medical care. Moreover, because custodial grandparents often have limited or fixed incomes, lack of adequate financial resources is often a significant stressor (Roe & Minkler, 1998). Finally, many grandparents report stress associated with parenting, particularly when their grandchildren have challenging emotional and behavioral problems.

Research on grandparent well being suggests that the stress associated with assuming caregiving responsibilities often results in negative outcomes. Physically, custodial grandparents experience health problems such as diabetes, hypertension, high cholesterol, and obesity (Kelley & Whitely, 2003). Custodial grandparents also experience limitations in tasks of daily living (Fuller-Thomson & Minkler, 2000), as well as declining mobility and energy. Psychologically, compared to noncustodial grandparents, custodial grandparents have higher rates of depression and psychological distress (Kelley & Whitley, 2003; Minkler, Fuller-Thomson, Miller & Driver, 1997; Pruchno & McKinney, 2000).

GRANDCHILDREN

Children being raised by grandparents often experience a variety of developmental, physical, behavioral, academic, and emotional difficulties (Billing, Ehrle & Kortenkamp, 2002; Grant, Gordon & Cohen, 1997; O'Reilly &

Morrison, 1993; Pruchno, 1999; Shore & Hayslip, 1994; Solomon & Marx, 1995). Although the severity of grandchildren's problems varies greatly, in one study, 70 percent of custodial grandparents reported feeling concerned about their grandchildren's behavior problems (Landry-Meyer, 1999). Thus, when a grandparent-headed family presents for therapy, it is likely that the presenting problem will be related to the grandchild. Therapists should be prepared to conduct an in-depth assessment of the grandchild, within the context of the larger family system.

Grandchildren's problems may be attributed to several factors. First, problems may result from the circumstances that brought the grandchildren into their grandparents' care. Problems may also result from the stress of transitioning between caregiving arrangements, or qualities of the grandparent's childrearing (Hayslip, Shore, Henderson & Lambert, 1998). Other aspects of grandparent-headed families that may exacerbate grandchildren's problems include poverty, custody battles, disruptive contact with the middle generation, new authority figures, unfamiliar household rules, uncertainly about the future, and disapproval from larger society (Webb, 1996).

Grandchildren's difficulties span the entire range of childhood disorders and include depression, anxiety, aggression, attachment disorders, acting out, hyperactivity, inattention, and impulsivity (e.g., Grant et al., 1997; O'Reilly & Morrison, 1993; Pruchno, 1999). Grandchildren may also experience health problems, as well as poor school performance (Billing et al., 2002). Interpersonally, grandchildren may demand attention, defy authority, test limits, and resist an emotional bond to their grandparent caregiver (Brown-Standridge & Floyd, 2000; Grant et al., 1997; Pruchno, 1999). Emotionally, grandchildren may struggle with feelings of grief, anger, loss, resentment, and confusion (O'Reilly & Morrison, 1993). They may also feel unwanted, worry that they are a burden to their grandparents, and worry about returning to their parents (Dolbin-MacNab, Nielson, & Keiley, 2005; Bratton, Ray, & Moffit, 1998).

THE FAMILY SYSTEM

The intersection of the individual issues experienced by custodial grandparents and their grandchildren results in complex family dynamics. These dynamics are further complicated by interactions with the middle generation and the larger extended family. Although a full consideration of the possible relationship dynamics within grandparent-headed families is beyond the scope of this update, there are some common relationship dynamics that have been observed in these families. Therapists should attend to these dynamics and any other interaction patterns that may be significant to the functioning of the family.

Although research suggests that custodial grandparents and grandchildren feel emotionally close (Dolbin-MacNab & Keiley, 2005; Dolbin-MacNab et al., 2005), there are also multiple sources of tension and conflict in the grandparent-grandchild relationship. One source of tension may be generational differences in expectations related to behavior, leisure, and social activities (Dolbin-MacNab & Keiley, 2005; Dolbin-MacNab et al., 2005). Tension can also arise from difficulty in negotiating rules and the grandparents' attempts at establishing authority. Grandparents and grandchildren may project their feelings of anger and resentment at the middle generation onto one another (O'Reilly & Morrison, 1993). Additionally, grandparents may approach parenting out of guilt, and as a result, overindulge and overprotect their grandchildren (O'Reilly & Morrison, 1993). This approach to parenting becomes especially problematic when trying to discipline a child with significant emotional and behavioral problems. Finally, because they often feel indebted to their grandparents (Dolbin-MacNab et al., 2005), grandchildren may assume an inappropriate level of responsibility for their grandparents' health and well-being.

Interactions with the middle generation can be stressful to both grandparents and grandchildren. Visits may be unpredictable and can disrupt important family routines and rules. Grandparents often feel hurt and disempowered when grandchildren are ecstatic to see parents who have not participated in their daily care. Frustration builds when promises to the grandchildren are not kept and the grandparents are left to "clean up the mess." Grandchildren may be triangulated into the grandparent-adult child relationship, and often struggle with loyalty conflicts. The middle generation may struggle to identify their role in the family system.

Within the extended family, there may be disagreement over the grandparent's decision to assume caregiving responsibilities. Other adult children may resent the attention being given to their sibling or the impact that caregiving is having on the grandparent. There may also be conflict arising from the perception that the grandparent does not spend enough time with the other grandchildren, or that the grandparent is showing favoritism to one portion of the family.

TREATMENT OPTIONS

SUPPORT GROUPS

Support groups represent the most widely used mental health intervention for custodial grandparents (Cox, 1999; Minkler et al., 1993; Smith, 2003). Although anecdotal evidence supports the notion that support groups are effective in meeting the needs of custodial grandparents and their grandchildren, empirical support for these claims is limited (Hayslip & Kaminski, 2005). Nevertheless, there is preliminary evidence that support group participation is associated with decreased negative affect and depression, greater social support, improved locus of control, increased parental knowledge and self-efficacy, and an improved grandparent-grandchild relationship (Hayslip, 2003; Kolomer, McCallion, & Janicki, 2002; Smith & Dannison, 2003). However, as there is also evidence that support group participation is associated with increased role strain, financial strain, and depression (Hayslip, 2003), more research about the implementation and effectiveness of support groups for custodial grandparents is needed.

Because of their ability to provide custodial grandparents with a supportive social network, community problem-solving, and psychoeducational information, support groups should be considered as one element of a multi-modal approach to meeting the needs of grandparent-headed families (O'Reilly & Morrison, 1993). However, therapists must be cautious in making referrals as the quality of support groups can vary widely. Furthermore, not all custodial grandparents and grandchildren are appropriate candidates for support groups. Some grandparent-headed families may have needs that are better met through individual or family therapy. Therapists should work with grandparents to determine, given their individual circumstances, whether participation in a support group would be appropriate.

Many support groups for grandparents raising grandchildren are ineffective and potentially harmful because they lack structure and skilled leadership, create an environment of self-pity and complaining, and do not have clear goals and objectives (Smith, 2003). Therapists interested in referring their clients to support groups should look for groups that feature the following characteristics:

- The support group offers meals, transportation, and childcare (Burnette, 1999; Dannison & Smith, 2003).
- Custodial grandparents have a voice in the conceptualization and implementation of the group (Dannison & Smith, 2003; Grant et al., 1997).
- Participants trust the group leaders and view them as credible (Dannison & Smith, 2003; Grant et al., 1997).
- While there is time for personal sharing (Dannison & Smith, 2003; Hayslip & Kaminski, 2005; Strom & Strom, 1993), the group has clear goals and objectives that emphasize advocacy, education, and skill building (Burnette, 1999; Cox, 1999; Hayslip & Kaminski, 2003; Strom & Strom, 2000).

Additionally, Strom and Strom (2000) recommend that support group leaders encourage optimistic attitudes, provide clear guidelines for discussion, facilitate social support from the larger community, and encourage goal setting.

Most support groups for grandparent-headed families focus on providing services to grandparents. When support groups provide services for grandchildren, they often take the form of childcare and do not formally address grandchildren's therapeutic needs. Therefore, therapeutic programming for grandchildren is a growing need (Dannison & Smith, 2003). Programs for grandchildren should include small adult to child ratios, therapeutic play, and consistent routines. Grandparents should also be given frequent feedback about their grandchildren's progress. In terms of content, Dannison and Smith (2003) advocate for programs that promote the development of self-esteem and social skills, as well as increased awareness of emotions and diversity in families.

TERMINOLOGY

Coresident Grandparents: Grandparents who are living with their adult child and grandchildren. There is significant variation in the degree to which coresident grandparents provide physical and financial support to their grandchildren. Some coresident grandparents function as traditional grandparents, while others are heavily involved in caregiving and parenting.

Custodial Grandparents: Grandparents who are serving as the primary caregiver for one or more of their grandchildren. These grandparents are primarily responsible for all physical and financial aspects of their grandchildren's care. The middle generation may or may not be present in these households. The U.S. Census refers to custodial grandparents as grandparent caregivers.

Grandfamilies: A term used to refer to grandparent-headed families.

Kinship Care/Kincare: Refers to families in which children are being raised by a relative, typically a grandparent. Kinship care families may or may not be skip generation families, depending on whether members of the middle generation are also living in the household.

Middle Generation: The parents of the children who are being raised by grandparents. They may or may not be living with the grandparent(s).

Second Time Around Parents: Refers to people who are parenting a second generation of children. The term is typically synonymous with custodial grandparents.

Skip Generation Household: Occurs when grandparents, or less frequently, great-grandparents, assume primary responsibility for the physical and financial care of their grandchildren or great-grandchildren. In a skip generation household, members of the middle generation are not living in the home of the grandparent or great-grandparent caregiver.

FAMILY THERAPY

Despite the popularity of support groups, therapy may be necessary in order to fully address the needs of custodial grandparents and their grandchildren. Because the presenting problems that bring grandparent-headed families to therapy are so varied, the exact course of treatment will be highly individualized and tailored to each family's particular constellation of strengths and stressors. Therapy with grandparent-headed families also requires a high degree of flexibility and a willingness to address issues as they become relevant. Additionally, as many custodial grandparents and grandchildren have needs that extend beyond the scope of therapy, therapists should be prepared to assist grandparents in locating public benefits, accessing medical care, and finding legal representation. Therapists may also need to coordinate with school personnel, child welfare professionals, and physicians.

Given that grandparent-headed families often encounter relational challenges, family therapy may be an ideal treatment modality. Although there have been few published examinations of family therapy's effectiveness with grandparent-headed families, several therapy approaches have been applied to this population. Because these therapy approaches are sensitive to the unique challenges experienced by grandparent-headed families, therapists working with grandparent-headed families may want to consider using these approaches or incorporating aspects of these approaches into their existing theoretical perspective. Other effective approaches should also be considered, depending on the presenting problem(s).

STRUCTURAL FAMILY THERAPY

Many of the difficulties reported by grandparent-headed families can be attributed to blurred boundaries, triangulation, and unclear hierarchies. Structural family therapy (Bartram, 1994; Minuchin, 1974) emphasizes helping grandparents maintain firm yet flexible boundaries and appropriate generational hierarchies. Specifically, because contact with the middle generation may be unpredictable and grandparents and grandchildren must negotiate new roles within the family system, grandparent-headed families may need assistance clarifying who is part of the family system and establishing clear boundaries (Miller & Sandberg, 1998). Clear boundaries are especially important in managing contact with the middle generation, so as to minimize stress and frustration for the grandparent and the grandchildren.

Due to their own ambivalence about caregiving, or a desire to protect their grandchildren from additional stress, custodial grandparents may have difficultly establishing a clear generational hierarchy. They may parentify their grandchildren, or avoid giving consistent discipline. Additionally, if the grandparent is single, the grandchild may assume a great deal of power in family decision making. In structural family therapy, therapists work with grandparents to create clear, appropriate hierarchies in which they have appropriate power and leadership over their grandchildren (Minuchin, 1974).

When treating custodial grandparents and their grandchildren, therapists should be attentive to coalitions, alliances, and triangulation (Minuchin, 1974). Triangulation may be especially problematic, as the grandchild may be triangulated in order to diffuse tension between the grandparent and the middle generation. Grandparents or the middle generation may also attempt to form a coalition with the grandchild against other family members. Therapists should work with grandparent-headed families to remove grandchildren from the triangles and help grandparents find more constructive ways of interacting with the middle generation.

CONTEXTUAL FAMILY THERAPY

In grandparent-headed families, it is very common to hear references to what is owed and what has been sacrificed. Further probing often reveals invisible loyalties and a lack of trust, particularly between grandparents and the middle generation. Because grandparents may want to correct past parenting mistakes (Dolbin-MacNab, 2006), and often speak in terms of commitments

PUBLIC BENEFITS AVAILABLE TO CUSTODIAL GRANDPARENTS

Census data reveals that approximately 19 percent of grandparent-headed families are living in poverty (Simmons & Dye, 2003). Grandparents may be eligible for a number of public benefits, some of which are listed here. As many grandparents are unaware of these resources, therapists play an important role in connecting grandparents to the appropriate assistance programs.

Temporary Assistance to Needy Families (TANF): Children may be eligible for a child-only grant, which does not consider the grandparent's income and does not include work requirements. Families may also apply for TANF, but these grants include a 60-month time limit and work requirements.

Supplementary Security Income (SSI): Grandparents over the age of 65 and children under the age of 18 can receive SSI if they have a disability.

Children's Health Insurance Program (CHIP): CHIP provides medical and dental insurance to children under the age of 18. CHIP is for families who are not eligible for Medicaid, but cannot afford private insurance.

Food Stamps: Families who meet income requirements can receive assistance to purchase nutritious foods.

Earned Income Tax Credit: Workers who meet income requirements and are raising children may be eligible for a federal tax credit. To qualify, the child must live with the grandparent half the year and be younger than 19, be a full-time student under the age of 24, or be completely disabled. Grandparent caregivers are not required to have legal custody or guardianship.

Child Tax Credit: Grandparents can receive a $1,000 federal tax credit for each grandchild they are raising. The grandchild must meet the IRS definition of a dependent.

Subsidized Guardianship: Grandparents who obtain legal guardianship of a grandchild who has been in the foster care system can receive financial assistance.

Adoption Assistance & Foster Care Payments: Grandparents who adopt their special needs grandchildren from the state welfare system may receive financial assistance. Grandparents can also receive foster care payments, if they are raising a grandchild who is in the state's custody.

As eligibility for these benefits varies widely from state to state, refer to the online resources for additional information.

and obligations, Contextual Family Therapy (CFT) (Boszormenyi-Nagy & Krasner, 1986) may prove useful.

CFT with grandparent-headed families promotes individual freedom while also acknowledging familial responsibilities (Brown-Standridge & Floyd, 2000). The goal of CFT is to rebalance ledgers of debts and entitlements so that future generations can develop healthier patterns of interaction (Miller & Sandberg, 1998). Once these new interaction patterns have developed, family members can develop a deeper appreciation and understanding of each other's experience (Miller & Sandberg, 1998).

When using CFT with grandparent-headed families, therapists work to expose transgenerational patterns that may be perpetuating problematic behavior. Through reviewing past experiences, grandparents and other family members work to see each other as suffering humans and repair their imbalanced ledgers within those particular relationships. Therapists can also help grandparents review their families of origin, for the purposes of discovering how they have transmitted imbalanced ledgers to their children and custodial grandchildren. Grandchildren can be helped to see how they might be holding their grandparents accountable for their parents' irresponsibility (Brown-Standridge & Floyd, 2000). The goal of CFT is not to blame the grandparent or grandchild, but to empower families to create a new legacy that is based on fairness and trust (Brown-Standridge & Floyd).

FILIAL THERAPY

In order to improve the grandparent-grandchild relationship, grandparents' parenting skills, and the functioning of the grandchild, Bratton, Ray and Moffit (1998) recommend filial/family play therapy. This approach is designed to help grandparents create a nonjudgmental environment in which their grandchildren can express their full range of feelings and experiences. Goals for the family include improving family interaction, enhancing problem-solving, and increasing positive feelings such as warmth, trust, and affection (Bratton et al., 1998). Goals for the grandchild include reducing symptoms, developing coping strategies, increasing self-esteem, and creating a positive relationship with the grandparent (Bratton et al., 1998). Within filial therapy, grandparents learn developmentally appropriate parenting skills, receive emotional support, and find new ways to be responsive to their grandchildren's emotional needs (Bratton et al., 1998).

Filial therapy involves using role-plays and demonstrations to teach grandparents child-centered play therapy techniques. Then, grandparents and their young grandchildren (i.e., age 2 to 10) participate in supervised play sessions, where they receive feedback from the therapist. Filial therapy can be adapted for older children and adolescents and has been shown to be effective with a variety of children and presenting problems (see Bratton et al., 1998). For additional information about filial therapy, please consult VanFleet (2005).

ABOUT THE AUTHORS

Megan L. Dolbin-MacNab, PhD, is an assistant professor in the marriage and family therapy program in the department of human development at Virginia Polytechnic Institute and State University. Dolbin-MacNab's experience related to grandparents raising grandchildren includes research, clinical practice, advocacy, and outreach. She has authored multiple publications related to family relationships within grandparent-headed families. Dolbin-MacNab is a Clinical Member of the AAMFT.

Ryan M. Traylor, MS, is a doctoral student in the marriage and family therapy program in the department of human development at Virginia Polytechnic Institute and State University and is a licensed LMFT in Colorado. His research interests include aging and family therapy, and how families cope with mental illness.

RESOURCES FOR PRACTITIONERS

BOOKS

Hayslip, B., & Patrick, J. H. (2003). *Working with custodial grandparents.* New York: Springer.

Hayslip, B., & Goldberg-Glen, R. S. (2000). *Grandparents raising grandchildren: Theoretical, empirical, and clinical perspectives.* New York: Springer.

Cox, C. B. (2000). *Empowering grandparents raising grandchildren: A training manual for group leaders.* New York: Springer.

Cox, C. B. (2000). *To grandmother's house we go and stay.* New York: Springer.

Callandar, J. (1999). *Second time around: Help for grandparents who raise their children's kids.* Wilsonville, OR: BookPartners.

de Toledo, S., & Brown, D. E. (1995). *Grandparents as parents: A survival guide for raising a second family.* New York: Guilford.

CURRICULA

Supporting the Kinship Triad: A Training Curriculum
http://www.cwla.org/pubs/pubdetails.asp?PUBID=7335
This five-day curriculum is designed for professionals and offers a service-delivery model that is time-limited, culturally sensitive, strength-based, and rooted in family preservation. The curriculum takes a systemic perspective on kinship care families.

Second Time Around … Grandparents Raising Grandchildren
http://homepages.wmich.edu/~dannison/grandparents.html
This curriculum is designed to assist grandparents with their parenting responsibilities. The curriculum includes material for 8 to 16 sessions and focuses on strategies for successful parenting.

Grandparents Raising Grandchildren: Double Stressed, Triply Blessed
http://agexted.cas.psu.edu/fcs/mk/Available.html
This multimedia curriculum is designed to introduce communities to the issues facing grandparent-headed families and to provide community-level strategies for assisting custodial grandparents and their grandchildren.

Grandparents Raising Grandchildren Educational Program
http://www.uwex.edu/ces/flp/grandparent/aarp.pdf
Designed to provide an introduction to the topic of grandparents raising grandchildren, this multimedia curriculum provides an overview of the topic and information about resources available to assist these families.

ONLINE RESOURCES

AARP Grandparent Information Center
www.aarp.org/families/grandparents/raising_grandchild
The AARP Grandparent Information Center provides a variety of resources for grandparents and other relatives raising children. The site includes a searchable listing of support groups, as well as detailed information about accessing public benefits. Also included are resources for addressing grandparents' legal, financial, education, health, and support challenges.

Generations United
www.gu.org
Generations United promotes awareness of grandparents raising grandchildren. The site offers a variety of information related to grandfamilies, including fact sheets specific to each state and the District of Columbia.

American Bar Association Kinship Care Legal Research Center
www.abanet.org/child/kinshipcare.shtml
The Kinship Care Legal Research Center is a central location for information related to the complex legal issues facing kinship caregivers.

Brookdale Foundation Relatives As Parents Program
www.brookdalefoundation.org/relativesasparents.htm
The Brookdale Foundation encourages the creation and expansion of services targeting grandparents and other relatives who are raising children. Seed grants are available to support the development of new service programs.

Child Welfare League of America
www.cwla.org

Children's Defense Fund
www.childrensdefense.org

REFERENCES

Bartram, M. H. (1994). Clarifying subsystem boundaries in grandfamilies. *Contemporary Family Therapy, 18,* 267-277.
Beltran, A. (2000, Summer). Grandparents and other relatives raising children: Supportive public policies. *The Public Policy and Aging Report, 1,* 3-7.
Billing, A., Ehrle, J., & Kortenkamp, K. (2002). Children cared for by relatives:

What do we know about their well-being? *New Federalism* (Policy Brief B-46). Washington DC: The Urban Institute.

Boszormenyi-Nagy, I., & Krasner, B. R. (1986). *Between give and take: A clinical guide to contextual therapy.* New York: Brunner/Mazel.

Bratton, S., Ray, D., & Moffit, K. (1998). Filial/Family play therapy: An intervention for custodial grandparents and their grandchildren. *Educational Gerontology, 24,* 391-406.

Brown-Standridge, M. D., & Floyd, C. W. (2000). Healing bittersweet legacies: Revisiting

contextual family therapy for grandparents raising grandchildren in crisis. *Journal of Marital and Family Therapy, 26,*184-197.

Bryson, K., & Casper, L. M. (1999). *Coresident grandparents and grandchildren.* U.S.

Census Bureau, Current Population Reports, Special Studies (P23-198).

Burnette, D. (1999). Custodial grandparents in Latino families: Patterns of service use and predictors of unmet needs. *Social Work, 44*(1), 22-34.

Cox, C. (Ed.). (1999). *To grandmother's house we go and stay: Perspectives on custodial grandparents.* New York: Springer.

Dannison, L. L., & Smith, A. B. (2003). Custodial grandparents community support program: Lessons learned. *Children and Schools, 25*(2), 87-95.

Dolbin-MacNab, M. L. (2006). Just like raising your own? Grandmothers' perceptions of parenting a second time around. *Family Relations, 55,* 564-575.

Dolbin-MacNab, M. L., & Keiley, M. K. (2005). A systemic examination of grandparents' emotional closeness with their custodial grandchildren. *Research in Human Development, 3,* 59-71.

Dolbin-MacNab, M. L., Nielson, L. R., & Keiley, M. K. (2005). *Family relationships of adolescents being raised by grandparents.* Paper presented at the annual meeting of the National Council on Family Relations, Phoenix, AZ.

Ehrle, J., & Day, H. D. (1994). Adjustment and family functioning of grandmothers rearing their grandchildren. *Contemporary Family Therapy, 16,* 67-82.

Fuller-Thomson, E., & Minkler, M. (2000). The mental and physical health of grandmothers who are raising their grandchildren. *Journal of Mental Health and Aging, 6,* 311-323.

Fuller-Thomson, E., Minkler, M., & Driver, D. (1997). A profile of grandparents raising grandchildren in the United States. *The Gerontologist, 37,* 406-411.

Goodman, C. C., & Silverstein, M. (2005). Grandmothers raising grandchildren: Ethnic and racial differences in well-being among custodial and coparenting families. *Journal of Family Issues, 27,* 1605-1626.

Grant, R., Gordon, S. G., & Cohen, S. T. (1997). An innovative school-based intergenerational model to serve grandparent caregivers. *Journal of Gerontological Social Work, 28,* 47-61.

Hayslip, B. (2003). The impact of a psychosocial intervention on parental efficacy, grandchild relationship quality, and well being among grandparents raising grandchildren. In B. Hayslip & J. Patrick (Eds.), *Working with custodial grandparents* (pp. 163-178). New York: Springer.

Hayslip, B., & Kaminski, P. L. (2005). Grandparents raising their grandchildren. *Marriage and Family Review, 37,* 147-169.

Hayslip, B., Shore, R. J., Henderson, C. E., & Lambert, P. L. (1998). Custodial grandparenting and the impact of grandchildren with problems on role satisfaction and role meaning. *Journal of Gerontology: Social Sciences, 53B,* S164-S173.

Kolomer, S., McCallion, P., & Janicki, M. (2002). African-American grandmother carers of children with disabilities: Predictors of depressive symptoms. *Journal of Gerontological Social Work, 37*(3/4), 45-64.

Jendrek, M. P. (1993). Grandparents who parent their grandchildren: Effects on lifestyle. *Journal of Marriage and the Family, 55,* 609-621.

Jendrek, M. P. (1994). Grandparents who parent their grandchildren: Circumstances and decisions. *The Gerontologist, 34,* 206-216.

Kelley, S. J., & Whitley (2003). Psychological distress and physical health problems in grandparents raising grandchildren: Development of an empirically based intervention model. In B. Hayslip & J. Patrick (Eds.), *Working with custodial grandparents* (pp. 127-144). New York: Springer.

Landry-Meyer, L. (1999). Research into action: Recommended intervention strategies for grandparent caregivers. *Family Relations, 48,* 381-389.

Lugaila, T., & Overturf, J. (2004). *Children and the households they live in: 2000.* U.S. Census Bureau, Census 2000 Special reports (CENSR-14).

Miller, R. B., & Sandberg, J. G. (1998). Clinical interventions in intergenerational relations. In M. E. Szinovacz (Ed.), *Handbook on grandparenthood* (pp. 218-229). Westport, CT: Greenwood Press.

Minkler, M. (1999). Intergenerational households headed by grandparents: Contexts, realities, and implications for policy. *Journal of Aging Studies, 12*(2), 199-218.

Minkler, M., Driver, D., Roe, K. M., & Bedeian, K. (1993). Community interventions to support grandparent caregivers. *The Gerontologist, 33,* 807-811.

Minkler, M., & Fuller-Thomson, E. (2005). African-American grandparents raising grandchildren: A national study using the Census 2000 American Community Survey. *Journal of Gerontology, 60B,* S82-S92.

Minkler, M., Fuller-Thomson, E., Miller, D., & Driver, D. (1997). Depression in grandparents raising grandchildren: Results of a national longitudinal study. *Archives of Family Medicine, 6,* 445-452.

Minuchin, S. (1974). *Families and family therapy.* Cambridge, MA: Harvard University Press.

O'Reilly, E., & Morrison, M. L. (1993). Grandparent-headed families: New therapeutic challenges. *Child Psychiatry and Human Development, 23,* 147-159.

Pruchno, R. A. (1999). Raising grandchildren: The experience of black and white grandmothers. *The Gerontologist, 39,* 209-221.

Pruchno, R. A., & McKinney, D. (2000). Living with grandchildren: The effects of custodial and co-resident households on the mental health of grandmothers. *Journal of Mental Health and Aging, 6,* 269-289.

Roe, K. M., & Minkler, M. (1998). Grandparents raising grandchildren: Challenges and responses. *Generations, 22*(4), 25-32.

Shore, R., & Hayslip, B. (1994). Custodial grandparenting: Implications for children's development. In A. E. Gottfried & A. W. Gottfried (Eds.), *Redefining families: Implications for children's development* (pp. 171-218). New York: Plenum Press.

Simmons, T., & Dye, J. L. (2003). Grandparents living with grandchildren: 2000. *Census 2000 Brief C2KBR-31.* Retrieved April 20, 2006, from http://www. census.gov/prod/2003pubs/C2kbr-31.pdf.

Smith, G. C. (2003). How caregiving grandparents view support groups: An exploratory study.

In B. Hayslip & J. Patrick (Eds.), *Working with custodial grandparents* (pp. 69-91). New York: Springer.

Smith, A. B., & Dannison, L. L. (2003). Grandparent-headed families in the United States:

Programming to meet unique needs. *Journal of Intergenerational Relationships, 1*(3), 35-46.

Solomon, J. C., & Marx, J. (1995). "To grandmother's house we go:" Health and school adjustment of children raised solely by grandparents. *The Gerontologist, 35*(3), 386-394.

Strom, R. D., & Strom, S. K. (1993). Grandparents raising grandchildren: Goals and support groups. *Educational Gerontology, 19,* 705-715.

Strom, R. D., & Strom, S. K. (2000). Meeting the challenge of raising grandchildren.

International Journal of Aging and Human Development, 51(3), 183-198.

Uhlenberg, P., & Kirby, J. (1998). Grandparenthood over time: Historical and demographic trends. In M. Szinovacz (Ed.), *Handbook on grandparenthood* (pp. 23-39). Westport, CT: Greenwood Press.

VanFleet, R. (2005). Filial therapy: Strengthening parent-child relationships through play (2nd ed.). Sarasota, FL: Professional Resource Press.

Webb, N. B. (1996). *Social work practice with children.* New York: Guilford.

Oppositional Defiant Disorder

J. Matthew Orr, PhD

Originally published as Clinical Update in Family Therapy Magazine
November-December 2008

WE'VE TRIED EVERYTHING AND NOTHING WORKS!

Marriage and family therapists (MFTs) have likely heard this familiar cry from parents who are exasperated, demoralized, and desperate for solutions to the chronically disruptive behavior of their children with Oppositional Defiant Disorder (ODD). Likewise, many MFTs may share in this "tried everything, nothing works" state of mind; ODD is a complex problem which seems to be characterized as much by its lack of clear etiology and its insidious onset as it is by the defiance and hostile disposition that mark its clinical presentation.

According to the *DSM-IV* (American Psychiatric Association [APA], 1994, 2000), ODD is characterized by a chronic pattern of negativity, hostility, and non-compliant child behavior that is most often directed toward authority figures. Specific symptoms often include argumentativeness, outward defiance of authority figures' reasonable commands or requests, blaming others for their own mistakes, annoying or being easily annoyed by others, and acting angry, resentful or aggressive. It is a relatively common problem in the community at-large with prevalence rates ranging from 2 to 16 percent, depending on how it is defined and measured (Loeber et al., 2000). While it appears to be true that boys tend to display more severe conduct problems at younger ages than girls, MFTs can expect to confront ODD in girls, especially as they enter into adolescence (Loeber et al., 2000). Clinicians should also be aware that in clinical settings, the rate of comorbidity between Attention Deficit Hyperactivity Disorder ADHD and ODD or Conduct Disorder (CD) is high and often signifies the presence of comorbid anxiety (Jensen et al., 2001). It is generally believed that ODD develops out of a complex interplay of risk and protective factors in the biopsychosocial milieu of the individual child and his or her environment. However, it is difficult to pin these factors down (Steiner & Remsing, 2007).

AACAP PRACTICE PARAMETER

There is not necessarily a consensus protocol for the evaluation, differential diagnosis, and treatment of ODD; however, the American Academy of Child and Adolescent Psychiatry (AACAP) and its Work Group on Quality Issues (Steiner & Remsing, 2007) recently established recommended guidelines for the assessment and treatment of ODD. The reader is strongly encouraged to review these guidelines in detail to determine whether their own practices in regard to ODD fall within this parameter, as they are only briefly mentioned here.

Based on the nature of MFT training and practice, it is expected that most MFTs will find that the AACAP recommendations resonate with their customary, or at least intended, approaches.

While the *DSM-IV* (APA, 1994, 2000) diagnostic criteria remain the essential standard for the actual diagnosis of ODD, it should also be pleasing to MFTs not only that the guidelines direct clinicians to carefully consider the parent-child relationship and the nature of the relational dynamics in the family system, but also that the quality of the therapeutic alliance is regarded as a critical ingredient to successful assessment and treatment of ODD (Steiner & Remsing, 2007).

DIAGNOSIS AND ASSESSMENT

Differentiating between the ordinary episodic disruptive behavior that often occurs during childhood and adolescence and the chronic and pervasive nature of the negativity, hostility, and defiance associated with ODD can be challenging. MFTs should consider three layers of assessment in accord with the AACAP recommendations: 1) Family-based *clinical interview;* 2) *DSM-IV* (APA, 1994, 2000) diagnostic criteria; 3) Standardized behavior rating scales.

1) Clinical Interview. The major emphasis of the parameter is placed on obtaining information from and observing both the child and family, especially the parents, in the evaluation and treatment process. A premium is placed on consideration of the cultural context in which that family lives, as well as the need to tailor the assessment process and the treatment plan on the individual needs of the child and family. It is also important for MFTs to recognize the presence of comorbid conditions when they are present. They should rely on the parents or other primary caregivers, as opposed to teachers, for example, for the core of the information about the symptomatic behavior—vis a vis the *DSM-IV* (APA, 1994, 2000) criteria—its onset, its duration, and its severity, because it is common for these behaviors to show up in some settings, especially at home, but not in others. Of course, teachers and other caregivers represent a rich source of additional information, especially if they are corroborated by the MFT's own observation of the child in the given social context, such as at school. Information from multiple outside informants can also help the clinician reconcile some of the confusion that may exist if parents or primary caregivers do not agree on the problem.

Therefore, it is important for MFTs to conduct a comprehensive psychosocial assessment of the child, including a thorough developmental history with the parents, as well as an interview with teachers or other outside caregivers, if at all possible. A format should be applied that provides both the requisite developmental/medical history and the information necessary to assess for and differentiate between the major disorders of childhood (e.g., Barkley, 1997). It is important that clinicians include the nuclear family so that they can assess family dynamics while paying particular attention to the patterns of interaction and levels of cooperation and conflict between and within the caregivers and children.

As with all disorders of childhood and adolescence, it is necessary for MFTs to be competent in normative child behavior so that they can better differentiate between age-appropriate behaviors, especially as they occur in specific contexts or situations, and those that are characteristic of more chronic and pervasive oppositionality and defiance. For example, it is common for four year olds to constantly fail to flush the toilet; this can typically be attributed to their sensitivity to, or fear of, loud noises or short attention spans rather than willful defiance.

2) DSM-IV Criteria: Defiant or Just Strong-Willed. "So, how *do* we tell the difference between a child who is simply strong-willed and one with ODD?" To answer this question, MFTs must be able to decide how often is "often," as any of the criterion-specific behavior the individual is displaying must occur "often." Employing the DSM criteria, a child would have to meet four of the eight individual criteria, which must have existed for at least six months and "must occur more frequently than what is typically observed in individuals of comparable age and developmental level" (APA, 2000). Frequency, then, is the key; however, it is difficult to know in all circumstances how often is "often." Fortunately, Angold & Costello (1996) have provided empirically-based recommendations for assessing symptom frequency. They suggest using the following cutoff rules to determine if a given *DSM-IV* symptom is occurring often enough to be considered clinically significant (keep in mind that this pattern must also have existed for at least six months):

- Has occurred at all during the last three months
  - spiteful or vindictive
  - blames others for his or her mistakes or misbehavior
- Occurs at least twice per week
  - touchy or easily annoyed by others
  - loses temper
  - argues with adults
  - actively defies or refuses to comply with adults' requests or rules
- Occurs at least four times per week
  - angry or resentful
  - deliberately annoys people

Angold & Costello (1996) also suggest reducing the diagnostic requirement for ODD from four out of eight symptoms to two or three, plus a requirement that the symptoms cause impairment in some area of functioning. They base this recommendation on data from their population-based study, which indicated that there were a significant number of children whose behavior (i.e., symptoms) did not cross the threshold of any particular diagnostic category, yet the level of their disruptive behavior was causing clinically significant impairment and half of them were still impaired one year later. Though children crossing this alternative threshold may be less disruptive than those meeting the full DSM-IV criteria, this approach may avail children and families to interventions that might not otherwise be offered if the problem behavior were not considered to be clinically significant.

3) Rating Scales. The use of standardized child behavior rating scales not only aids in differential diagnostic procedures by offering objective data regarding the clinical significance of symptoms, but it also allows the clinician to focus attention on the child and family's story, which is important for establishing the therapeutic alliance, as well as learning about the nature of the behavior and the way it interacts with individual and family functioning. Instruments, such as the Child Behavior Checklist (CBCL; [Achenbach, 1991]), offer the clinician objective data about children's functioning across multiple areas of their lives, which is useful for determining areas in which they are having problems and may be in need of further attention. In fact, recent evidence (Biederman et al., 2008) suggests that the "Aggression" scale of the CBCL is a reliable screening tool for ODD among children and adolescents with ADHD. The CBCL also appears to be a reliable screening tool for pediatric bipolar disorder, which can often be difficult to differentiate from ODD (Faraone et al., 2005), given the explosive nature of the tantrums associated with each disorder. Another area of screening afforded by the CBCL is substance use. In ODD that does not occur until the middle to high school ages (i.e., adolescence) consideration must be given to the possibility that these behaviors are related to (not necessarily caused by) possible substance use or abuse issues. In these cases, substance abuse would be a primary focus of treatment.

In terms of symptom-specific scales for ODD, the Vanderbilt AD/HD Rating Scales developed by Wolraich and colleagues (2003) include parent and teacher measures for ODD based on DSM diagnostic criteria. These resources are made available by the National Initiative for Children's Healthcare Quality (http://www.nichq.org/NICHQ/Topics/ChronicConditions/). This site contains a wealth of resources for AD/HD, which is significant due to its comorbidity with ODD. In addition, the Vanderbilt scales include items that screen for problems with anxiety and depression, as well as items that help identify in which areas the child is experiencing functional impairment. The SNAP-IV (Swanson, 1992) scales are similar in nature and are available at www.adhd.net.

TREATMENT

What about that "tried everything, nothing works" state of mind? Parents and even therapists who experience this are not usually exaggerating; the issue is that they *have* tried everything, at least all of the conventional methods known or suggested to them. It is the assumption herein that those cases which clinicians refer to as "difficult" are those for which intervention does not result in *sustainable* change over the long term. That is, they may have success applying conventional treatment approaches, such as parent training in child behavior management strategies, with some cases of ODD, but they may find that such conventional interventions do not "stick" in other cases. Therefore, it is important for MFTs to be aware not only of empirically-supported treatment approaches, but also of some of the predominant features often associated with ODD, which can act as impediments to changes that families can sustain over time.

While there is not clear evidence to help us discern the etiology of ODD, there is a hardy body of evidence suggesting what works to treat the disorder. It appears that family-based approaches, especially those that emphasize behavior management training, such as parent training (PT), are the most effective treatment for ODD (Burke, Loeber, & Birmaher, 2002; Pelham, Wheeler, & Chronis, 1998; Steiner & Remsing, 2007). In fact, there are an abundance of models that have been developed, studied, and achieved the distinction as "model programs" by one or all of the following:

- Substance Abuse and Mental Health Services Administration's (SAMHSA) National Registry of Evidenced-based Programs and Practices (NREPP) http://nrepp.samhsa.gov/index.asp
- Office of Juvenile Justice and Delinquency (OJJDP) Prevention's Model Programs http://www.dsgonline.com/mpg2.5/mpg_index.htm
- Center for the Study and Prevention of Violence at the University of Colorado   http://www.colorado.edu/cspv/blueprints/

Many of these programs require training and certification prior to implementing them into practice. The reader should pay close attention to the age groups for which each model is designed, as some focus on children and others adolescents. In addition, many of them, especially those related to preschool and elementary-age children, are not focused on ODD specifically, but focus on disruptive behavior or conduct problems, in general. This caveat is significant because there is evidence to suggest that such models may not be as effective unless they address the complex factors related to ODD (Burke, Loeber, & Birmhaier, 2002), especially in regard to family conflict and low parental motivation (Lindahl, 1998; Pelham, Wheeler & Chronis, 1998). Perhaps, for many MFTs, training in an evidence-based model may provide the methods their practices need to overcome many of the challenges of treating ODD. However, it seems that there will always be difficult cases of ODD no matter which model or approach an MFT employs. Given this latter point, as well as the reality that thorough reviews and discussions of the evidence-based models are available at the sources listed, it is essential that attention is given to several key family and individual factors of which MFTs should be aware.

PROMOTING SUSTAINABLE CHANGE: FAMILY AND INDIVIDUAL FACTORS

Family conflict. Evidence indicates that family conflict is one of the primary factors associated with ODD (Burke, Loeber, & Birmhaier, 2002) and it also appears that the more severe the discord, the more severe the conduct problems (Lindahl, 1998). In fact, Lindahl's (1998) study of families of children with only ADHD, children with comorbid ADHD and ODD, children with only ODD, and children without behavior problems revealed that disruptions to emotional connectedness within the parental subsystem and between the parent and child subsystems, as well as lax and inconsistent parenting efforts, seem to contribute significantly to the development of ODD and complicated the clinical picture of ADHD, which is much more manageable on its own. Rather than pointing to specific negative parenting behaviors or skills, per se, this study suggests that it is primarily the lack of interconnectedness among family members and a lack of dyadic parental responsiveness or effectiveness that seems to give rise to the presence of ODD as far as family functioning is concerned.

Consequently, MFTs must be aware that, in these cases, the effectiveness of PT can be compromised because parents' level of effort is often insufficient, and the distress in the emotional atmosphere erodes the motivation to stick it out with their children who display such high-intensity, high-demand behavior. Moreover, Pelham, Wheeler, & Chronis (1998) warn that the positive effects of such behavioral interventions, whether at home or in the classroom, seem to be lost once the treatments are removed, and that their potential effectiveness in the "real-world" is dependent upon the "motivation and capabilities of the significant adults in the child's life" (p. 200). Therefore, not only must MFTs be attuned to the nature and effectiveness of the strategies and skills parents are using, but they must also be prepared to target family conflict, which is often severe. It is crucial to intervene in ways that promote harmonious parent-child and marital relational processes or patterns of behavior. This intervention is a means of increasing the motivation and effort of parents and children to implement learned strategies and, more importantly, maintain them during times of high stress, which can be a lot to ask of parents who may be under siege by unrelenting opposition.

"Some examples please?" While designed more for older children and teenagers, programs by Alexander (1998) and Sells (1998), for example, are family therapy-based and may help clinicians more effectively intervene in this area. Another family therapy model for ODD is one developed by Keim (2000). Although it is not considered an evidence-based model, it offers a cogent systemic framework for understanding the interactional nature of ODD and corresponding methods of intervention. Programs for younger children, such as by Webster-Stratton (2000), are oriented toward family therapy in that they include work with parents and children, although the emphasis is still placed on teaching parenting skills and social skills training for children, rather than family therapy, specifically.

Engaging parents. Perhaps the most critical element of all the treatment issues is the need to fully engage parents in the process. This is not an easy task considering that these parents are often exhausted, demoralized, and skeptical of any approach that suggests that they need to change their behavior in order to change their children's behavior. Therefore, it is critical that MFTs be able to reduce parents' defensiveness and skepticism from the outset before at-

SENSORY PROCESSING DISORDER

Sensory Processing Disorder (SPD), or Sensory Integration Dysfunction, refers to problems with the unconscious neurophysiologic process of organizing sensory information, such as movement, sight, sound, smell, etc., and the way in which one perceives that information (e.g., pleasant or threatening), as well as the manner in which she responds to it (Ayres, 2005). As Ayres puts it, "When the flow of sensations is disorganized, life can be like a rush hour traffic jam" (p. 5, 2000). Since so much of learning and behavior is about sending and responding to these messages, problems in any one of these areas can impair academic and social functioning. It is primarily a disorder, or group of disorders, that are evaluated and treated by occupational therapists. Although, it is not a disorder yet in the mainstream of mental health practice; however, efforts are underway to have SPD recognized by the APA in the DSM-V (see www.spdfoundation. net for more information).

What is the significance of this to ODD? Anecdotally, it seems that many, if not most, of the children with chronic and more severe oppositionality and defiance have some level of sensory integration impairment, in that they get overwhelmed or over-stimulated quite easily. From this perspective, ODD behaviors, such as argumentativeness, defiance, anger, tantrums, etc., might be considered indicative of "sensory defensiveness," or maladaptive versions of primitive behaviors designed to protect one from threats of danger (Ayres, 2005). That is not to say that all of ODD is explained by SPD or that this framework definitely applies in all cases; however, it may be worthy of consideration in those "difficult" cases where conventional treatment methods seem to be ineffective and for which MFTs may be seeking alternative explanations and adjunctive treatment strategies.

The purpose of shedding light on this topic is not only related to ODD, but also to make MFTs aware of it in the first place, as treatments for SPD can require a great deal of parent involvement and, subsequently, adjustment of family routines and relationships and MFTs are naturally in a position to assist families in this situation.

REFERENCES AND RESOURCES

Ayres, A. J. (2005). *Sensory integration and the child: Understanding hidden sensory challenges.* (Revised and updated by Pediatric Therapy Network). Los Angeles, CA: Western Psychological Services.

Sensory Integration Global Network (www.siglobalnetwork.org)

Sensory Processing Disorder Foundation (www.spdfoundation.net)

tempting any interventions. How is this done? The author has found that the answer to this question depends on the MFT's ability to answer another question—the one most parents ask: "But why does he act that way?" There is no ironclad method or framework for answering this question, especially given the lack of evidence clearly defining the origins of ODD. However, there are several key issues related to the process of connecting with parents, as well as offering them information regarding ODD, that may help clarify the purpose for the interventions that the MFT recommends to the parents.

Culture and context. MFTs must be sensitive to cultural issues in therapy, especially as it pertains to similarities and differences between the therapist and family in conceptualization of the behavior and discipline practices (Steiner & Remsing, 2007). The therapist must be attuned to the natural tendency for people to find a better fit with approaches that more closely match the attitudes and viewpoints with which they are most familiar. MFTs must also be savvy in the way that they approach marital discord; even though it can play a substantial role in the level of conflict a family experiences, it is not uncommon for parents to become aversive to the therapy process when marital intervention is suggested, despite the fact that they came in for help with their child. Clinicians should think of working with the couple's relationship as one aspect of the process rather than the target, as far as the clients are concerned. That is, the clinician should always discuss the parent-child relationship as the primary target and promoting any couples work as a means to helping them meet their goals as parents.

Temperament. In addition to becoming familiar with the essential elements of the evidence-based models, approaches that incorporate an understanding of temperament, both child and adult, may hold the most promise for difficult cases of ODD, especially in terms of engaging parents. Why? Loosely defined, temperament refers to the inborn traits that comprise how we react and respond to the world around us. From this perspective, ODD behavior can be viewed as a product of a child's tendency to become overwhelmed by the demands of a given situation and having inadequate problem-solving skills to meet those demands (Greene & Ablon, 2006).

This view usually fits well for parents, even though they are still being encouraged to change their own behavior, as it emphasizes the child's intrinsic characteristics and basic nature rather than going straight for parenting skills. Treatment then focuses on helping parents learn how to modify the child's environment, including changing their own typical responses to non-compliance and trying to avoid situations in which the child is likely to get overwhelmed and meltdown. See the resources section for examples.

ABOUT THE AUTHOR

J. Matthew Orr, PhD, is an AAMFT Clinical Member and Approved Supervisor. He is an associate professor and director of Behavioral Medicine in the Department of Family and Preventive Medicine at the University of South Carolina School of Medicine. Orr practices as an LMFT at the University Special Clinics where he specializes in working with families of children with ADHD, ODD, and anxiety. He has taught on the topic of ADHD and ODD at the AAMFT Institutes for Advanced Clinical Training. Orr is recently a former faculty member of the MFT program at the Mercer University School of Medicine.

PROFESSIONAL RESOURCES

Barkley, R. A. (1997). *Defiant children: A clinicians manual for assessment and parent training (2nd ed.).* New York: Guilford Press. This manual describes Barkley's approach to classic behavior management with a comprehensive theory for the development of ODD behavior, including consideration of factors related to temperament. This is an empirically-supported model.

DeGangi, G. A., & Kendall, A. (2007). *Effective parenting for the hard-to-manage child: A skills-based book.* New York: Routledge. Although this book is written for parents, it will provide MFTs with a wealth of information regarding basic concepts and skills, such as temperament, anxiety and sensory integration problems (see sidebar), which are critical factors MFTs should consider when conventional behavior management methods seem not to stick. It is not a therapy model; however, it offers a number of ideas regarding some of the underpinnings of child irritability and non-compliance, and the corresponding intervention strategies that MFTs can use to educate parents as they try to engage them in the therapy process.

Greene, R. (1998). *The explosive child: Understanding and helping easily frustrated, "chronically inflexible" children.* New York: HarperCollins. This book for parents is the predecessor to the clinician's guide (Greene & Ablon, 2006) and is useful for MFTs looking for an alternative approach to traditional behavior management. It emphasizes the contemporary framework that defiant and explosive child behavior is usually the product of the child's inability to meet the emotional demands of a situation due to poor or immature cognitive problem-solving skills. The model has received acclaim in institutional settings and may represent a better fit conceptually for parents who may struggle with conventional behavior management approaches.

Kazdin, A. (2008). *The Kazdin Method for parenting the defiant child: With no pills, no therapy, no contest of wills.* New York: Houghton Mifflin. The Kazdin Method is the author's approach to classic behavior management principles based on the distillation of several decades of the author's work in the area of child conduct. The approach is developed out of 30 years of research regarding what works to shape child behavior and remove non-compliance. The book is written for parents and clinicians will likely find it useful as well.

Kurcinka, M. S. (1998). *Raising your spirited child: A guide for parents whose child is more intense, sensitive, perceptive, persistent, energetic.* New York: HarperCollins.

Turecki, S. (2000) *The difficult child.* New York: Bantam.
These two books offer rich insights into the nature of child behavior based on the concept of temperament. While both books are designed for par-

ents, Turecki weaves together basic behavior management strategies and a temperament-sensitive approach todiscipline. Kurcinka is a non-clinical parent education approach and emphasizes heavily ways in which parents can create a better fit between themselves, the child, and the environment.

REFERENCES

Alexander, J., Barton, C., Gordon, D., Grotpeter, J., Hansson, K., Harrison, R., Mears, S., Mihalic, S., Parsons, B., Pugh, C., Schulman, S., Waldron, H., & Sexton, T. (1998). Functional family therapy: Blueprints for violence prevention, book three. Blueprints for violence prevention series (D. S. Elliott, Series Editor). Boulder, CO: Center for the Study and Prevention of Violence, Institute of Behavioral Science, University of Colorado.

American Psychiatric Association. (1994). *Diagnostic and statistical manual of mental disorders* (4th ed.). Washington, DC: Author.

American Psychiatric Association. (2000). *Diagnostic and statistical manual of mental disorders, fourth edition, text revision (DSM-IV-TR)*. Washington, DC: Author.

Angold, A., & Costello, J. (1996). Toward establishing an empirical basis for the diagnosis of oppositional defiant disorder. *Journal of the American Academy of Child & Adolescent Psychiatry*, 35(9), 1205-1212.

Angold, A., Costello, E., & Erkanli, A. (1999). Comorbidity. *The Journal of Child Psychology & Psychiatry*, 40, 57-88.

Barkley, R. A. (1997). Defiant children: A clinician's manual for assessment and parent training (2nd ed.). New York: Guilford Press.

Barkley, R. A., Edwards, G. H. Robin, A. L. (1999). *Defiant teens: A clinician's manual for assessment and family intervention*. New York: Guilford Press.

Biederman, J., Ball, S., Monuteaux, M., Kaiser, R., & Faraone, S. (2008). CBCL Clinical Scales discriminate ADHD youth with structured-interview derived diagnosis of oppositional defiant disorder (ODD). *Journal of Attention Disorders*, 12(1), 76-82.

Burke, J. D., Loeber, R. Birmaiher, B. (2002). Oppositional defiant and conduct disorder: A review of the past 10 years, part II. *Journal of the American Academy of Child and Adolescent Psychiatry*, 46, 126-141.

Faraone, S., Althoff, R., Hudziak, J., Monuteaux, M., & Biederman, J. (2005). The CBCL predicts DSM bipolar disorder in children: A receiver operating characteristic curve analysis. *Bipolar Disorders*, 7(6), 518-524.

Greene, R. W., & Ablon, J. S. (2006). Treating explosive kids: The collaborative-problem solving approach. New York: Guilford.

Jensen, P., Hinshaw, S., Kraemer, H., Lenora, N., Newcorn, J., Abikoff, H., et al. (2001). ADHD comorbidity findings from the MTA study: Comparing comorbid subgroups. *Journal of the American Academy of Child & Adolescent Psychiatry*, 40, 147-158.

Keim, J. (2000). Oppositional behavior in children. In C. E. Bailey (Ed.), *Children in therapy: Using the family as a resource*. New York: W.W. Norton.

Kurcinka, M. S. (1998). Raising your spirited child: A guide for parents whose child is more intense sensitive, perceptive, persistent, energetic. New York: HarperCollins.

Lindahl, K. M. (1998). Family process variables and children's disruptive behavior problems. *Journal of Family Psychology*, 12, 420–436.

Pelham, W. E., Wheeler, T., & Chronis, A. (1998). Empirically supported psychosocial treatments for Attention Deficit Hyperactivity Disorder. *Journal of Clinical Child Psychology, 27,* 190–205.

Sells, S. P. (1998). *Treating the tough adolescent: A family-based step-by-step guide.* New York: Guilford Press.

Swanson, J. (1992). School-based assessments and interventions for ADD students. Irvine, CA: K. C. Publishing.

*Steiner, H., & Remsing, L. (2007). Practice parameter for the assessment and treatment of children and adolescents with oppositional defiant disorder. *Journal of the American Academy of Child & Adolescent Psychiatry, 46,* 126-141.

Turecki, S. (2000) *The difficult child.* New York: Bantam.

Webster-Stratton, C. (2000). The incredible years training series. *Juvenile Justice Bulletin.* Washington, DC: U.S. Department of Justice, Office of Justice Programs, Office of Juvenile Justice and Delinquency Prevention.

Wolraich, M., Lambert, W., Doffing, M., Bickman, L., Simmons, T., & Worley, K. (2003, December). Psychometric properties of the Vanderbilt ADHD Diagnostic Parent Rating Scale in a referred population. *Journal of Pediatric Psychology, 28*(8), 559-568.

*Essential reading for the MFT practitioner

Problem Gambling: Taking Chances

Bonnie K. Lee, PhD

Originally published as Clinical Update in Family Therapy Magazine
January-February 2010

BACKGROUND

From the rattling of divination sticks, to the clatter of hucklebone dice, games of chance have been practiced by humans since prehistory (Grunfeld, Zangeneh, & Diakoloukas, 2008; Reith, 1999). Gambling behavior as a form of play (Smith & Abt, 1984) has evolved into what is now a multibillion-dollar industry worldwide, fueled by capitalistic appetites, tourism and technology. Casinos have become part of the landscape. Electronic gambling machines, Internet gambling, and the ubiquitous lure of lotteries are a part of 21st century culture. Legalized gambling is now found in every state in the United States except Hawaii and Utah (American Gaming Association, 2009). Some form of legalized gambling is found in every province and territory in Canada (Statistics Canada, 2009).

Gambling is defined as staking something of value upon a game or event with an uncertain outcome based on luck or chance. Social acceptance of gambling and its accessibility have increased the risk for problem outcomes (Gerstein, Murphy, Toce, Hoffman, Palmer, Johnson, 1999). Although it has been argued that gambling and casinos can act as a catalyst for economic growth with spinoffs in social benefits, it also poses a public health and mental health concern (Shaffer & Korn, 2002). Hence, marriage and family therapists need to be alerted to symptoms of problematic gambling and its impact on couples and families, and to the types of therapies available, especially empirically-supported forms of treatment.

PROBLEM AND PATHOLOGICAL GAMBLING

Gambling exists along a dynamic continuum from social, recreational gambling to problem and pathological gambling. Problem gambling is a term commonly used to describe a range of gambling behaviors that result in nega tive consequences for the gambler, family and friends. Approximately three to four percent of the adult population in North America gamble excessively, and one to two percent of the population experience serious recurrent disruptions of their personal, family and vocational lives that fit with the diagnosis of "pathological gambling" (Stucki & Rihs-Middel, 2007).

Problem gambling needs to be viewed as a family problem because it has adverse consequences, not only for gamblers, but for spouses, children and extended family members (Grant Kalischuk, Nowatzki, Cardwell, Klein, & Solowoniuk, 2006; McComb, Lee & Sprenkle, 2009). On average, at least seven other people are said to be affected by each problem gambler's behavior (Productivity Commission, 1999), with fallout ranging from enormous financial and family pressures, to relationship breakdown, and domestic violence. Compared to the general population, problem gamblers are more likely to report legal issues, crime and incarceration (Potenza et al., 2000), impaired physical and mental health (Pietrzak & Petry, 2005), and suicide attempts (Maccallum & Blaszczynski, 2003).

Adolescents and college students show markedly higher rates of problematic gambling than the general population (Shaffer & Hall, 2001). Older adults are also considered a population that is potentially vulnerable to problem gambling (Shaffer, LaBrie, LaPlante, Nelson, & Stanton, 2004) with their increased leisure, personal losses and loneliness. In fact, Gerstein et al. (1999) found that those over age 65 show the most dramatic rise in lifetime gambling. Traditionally, men have gambled more than women and are more likely to develop gambling problems, but more recently, disordered gambling rates among women have increased and are now comparable to men's (Hing & Breen, 2001; Hraba & Lee, 1996). Ethnic minority groups, notably Native Americans (Volberg, 1994; Wardman, el-Guebaly, & Hodgins, 2001) and Asian immigrants (Blaszczynski, Huynh, Dumlao, & Farrell, 1998; Petry, Armentano, Kuoch, Norinth, & Smith, 2003) have been found in several studies to have a higher prevalence of gambling-related problems and are at greater risk for gambling problems than the general population. Social determinants such as social and cultural marginalization, trauma history, and socio-economic stresses need to be considered in understanding this over-representation (Yanicki, Gregory, & Lee, 2010). Gamblers of lower socio-economic status spend a higher proportion of their personal income on gambling and hence are at higher risk for adverse consequences (Shaffer, 2003).

ASSESSMENT

A variety of measures and instruments are available for the assessment of the severity of gambling and related problems, and for the diagnosis of "pathological gambling." However, an assessment is always more than test administration, so the following discussion hopes to assist practitioners in covering areas of inquiry and exploration in the clinical interview with individuals and couples.

TABLE 1. DSM-IV (APA, 2000) CRITERIA:

Pathological Gambling

A. Persistent and recurrent maladaptive gambling behavior as indicated by five (or more) of the following:

1. is preoccupied with gambling (e.g. preoccupied with reliving past gambling experiences, handicapping or planning the next venture, or thinking of ways to get money with which to gamble)

2. needs to gamble with increasing amounts of money in order to achieve the desired excitement

3. has repeated unsuccessful efforts to control, cut back, or stop gambling

4. is restless or irritable when attempting to cut down or stop gambling

5. gambles as a way of escaping from problems or of relieving a dysphoric mood (e.g. feelings of helplessness, guilt, anxiety, depression)

6. after losing money gambling, often returns another day to get even ("chasing" one's losses)

7. lies to family members, therapist, or others to conceal the extent of involvement with gambling

8. has committed illegal acts such as forgery, fraud, theft, or embezzlement to finance gambling

9. has jeopardized or lost a significant relationship, job, or educational or career opportunity because of gambling

10. relies on others to provide money to relieve a desperate financial situation caused by gambling

B. The gambling behavior is not better accounted for by a Manic Episode.

DIAGNOSIS

Pathological gambling is currently classified as an "impulse control disorder" in the Diagnostic and Statistical Manual of Mental Disorders (American Psychiatric Association, 2000). The 10 criteria seen in Table 1 assess persistent and recurrent maladaptive gambling that interferes with personal, family or occupational functioning. Similar to cases of substance dependency, pathological gamblers exhibit signs of tolerance and withdrawal. These are captured on the DSM-IV-TR as preoccupation with gambling; a need to gamble with increasing amounts of money; repeated, unsuccessful efforts to control or stop gambling; and restlessness or irritability when attempting to cut back or stop gambling. At least five of the ten criteria must be met for a diagnosis of pathological gambling, provided that the gambling behavior is not better accounted for by a manic episode.

CONCURRENT MENTAL HEALTH CONCERNS

Screening for pathological gambling for clients with a history of mental illness or substance abuse is important since these issues commonly co-occur with gambling problems (Cunningham-Williams, Cottler, Compton, & Spitznagel, 1998; Rush, Bassani, Urbanoski, & Castel, 2008). Major depression and mood disorders, anxiety disorders, obsessive-compulsive disorder, personality disorders (Boughton & Falenchuk, 2007; Zimmerman, Chelminski, & Young, 2006), and attention deficit disorder (Nower & Blaszczynski, 2006) have been associated with pathological gambling. The link between pathological gambling and adverse childhood experiences and trauma has received increasing attention in recent years (Kausch, Rugle, & Rowland, 2006; Lee, 2002; Petry & Steinberg, 2005).

ASSESSMENT TOOLS

One of the most commonly used DSM-based assessment instruments is the South Oaks Gambling Screen or SOGS (Lesieur & Blume, 1987). Gamblers are asked about their gambling behavior in lifetime and past 12-month timeframes, including types and frequency of gambling and the largest sum of money they have lost in a day, thus revealing the extent of spending related to gambling. Gambling debts and their sources are also assessed by the SOGS. More recently, the Canadian Problem Gambling Index or CPGI (Ferris & Wynne, 2001) was developed to provide a meaningful measure of problem gambling with further indicators of the social and environmental context of problem gambling. Like the SOGS, the CPGI overlaps with DSM criteria for assessment.

The Gambling Symptom Assessment Scale or G-SAS (Kim, Grant, Adson, & Shin, 2001) is a useful tool for assessing past-week gambling behavior. The scale consists of 12 items that reflect frequency, intensity, and duration of gambling urges, and frequency and intensity of gambling thoughts and behaviors, and may be either self-administered or clinician-administered.

A timeline follow-back procedure (G-TLFB), initially developed to assess alcohol consumption, has been applied to assess gambling behavior (Weinstock, Whelan, & Meyers, 2004). This interviewer-administered instrument uses calendar prompts to cue clients to remember the frequency and duration of their gambling. Results match those of other gambling screening instruments.

COGNITIVE BEHAVIORAL ASSESSMENT

The premise of cognitive behavioral therapy is that thoughts underlie behaviors and if we change the thoughts, we change the behaviors. Erroneous thought patterns related to problem gambling include illusions of control in games of chance, superstitious and magical beliefs, selective memory of past wins over past losses, overestimating one's abilities, and irrational interpretation of events during a gambling session (Ladouceur, Sylvain, Boutin, & Doucet, 2002). Cognitions immediately prior to gambling are assessed to identify triggers. Cognitions during and after a gambling session are assessed for the sequence of erroneous thoughts related to gambling problems. Cognitive approaches are often integrated with behavioral approaches focusing on stimulus control; hence assessment would include obtaining information on money control, risky situations, triggers. social skills and ways of coping with stress (Jimenez-Murcia et al., 2007; Petry, 2005).

COUPLE ASSESSMENT

Family and couple problems are among the most common reasons that lead problem gamblers to seek treatment, next to negative emotions and financial concerns (Ladouceur et al., 2002). Referrals to financial advisors to help couples develop a plan to pay off debt, consider declaration of bankruptcy and to get back on track financially are recommended. A high percentage of calls for help is initiated by concerned significant others (Hodgins, Shead, & Makarchuk, 2007). Strategies for engaging the absent partner are important and should be developed (Lee, 2009a). Increased marital distress (Abbott, Cramer & Sherrets, 1995; Hodgins et al.; Lorenz & Yaffee, 1986), and separation or divorce (National Gambling Impact Study Commission, 1999; Tepperman, Korn & Reynolds, 2006), are common sequelae.

The relationship between couple distress and problem gambling is complex. There is evidence that couple difficulties and "fault-lines" in communication existed prior to pathological gambling, which in turn exacerbate couple distress in recursive cycles (Lee, 2009b). Therefore, the therapist needs to assess and observe not only the couple relationship impacted by the gambling, but also inquire into the history of the couple relationship—level of trust, intimacy, quality of communication and how problems were dealt with before the gambling onset (Lee, 2009b). Such inquiry provides an understanding of the couple's pervasive patterns and communication impasses. Couple communication breakdowns often reflect family-of-origin patterns, and childhood maltreatment in the form of abuse, neglect, loss and abandonment, experiences that are over-represented among pathological gamblers (Lee, 2002; Kausch et al., 2006; Petry & Steinberg, 2005) and potentially among their partners (Lee, 2002). Therefore, obtaining a family-of-origin history of communication patterns, traumatic events, and their impacts on current individual and couple functioning should be illuminating. Prior adult relationship traumas could also intensify the couple's reactions to the gambling, amplifying the repercussions (Lee, 2009b). A history of addictions and problem gambling in the family-of-origin of the gambler is common and should be noted.

Family life cycle transitions (Carter & McGoldrick, 1989), losses, crises and setbacks in the gambler's or couple's life are pressure points that often set off the onset or escalation of problem gambling (Lee, 2002; 2009b). At such times, couples could experience overwhelming emotional and coping challenges that overtax their responsive capacity, especially if the couple lack awareness of themselves and their communication is limited in range and depth that pre-empt support and negotiations.

Because gamblers and partners often have poor coping and relational skills (Wood & Griffiths, 2007), assessing the couple's cycle of communication and ways of handling stress and distress is important. What is commonly called "family programs" may mean seeing spouses in groups separate from the gamblers. Conjoint sessions are lacking in many existing treatment programs, despite their advantage of allowing the clinician to observe the couple interaction and to assess their different perspectives on the issue systemically. Building a strong therapeutic alliance with both partners and containing the volatility in couple sessions are integral to therapeutic progress and require systemic skills. Engaging the hesitant partner to come in for conjoint therapy also requires some strategizing, as fear, mistrust and a lack of understanding of how pathological gambling is a couple and family issue can get in the way.

Screening for domestic violence is recommended, as problem gamblers have shown higher risks of intimate partner violence (Afifi, Brownridge, MacMillan, & Sareen, 2009; Korman et al., 2008). Physical and verbal abuse by both gamblers and spouses could occur (Gerstein et al., 1999; Lee, 2009b; Lesieur & Blume, 1991). Anger, guilt, isolation, helplessness and depression as well as physical symptoms have been reported by spouses of problem gamblers (Hodgins, Shead, & Makarchuk, 2007; Lorenz & Shuttlesworth, 1983). Spouses experience loss of trust, a sense of betrayal and being left with the burden of responsibilities (Dickson-Swift, James, & Kippen, 2005). The HITS Scale (Sherin, Sinacore, Li, Zitter, & Shakil, 1998) is a screening tool for identifying the frequency and type of domestic violence that could be present to allow the clinician to assess for appropriateness of couple therapy. The Dyadic Adjustment Scale (Spanier, 1976) is useful in gauging the degree of couple distress and cohesion as a baseline for comparison as therapy progresses.

FAMILY ASSESSMENT

Children of pathological gamblers experience a theme of "pervasive loss" affecting their physical and existential well-being with loss of trust, sense of home, as well as material and relational security (Darbyshire, Oster & Carrig, 2001). They are caught in family stress and triangles and become family scapegoats or peace-makers (Lesieur & Rothschild, 1989; Shaw, Forbush, Schlinder, Rosenman, & Black, 2007). Adolescent children are at increased risk of depressive feelings, adjustment and conduct problems, as well as gambling and substance use problems (Jacobs, Marston, Singer, et al., 1989; Vitaro, Wanner, Brendgen, & Tremblay, 2008).

STAGES OF CHANGE

The "stages of change" model (Prochaska & DiClemente, 1983) has been valuable in working with addictions and other client changes. Clients' readiness to change is assessed in terms of six stages: (1) pre-contemplation; (2) contemplation; (3) preparation; (4) action; (5) maintenance; and (6) relapse. At each stage, clients focus on specific tasks that will lead them to the next stage of change. By noting clients' readiness to change in relation to each target area, e.g. gambling, couple relationship, parenting, mental health, the therapist can capitalize on the goal that represents the client's greatest readiness and motivation to lever the therapeutic process in a positive direction. In effect, all aspects of a problem are linked and interwoven.

TREATMENT

Most problem gamblers do not seek or receive treatment despite its availability (National Research Council, 1999; Petry & Armentano, 1999). At the lower end of problem gambling severity, many gamblers naturally recover without self-help or formal treatment interventions (Hodgins, & el-Guebaly, 2000). For those who seek formal treatment, gambling problems that range along a continuum of severity respond to a variety of therapies and treatment modalities offered in clinical settings.

INDIVIDUAL AND GROUP APPROACHES

Brief therapy models such as motivational interviewing (Miller & Rollnick, 1991) utilize open-ended questions, affirmations, reflective listening, and summaries to support client's self-efficacy. Questions help clients work with their ambivalence towards change by having them explore the positive and negative consequences of problem gambling. Clients can come to realize the payoffs of problem gambling and how these may need to be compensated for by other alternatives; they also come to appreciate what benefits can be anticipated by stopping/reducing gambling behavior. The goals of brief intervention include instilling hope, increasing awareness of risky habits, offering feedback, and obtaining information about the client's healthier behavior patterns. Psycho-education and client-centered interviewing raise awareness of factors that may be contributing to problem gambling (e.g., family history; habitual ways of dealing with stress and boredom). Brief interventions consisting of one to two sessions are valued for their cost-effectiveness and for the purpose of engaging the gambler while opening up the potential for change. Once engaged, continuing therapy is much easier and the drop-out rate is substantially lower (Wulfert, Blanchard, Freidenberg, & Martell, 2006). Treatment dropout rate averages around 31 percent (Melville, Casey, & Kavanagh, 2007). Motivational interviewing is an empirically supported method to engage clients in weighing the costs-benefits of problem gambling and empowering them to reach a decision for change (Hodgins & Makarchuk, 2002; Robson, Edwards, Smith, & Colman, 2002).

Cognitive-behavioral approaches may involve recording the number of gambling and non-gambling days in a month, rewarding the non-gambling days, noting times for greater risks for gambling and restructuring these times to prevent access to gambling, and looking for other pleasurable activities (Petry, 2005). Cognitive interventions explore thoughts that occurred before, during and after the client's last gambling session, and challenge faulty thoughts and beliefs (Ladouceur et al., 2002). Problem gamblers are educated on the difference between chance and skill in gambling, and a primary focus is to increase awareness of the impersonal and unpredictable nature of most gambling games (where outcomes are entirely random). Exercises are set up to increase gamblers' awareness of their own thoughts and behaviors and to help them control their losses. Maintaining healthy thought patterns, finding strategies to support abstinence, and being aware of risks of relapse are part of a cognitive-behavioral program. Cognitive-behavioral therapy has often been conducted in group treatment with comparable results to individual treatments at 3 months (Ladouceur et al., 2003; Gooding & Tarrier, 2009).

Psychodynamic and psychoanalytic approaches view problem gambling as arising from and motivated by internal conflicts and unconscious forces and its understanding of "compulsive gambling" held sway in the 1950s and 1960s (Hodgins & Holub, 2007). Delivered in individualized or group format, psychodynamic therapy aims to increase the clients' insight into the unconscious drives and id impulses behind the gambling behavior and helps the clients resolve unconscious conflicts to reduce the compulsion to gamble. Requirements for longer-term treatment and client propensity for high-level verbalization of psychological insights may be barriers to clinical application of formalized psychodynamic therapies. Psychodynamic approaches depend on the orientation of the therapist and are not standardized, hence difficult for controlled outcome studies.

Although medications specific to the treatment of problem gambling have not been approved (Hodgins & Holub, 2007), a small body of research exists to demonstrate the treatment effectiveness of some pharmaceuticals (e.g., selective serotonin re-uptake inhibitors; opioid agonists; mood stabilizers) that reduce urges to gamble, anxiety, and compulsive symptoms (Grant, Williams, & Kim, 2006; Pallesen et al., 2007). Problems of medication research are side effects, lack of treatment compliance, and high treatment drop-out rates (Hodgins & Holub, 2007).

COUPLE APPROACHES

Despite the fact that problem gambling takes a toll on the gambler, as well as the partner and the couple relationship, relatively little attention has been given to couple treatment models until recently (Bertrand, Dufour, Wright, & Lasnier, 2008; McComb, Lee, & Sprenkle, 2009).

Couple Behavioral-Cognitive Models. Behavioral-cognitive models for couples treatment have been adapted from such models for substance abuse disorders. Ciarrocchi (2002) adapted integrative behavioral couple therapy (Jacobson & Christensen, 1996) to provide a self-regulation manual for individuals and couples. Strategies are directed towards task-oriented goals, such as developing environmental controls, restoring the couple's financial situation, managing legal problems, and permitting partners to ask questions and give feedback to gamblers. The approach favors tolerance and acceptance to motivate change and create a climate to explore trust, fairness and self-esteem (Ciarrocchi, 2002).

More recently, Adapted Couple Therapy (Bertrand et al., 2008) is proposed as a promising adjunct to individual cognitive behavioral therapy that corrects the gambler's erroneous cognitions concerning randomness. Adapted Couple Therapy commences only after the crisis situation is resolved and the financial crisis is settled. The model subscribes to the gambler being the identified patient and that the responsibility of the pathological gambling "rests on the shoulders of the IP" (Bertrand et al., 2008, p. 403). The therapy begins with a functional analysis of the gambling behavior, to identify the sequence of trigger-behaviors-consequences. Analysis of this chain of events leads to strategies to sustain abstinence and prevent relapse. Spouses are helped to avoid behaviors that could undermine these goals, sometimes unintentionally through control and checking on the spouse, and through criticism, and protecting the spouse from negative consequences. Spouses are encouraged to look after their own needs and explore social support, to set limits, and to use specific help services. A couple recovery contract establishes that the couple discuss at predetermined intervals the status of the gambler's abstinence from gambling, secures commitment from the gambler to maintain abstinence, and requires the spouse's recognition of the gambler's abstinence in a positive manner. Other elements in ACT include couple work such as the demonstration of caring behaviors, sharing pleasure and expression for affection, constructive anger and frustration management, and problem-solving skills. This model has not been empirically validated.

CASE EXAMPLE

Cindy has been feeling depressed after the death of her brother and her gambling problems began when the casino opened in town. Her gambling increased to the point where she now meets all ten of the DSM criteria for pathological gambling. She has lost $15,000 of her retirement funds and kept this a secret from her husband Rob until she was charged for defrauding her employer. Unlike substance abuse, gambling problems can be better hidden which makes its discovery more sudden and devastating. Cindy was under house arrest while her husband took control of the family finances and kept a close eye on her use of the Internet and other activities. Resentful of being "treated like a child" and berated by Rob for her crime, Cindy bottled up her shame and resentment while feeling she was given no credit for her efforts. This eventually led to her relapse. "What's the point," she thought, "I have tried so hard to make other people happy all my life; now is my turn to have some fun." After her arrest, Cindy received a few individual counseling sessions focused on modifying her erroneous cognitions regarding her chances of winning at casino games. She also attended Gamblers Anonymous (GA) and felt less alone in her struggles in fellowship with other gamblers. GA gave her a place to talk about the twists and turns of her recovery, something she was not able to do at home. The couple therapist at the agency coaches Cindy in approaching Rob to see if he might be willing to try a few conjoint couple sessions. The therapist balances hearing and validating each of Cindy's and

Rob's perspectives and concerns. Fears, anger, and hurt expressed from both sides are acknowledged in a non-blaming way. Patterns of the couple's communication are pointed out to them—how Cindy tends to placate and hide her feelings because of her fear of rejection and Rob's self-preoccupation, dismissiveness and oblivion to Cindy's ongoing distress and loneliness. The therapist helps the couple see that the impasses in interaction they have in the present reopen the hurts and unresolved issues they suffered in their respective families of old. With new clarity and awareness of themselves and their past, the couple rehearse new patterns of congruent communication with each other, and learn to acknowledge themselves and their partner. Through these conjoint sessions, Cindy and Rob gain a deeper understanding and respect for each other that heal the breach in their relationship. They recognize problem gambling as a symptom of a prolonged and profound disconnection they have with themselves and each other with influences from their family-of-origin. Less ashamed and alone, Cindy's urges to go back to the casino have drastically reduced. When she has the odd relapse, she and Rob are able to talk in order understand what happened, and to strategize ways to pre-empt the possibility of a future episode. She and Rob have started renovating their house and are planning a vacation together for the first time in eight years.

Systemic Humanistic Integrative Model. Congruence Couple Therapy (CCT) was developed as a short-term, integrative, humanistic systemic model for working with pathological gamblers and spouses conjointly (Lee, 2002; 2009a). Designed around the concept of congruence, CCT provides a clear therapy structure for working with couples along four dimensions (Lee, 2002; 2009a). Rather than targeting the behavior of gambling, the aim is to reduce or end problem gambling through addressing underlying systemic disconnections (Lee, 2009a, 2009b). Pathological gambling is viewed as a symptom of a distressed system, delineated in "five circuits" of couple interactions (Lee, 2009b). Within these five circuits are the four recursive circuits of escalating couple distress: (1) fault-lines; (2) pressure points; (3) exacerbation; and (4) relapse, with the fifth circuit, congruence, interrupting the recursive cycles to bring about reconnection and healing hence displacing gambling urges and behaviors. Couple communication often lack depth and openness prior to pathological gambling. Onset and escalation of pathological gambling are set off by pressure points of life transition and setbacks overwhelming the adaptive capacity of the gambler who cannot turn to his/her spouse. Gambling is a way of finding solace, relief or boosting one's self-esteem. The couple relationship further deteriorates in the aftermath of pathological gambling, precipitating relapse. Healing of the couple relationship and both partners through increased congruence is facilitated by CCT (Lee, 2009b). Congruence is defined as awareness, attention, acknowledgment, and alignment of four dimensions of being: intrapsychic, interpersonal, intergenerational, and universal-spiritual (Lee, 2009a). Living congruently breaks individual isolation and reduces relationship distress commonly experienced by pathological gamblers and their spouses. Congruence Couple Therapy is generally conducted in blocks of 12 sessions and places emphasis on generating hope, developing realistic goals collaboratively, reframing blame, and building on the foundation of a strong therapeutic alliance with both partners. As interpersonal and intrapsychic experiences intertwine, CCT facilitates self awareness and acknowledgment which lead to congruent communication. Conversely, respectful communication that is safe and acknowledging invites greater self-awareness and disclosure. Intergenerational underpinnings to current couple patterns are brought to awareness prompting new choices in the present. A vital context is created for fulfillment of human yearnings and an affirmation of the positive qualities of the unique spirit and being of each person (Lee, 2009a; 2009b). Congruence Couple Therapy has been taught to a cohort of Canadian problem gambling counsellors and has obtained promising empirical support for both its training and client outcomes (Lee, 2002; Lee & Rovers, 2008; Lee, Rovers, & MacLean, 2008).

RELAPSE AND MAINTENANCE

Similar to other addictions, relapse rates among pathological gamblers are high, and can be up to 75 percent (Hodgins, Currie, el-Guebaly & Diskin, 2007). Financial and emotional concerns are frequently cited reasons for relapse (Hodgins et al., 2007). Unresolved relationship problems perpetuate the gambler's distress, rendering the gambler vulnerable to relapse (Lee, 2009b).

In contrast to approaches for directly treating the gambling behavior, an important consideration of conjoint systemic couple therapy is to interrupt underlying recurring difficult relationship patterns that create distress and undermine mutual support in life's storms. Improved relationship with self and one's partner increases resiliency, so that a person can better respond to the challenges life throws at us. Problem gambling as a symptom of unmitigated personal and relationship distress then dissipates. Marriage and family therapists are poised to rise to the task of bringing true systemic couple therapy options into the arena of problem gambling treatment.

ABOUT THE AUTHOR

Bonnie Lee, PhD, assistant professor in the Faculty of Health Sciences, Addictions Counselling Program, is an AAMFT Clinical Member and Approved Supervisor, and a board member with the Alberta Association of Marriage and Family Therapy (2007-2009). Lee has been the principal researcher and trainer in a program of research since 2001 in the development and application of Congruence Couple Therapy, a systemic, relationship model for pathological gambling, a model she is now extending to other addictions. Her work aims to bring together training, practice and research in service of human growth and healing.

The author gratefully acknowledges the editorial and research assistance of Michelle Browne, Bev West, Rhys Stevens, Beth Johnson, and Jason Solowoniuk.

RESOURCES FOR PRACTITIONERS

Berman, L. & Siegal, M. E. (1999). *Behind the 8 ball: A guide for families of gamblers.* New York: Simon & Schuster.

Lee, B. K. (2009). Congruence Couple Therapy for pathological gambling. *International Journal of Mental Health and Addiction, 7,* 45-67.

Lee, B. K. (2009). *Five circuits: A systemic relationship framework for pathological gambling.* Manuscript submitted for publication.

Federman, E. J., Drebing, C. E., & Krebs, C. K (2000). *Don't leave it to chance: A guide for families of problem gamblers.* Oakland, CA: New Harbinger Publications Inc.

McCown, W. G., & Howatt, W. A. (2007). *Treating gambling problems.* New Jersey: John Wiley & Sons.

Petry, N. M. (2005). *Pathological gambling: Etiology, comorbidity, and treatment.* Washington, DC: American Psychological Association.

National Council on Problem Gambling (U.S.)
www.ncpgambling.org
The mission of the National Council on Problem Gambling is to increase public awareness of pathological gambling, ensure the widespread availability of treatment for problem gamblers and their families, and to encourage research and programs for prevention and education.

National Problem Gambling Helpline: 1-800-522-4700 (U.S.)
Confidential-Nationwide-24/7

Gamblers Anonymous (International)
http://www.gamblersanonymous.org
Gamblers Anonymous is a fellowship of men and women who share their experience, strength and hope with each other that they may solve their common problem and help others to recover from a gambling problem.

Gam-Anon (International)
www.gam-anon.org
The self-help organization of Gam-Anon provides assistance for the spouse, family or close friends of compulsive gamblers.

Journal of Gambling Issues
www.camh.net/egambling
An on-line publication on gambling research, treatment, policy and people's experience with gambling.

Responsible Gambling Council (Canada)
www.responsiblegambling.org/en/help
This non-profit organization provides useful information, articles, audio and video resources and research on problem gambling and to support responsible gambling.

ProblemGambling.ca (Canada)
www.problemgambling.ca
An online community supported by the Centre for Addiction and Mental Health (CAMH). This web site contains information about problem gambling for individuals concerned about their own, or someone else's gambling. ProblemGambling.ca also provides an online space for professionals to exchange knowledge and resources about problem gambling.

Youth Gambling (Canada)
www.youthgambling.com
The Centre advances knowledge on youth gambling and risk-taking behaviors. Information for adolescents and parents are available on this site.

REFERENCES

Abbott, D. Cramer, S. L., & Sherrets, S. D. (1995). Pathological gambling and the family: Practice implications. *Families in Society, 76*(4), 213-219.

Afifi, T. O., Brownridge, D. MacMillan, H., & Sareen, J. (2009). The relationship of gambling to intimate partner violence and child maltreatment in a nationally representative sample. *Journal of Psychiatric Research.*

American Gaming Association. (2009). *U.S. commercial casino industry: Facts at your fingertips.* Washington, DC: Author. Retrieved September 17, 2009, from http://www.americangaming.org/assets/files/AGA_Facts_Web.pdf

American Psychiatric Association (APA). (2000). *Diagnostic and statistical manual of mental disorders (4th ed., Text Rev.).* Washington, DC: Author.

Bertrand, K., Dufour, M., Wright, J., & Lasnier, B. (2008). Adapted Couple Therapy (ACT) for pathological gamblers: A promising avenue. *Journal of Gambling Studies, 24,* 393-409.

Blaszczynski, A., Huynh, S., Dumloa, V., & Farrell, E. (1998). Problem gambling within a Chinese-speaking community. *Journal of Gambling Studies, 14,* 359-380.

Boughton, & Falenchuk, O. (2007). Vulnerability and comorbidity factors of female problem gambling. *Journal of Gambling Studies, 23,* 323-334.

Carter, E. A., & McGoldrick, M. (Eds.). (1989). *The changing family life cycle: A framework for family therapy (2nd ed.).* Boston: Allyn and Bacon.

Ciarrocchi, J. W. (2002). *Counseling problem gamblers: A self-regulation manual for individual and family therapy.* New York: Academic Press.

Cunningham-Williams, R., Cottler, L., Compton III, W., & Spitznagel, E. (1998). Taking chances: Problem gamblers and mental health disorders—Results From the St. Louis Epidemiologic Catchment Area Study. *American Journal of Public Health, 88(7),* 1093-1093.

Darbyshire, P., Oster, C., & Carrig, H. (2001). The experience of pervasive loss:

Children and young people living in a family where parental gambling is a problem. *Journal of Gambling Studies, 17,* 23-45.

Dickson-Swift, V. A., James, E. L., & Kippen, S. (2005). The experience of living with a problem gambler: Spouses and partners speak out. *Journal of Gambling Issues, 13,* Retrieved December 1, 2009, from http://www.camh.net/egambling/archive/pdf/JGI-issue13/JGI-Issue13-dicksonSwift.pdf

Ferris, J., & Wynne, H. (2001). The *Canadian Problem Gambling Index final report.* Ottawa, Ontario: Canadian Centre on Substance Abuse.

Gerstein, D., Murphy, S., Toce, M., Hoffman, J., Palmer, A., Johnson, R., et al. (1999). *Gambling impact and behavior study: Report to the National Gambling Impact Study Commission.* Chicago: National Opinion Research Centre.

Gooding, P., & Tarrier, N. (2009). A systematic review and meta-analysis of cognitive behavioural interventions to reduce problem gambling: Hedging our bets? *Behaviour Research and Therapy, 47,* 592-607.

Grant, J. E., Williams, K. A., & Kim, S. W. (2006). Update on pathological gambling. *Current Psychiatry Reports, 8,* 53-58.

Grant Kalischuk, R., Nowatzki, N., Cardwell, K., Klein, K., & Solowoniuk, J. (2006). Problem gambling and its impact on families: A literature review. *International Gambling Studies, 6*(1), 31-60.

Grunfeld, Zangeneh, M., & Diakoloukas, L. (2008). Religiosity and gambling rituals. In M. Zangeneh, A. Blaszczynski, and N. E. Turner (Eds.), *In the pursuit of winning: Problem gambling theory, research and treatment* (pp. 155-166). New York: Springer.

Hing, N., & Breen, H. (2001). Profiling lady luck: An empirical study of gambling and problem gambling amongst female club members. *Journal of Gambling Studies, 17,* 47-39.

Hodgins, D. C., Currie, S. R., el-Guebaly, N., & Diskin, K. M. (2007). Does providing extended relapse prevention bibliotherapy to problem gamblers improve outcome? *Journal of Gambling Studies, 23*(1), 43-54.

Hodgins, D. C., & el-Guebaly, N. (2000). Natural and treatment-assisted recovery from gambling problems: A comparison of resolved and active gamblers. *Addiction,* 95(5), 777-789.

Hodgins, D. C., & Holub, A. (2007). Treatment of problem gambling. In G. Smith, D. C. Hodgins, & R. J. Williams (Eds.), *Research and measurement issues in gambling studies* (pp. 371-397). Burlington, MA: Elsevier.

Hodgins, D. C., & Makarchuk, K. (2002). *Becoming a winner: Defeating problem gambling.* Edmonton, Alberta: Alberta Alcohol and Drug Abuse Commission (AADAC).

Hodgins, D., Shead, N., & Makarchuk, K. (2007). Relationship satisfaction and psychological distress among concerned significant others of pathological gamblers. *The Journal of Nervous and Mental Disease, 195*(1), 65-71.

Hraba, J., & Lee, G. (1996). Gender, gambling, and problem gambling. *Journal of Gambling Studies, 12,* 83-101.

Jacobs, D. F., Marston, A. R., Singer, R. D., Widsman K., Little, T., Veizades, J. (1989). Children of problem gamblers. *Journal of Gambling Behaviour, 5,* 261-268.

Jacobson, N., & Christensen, (1996). Studying the effectiveness of psychotherapy. How well can clinical trials do the job?. *The American Psychologist, 51*(10), 1031-1039.

Jimenez-Murcia, S., Alvarez-Moyer, M., Granero, R., Aymami, M. Gomez-Pena, M.,

Jaurrietta, et al. (2007). Cognitive-behavioral group treatment for pathological gambling: Analysis of effectiveness and predictors of therapy outcome. *Psychotherapy Research, 17*(5), 544-552.

Kausch, Rugle, L., & Rowland, D. (2006). Lifetime histories of trauma among pathological gamblers. American Journal on *Addictions, 15*(1), 35-43.

Kim, S. W., Grant, J. Adson. D. & Shin, Y. C. (2001). Double-blind naltrexone and placebo comparison study in the treatment of pathological gambling. *Biological Psychiatry, 49*, 914-921.

Korman, L., Collins, J., Dutton, D., Dhayananthan, Littman-Sharp, N., & Skinner, W. (2008). Problem gambling and intimate partner violence. *Journal of Gambling Studies, 24*(1), 13-23.

Ladouceur, R., Sylvain, C., Boutin, C., & Doucet, C. (2002). *Understanding and treating the pathological gambler.* West Sussex, England: John Wiley & Sons.

Ladouceur, Sylvain, C., Lachance, S., Doucet, C., & Leblond, J. (2003). Group therapy for pathological gamblers: A cognitive approach. *Behaviour Research and Therapy, 41,*587-96.

Lesieur, R., & Rothschild, J. (1987). Children of Gamblers Anonymous members. *Journal of Gambling Behaviours, 5,* 269-81.

Lee, B. (2002). *Well-being by choice not by chance: An integrative, system-based couple treatment model for problem gambling.* Final Report submitted to the Ontario Problem Gambling Research Centre (OPGRC). Guelph, Ontario.

Lee, B. K. (2009a). Congruence Couple Therapy for pathological gambling. *International Journal of Mental Health and Addiction, 7,* 45-67.

Lee, B. K. (2009b). *Five circuits: A systemic relationship framework for pathological gambling.* Manuscript submitted for publication.

Lee, B. K., & Rovers, M. (2008). 'Bringing torn lives together again': Effects of the first Congruence Couple Therapy application to clients in pathological gambling. *International Gambling Studies, 8*(1), 113-129.

Lee, K., Rovers, M., & MacLean, L. (2008). Training problem gambling counsellors in Congruence Couple Therapy: Evaluation of training outcomes. *International Gambling Studies, 8,* 95-111.

Lesieur, H. & Blume, S. B. (1987). The South Oaks Gambling Screen (SOGS): A new instrument for the identification of problem gamblers. *American Journal of Psychiatry, 144*(9), 1184-1188.

Lesieur, H., & Blume, S. (1991). Evaluation of patients treated for pathological gambling in a combined alcohol, substance abuse and pathological gambling treatment unit using the Addiction Severity Index. *British Journal of Addiction, 86*(8), 1017-1028.

Lorenz, V. C., & Shuttlesworth, D. E. (1983). The impact of pathological gambling on the spouse of the gambler. *Journal of Community Psychology, 11,* 67-76.

Lorenz, V. C., & Yaffee, R. A. (1986). Pathological gambling: Psychosomatic, emotional and marital difficulties as reported by the gambler. *Journal of Gambling Behavior, 2,* 40-49.

Maccallum, F., & Blaszczynski, (2003). Pathological gambling and suicidality: An analysis of severity and lethality. *Suicide and Life-Threatening Behaviour, 33*(1), 88-98.

McComb, J. Lee, B. K., & Sprenkle, D. H. (2009). Conceptualizing and treating problem gambling as a family issue. *Journal of Marital and Family Therapy, 35*(4), 415-431.

Melville, K. M., Casey, L. M., Kavanagh, D. J. (2007). Psychological treatment dropout among pathological gamblers. *Clinical Psychological Review, 27*, 944-958.

Miller, W., & Rollnick, N. (1991). *Motivational interviewing: Preparing people to change addictive behaviors.* New York: Guilford.

National Gambling Impact Study Commission. (1999). *Final report.* Washington, DC: Author.

National Research Council. (1999). *Pathological gambling: A critical review.* Washington, DC: National Academy Press.

Nower, L., & Blaszczynski, (2006). Characteristics and gender differences among self-excluded casino problem gamblers: Missouri data. *Journal of Gambling Studies, 22*(1), 81-99.

Pallesen, S., Molde, H., Arnestad, H. M., Laberg, J. C., Skutle, Iversen, et al. (2007). Outcome of pharmacological treatments of pathological gambling: A review and meta-analysis. *Journal of Clinical Psychopharmacology, 27*(4), 357-364.

Petry, N. M. (2005). *Pathological gambling: Etiology, comorbidity, and treatment.* Washington, DC: American Psychological Association.

Petry, N. M., & Armentano, C. (1999). Prevalence, assessment and treatment of pathological gambling: A review. *Psychiatric Services, 50*, 1021-1027.

Petry, N. M., Armentano, C., Kuoch, T., Norinth, T., & Smith, L. (2003). Gambling participation and problems among South East Asian refugees to the United States. *Psychiatric Services, 54*, 1142-1148.

Petry, N. M., & Steinberg, K. (2005). Childhood maltreatment in male and female treatment-seeking pathological gamblers. *Psychology of Addictive Behaviors, 19*(2), 226-229.

Pietrzak, R., & Petry, N. (2005). Antisocial personality disorder is associated with increased severity of gambling, medical, drug and psychiatric problems among treatment-seeking pathological gamblers. *Addiction, 100*(8), 1183-1193.

Potenza, M., Steinberg, M., McLaughlin, S., Wu, Rounsaville, B., & O'Malley, S. (2000). Illegal behaviors in problem gambling: Analysis of data from a gambling helpline. *Journal of the American Academy of Psychiatry & the Law, 28*(4), 389-403.

Prochaska, J. O., & DiClemente, C. C. (1983). Stages and processes of self-change of smoking: Toward an integrative model of change. *Journal of Consulting and Clinical Psychology, 51*, 390-395.

Productivity Commission. (1999). *Australia's gambling industries* (Report No. 10). Canberra: AusInfo.

Reith, G. (1999). *The age of chance: Gambling and western culture.* New York: Routledge.

Robson, E., Edwards, J., Smith, G., & Colman, I. (2002). Gambling decisions: An early intervention program for problem gamblers. *Journal of Gambling Studies, 18*(3), 235-255.

Rush, B., Bassani, D., Urbanoski, K., & Castel, S. (2008). Influence of co-occurring mental and substance use disorders on the prevalence of problem gambling in Canada. *Addiction, 103*(11), 1847-1856.

Shaffer, H. J. (2003). A public health perspective on gambling: The four principles. *AGA Responsible Gaming Lecture Series, 2*(1), 1-27.

Shaffer, J., & Hall, M. (2001). Updating and refining prevalence estimates of disordered gambling behavior in the United States and Canada. *Canadian Journal of Public Health, 92*, 68-172.

Shaffer, H. J., & Korn, D. A. (2002). Gambling and related mental disorders: A public health analysis. *Annual Review of Public Health, 23,* 171-212.

Shaffer, J., LaBrie, R. A., LaPlante, D. Nelson, S. E., & Stanton, M. V. (2004). The road less travelled: Moving from distribution to determinants in the study of gambling epidemiology. *Canadian Journal of Psychiatry, 49*(8), 504-516.

Shaw, M.C., Forbush, K.T., Schlinder, J., Rosenman, E., & Black, D.W. (2007). The effect of pathological gambling on families, marriages, and children. CNS Spectrums: *The International Journal of Neuropsychiatric Medicine, 12*(8), 615-622.

Sherin, K. M., Sinacore, J. M., Li, X-Q, Zitter, R. E., & Shakil, A. (1998). HITS: A short domestic violence screening tool for use in a family practice setting. *Family Medicine, 30,* 508-512.

Smith, G., & Abt, V. (1984). Gambling as play. *The ANNALS of the American Academy of Political and Social Science, 474,* 122-132.

Spanier, C. B. (1976). Measuring dyadic adjustment: New scales for assessing the quality of marriage and similar dyads. *Journal of Marriage and the Family, 38,* 15-28.

Statistics Canada. (2009). Gambling. *Perspectives on Labour and Income, 10*(7), 26-30. Retrieved September 17, 2009, from http://www.statcan.gc.ca/pub/75-001-x/75-001-x2009107-eng.pdf

Stucki, S., & Rihs-Middel, M. (2007). Prevalence of adult problem and pathological gambling between 2000 and 2005: An update. *Journal of Gambling Studies, 23*(3), 245-257.

Tepperman, L., Korn, D., & Reynolds, J. (2006). *Partner influences on gambling: An exploratory study.* Final Report submitted to the Ontario Problem Gambling Research Centre (OPGRC).

Vitaro, F., & Wanner, Brendgen, M., & Tremblay, (2008). Offspring of parents with gambling problems: Adjustment problems and explanatory mechanisms. *Journal of Gambling Studies, 24,* 535-553.

Volberg, (1994). The prevalence and demographics of pathological gamblers: Implications for public health. *American Journal of Public Health, 84,* 237-41.

Wardman, D., el-Guebaly, N., & Hodgins, D. (2001). Problem and pathological gambling in North American Aboriginal populations: A review of the empirical literature. *Journal of Gambling Studies, 17,* 81-100.

Weinstock, J., Whelan, J. P., & Meyers, A. W. (2004). Behavioral assessment of gambling: An application of the timeline followback method. Psychological Assessment 16(1), 72-80.

Wood, R. T. & Griffiths, M.D. (2007). A qualitative investigation of problem gambling as an escape-based coping strategy. *Psychology and Psychotherapy: Theory, Research and Pratice, 80,* 107-125.

Wulfert, E., Blanchard, E. B., Freidenberg , B. M., & Martell, R. S. (2006). Retaining pathological gamblers in cognitive behavior therapy through motivational enhancement, *Behavior Modification, 30*(3), 315–340.

Yanicki, S., Gregory, D., & Lee, B. K. (in press). Exploring gambling behaviours among Aboriginal peoples: A critical socioecological model. In Y. D. Belanger (Ed.), *First Nations gaming and gambling in Canada: Perspectives.* Winnipeg, MB: University of Manitoba Press.

Zimmerman, M., Chelminski, I., & Young, D. (2006). Prevalence and diagnostic correlates of DSM-IV pathological gambling in psychiatric outpatients. *Journal of Gambling Studies, 22,* 255-262.

Same-Sex Parents and Their Children: The Role of Family Therapists

Deanna Linville, PhD & Maya O'Neil, PhD

Originally published as Clinical Update in Family Therapy Magazine
July-August 2008 • Revised by authors June 2011

Studies estimate that between one and nine million children in the United States have at least one parent who is lesbian or gay (Laumann, 1995; Perrin, 2002). There are approximately 594,000 same-sex partner households, according to the 2000 Census, and there are children living in approximately 27 percent of those households (Meezan & Rauch, 2005; U.S. Census Bureau, 2003). Data are not provided on how many children are in each of these same-sex households. It is difficult to obtain an accurate count of same-sex parent families because many lesbians and gay men are not out due to fears of discrimination, such as loss of employment, loss of child custody, and antigay violence (Ariel & McPherson, 2000). Even with conservative estimates, it is reasonable to conclude that there are a large number of same-sex parents who are potential seekers of mental health services. Yet, when Doherty and Simmons (1996) surveyed licensed marriage and family therapists (LMFTs) about their perceived clinical competence in working with lesbian and gay clients, they found that 50 percent of LMFTs reported that they did not feel competent to treat gay and lesbian clients.

It is important to note that there is not a "usual" gay family, as there is diversity among family constellations (Biblarz & Stacey, 2010; Patterson, 2000). Some same-sex couples may decide to have a child within their relationship, while others may bring children from previous heterosexual or same-sex unions. The rise in same-sex parenting is partially due to the increase in options available for same-sex couples to become parents. Although most children of same-sex couples are biological children of one of the parents, a growing number are the result of donor insemination, surrogacy, foster care and adoption. There are many factors for same-sex couples to consider when deciding on an option for becoming parents. For example, in the case where one partner is the biological parent and the other parent is not biologically related to the child, the biological parent will have more legal rights to the child if the relationship were to dissolve. The non-biological parent may feel a sense of loss and/or yearning because they did not conceive and bear the child themselves, while the biological parent may feel guilty for the power they hold in the relationship.

Most research studies demonstrate that children with two moms or two dads fare just as well as children with heterosexual parents (Patterson, 2000). In fact, Anderssen, Amlie, and Ytteroy (2002) reviewed 23 empirical studies published between 1978 and 2000 on a non-clinical sample of children raised by lesbian mothers or gay fathers and concluded that children raised by same-sex parents did not systematically differ from other children on any of the examined outcomes including: emotional functioning, sexual orientation, stigmatization, gender role behavior, behavioral adjustment, gender identity, and cognitive functioning. Lesbian mothers and gay fathers are similar to other parents, and where research differences have been found, they have sometimes favored same-sex parents (Meezan & Rauch, 2005). For example, in one study, researchers drew on a nationally representative sample of more than 12,105 adolescents in the National Study of Adolescent Health, and compared 44 adolescents being raised by female same-sex couples with 44 raised by heterosexual couples (Wainrwright, Russell, & Patterson, 2004). No differences were found in adolescents' psychological adjustment, grade point averages, and problems in school. Adolescents with same-sex parents reported feeling more connected at school. Another study reported that children in gay and lesbian households are more likely to talk about emotionally difficult topics, and they are often more resilient, compassionate and tolerant (Erich, Leung, & Kindle, 2005).

Researchers have suggested that processes within the family affect child outcomes more than family forms. In other words, the quality of the parent-child relationship matters more than the structural features of the parent-child relationships (Wainwright, Russell, & Patterson, 2004). To illustrate this point, Wainright and Patterson (2006) examined associations among family type (same-sex versus different-sex parents), family and relationship variables, substance use, delinquency and victimization of adolescents and found that adolescents who described closer relationships with their parents reported less delinquent behaviors and substance abuse. The 2005 AAMFT Task Force on Relationships, Health and Marriage drew similar conclusions when they summarized the literature on same-sex parenting and further stated that researchers examining same-sex parenting outcomes report mixed results in only one area: social stigma. According to two studies, there are some data that children of same-sex parents may experience more peer teasing than children of heterosexual parents (Green, 1978; Tasker & Golombok, 1997), though more current research on the topic is necessary.

Despite the lack of evidence to support claims of negative child outcomes associated with same-sex parenting, living in a culture that supports heterosexist and homophobic attitudes and beliefs can affect same-sex parents and their children in a variety of ways. It is important to consider both the similarities with heterosexual families, as well as different contextual influences for same-sex parent families (Tasker, 1999).

The same concerns that face many heterosexual parents when they are deciding to have children also face same-sex parents including time, money, and responsibilities of parenthood (Perlesz et al., 2010; Perrin, 2002). Likewise, many of the parenting tasks faced by same-sex parents are similar to those faced by heterosexual parents, such as providing appropriate structure for children, while also being warm and accepting, setting limits, teaching open and honest communication, healthy conflict resolution, and monitoring of child's peer network and extracurricular activities. Some differences may include adapting to different types of family forms, the impact of social stigma on the family, and dealing with extra familial systems who may not be supportive of same-sex parenting (Tasker, 1999).

DIAGNOSIS AND ASSESSMENT

The issue of same-sex parenting does not generally involve diagnosis, as same-sex parenting, in itself, is not diagnosable. No diagnoses based on a person's sexual orientation are supported by medical, psychological, or counseling related professional organizations. Many mental and medical health professional organizations, such as the AAMFT and the American Psychological Association (APA), provide position statements related to issues pertaining to sexual minority individuals in general and LGBTQ parenting in particular. For example, the APA Public Interest Directorate provides a publication on same-sex parenting (APA, 2005). This publication includes position statements on LGBTQ parenting from other medical, research, and mental health professional organizations, such as the American Academy of Child and Adolescent Psychiatry, the American Academy of Family Physicians, and the American Academy of Matrimonial Lawyers. All of the aforementioned position statements are statements in support of same-sex parenting, and none support including same-sex relationships or attraction as criteria for any medical or mental health diagnosis. Likewise, the AAMFT provides a statement in support of all committed couples and families (AAMFT, 2005).Clinicians can utilize such resources, as well as the information provided to them by their own professional organization(s), to obtain up-to-date information on diagnoses related to sexual orientation and gender identity.

The complexities of being a sexual identity minority in the United States can exacerbate the problems that same-sex parented families face, making assessment essential. During the assessment phase, it is suggested that therapists take a four-pronged approach toward understanding what is happening for the family. First, it is important for the therapist to be aware of their own biases related to sexual orientation minority statuses. A therapist who has not examined these biases (their meaning, related countertransference, etc.), and who is not regularly attending to these biases through supervision and education, may inadvertently undermine the therapeutic process or even do damage.

Second, since same-sex parents may approach therapy feeling defensive or fearful about being judged, it is crucial that the therapist assess and build on the resiliency, strengths, and protective factors of the family. Asking about how the family has mastered the challenges of living in a society that often times stigmatizes same-sex parenting can give the therapist useful information on the family's strengths, and at the same time, empower the family to think about their resiliency and agency.

Third, it is important to assess the quality of the support system for same-sex parents. Green and Mitchell (2002) discussed the importance of the therapist doing a sociogram, as well as a genogram, to diagram the "family of choice" since this is how LGBTQ families often receive their support, versus receiving support from a biological family. Green and Mitchell offer some factors with which to evaluate the support network including: size and composition, frequency/length of contact, type of activities together, multiplicity and complexity of roles, type and quality of support, reciprocity, density, and stability. These family diagrams can help elucidate relevant treatment issues related to family structure, conflict, and relationships. Since it is common for same-sex parents to also be part of a blended family and to have children from previous heterosexual marriages, some of these families may deal with a disagreement from other family members about the authenticity and validity of these family patterns. This lack of support from a previous heterosexual partner and/or the other biological parent can cause major conflict and distress within the family system. Understanding who is in the full parental subsystem and the cohesiveness of this parenting unit can provide an essential road map for treatment. Furthermore, it is important for the therapist to assess how the children are understanding, identifying and making sense of their identity as a child of same-sex parents.

Fourth, as with any relational client, the couples and family therapist is best equipped to think about diagnosis relationally versus from an individual pathology standpoint (Kaslow, 1996). The therapist develops a relational diagnosis for the family based on concepts such as the process of communication for the family, power differentials, rules and roles in the family, how contextual variables and worldviews affect family dynamics, division of labor, and family connectedness (Kaslow, 1996; Rigazio-Digilio, 2000).

Additionally, while there are no diagnoses based on sexual orientation, there are concerns related to the use of assessment tools and diagnoses with diverse populations that every clinician should be aware of, and these considerations apply when working with same-sex parents and their children. When using assessment tools, clinicians need to examine their relevance and whether there is any information pertaining to how the tools have been used previously with people who identify as LGBTQ. If not, a clinician should consider whether any of the questions or assessment procedures are biased, homophobic, heterosexist, stereotyping, or discriminatory in nature. A common example is found in demographic questions. Children are frequently asked questions in a variety of contexts that include assumptions about their parents. For example, a child who is asked, "What jobs do your daddy and mommy do when they go to work each day?" may feel uncomfortable having to explain that he has two mommies, or that he has one mommy and one meema, or he may answer the question inaccurately. Keeping questions or assessment tools

TERMINOLOGY

Given that the people who are a part of Lesbian, Gay, Bisexual, Transgender, Queer, and Questioning (LGBTQ) communities are a large and diverse group of individuals, and because the make-up of these communities is constantly changing, the terminology used to describe these communities and individuals is also frequently changing. The following terminology is proposed by the Human Rights Campaign Foundation (HRC), among others (e.g., Bieschke, Perez, & DeBord, 2006), though we acknowledge that this language may not be the preferred language of all individuals who are part of LGBTQ communities. We recommend clinicians ask their clients how they identify, in terms of sexual orientation and gender identity, and that clinicians ask about clients' preferred terminology and how they would like to be referred to by others.

Bisexual: Describes a person who has a sexual orientation, attraction, and/or emotional/erotic/relational preference to persons of either the same or opposite sexes, and at least a part of their identification includes attraction to people of the same sex.

Gay: A person who has a sexual orientation, attraction, and/or emotional/erotic/relational preference to persons of the same sex, often used to refer to men (e.g., the term "gay" man).

Heterosexism: Systemic in nature, referring to privileging heterosexuality over LGBTQ identities. This privilege is based on the assumption that heterosexuality is normal and should be the ideal. Similar to racism, sexism, etc., heterosexism involves both privilege and power.

Homophobia: Refers to discomfort with, fear or disgust of, or discrimination against people who are LGBTQ.

Lesbian: A woman who has a sexual orientation, attraction, and/or emotional/erotic/relational preference to other women.

LGBTQ: Stands for Lesbian, Gay, Bisexual, Transgender, Queer and Questioning.

Sex: Refers to the sex or gender label a person was assigned at birth (this is frequently assigned by a medical professional after a visual inspection of genitalia). This term can be based on a person's physical make-up in terms of anatomy, chromosomes, and/or hormones.

Sexual Orientation: Refers to the way that a person perceives and/or enacts his or her sexual desires and/or expressions. Sexual orientation does not require that a person is sexually active, engage in any particular types of sexual behaviors, or identify in a particular way.

Queer: Of or relating to LGBTQ individuals or identities. The term "queer" has been reclaimed and is preferred by some members of the LGBTQ community, but can be used or perceived as being a derogatory term in certain contexts or by certain people.

open to a variety of possible responses from a client can help obtain a more accurate assessment of a situation, and can put clients at ease.

TREATMENT ISSUES

Frequently, lesbian and gay families will seek therapeutic help for guidance, support, and recognition that they may not be receiving from the broader so-

LEGAL ISSUES FOR SAME-SEX PARENTS

Legal discrimination against same-sex parents can pertain to housing choices, employment, religious support, adoption rights, and medical rights of access and decision-making, which all affect family life. Problems associated with illegality of marriage in same-sex couples include, but are not limited to, difficulty with adoptions, inability to make emergency medical decisions for a partner, possible loss of custody of children or loss of property upon death of one partner, and lack of tax breaks that married heterosexual couples enjoy (Lambda Legal, n.d.). All of these legal issues can tremendously affect the lives of same-sex parented families and need to be understood by their support and healthcare systems. Because these laws are changing frequently, and because they vary state by state, and even county by county, practitioners should gather up-to-date information on these topics when assisting clients with related concerns. The Lambda Legal Web site, www.lambdalegal.org, provides one location for dissemination of LGBTQ-related legal concerns, with information available for states and counties across the Unites States (Lambda Legal, n.d.).

Many of the legal issues that same-sex parents contend with vary greatly by their state of residence (Lambda Legal, n.d.). For example, in the case of second-parent adoptions, the non-biological parent holds the same rights as a legal parent, ensuring that relationship dissolution would be treated similarly to a divorce among heterosexual parents; however, second-parent adoption is not allowed in all states (Lambda Legal, n.d.). In fact, there are still many states where lesbian and gay parents are not allowed to adopt a child; they may be forced to hide their sexual orientation or adopt as single parents and then fight to gain parental rights for the second parent in the courts (Ariel & McPherson, 2000; Lambda Legal, n.d.). In states that recognize civil unions or domestic partnerships that include parental rights, the child custody laws will often look the same as the child custody laws for heterosexual parents. Unfortunately, in other states, the non-biological parent is a legal nonentity and ends up with virtually no rights at all (Lambda Legal, n.d.).

Moreover, many same-sex couples are choosing to have children conceived through methods such as artificial insemination, co-parenting teams (between gay male and lesbian couples) or surrogacy. With these methods of conception come complex questions, such as: a) who will be the biological parent of the child?; b) will the legal rights of each partner in the couple be the same?; c) does the donor have any custody rights and parenting responsibilities to the child?; d) will the non-biological parents maintain custody if the biological parent leaves the family or dies? These questions and, more importantly, the answers to these questions, can greatly affect power dynamics, security, communication, and roles within families, and need to be included as a treatment consideration when working with same-sex parented families.

cial arena (Ariel & McPherson, 2000). The impact of the coming out process on lesbian and gay parents has not been well researched; however, existing evidence suggests that disclosing one's sexual orientation to self and others is strongly associated with healthy psychological and emotional functioning (Armesto, 2002). Competent parenting may be influenced by gay and lesbian parents' ability to accept and acknowledge their LGBTQ identity and how they are able to negotiate living in a heterosexist, homophobic, or otherwise discriminatory society, while rearing their children in a family unit that is not socially sanctioned (Parks, 1998). It is important for therapists to acknowledge the prevalence both of homophobia that is experienced by the family as a result of the actions of others, as well as the existence of internalized homophobia and how this may impact families (Butler, 2009; McGeorge & Carson, 2011). According to Shidlo (1994), internalized homophobia is defined as, "A set of negative attitudes and affects toward homosexuality in other persons and toward homosexual features in oneself" (p.178). Again, the impact of internalized homophobia on parenting has not been well researched, but therapists should nonetheless be aware of whether or not, and how, all forms of homophobia could be impacting families. Both internalized homophobia and experiences of overt discrimination may mean that clients need more time in therapy to build rapport with the therapist and to feel comfortable disclosing personal and family-related concerns.

When working with diverse populations, it is important for clinicians to know where to access information that could be relevant to the presenting concerns of clients who are not always well represented by U.S. socio-cultural norms. When working with same-sex parents, clinicians can refer to (or refer their clients to) the HRC website for information related to a variety of concerns that impact parenting. Current topics on the site include adoption, donor insemination, custody, foster parenting, schools and youth, and surrogacy. Information can also be obtained through websites of professional organizations, such as the APA and the AAMFT, or associated publications that are specific to parenting (e.g., APA, 2005).

The following are some examples of treatment issues that may be unique to same-sex parent families:

1. Concerns about discrimination in parenting/custody arrangements. LGBTQ families may have concerns about discrimination in parenting/custody arrangements for many reasons. For example, a parent's minority sexual orientation and/or gender identity status may be brought up in custody disputes as a reason to restrict or deny custody by the child(ren)'s other parent and/or by the courts.

2. Co-parenting relationships in blended families. Co-parenting relationships in blended families may look different when one or more parents identifies as LGBTQ because family, friends, coworkers, and school professionals may have difficulty identifying salient relationships in blended families due to stereotypes and assumptions related to gender, sexual orientation, and family makeup. Parents and/or children may react to newly-identified LGBTQ parent(s) in many ways, including possibly blaming a parent or a parent's sexual orientation for "breaking up the family." The many co-parenting and blended family complexities present for heterosexual parents can also be present for same-sex parents with the additional complexities of discrimination, stereotypes, and assumptions.

3. Relationships with non-biological parent figures and donor relationships.

Though relationships with non-biological parent figures can be present in heterosexual families, they are far more common among LGBTQ families simply due to the biological complexities involved with conceiving children when parents are the same sex. Literature related to adoption and blended families can be consulted and used as a model for treatment issues related to relationships with non-biological parents; however, same-sex parents also face unique treatment issues in this area. Children and parents may be more open about non-biological relationships due to the impossibility of conception between same-sex parents. They may or may not be open within and outside of their immediate family about donor relationships or how the child was conceived/became part of the family. Children may be presented with a variety of ways that their biological relationship to their parents matters or does not matter (e.g., being told that both parents love them equally and that this is what makes a family rather than solely biological relationships).

4. Relationship acknowledgement/discrimination from extended family members. In same-sex relationships, it is common for extended family to acknowledge romantic relationships differently from heterosexual relationships; this discriminatory treatment can be confounded by parenting relationships as well. Extended family may see parenting as a necessary step in validating a relationship for same-sex couples or they may view parenting with similar biased and discriminatory views, even denying one parent's relationship to the child(ren).

5. Explanation of relationship status and family make-up to children and people outside of the family. Explaining relationship status and family make-up to people outside of the family (e.g., school professionals, medical professionals, children's friends/parents), as well as explaining relationship status and family make-up to children, can be uniquely complex for same-sex parents. Though many family relationships may be complex, explaining family relationships is uniquely complex for LGBTQ families because of the lack of societal norms and relevant examples in media, stereotyped notions about LGBTQ relationships that are common, and the fear of discrimination faced by these families.

Children of same-sex parent families will likely experience prejudice, because if the children are aware of their parent's sexuality, they will have to contend directly with the frequently made heterosexist assumption that all families have heterosexual parents (Tasker, 1999). Children, just like their parents, are forced to make decisions about whether it is safe to come out about their family. Children may experience greater mastery over this decision making process if they have a clear understanding of who their family members are and their parents are able to model navigating the coming out process successfully.

Though there are several treatment issues that are unique to working with same-sex parent families, it is essential for therapists to realize that many presenting concerns are the same for families with same-sex parents and families with heterosexual parents. Same-sex parented families may experience their sexual orientation or relationship status as a major influence on treatment issues, or this may not be a central part of family therapy at all. In all cases, it is important for the therapist to acknowledge the multifaceted nature of family culture (including salient cultural identities for the family such as ethnicity, ability/disability status, social class/socio-economic status, and other cultural identities), and it is equally important for the therapist to follow the client's lead related to the influence and impact that these cultural identities have on the presenting treatment issues.

For further information, see the *Clinical Updates* on "Same-Sex Couples" and "Transgender in Family Therapy" in Vol. 3 of this book series.

ABOUT THE AUTHORS

Deanna Linville, PhD, LMFT is an assistant professor and program director in the Couples and Family Therapy Program at the University of Oregon. She received an award for "Commitment to the Lesbian, Gay, Bisexual, Transgender community" in 2004, has conducted research to better understand the needs of lesbian, gay, bisexual and transgender individuals and couples for the last several years, and has been working with same-sex parents and LGBTQ communities for 12 years.

Maya O'Neil, PhD, is a clinical psychologist with the Portland VA Medical Center and assistant professor of psychiatry at Oregon Health and Science University. She works as a statistician and core investigator for the VA, researching topics including health disparities, suicide prevention, and neuropsychological assessment.

RESOURCES FOR PRACTITIONERS AND CLIENTS

American Psychological Association's Division 44: Society for the Psychological Study of Lesbian, Gay, and Bisexual Issues
www.apadivision44.org
Among several objectives, Division 44 aims to advance the understanding of lesbian, gay, and bisexual issues through basic and applied research.

Bieschke, K. J., Perez, R. M., & DeBord, (Eds.). (2006). *Handbook of counseling and psychotherapy with lesbian, gay, bisexual, and transgender clients.* Washington, DC: American Psychological Association.
Includes chapters on transgender communities and providing affirmative psychotherapy and counseling with transgender clients.

Children of Lesbians and Gays Everywhere (COLAGE)
www.colage.org
COLAGE engages, connects, and empowers people to make the world a better place for children of lesbian, gay, bisexual, and/or transgender parents and

families.

The Gay, Lesbian & Straight Education Network (GLSEN)
www.glsen.org
GLSEN strives to assure that each member of every school community is valued and respected regardless of sexual orientation or gender identity/expression.

Gay Parent Magazine
www.gayparentmag.com
Gay Parent features personal stories of lesbian, gay, bisexual, and transgender parents about their experiences with international and domestic adoption, foster care, donor insemination, using a surrogate and what it is like to raise their children.

Human Rights Campaign Foundation (HRC)
www.hrc.org
HRC is America's largest civil rights organization working to achieve gay, lesbian, bisexual and transgender equality.

Parents, Families, and Friends of Lesbians, Gays, Bisexual and Transgender (PFLAG) www.pflag.org
PFLAG is devoted to educating and supporting everyone involved in the life of a sexual minority individual. There are local chapters all over the United States.

Ritter, K. Y., & Terndrup, A.I. (2002). *Handbook of affirmative psychotherapy with lesbians and gay men*. New York: Guilford. The *Handbook* includes sociopolitical contexts, psychological theory and clinical practice about sexual minority individuals. It reviews the literature on the history, terminology, and research about this population.

World Professional Association for Transgender Health, Inc. (WPATH)
www.wpath.org
Provides comprehensive ethical guidelines concerning the care of patients with gender identity disorders. WPATH has established internationally accepted Standards of Care (SOC) for the treatment of gender identity disorders.

REFERENCES

American Association for Marriage and Family Therapy (2005). *AAMFT position on couples and families*. Retrieved June 27, 2011, from http://www.aamft.org/imis15/Content/About_AAMFT/Position_On_Couples.aspx.

American Psychological Association, (2005). *Lesbian and gay parenting*. Washington, DC: Author.

Anderson, N., Amlie, C., & Yttteroy, (2002). Outcomes for children with lesbian or gay parents. A review of studies from 1978-2000. *Scandinavian Journal of*

Psychology, 43, 335-351.

Ariel, J. & McPherson, D. (2000). Therapy with lesbian and gay parents and their children. *Journal of Marital and Family Therapy, 26*(4), 421-423.

Armesto, J. (2002). Developmental and contextual factors that influence gay father's parental competence: A review of the literature. *Psychology of Men and Masculinity, 32*(2), 67-78.

Biblarz, T. J., & Stacey, J. (2010). How does the gender of parents matter? *Journal of Marriage and Family, 72*(1), 3-22. DOI:10.1111/j.1741-3737.2009.00678.

Bieschke, K. J., Perez, R. M., & DeBord, (Eds.). (2006). *Handbook of counseling and psychotherapy with lesbian, gay, bisexual, and transgender clients.* Washington, DC: American Psychological Association.

Butler, C. (2009). Sexual and gender minority therapy and systemic practice. *Journal of Family Therapy, 31*(4), 338-358.

Diamond, M. (2002). Sex and gender are different: Sexual identity and gender identity are different. *Clinical Child Psychology and Psychiatry, 7*(3), 320-334.

Doherty, W. J., & Simmons, D. S. (1996). Clinical practice patterns of marriage and family therapists: A national survey of therapists and their clients. *Journal of Marital and Family Therapy, 22,* 9-25.

Erich, S., Leung, P., & Kindle, P. (2005). A comparative analysis of adoptive family functioning with gay, lesbian, and heterosexual parents and their children. *Journal of GLBT Family Studies, 1*(4), 43-60.

Green, R. J. (1978). Sexual identity of 37 children raised by homosexual or transsexual parents. *American Journal of Psychiatry, 135,* 692-697.

Green, R. J. & Mitchell, V. (2002). Gay and lesbian couples in therapy: Homophobia, relational ambiguity, and social support. In Alan S. Gurman and Neil S. Jacobson (eds), *Clinical handbook of couple therapy* (3rd Edition). New York: Guilford.

Human Rights Campaign Foundation (n.d.). *Transgender Americans: A handbook for understanding.* Retrieved on June 13, 2006, from http://www.hrc.org/Content/ContentGroups/Publications1/TransgenderAmericans.pdf.

Kaslow, F., W. (1996). *Handbook of relational diagnosis and dysfunctional family patterns.* New York: Wiley.

Lambda Legal (n.d.). *Lambda legal: Making the case for equality.* Retrieved February 17, 2008, from http://www.lambdalegal.org/our-work/issues/marriage-relationships-family/parenting/.

Laumann, E. (1995). *National health & social life survey.* Chicago, IL: University of Chicago and National Opinion Research Center.

McGeorge, C., & Carlson, T. S. (2011). Deconstructing heterosexism: Becoming an LGB affirmative heterosexual couple and family therapist. *Journal of Marital and Family Therapy, 37*(1), 14-26. Alexandria, VA: AAMFT.

Meezan, W. & Rauch, J. (2005). Gay marriage, same-sex parenting, and America's children. *The Future of Children, 15*(2), 97-115.

Parks, C. (1998). Lesbian parenthood: A review of the literature. *American Journal of Orthopsychiatry, 68*(3), 376-389.

Patterson, C. (2000). Family relationships of lesbians and gay men. *Journal of Marriage and the Family, 62,* 1052-1069.

Perrin, E. C., and the Committee on Psychosocial Aspects of Family Health (2002). Technical Report: Coparent and second-parent adoption by same-sex parents. *Pediatrics, 109,* 341-344.

Rigazio-Digilio, S. (2000). Relational diagnosis: A coconstructive-developmental perspective on assessment and treatment. *Journal of Clinical Psychology, 56*(8), 1017-1036.

Shidlo, A. (1994). Internalized homophobia: Conceptual and empirical issues in measurement. In Greene, B. & Herek, G.M. (Eds.), Psychological perspectives on lesbian and gay issues: Vol.1 *Lesbian and gay psychology: Theory, research, and clinical applications* (pp.176-205). Sage Publications: Thousand Oaks, CA.

Tasker, F. (1999). Children in lesbian-led families. *Clinical Child Psychology and Psychiatry, 4,* 153-166.

Tasker, F. & Golombok, S. (1997). *Growing up in a lesbian family: Effects on child development.* London: Guilford.

U.S. Census Bureau (2003). *Married couple and unmarried partner household 2000: Census 2000 special reports.* Retrieved from http://www.census/gov/prod/2003pubs/censr-5.pdf.

Wainright, J. & Patterson, C. (2006). Delinquency, victimization, and substance use among adolescents with female same-sex parents. *Journal of Family Psychology, 20*(3), 526-530.

Sibling Violence

John Caffaro, PhD

Originally published as Clinical Update in Family Therapy Magazine
May-June 2008 • Revised by author June 2011

Despite dramatic declines in family size in the United States over the past century, in the mid-1990s almost 90 percent of children lived in a home with a sibling (Hernandez, 1997). Brothers and sisters provide life's longest lasting intimate relationship, generally outlasting ties with parents by 20 to 30 years. Researchers say, and siblings agree, that there is a deep-seated sense of obligation felt among many brothers and sisters. And sibling interdependence begins early: in the majority of societies, siblings are principle caretakers and companions of younger children (Caffaro, 2007). There is also a shared family history. What if that history is filled with aggression and violence? Until recently, there has been less interest in sibling violence relative to concerns about violence toward children and women in families.

SIBLING VIOLENCE

Although parent-child and partner violence has received more public attention, physical violence between brothers and sisters is by far the most common form of family conflict. Data reported in several studies over the past three decades suggest that sibling abuse is pandemic and can have serious consequences. Sibling violence is estimated to occur in 60 percent of American families with more than one child living in the home and the violence is believed to peak as the oldest sibling in the dyad reaches the age of 10 to 14 years (Noland, Liller, McDermott, Coulter, & Seraphine, 2004). Results of a more recent study (Finkelhor et al., 2006) indicate that 35 percent of a national survey of 2,030 children interviewed were "hit or attacked" by a sibling, and 14 percent were repeatedly attacked in the past year. Sibling victimizations were most common for six to nine year olds. And the experience associated with the most symptoms was chronic sibling violence against

---

younger children (defined as five or more episodes in one year).

Additionally, research (Nolan et al., 2004; Simonelli, Mullis, Elliot, & Pierce, 2002) suggests a link between young adult dating violence and sibling abuse. These studies support the hypothesis that violence in the sibling relationship may act as a blueprint for subsequent peer relationships. Indeed, it has been argued that violent sibling interactions, particularly for the child in the perpetrator role, may be a better predictor of later adult violence than exposure to spousal abuse (Gully, Dengerink, Pepping, & Bergstrom, 1981). Despite such evidence, sibling violence receives relatively little attention in the child maltreatment or family therapy literature. Acts of sibling violence tend to be underreported because there is a tendency for families to dismiss the abuse as normal sibling rivalry and to consider aggression an acceptable form of conflict resolution (Patterson, 1975, 1982; Wiehe, 2000). Perhaps because it is so commonplace, sibling violence tends to be accepted as a normal characteristic of family life.

Sibling violence can be defined as *a repeated pattern of aggression directed toward a sibling with the intent to inflict harm, and motivated by an internal emotional need for power and control* (Caffaro & Conn-Caffaro, 1998). When parents frequently disagree over how to resolve disputes between siblings, children may decide to reject parental authority and "fight it out" between themselves. Overt parental conflict in the family provides a model of authority for siblings to eventually emulate both within and outside of the family.

CONTRIBUTING FACTORS

Sibling rivalry is a normal and mostly harmless part of growing up. The sometimes fierce, but balanced comparisons regarding achievement, attractiveness, or social relations with peers may actually strengthen sibling attachments in more functional families. However, rivalry alone is not sufficient to explain the presence or absence of sibling violence. The family is an interdependent unit and the actions of one family member have an impact on all of the others.

In troubled families, parents frequently scapegoat one child; thus indirectly favoring another. Conflict between siblings in these situations may reflect the child's way of coping with power imbalances brought on by parent-child coalitions. Children who are treated unequally or unfairly by their parents are more likely to fight with one another. Their future adult sibling relationship may also suffer. When parental relationships with children are characterized by favoritism or cross-generational coalitions, the child who is "left out" may become increasingly resentful and aggressive toward the preferred sibling. Parental intervention is critical.

Key determinants include how often and how long the behavior has been occurring, whether the behavior is appropriate to the children's ages, and whether one child is consistently the victim of the other. Frequently, what begins as normal rivalry can escalate into something more when parents fail to adequately supervise their children and teach them appropriate means of resolving conflict. In one fairly common set of circumstances, parents may leave an older sibling in charge of younger children. The child in charge may not know how to mete out appropriate discipline. When a child misbehaves, the older sibling may resort to extreme behavior to obtain the younger child's compliance.

Age differences appear to be more important between children reared with siblings as caretakers, though this depends somewhat on the role and function assumed by older siblings in the family. One of the most consistent research findings in this area is that each child's contribution to a sibling interaction is strongly influenced by whether the child is older or younger. Overall, older siblings are a salient feature in the lives of their younger brothers and sisters. Baskett (1984) observed that younger siblings were more likely to attend to an older sibling's behavior than to that of a parent. In addition, younger siblings often passively accept aggressive acts initiated by older siblings.

Firstborns, especially boys who use physical force, are viewed as more powerful and bossier than younger siblings (Bryant, 1982). Several explanations are hypothesized: firstborns generally are considered more likely to engage in hierarchical power relationships with their parents; in relationships with younger siblings, they tend to model their parents' power tactics. In response, younger siblings often react in ways aimed at upsetting the older sibling's power.

A common characteristic of families with ineffective parenting is harsher, more frequent punishment of an older, dominant sibling. Felson and Russo (1988) report that such parents are more likely to punish the more powerful sibling; this, in turn, stimulates more aggression on the part of the "weaker" sibling. Such a response begins a repetitive, nonproductive sequence of events that can escalate into sibling violence. Research findings indicate that the rate of sibling violence is highest among children in families in which both child and spousal assault are present (Hotaling, Straus, & Lincoln, 1990).

SIBLING ABUSE FAMILY CONFIGURATIONS

Peripheral Parent Families. One of the more common family configurations vulnerable to sibling violence is the family where one parent or caretaker is maintained in a peripheral role. In such families, one parent assumes a role exterior to the others. In many cases, he or she re-enters the family system in an authoritarian or abusive manner. The parent who is more available in the family may be nurturing, but unable to protect him or herself and the children when the peripheral parent becomes abusive. Conversely, the nonperipheral parent may be the one who abuses the children. An absence of parental contact and support renders children vulnerable to sibling violence for a number of reasons. Children in peripheral-parent homes may feel that there is not enough love, attention, or support for everyone. These feelings can create adversarial relationships among siblings who are attempting to meet their needs in a family with limited resources. In addition, sibling interactions often are not supervised adequately; this situation creates structural deficits, and a lack of parental authority and control. When adult caretakers are not available to facilitate problem solving, siblings are left to resolve conflicts using their own inadequate (albeit developing) skills. Thus the benefits of learning effective communication, sharing, and natural and logical consequences are not integrated readily into their abilities to resolve problems (Caffaro & Conn-Caffaro, 1998).

Pseudo-parent Sibling Families. In pseudo-parent sibling families, neither parent is reliably available and the pseudo-parent child becomes a highly relied upon family member, but simultaneously cannot fully join or maintain membership in either the sibling or the parental generation. When parents abdicate caretaking responsibilities to the functional oldest child, they place him or her in a unique generational position in relation to the other siblings. Brothers or sisters in this role sometimes lack the authority to create appropriate limits governing sibling behavior. The caretaking child in these families tends to be four to five years older than his or her next youngest sibling. Furthermore, it is frequently the pseudo-parent child who initiates the abuse of his or her younger sibling(s). Dynamics within the pseudo-parent sibling family (dual and single parent) are somewhat alike. The primary difference is that the parental child in the single parent family assumes caretaking responsibility for both his or her younger siblings and the single parent. This child is actually drawn into the spousal subsystem as more of an equal, and therefore has greater influence with regard to younger siblings.

Gender and Sibling Aggression. Boys are less likely to report being a victim because of the embarrassment they experience about seeking help and admitting that they have been abused (Duncan, 1999; Goodwin & Roscoe, 1990). This is an important consideration regarding professional outreach with sibling abuse victims because male victims tend to be overlooked. Boys are also more likely to be perpetrators of sibling violence and this tendency may be linked to societal messages boys receive about being tough. Marriage and family therapists should be willing to explore with male perpetrators their attitudes about masculinity and what it means to be a man.

Conversely, the lack of attention directed toward girls who perpetrate sibling violence may be linked to the societal gender stereotype that boys are aggressive and girls are not. Parents and professionals tend to have trouble accepting and confronting sibling abuse in girls. Adults may deny that girls can be perpetrators and dismiss aggressive acts as minor and not harmful due to the mistaken belief that girls are not strong enough to do serious damage to others.

Fathers and Sibling Aggression. A father's role may be particularly salient in forecasting the quality of the sibling relationship. For example, father-to-child violence is a significant predictor of sibling violence (Noland et al., 2004). This is supported by evidence that males in general report higher levels of sibling violence and more closely identify with, and imitate, behaviors exhibited by their male parent. In addition, peripheral fathers are over-represented in families experiencing sibling violence. Lower levels of paternal acceptance and involvement have pervasive negative effects on children, and are associated with higher levels of sibling conflict.

Studies report that siblings who characterized their father as warm and treated siblings equally had lower levels of sibling conflict (Stocker & McHale, 1992). This suggests that family intervention should include fathers whenever possible. The father's role with male children has also been related to empathy development. Koestler (1990) demonstrated that the amount of time a father spends with his children, and specifically, a father who is able to *display tender emotions,* contributes an important ingredient for the development of empathy in his male children. Empathy is a critical component of high-quality functional sibling relationships.

ASSESSMENT CONSIDERATIONS

For a thorough assessment of sibling violence, it is often necessary to evaluate a child's behavior under varying conditions of separation from his or her offender and parents. The process of interviewing siblings alone without parents is not well established in family therapy. Researchers, however, increasingly suggest the efficacy of this approach. Assessment must also include an evaluation of risk and protective factors present in the family (see Table 1).

Assessment of sibling violence can be challenging for other reasons. Sibling offenders, unlike their adult counterparts, are more often likely to remain in the same home, school, and community as their victims, even after a child welfare services report has been filed. Therefore, the therapist must make every effort to conduct a thorough family-based risk assessment that can determine an appropriate treatment plan, including whether to recommend removal of an offender. And if removal is indicated, one must plan how to proceed with reunification.

Areas of strength and vulnerability, both for individuals and throughout the family system, must be identified. Information about interactional patterns and individual personalities, as well as an evolutionary sibling history, is important in arriving at a clear diagnosis and treatment plan. Like risk factors, protective factors can be characteristics of the individual (e.g., personality) or larger ecological setting (e.g., family, school, peers). For example, good sibling relations appear to buttress children from some of the risks posed by parental conflict (Cummings & Davis, 2002).

A structured interview generally begins with an individual assessment of the sibling victim and offender. By obtaining information from individual interviews with siblings before meeting with the family, one gains an opportunity to establish relationships with the children involved and gather important individual perspectives on abusive events. Sometimes the protocol must be modified to allow for each family's characteristics. In some families, for example, it may be more prudent to meet initially with the sibling victim in the context of the family. Consultation with the victim about any meetings with a sibling offender should guide the decision about whether or not to hold such a meeting. Some victims may be opposed to, or upset by, the prospect of their therapist meeting with their offender. Sometimes, therapists do not have access to all family members in cases of sibling violence. In this situation, it is essential to maintain close contact with other clinicians who may be involved in treating other fam-

FIGURE 1: CRITICAL COMPONENTS OF THE SIBLING ABUSE INTERVIEW (SAI)

Adapted from Caffaro & Conn-Caffaro (1998)

Subsystem   Item

SIBLING VICTIM

Do boys or girls have the most say in your family?

- If you were to look at your family as being made up of two teams, who would be on each team?
- Pretend there is something that you and your sibling both really want, and only one of you can have it. Who gets it, and how?
- If your sibling is teasing you, or doing something to you that you don't like, will he or she stop when you ask him or her to?
- When your brother or sister hits you, are you able to go and tell your parents? Will they help you?
- When a sibling shouts at you or teases you, do you believe that it is usually because you have done something to deserve it?

SIBLING OFFENDER

How do you know when people in your family are mad at you?

- How are you able to get your sibling to do things that you want him or her to do?
- What is one of the worse days or experiences that you think your brother or sister has ever had? How do you imagine that she or he felt about it?
- Has anyone inside or outside of your family ever bothered you a lot, made you feel scared, hit you, or hurt you in other ways? If so, who was it, ands how did she or he hurt you? How did you feel about it?

NONTARGETED SIBLINGS

If you and your brother or sister made the same mistake at home, would you each get punished in the same way?

- Does it usually seem that the punishment "fits the crime" in your family?
- When your brother or sister is punished, does it usually seem that he or she deserved it?

ily members, and to coordinate therapeutic efforts accordingly.

Working through sibling abuse issues generally involves some combination of individual, sibling, family and group sessions. We developed a psychosocial assessment tool, the Sibling Abuse Interview*, to enhance evaluation and intervention with sibling abuse families. The SAI explores the history and current status of sibling relationships through a series of questions presented to each member of the family and the relevant subsystem over a series of meetings (Caffaro & Conn-Caffaro, 1998). Areas of inquiry are arranged in developmental sequence and address the effects of traumatic stress on individual, subsystem, and family functioning. The SAI also highlights sibling strengths in order to evaluate safety concerns and sources of individual and family resilience.

SIBLING SUBSYSTEM

What are some amusing, funny, interesting experiences that you have gone through together that are unique to your relationship as siblings?

- When you do a good job at something---such as in school, work around the house, or things that your parents ask you to do---what does Dad usually do or say about that? What does Mom usually do or say?
- Tell me about some times when you have been fighting, and describe how each of your parents have responded.
- What are some rules or things your parents expect you to do or not do? Which of these rules or expectations seem fair and which seem unfair?

INDIVIDUAL PARENT INTERVIEWS

In every family, members have different roles, such as the smart one, the athletic one, the one who gets into trouble, etc. What roles did you and your siblings occupy in your family of origin?

- At times in every family, a parent feels closer to one child than another. This may be related to the child's age, personality, physical appearance, or ability. Which of your children do you currently feel more connected to? Have you always felt closer to one child in particular?
- Who do your children feel is the "favored" sibling in your family?

PARENTAL SUBSYSTEM

How do you know when each of your children is angry, sad, afraid, happy, etc.

- What does each of you do when you're angry with the other?
- How do you show affection for each other in front of your children?
- Describe some of your children's "roughhousing" behavior.
- How do you disciple your children? What are differences between your styles of discipline?
- Which of your children generally "requires" more discipline? How is he or she disciplined differently than the others?

FAMILY INTERVIEW

Beginning with the adults, please tell me two or three things you really like about each other

- When one of you doesn't want your brothers, sisters, or parents to use something of yours, are you able to tell them?
- If a family member started to say something that you wanted to keep private and you asked him or her to stop, would he or she respect your wishes? And would your other family members also agree to not do this again?

Clinicians must remember that each family relationship is set in a particular cultural context. Indeed, Weisner (1993) argued that culture is the single most important factor to consider when understanding sibling relationships. Differing cultural expectations influence the developmental course of relationships between parents and children, as well as between siblings. For example, one study (Horwitz & Reinhard, 1995) reported that African American siblings tended to have more caregiving responsibilities than Caucasian siblings.

However, at equivalent levels of caregiving, Caucasian siblings felt the burden of care more strongly. The ability to recognize these differences is important when assessing and intervening in sibling violence. Sociocultural experiences, such as discrimination, may also have a negative impact on sibling relationships, suggesting that intervention efforts take into account forces operating in the larger context within which families are embedded (McHale, Whitman, Kim, & Crouter, 2007). In addition, because sibling violence is likely to involve multiple areas of functioning, sibling assessment must be an ongoing aspect of treatment rather than a static process that precedes therapy.

INTERVENTION

Family therapy may be viewed as varying along a continuum from individual treatment, in which family influences are considered, to conjoint family therapy, in which all family members are present. Therapists treating sibling violence must have not only clinical training in family therapy, but also family violence. The unique circumstances of sibling abuse treatment frequently require a modification of traditional systemic approaches. In treating victims or perpetrators of sibling violence, safety and accountability become front and center issues. Family-based therapy may be one aspect of a multidimensional approach to treatment that includes individual, group, and family intervention. A prime criterion for determining the wisdom of an individual family member's involvement in family therapy must take into account the developmental stage and "readiness" of the sibling violence survivor and be coordinated with his or her needs and capacities. Siblings frequently perceive the same family events differently. In cases of sibling violence, this developmental concept assumes increased significance. Each child's perception of an event may be as clinically significant as the actual event itself in determining where, how, and when to intervene. There is a clear danger inherent in rigid approaches, which expect all families to fit the same theories of causation and methods of treatment.

One question that remains unanswered is what kind of treatment works best. While the literature on evidenced-based approaches remains sparse, some studies suggest possible directions. In developing a family intervention strategy, it is important to determine if other family members can maintain clear boundaries between the different subsystems. Sometimes, for example, parents may need to distance themselves from the sibling subgroup in order to allow the development of productive sibling relationships. In underfunctioning families, relationship boundaries tend to fall on extreme ends of a continuum, ranging from enmeshment to disengagement (Minuchin, 1974). In both types of dysfunctional families where sibling violence occurs, the family system tends to rely on coercive control. A focus on family dynamics, strengthening boundaries, and improving parent-child bonds seems universally accepted. This approach adapts interventions from pragmatic, problem-focused treatments that have at least some empirical support. These include strategic family therapy (Haley, 1987; Szapocznik & Kurtines, 1990), structural family therapy (Minuchin, 1974, 1996) and cognitive behavior therapies (Kendall & Braswell, 1993). One frequent goal of treatment at the family level is to enhance a caregiver's capacity to effectively monitor sibling behavior and provide positive consequences for responsible behavior and sanctions for irresponsible behavior. One must also be able to identify and address barriers to the effective implementation of these new rules and consequences. Such barriers might include caregiver substance abuse, mental health difficulties, high levels of family stress, etc.

In the initial stages of intervention, parents and siblings are seen together and separately. The therapist must create a context that is conducive to the desired change and create a balanced alliance with each family member. Family patterns of interaction and communication, as well as resources for settling disputes, are observed. Problematic sibling interactions are discussed in the context of family rules and structure. During this phase, the parental dyad must also be seen alone to develop rules of cooperation between them. A parental alliance is essential in developing family rules to curb sibling violence. An inappropriate, but all too common initial parental response is to minimize or ignore the abuse. In one family, where parents disagreed about the seriousness of the sibling conflict and the need to provide increased structure and supervision, the therapist decided to frame the abusive child as depressed. She explained how common it was for depressed children and adolescents to express their despair by becoming irritable and aggressive, even to the point of being physically assaultive. She suggested the offending sibling's behavior was linked to a serious increase in his depression, which, of course, required immediate attention. The father responded empathically to this conceptualization of his child's problem and together the parents worked harder to establish clearer boundaries and increased supervision of their children's interactions at home.

Subsequent intervention must focus on treating the family as a unit. They must work together to develop effective ground rules for facilitating structural changes agreed upon by the family, including guidelines for avoiding or controlling sibling aggression. Key rules that prevent the escalation of sibling violence (e.g., parental alignment with each other rather than an alignment with one sibling), are of particular importance. The therapist must address cross-generational coalition patterns in this phase. For example, a therapist may ask a father to problem solve with his son, if normally he aligns with his daughter. A grandparent can be brought in to temporarily buttress efforts by the parents to supervise and monitor sibling aggression. Therapy should be focused on restructuring family relations in ways that will facilitate the desired behavioral change.

TRAUMATIC EFFECTS

The conventional wisdom that sibling violence is less injurious for younger children is not supported by empirical evidence. There is the potential for both short and long-term consequences. Finkelhor et al. (2006) reported that

---

SIBLING VIOLENCE
RISK AND PROTECTIVE FACTORS

Risk factors

- Parental unavailability
- Attachment difficulties where parents may be physically available but emotionally absent
- Ineffective parenting
- Low levels of paternal acceptance and involvement are linked to higher levels of sibling conflict.
- Ideally, parents learn to create a balance between over-involvement in sibling affairs and a lack of protective, competent parenting
- Sibling relationships characterized by power imbalances, role rigidity, and unclear boundaries
- Consistent disregard for sibling's personal and psychological space usually indicates more serious problems
- Parental favoritism and differential treatment of siblings

Protective factors

- Father's levels of positive involvement with sons most closely associated with stability of sibling behavior problems
- Quality of mother-child interaction mediates the effects of overt marital conflict on older sibling's tendency to behave aggressively toward younger siblings
- Parental warmth and involved interactions; and consistent, non-punitive discipline management

---

children who were repeatedly attacked by a sibling were twice as likely as others their age to demonstrate severe symptoms of trauma, anxiety, and depression, including sleeplessness, suicidal ideation and fear of the dark. Reports from the adult survivors in our study (Caffaro & Conn-Caffaro, 1998; 2005) suggest that sibling violence may also leave lasting effects on the sibling relationship. For example, Cicirelli (1982) estimated that only three percent of siblings reared in healthy families ever permanently sever emotional ties with one another. However, 34 percent of participants said they had no contact with the sibling who abused them; practicing an "emotional cutoff" pattern with at least one adult brother or sister.

A consistent theme raised by research participants was the failure of family members to acknowledge the sibling violence. Family members' reluctance to validate and support a survivor increases the likelihood of impaired adult sibling relationships. Furthermore, relationships between sibling victims in the same family may be fractured. Some families will remain silent to protect children (and themselves) from the stigma of treatment rather than seek intervention that would benefit both victim and offender. Psychological maltreatment is a core element of sibling violence. Many sibling violence survivors suffer from multiple traumatizations. "Teasing" often precedes physical violence and may include ridiculing, insulting, threatening and terrorizing, as well as destroying a sibling's personal property.

There are individual traumatic effects as well. Graham-Bermann and Cutler (1992) observed that adults from high conflict sibling dyads experienced lower self-esteem and greater anxiety than did those from sibling dyads involving less conflict. They concluded that childhood sibling violence has the power to shape the adult survivor's emotional life and worldview.

Another important theme from our research is that a significant number of research participants had not sought treatment, nor previously shared their stories of sibling violence. Forty-five percent of the adult sibling violence survivors in our study had not disclosed their abuse to anyone (Caffaro & Conn-Caffaro, 2005). Those who were in therapy often remarked how their therapists did not focus on their abusive relationships with siblings. Clinical experience suggests another explanation for why an individual with a history of sibling violence may be less inclined to reveal his or her experience: small age differences between children may lead victims to assume they were willing participants.

CLINICAL AND RESEARCH IMPLICATIONS

Schools and parents must take sibling violence more seriously. We may need to set clearer standards against such violence and intervene earlier to prevent recurrence and protect victims. Families must be encouraged to establish no hitting policies among their children, and parent education regarding sibling violence is necessary. Underreporting by families is a significant concern despite the high incidence rates of sibling violence in the literature. There is evidence (Caffaro & Conn-Caffaro, 1998, 2005; Finkelhor et al., 2006) that sibling violence will not be disclosed unless mentioned specifically by the researcher or practitioner. This underscores the importance of comprehensive sibling violence assessment since it may turn out to be an important precursor to other kinds of victimization.

Finally, sibling violence data collection efforts are often hampered because incidents of child-on-child violence (under 12 years old) are currently excluded from the National Crime Victimization Survey (NCVS), one of the nation's most important and widely cited sources of crime information. This is not to suggest that sibling violence against younger children should be considered a crime. Rather, that children face elevated frequencies of violence, higher levels than most adults encounter. Sibling and peer violence against younger children, therefore, represents an important public policy and societal concern.

John Caffaro, PhD, is an internationally recognized expert on sibling abuse. He currently serves as distinguished professor at the California School of Professional Psychology–Los Angeles, and assistant clinical professor of psychiatry at the University of California, San Diego, School of Medicine, Child Psychiatry Residency Training Program. He is a former expert consultant for California Statewide Child Welfare Services Redesign and has authored numerous peer-reviewed publications on child maltreatment, sibling abuse, and family systems approaches to treating post-traumatic stress. Caffaro draws on more than 20 years of private practice clinical experience working with trauma treatment in Del Mar, CA, and currently divides his time between psychotherapy, teaching, and training. He is an AAMFT Clinical Member and Approved Supervisor.

RESOURCES FOR PRACTITIONERS

American Professional Society on the Abuse of Children
http://www.apsac.org/mc/page.do

Caffaro, J. (2010). *Sibling violence and systems-oriented therapy.* In Caspi, J. (Ed.). Sibling development: Implications for mental health practitioners. NY: Springer

Caffaro, J. & Conn-Caffaro, A. (1998). *Sibling abuse trauma.* New York: Haworth Press.

Sibling Abuse Survivors Information and Advocacy Network
http://www.sasian.org/

Sound Medicine. (2006). *Sibling abuse.* Public Radio (WFYI 90.1 FM). Live interview with J. Caffaro. Indiana Univeristy School of Medicine. Located online at http://soundmedicine.iu.edu/segment.php4?seg=847.

Sidran Institute
http://www.sidran.org/

American Psychological Association (Division 37: Child Maltreatment)
http://www.apa.org/divisions/div37/child_maltreatment/child.html

American Psychological Association (Division 56: Trauma Psychology)
http://www.apatraumadivision.org/

*The Sibling Abuse Interview may be obtained from the author.

REFERENCES

Baskett, L. M. (1984). Ordinal position differences in children's family interactions. *Developmental Psychology, 20,* 1026-1031.

Bryant, B. K. (1982). Sibling relationships in middle childhood. In M. E. Lamb and B. Sutton-Smith (Eds.), *Sibling relationship: Their nature and significance across the life span* (pp. 87-121). Hillsdale, NJ: Lawrence Erlbaum.

Caffaro, J. (2007). Sibling violence and aggression: Assessment and clinical intervention with children, families and adults. In Proceedings of the 5th European Congress on Violence in Clinical Psychiatry, Callaghan, P., Nijman, H., Palmstierna, T., & Oud, N. (Eds.) Netherlands: KAVANAH Publications.

Caffaro, J. & Conn-Caffaro, A. (2005). Treating sibling abuse families. *Aggression and violent behavior, 10* (5), 604-623. UK: Elsevier Press.

Caffaro, J. & Conn-Caffaro, A. (1998). *Sibling abuse trauma.* New York: Haworth Press.

Cicirelli, V. (1982). Sibling influence throughout the life span. In M. Lamb & B. Sutton-Smith (Eds.), *Sibling relationships: Their nature and significance across the life span.* Hillsdale, NJ: Erlbaum.

Cummings, E. M. & Davis, P. T. (2002). Effects of martial conflict on children: Recent advances and emerging themes in process-oriented research. *Journal of Child Psychology and Psychiatry, 43*, (1), 31-63.

Duncan, R. (1999). Peer and sibling aggression: An investigation of intra-and extra-familial bullying. *Journal of Interpersonal Violence, 14*, 871-886.

Finkelhor, D., Turner, H., & Ormrod, R. (2006). Kids stuff: The nature and impact of peer and sibling violence on younger and older children. *Child Abuse & Neglect, 30*, 1401-1421.

Felson, R. B., & Russo, N. (1988). Aggression and violence between siblings. *Social Psychology Quarterly, 46*, 271-285.

Goodwin, M. P., & Roscoe, B. (1990). Sibling violence and agonistic interactions among middle adolescents. *Adolescence, 25*, 451-467.

Graham-Bermann, S. A., & Cutler, S. E. (1992, August). Sibling violence and abuse: Prevalence, emotional and social outcome. Paper presented at the 100th Annual Convention of the American Psychological Association, Washington, D.C.

Gully, K. J., Dengerink, H. A., Pepping, M., & Bergstrom, D. (1981). Research note: Sibling contribution to violent behavior. *Journal of Marriage and the Family, 43*, 333-337.

Haley, J. (1987). *Problem-solving therapy.* San Francisco, CA: Jossey-Bass.

Hernandez, D. J. (1997). Child development and social demography of childhood. *Child Development, 68*, 149-169.

Horwitz, å.V., & Reinhard, S. C. (1995). Ethnic differences in caregiving duties and burdens among parents and siblings of persons with severe mental illness. *Journal of Health and Social Behavior, 36*, (2), 138-150.

Hotaling, G. T., Straus, M., & Lincoln, A. J. (1990). Intrafamily violence and crime and violence outside the family. In M.S. Straus & R. J. Gelles (Eds.), *Physical violence in American families: Risk factors and adaptations to violence in 8,145 families* (pp. 431-470). New Brunswick, NJ: Transaction.

Kendall, P., & Braswell, L. (1993). *Cognitive-behavioral therapy for impulsive children.* 2nd Edition. New York: Guilford Press.

Koestler, R., Franz, C., & Weinberger, J. (1990). The family origins of empathic concern: A 26-year longitudinal study. *Journal of Personality and Social Psychology, 58*, (4), 709-717.

McHale, S., Whitman, S., Kim, J., & Crouter, A. (2007). Characteristics and correlates of sibling relationships in two-parent African American families. *Journal of Family Psychology, 21*, (2), 227-235.

Minuchin, S. (1974). *Families and family therapy.* Cambridge, MA: Harvard University Press.

Minuchin. S., Lee, W. Y., & Simon, G. (1996). *Mastering family therapy.* New York: Wiley.

Noland, V., Liller, K., McDermott, R., Coulter, M., & Seraphine, A. (2004). Is adolescent sibling violence a precursor to college dating violence? *American Journal of Health Behavior, 28,* S13-S23.

Patterson, G. R. (1975). The aggressive child: Victim and architect of a coercive system. In E. J. Marsh, L. A. Hamerlynck, & L. C. Handy (Eds.), *Behavior modification and families* (pp. 267-316). New York: Bruner/Mazel.

Simonelli, C., Mullis, T., Elliot, A., & Pierce, T. (2002). Abuse by siblings and subsequent experiences of violence within the dating relationship. *Journal of Interpersonal Violence, 17,* 103-121.

Stocker, C., & McHale, S. M. (1992). The nature and family correlates of preadolescent's perceptions of their sibling relationships. *Journal of Social and Personal Relationships, 9,* 179-195.

Szapocznik, J., & Kurtines, W. M. (1989). *Breakthroughs in family therapy with drug abusing and problem youth.* New York: Springer

Weisner, T. S. (1993). Overview: Sibling similarity and difference in different cultures. In C. W. Nuckolls (Ed.), *Siblings in South Asia* (pp. 1-18). New York: Guilford Press.

Wiehe, V. R. (2000). Sibling abuse. In H. Henderson (Ed.) *Domestic violence and child abuse resource sourcebook* (pp. 409-492). Detroit, MI: Omnigraphics

**VOLUMES 1, 2 AND 3 OF THIS SERIES
CONTAIN THE FOLLOWING TOPICS:**

VOL. 1

Male Sexual Dysfunction

Depression

Alcohol Use Disorders

Female Sexual Dysfunction

Adolescent Disruptive Behavior Disorders

Eating Disorders

Children and Divorce

Domestic Violence

Attention-Deficit Hyperactivity Disorder

Post-Traumatic Stress Disorder

Bereavement and Loss

Infertility

Children's Attachment Relationships

Adolescent Substance Abuse

Chronic Illness

Schizophrenia

Suicidal Ideation and Behavior

VOL. 2

Postpartum Depression

Adolescent Self-Harm

Premarital Assessment

Caregiving for the Elderly

Panic Disorder

Alzheimer's Disease

Adoption Challenges

Bipolar Disorder

Borderline Personality Disorder

Obsessive Compulsive Disorder

Childhood Onset Mental Illness

Substance Abuse and Intimate Relationships
Intrafamilial Childhood Sexual Abuse
Juvenile Sexual Offenders
Sexual Minority Youth
Body-focused Repetitive Behaviors
Treating Anger
Asperger's Syndrome

VOL. 3

Suicide in the Elderly
Multiracial Families
Marital Distress
Parental Grief After the Death of a Child
Bipolar Spectrum Disorders in Children and Adolescents
Children of Alcoholics
Sexual Assault and Intimacy in the Marriage
Online Infidelity
Stepfamilies
Phobias
Genomics and MFT
Dissociative Identity Disorder
HIV Disease
Sexual Addiction and Compulsivity
Transgender in Family Therapy
Reducing Divorce Conflicts
Physical Abuse and Neglect
Same-sex Couples